CULTURAL FOUNDATIONS

of

POLITICAL PSYCHOLOGY

Also by Paul Roazen

Freud: Political and Social Thought (1968, 1986, 1999)
Brother Animal: The Story of Freud and Tausk (1969, 1990)
Freud and His Followers (1975)
Erik H. Erikson: The Power and Limits of a Vision (1976)
Helene Deutsch: A Psychoanalyst's Life (1985,1992)
Encountering Freud:
The Politics and Histories of Psychoanalysis (1990)
Meeting Freud's Family (1993)
How Freud Worked: First-Hand Accounts of Patients (1995)
Heresy: Sandor Rado and the Psychoanalytic Movement
(with Bluma Swerdloff) (1995)
Canada's King: An Essay in Political Psychology (1998)
Oedipus in Britain: Edward Glover and the Struggle
Over Klein (2000)
Political Theory and the Psychology of the Unconscious (2000)
The Historiography of Psychoanalysis (2001)
The Trauma of Freud: Controversies in Psychoanalysis (2002)

Edited by Paul Roazen

Sigmund Freud (1973)
Walter Lippmann, *The Public Philosophy* (1989)
Louis Hartz, *The Necessity of Choice:*
Nineteenth Century Political Theory (1990)
Helene Deutsch, *The Psychoanalysis of the Sexual Functions*
of Women (1991)
Victor Tausk, *Sexuality, War, and Schizophrenia:*
Collected Psychoanalytic Papers (1991)
Helene Deutsch, *The Therapeutic Process, The Self, and*
Female Psychology: Collected Psychoanalytic Papers (1991)
Walter Lippmann, *Liberty and the News* (1995)

CULTURAL FOUNDATIONS
of
POLITICAL PSYCHOLOGY

Paul Roazen

Transaction Publishers
New Brunswick (U.S.A.) and London (U.K.)

Library of Congress Catalog Number: 2003050773
ISBN: 0-7658-0182-5
Printed in the United States of America

Library of Congress Cataloging-in-Publication Data

Roazen, Paul, 1936–
    Cultural foundations of political psychology / Paul Roazen.
        p. cm.
    Includes bibliographical references and index.
    ISBN 0-7658-0182-5 (alk. paper)
        1. Political psychology. 2. Political science. 3. Culture. I. Title.

JA74.5R63 2003
320'01'9—dc21

                                                    2003050773

In Memory of Anthony Storr

Contents

Preface

Although it is now almost three-quarters of a century since Harold Lasswell first insisted on the central importance of modern depth psychology for an understanding of politics, even today not much legitimacy attaches to the professional links Lasswell had sought to establish. Even before Lasswell tried to bring together psychology and politics, a thinker like Graham Wallas had, in a different way, also attempted to make the problem of human nature central to the study of politics; and in many of his books Walter Lippmann shared a similar agenda to Wallas, who had been one of Lippmann's teachers. If one takes an even longer perspective than the last hundred years, the greatest thinkers of ancient Greece had thought that it would be impossible to conceive of political life without insights into the human soul. Over the centuries, all the greatest philosophers had made psychology central to their understanding of social life.

At various times throughout this past century, the possible interconnections between psychology and politics have seemed of key importance. But when someone like Wilhelm Reich, for example, proposed the subject of political psychology, he had such clear Marxist ideological objectives that the enterprise of bringing psychology and politics together seemed a partisan endeavor. But unspoken moral purposes throughout the social sciences proved more pervasive than many have wanted to acknowledge; ideologizing helps to explain why there has been so much sectarian intolerance. Part of the reason the history of psychoanalysis has held my attention is because of the rival conceptions of the good life that could be advanced by means of psychological categories. Still, the contentiousness among analysts has had its distinctly unattractive sides, and many fair-minded observers have been put off by psychological infighting. The whole subject of psychology has appeared to be such a challenge to the more conventional ways of thinking politically that it has been too easy for the so-called mainstream of the field of political science to ignore the possibilities of acknowledging the extent to which intellectual events have moved almost everyone, at least in the West, in a distinctly psychological direction.

When people have thought about the possible juncture of psychology and politics, too often it has been tempting to think in terms of conventional social psychology, often reducing the matter to one more careerist stepping-stone. As someone like Lasswell knew, the exposure to clinical work differs from what is customarily encountered in university life. It remains a problem that when professional work on political psychology has proceeded, it has had a distinctly anti-theoretical orientation. Lasswell felt that political theory deserved to pay a price for its earlier arrogances—the pretension to be master of the universe—and as part of a kind of class warfare within the profession he downplayed what he had learned from the humanities. And so it seemed in nobody's interest to see modern psychology as part of great literature. In fact, the spirit of philosophic inquiry should involve valuing uncertainty and indeterminancy, qualities not apt to be appreciated by pioneering social scientists.

We seem to live in a time that demands immediate intellectual pay-offs, and so trying to solve even the most intractable-seeming political issues, such as the Arab-Israeli conflict, appears to be a tempting, plausible, near-term objective. Lasswell himself was interested in what he called the policy sciences. But my own view of political psychology has not had any such large-scale practical aims, which I view as intellectual short-cuts, even if in another sense my own philosophical inclinations may appear even more ambitious. Following the spirit of Henry Adams, I consider getting an education to be a life-long endeavor, and I regard it as unquestionably the case that it is impossible, at a minimum, for students of politics to proceed without unacknowledged psychological assumptions.

A bit of my own personal history may clarify things, since I believe that chance plays a larger role in life than may be commonly assumed. During the summer of 1954, after I had been admitted to Harvard College earlier that spring, I was away traveling in Europe with my older brother. A notice had arrived at our parents' home inquiring about what "field of concentration" (Harvard's term for major) I would like to plan enrolling in. On returning from Europe, I found that although neither my mother or father had gone to college, they happened to send in for me the choice of Government; I had been avidly interested in politics at least since the mid-term 1950 elections, so it could have seemed a reasonable idea to them. The Army-McCarthy hearings had recently been spellbinding to me, and each day after school I had been glued to the television set. But it was as a result of my parents' summertime decision that in the fall of 1954 I had the good fortune to find myself in Cambridge with an excellent freshman adviser in the field of Government.

I cannot say that there were not many other forces that kept me in the Government Department. I had had a solid background in European history in public high school, and soon found the study of political philosophy challenging and exhilarating. The intellectual historians then at Harvard seemed to me comparatively on the lightweight side, displaying a kind of upper-class dilettantish interest in the history of ideas. But the Government

Department's political theorists impressed me as more passionately concerned with the life of the mind, and I stuck with them. Even after a year of graduate work in political science at the University of Chicago in 1958-59 alerted me to how exceptional, and apart from the center of the discipline, the study of Government was at Harvard, I was not lured by the fashionable behavioral persuasion or the prospect of immediate empiricism. Leo Strauss was also then holding forth at Chicago, but I was partly put off by the cult that seemed to surround him; I did not suppose that natural rights thinking was the only option open to those in quest of social values. So, as for the behaviorists and the Straussians, I responded with the reaction of a plague on both their houses. The next year at Magdalen College, where I was supervised in the graduate study of Politics at Oxford by Sir Isaiah Berlin, served to reinforce my earlier allegiances, and my commitment to exploring liberal democratic thinking. Even today I remain grateful for the luck I had in early on getting a good general education.

Berlin still stands out as someone singularly unimpressed by Freud, as Strauss was too; I remember Strauss not being able even to see similarities between Nietzsche and Freud on the subject of sublimation. (Since the reader is entitled to some sort of advance roadmap of what will follow here, Hannah Arendt's ability to work without Freud will be examined in chapter 11.) Berlin's own judgment about psychoanalysis was partly a personal matter, and when Berlin had met Freud in London his skepticism was reinforced by the specifics of what he felt he had encountered. Although Berlin published essays about various of the great and famous he happened to come in contact with, it seems striking to me that he did not bother to write up his impressions of meeting Freud.

A small literature has started to appear on Berlin's standoffishness toward Freud's place in the history of thought, and we will return to the subject while examining Berlin's authorized biography in chapter 7. Berlin's first book had been on Karl Marx, and I have little doubt that he saw Freud as among those whom he considered the modern enemies of freedom. When I once later saw Berlin in America he had just bought the big Modern Library edition of Freud, even though the best new collections of Freud's works had come out in England. While Berlin was talented enough to be able to sprinkle in Freud's name in various of his essays, I always doubted how much by the founder of psychoanalysis Berlin had ever felt the need actually to read.

Berlin's famous 1958 inaugural lecture at Oxford, distinguishing between what he called negative as opposed to positive liberty, was as directly related to Freudianism as to Marx's socialism. Although Berlin had to acknowledge the legitimate historic role of the school of socialism, he was so opposed to the moral implications of all theories of self-development that I think it blinded him to the implications for his work of the tradition of thought that Freud had started. Berlin acknowledged to me how friends of his like Stuart

Hampshire and Richard Wollheim were taking psychoanalysis seriously; while I was at Oxford the philosophers there were more concerned with the implications of depth psychology than any other single academic group. As we shall see in chapter 6, Ludwig Wittgenstein, then the central figure in Oxford philosophy, could be remarkably perceptive about what Freud's work amounted to.

But Berlin's distance towards psychology, and his notable detachment from all modern social science theorizing for that matter, was characteristic of mainline British political theorists. Berlin and I scarcely ever engaged in any give-and-take when it came to Freud. He gave me some analogies in the history of music to the psychoanalytic sectarianism I was to encounter, and he listened in wonderment to my tales of censorship in Freud's published correspondences, exceeding what had happened with Marx's own letter-writing. The one bit of my publications that attracted Berlin's interest and comment consisted of my contribution to discussing the thought and career of a political theory teacher of mine, Louis Hartz, who later became my Ph.D. supervisor.

I had returned from Oxford in 1960 to Cambridge, Massachusetts, where I got my Ph.D. in Government, with a dissertation on Freud and Political Theory (my undergraduate thesis had been on the ideas of Walter Lippmann); after having been a teaching fellow for four years, I then taught full time at Harvard for six years thereafter. My own courses in Government (and also General Education) were designed as forums for working out my ideas, and were called Psychology and Politics, Political Psychology, Human Nature in Political Thought, as well as American Political Thought. I approached everything I taught within the context of the history of political theory. Living afterwards in Canada between 1971 and 1995 was a luxury in that academic life there was old-fashioned enough to be tolerant of those centrally concerned with the history of thought. Now that I have returned to Cambridge in my retirement, I find I am as concerned as I ever was about thinking about how we think, which is how I look on social theorizing. Although I have to admit that I feel as alienated as ever from political science as a whole, staying in the field did allow me to do pretty much what I wanted, and for that I have to remain grateful.

My professional background has meant that I have always approached the history of psychoanalysis with a conviction that ethical issues are implicit in every clinical encounter. Such problems as confidentiality, or theories connected with privacy, should clearly be subjects of concern to political theorists. What we might mean by human individuality, and the sources of distortion or oppression, can benefit from a psychological perspective. But other theoretical approaches, like game theory or rational choice models, are alternatives that ought not to go without examination and criticism.

Although in some abstract sense one would have to delve a good deal deeper to help explain why the study of psychology and politics so succeeded in capturing my imagination, I never plan to engage in any sort of systematic introspective self-exploration. In my view, that sort of enterprise should be reserved for people as talented as Henry Adams, or, to move even higher up in the scale of things of the mind, Saint Augustine or Jean-Jacques Rousseau. Even Alexis de Tocqueville, when he wrote memoirs, was conflicted enough to leave instructions that they not be published, although one might wonder why he did not personally see that they got destroyed. (Tocqueville will come up in chapter 7.)

The pieces I've collected here represent a lifetime's range of thinking. My other writings may appear to have been on other subjects, but I have to confess that in my work on the history of psychoanalysis I only temporarily stumbled on intellectual matters that I could not resist working on. Interviewing so many of the early analysts, including those who had known Freud personally, handed me material that was compelling in a way that I was unable to dodge. I had always looked on Freud, whose *Civilization and Its Discontents* had been assigned reading in a freshman introductory course in the Government Department, as one in a long line of previous political philosophers. And I hope that on inspection this work of mine will show a breadth of interests that is genuinely reflective of what my real long-term aims have been.

In life one does make choices, even those whose ramifications are far beyond what any of us can anticipate; but existence does also come at least half-way to meet us, and in multiple ways that are hard to define. I hope that even though the academic study of politics may now seem largely a matter of mathematical equations, a longer humanistic tradition of how to proceed will someday succeed in also being adequately recognized. As a teacher myself, I always sought to live up to the ancient Socratic example, and I hope that these various attempts by me will be taken in the most generous spirit of Montaigne's ideal of what essays ought to be.

The opening chapter on Erich Fromm's exclusion from the International Psychoanalytic Association touches on a host of interesting political matters; collaboration with tyranny, as opposed to how it can be resisted, acquired new dimensions in the last century. How organized psychoanalysis dealt with Nazism, and the way in which a Marxist like Fromm suffered professionally in North America, amounts to a tale that deserves being remembered.

Chapter 2 deals with the once-famous story of Alger Hiss and Whittaker Chambers, a troubling case in American liberalism that has attracted a good deal of psychological conjecture. The historic encounter between them remains a telling example of how psychology and politics can intersect; although formal treason could not be the legal accusation against Hiss, themes of betrayal as opposed to fidelity do crowd the stage of what needs to be understood in reconstructing what was going on. And chapter 3 deals with another set of conundrums, this time having to do with the great novelist

Virginia Woolf, her madness, and what role others played in her efforts to deal with her demons. Even if psychology cannot hope to "solve" the question of artistic creativity, we will find that how Virginia Woolf's life has been recounted reflects various psychological and social fashions that have not often enough been critically examined.

With chapter 4, I try to deal with the fate of psychologizing in twentieth-century America, in contrast to what has been the case in other countries within the Old World. Incidentally, the future of psychology in the non-Western parts of the globe may prove not only the most significant set of issues yet to be decided, but may also shape how later generations will come to evaluate the ideas that Freud initiated. As traditionalist family systems change, presumably more in line with what the West has been familiar with, human problems that have been at the heart of Freud's thinking should prove even more relevant.

In chapter 5, I move to a particular historical example, how the American Central Intelligence Agency funded the magazine *Encounter*, and what the implications of this hidden public subsidy are for our understanding of the survival of democratic government. Such intellectual history has, I think, direct relevance for political psychology, in that values and beliefs deserve to be subjected to critical scrutiny as part of studying this field of knowledge. Chapter 6, dealing with the reaction to psychoanalysis of three major philosophers, fills out a range of theoretical moral matters that are inevitably part of any political psychology. Carl Jung too, like Freud, had his own uncritical believers as well as passionate critics, and looking at philosophical thinking helps to round out the social and human context in which all these ideas need to be considered.

Chapter 7, dealing with various of the grand theorists in the history of political theory, reminds us of the relevance of people with whose ideas every educated person needs to be acquainted. For a direct line runs from Machiavelli, Rousseau, Burke, and Tocqueville down to Freud, as well as, in our own day, to Fromm and Berlin. Studying this whole tradition of thought enhances anyone's ability to deal with particular problems associated with psychology and politics. Chapter 8, grappling with the Vietnam and the Cold War, illustrates how political psychology inevitably has to be concerned with questions of an "ought" character; my own personal resolution of these matters seems to me less important than my objective of illustrating the centrality of ethics to all political problems.

Chapter 9, covering the matter of intellectuals and exile, should raise the question of what are the social bases for political theorizing, a subject too often taken for granted. And chapter 10 deals with a variety of the methodological issues associated with psychology and politics; part of the interest that this subject evokes comes from the fact that bringing together two such different fields means that both of them need to change and redefine themselves as a result of their interaction.

Chapter 11 discusses the famous theorist Hannah Arendt, about whom there is today a considerable secondary literature. Although she pointedly disdained all forms of introspection, including psychoanalysis, her work inevitably meant coming to terms with familiar problems we have already encountered, like normality, democracy, and the vexing matter of collaboration with tyranny. In chapter 12 I try also to revive the little-known name of Geoffrey Gorer; even though he is now mainly forgotten, he was once an influential man of letters whose independent thinking deserves a place alongside that of more celebrated figures.

With chapter 13 I present the problem of biography by means of a series of concrete examples; biographical work has for too long labored under the bias shared by too many that it constitutes a kind of low-level activity. Psychological matters are inevitably an essential constituent of any biographical approach. And finally in chapter 14, "Affairs of State," I try to illustrate, by means of a series of observations about works dealing with practical politics, some of the implications of psychological thinking for political observations.

For the concluding chapter, I turn to the "Psychology of Women." Although feminist theory is now an acknowledged part of today's university curriculum, I think it needs to be pointed out how political psychology has long been trying to deal with the issues posed by changing conceptions of femininity. Although Freud has often enough been criticized, the case against him has largely been, I think, made on ahistorical grounds; any psychological thinker, when taken away from his own cultural context, is going to be bound to look responsible for having advanced what might now appear to be dubious ideas. But in historical perspective, Freud played a significant role in the emancipation of women; his profession of psychoanalysis proved to be more open to female talent than almost any other alternative calling, and one chorus of his critics has taken the theme that he is responsible for undermining old-fashioned family life. Although it should not be necessary to accept credulously any particular idea Freud may have advanced about women, any more for that matter than what he might have ever said about men, I think that no survey of intellectual history is going to be able to ignore the role his work has played in helping to change our ideas about gender and sexuality. I believe it would be hard to imagine how the topic of political psychology could proceed without coming to terms with the challenge Freud's ideas represent.

1

The Exclusion of Erich Fromm from the IPA

The subject of psychoanalytic lineage has recently acquired a new respectability among historians in the field; although privately analysts have known and acknowledged how critical it is who has gone where and to whom for training, it is only relatively rarely that public attention has been focused on the unusually powerful impact that such training analyses can have. The special suggestive role of analytic training experiences was long ago pointed out in the course of controversial in-fighting by such differently oriented pioneers as Edward Glover[1] and Jacques Lacan, but it has been unusual to find the institution of training analysis itself publicly challenged. It remains too little known that historically the requirement that all analysts be themselves analyzed for purposes of training only officially got going under the auspices of the International Psychoanalytic Association (IPA) in 1925, after Freud became ill with cancer and had implicitly to concede his inability personally to control the future of his movement.[2]

At the same time, however, that analytic lineage—family tree matters[3]—deserve to get full attention, it can be too easy to forget the role that books themselves play, especially for intellectuals, in spreading ideas. One might think it a truism that people not only go for treatment but respond powerfully to what they come across in print. Many of us were first attracted to psychoanalysis by reading the writings of Erich Fromm (1900-80). Erich Fromm's powerful papers from the early 1930s were once almost unknown, but a book of his like *Escape From Freedom*[4] became for years a central text in the education of social scientists. Works of Fromm's like *Man For Himself, Psychoanalysis and Religion, The Forgotten Language*, and also *The Sane Society*[5] formed an essential part of my generation's general education. Fromm's most hortatory last writings, and his specifically political ones, fall, I think, into a different category as far as the general influence that he had; still, the book Fromm co-authored with Michael Maccoby, *Social Character in a Mexican Village*, deserves more attention.[6] Fromm's *The Art of Loving* has meanwhile sold millions of copies, and *To Have Or To Be?* succeeded in selling a million copies in Germany alone; *The Anatomy of Human Destructiveness* was also a notable achievement.[7]

Ernest Jones's biography of Freud was also formative in the psychoanalytic education of my time, as was Fromm's short and relatively neglected retort to Jones: *Sigmund Freud's Mission: An Analysis of His Personality and Influence*.[8] Jones's multiple distortions are so built into his heavily documented narrative that they continue to slide by even many of the most conscientious researchers. Let me give just one example from *Sigmund Freud's Mission* of the persuasiveness of Fromm's reasoning, as he follows an interpretive line entirely his own—and at odds with Jones. In the following passage Fromm was writing about the "secret" Committee, made up of Karl Abraham, Jones, Otto Rank, Sandor Ferenczi, Hanns Sachs, and Max Eitingon, which was designed before World War I to safeguard the psychoanalytic "cause" after the so-called defection of Carl G. Jung:

> Who were these first most loyal disciples, the wearers of the six rings? They were urban intellectuals, with a deep yearning to be committed to an ideal, to a leader, to a movement, and yet without having any religious or political or philosophical ideal or convictions; there was neither a socialist, Zionist, Catholic nor Orthodox Jew among them. (Eitingon may have had mild Zionist sympathies.) Their religion was the Movement. The growing circle of analysts came from the same background; the vast majority were and are middle-class intellectuals, with no religious, political or philosophical interests or commitments. The great popularity of psychoanalysis in the West, and particularly in the United States, since the beginning of the thirties has undoubtedly the same social basis. Here is a middle class for whom life has lost meaning. They have no political or religious ideals, yet they are in search of a meaning, of an idea to devote themselves to, of an explanation of life which does not require faith or sacrifices, and which satisfies this need to feel part of a movement. All these needs were fulfilled by the Movement.[9]

These words seem to me still strikingly valid. Entirely aside from any of Fromm's other clinical and theoretical contributions, one essay of his (which originally appeared in the old *Saturday Review of Literature*) played a notable role, despite an effort to rebut it by an orthodox analyst, in helping to start the "rehabilitation" of the historical reputations of both Ferenczi and Rank[10]; Jones had been singularly unfair to both. In fact, I think that the recent renaissance in Ferenczi's clinical reputation is the one great success story in contemporary psychoanalytic historiography.

Yet bureaucratic struggles, as we shall see, were to limit Fromm's own historical place. By now, he can be accurately described as a "forgotten intellectual," and the whole school of thought once known as "neo-Freudianism" (Fromm did not like having the term applied to himself) has been considered as a "failure" within intellectual history.[11] Even while he was alive, Fromm saw how peculiar and wayward a direction the history of ideas seemed to be moving in, as his rightful standing seemed to sink ever since the late 1960s.

When the term "psycho-history," thanks largely to the initiative of the work of Erik H. Erikson, had first started to take hold in the late 1950s and early 1960s, Fromm justifiably felt somehow left out of the whole story. (Freud's own most speculative works might appeal to political philosophers, but not to most practicing social scientists.) Fromm could not understand how Erikson could proceed in ignoring Fromm's own pioneering work in this area; after all, Fromm's *The Dogma of Christ*[12]—a text among those the Nazis banned— had originally come out as long ago as 1930.

We only now know that Erikson had explicitly discussed Fromm's *Escape From Freedom* at a meeting of the San Francisco Psychoanalytic Society in March 1943, well before Erikson's own *Childhood and Society* saw the light of day in 1950.[13] Erikson always proceeded more than warily about ever even citing Fromm. And so Erikson could be fearful of risking the fate of Fromm's having been excluded as a psychoanalyst, even more than the consequences of Erikson's favorably mentioning—in his last works—the otherwise dread name of Jung; Erikson publicly idealized Freud at the same time he was moving away from orthodox thinking in an original direction.[14] (Fromm would remain intransigently unforgiving about Jung's work, and in good part this was related to Jung's politics in the 1930s that we will be touching on.)

Yet Erikson had himself played a subtle part in assisting in the process of Fromm's being stigmatized as a professional alien; Fromm seems to have been virtually alone in pointing out, in reading Erikson's *Young Man Luther*, the significance of the passage where Erikson refers to "sociological treatises of our time by authors from Weber to Fromm."[15] The word "sociological" was clearly meant to distance Erikson from Fromm, and the very designation of being a sociologist (rather than an analyst) Erikson had feared being used about himself by his own analyst, Anna Freud. (This was part of a tradition in which on December 19, 1934, Jones had written to Anna Freud: "Like [Franz] Alexander and many others she [Karen Horney] seems to be replacing Psychoanalysis by a pseudo-sociology.") Karl Menninger's harsh 1942 critique of Fromm's *Escape From Freedom* helped establish the party line which Erikson was dutifully following; for Menninger had maintained in a review in the *Nation* that "Erich Fromm was in Germany a distinguished sociologist. His book is written as if he considered himself a psychoanalyst."[16] Otto Fenichel had also been thoroughly severe, and pointedly described his review as "psychoanalytic remarks" on Fromm's book.[17] Freud had himself set the unfortunate pattern, in arguing against Alfred Adler and Jung, of polemically depriving free-thinkers, who then were categorized as "mavericks" if not "heretics," of the right to call themselves analysts.

Erikson continued to steer clear of the "controversial" status of Fromm's name, even though so much of what Erikson was trying to accomplish through re-naming more positively early libidinal phases, and by bringing ethics and psychoanalysis together, had in reality been anticipated by Fromm. For *Es-*

cape From Freedom, through Fromm's powerful concept of "social character," really put the social environment on the map for all future analytic thinkers. By the time of *Young Man Luther,* Fromm was training his own school of candidates in Mexico, a "heretical" offense to the organizational powers-that-be within psychoanalysis that Erikson never risked duplicating. (And in New York City, Fromm, once allied with Karen Horney, had notably continued to teach at the William Alanson White Institute, also outside of the IPA.) But everything Fromm had done to incorporate the social perspective within psychoanalytic thinking, including an interest in matters of identity and conformity, was swamped by the immense, if perhaps transitory, success of Erikson's own teachings.[18] (To be fair to psychoanalysis's intra-mural feuding, Marxists had their own brand of sectarianism, and Fromm had to struggle against the criticisms of his former allies at the Frankfurt Institute for Social Research; Herbert Marcuse's ill-founded charges against Fromm and other "revisionists" like Horney and Harry Stack Sullivan were to gain notoriety starting in the mid-1950s.)

Fromm's organizational problems within psychoanalysis, which culminated in his finally being excluded from the IPA in the early 1950s, really got their start with the coming to power of the Nazis in Germany in early 1933. It is essential to start out by providing the full specifics of Fromm's official standing as an analyst in Germany. On June 18, 1927. Fromm, who was then living in Heidelberg, delivered his first paper, as a "guest" of the Germany Psychoanalytic Society—the "DPG"—in Berlin. (The name of the old Berlin Psychoanalytic Society had been changed in 1926 to become the German Psychoanalytic Society, and it continues to be known there as the "DPG.") Some five years earlier, Fromm had received his doctorate in sociology, working under Max Weber's younger brother Alfred, at Heidelberg. It is also historically significant that in early 1927 Fromm's first wife Frieda Fromm-Reichmann had been elected an associate member of the German Society; she became a full member in 1929.

The first "sub-section" of the German Psychoanalytic Society (DPG) was located in Frankfurt and started in October 1926; Fromm, Fromm-Reichmann, along with Clara Happel, Karl Landauer, and Heinrich Meng were listed as members. (Landauer, who had been analyzed by Freud but died in the concentration camp at Bergen-Belsen, was one of Fromm's analysts, along with Fromm-Reichmann herself, Sachs, Wilhelm Wittenberg, and Theodor Reik.) In February 1929 the South-West German Psychoanalytic Society in Frankfurt created an Institute of its own, mainly directed to giving public lectures. This Institute, with Landauer as director, was associated with the Institute for Social Research, a Marxist group that was headed by Max Horkheimer and linked to the University of Frankfurt.

Fromm, along with Landauer, Meng, and Fromm-Reichmann, was one of the original four lecturers at the Frankfurt Psychoanalytic Institute. (S. H.

Fuchs, who later immigrated to England where he changed his name to Foulkes and became prominent especially in group analysis, was to be another early notable figure at the Frankfurt Psychoanalytic Institute.) Fromm gave another paper in Berlin at the German Psychoanalytic Society, where he was elected an associate member on October 7, 1930. Finally Fromm was moved up to being a full member on October 8, 1932; he was fully entitled to IPA membership. Besides the study group in Frankfurt, the German Society had ones in Leipzig, Hamburg, and later Stuttgart. Fromm had been ill with tuberculosis since 1931, and was abroad when Hitler became German Chancellor in January 1933; Fromm remained in Switzerland until the autumn of 1933,[19] when he moved to the United States as a lecturer at the Chicago Institute of Psychoanalysis, where Franz Alexander and Horney (both from the German Psychoanalytic Society) had preceded him.

Once the Nazis had come to power at the end of January 1933, a well-known series of political events followed. The Reichstag fire took place in the night of February 27. A further parliamentary election was held in early March, the Nazis getting 43.9 percent of the vote and a bare working majority in the new Reichstag. Finally the Enabling Act was passed on March 23rd, after which the government had the dictatorial powers in its hands that we now know of as characteristic of Hitler's regime. Virtually the whole of the Frankfurt study-group promptly emigrated – Marxist Jewish analysts did not need to find it hard to read the writing on the wall, although Landauer's going only as far as the Netherlands meant that he eventually got caught in the net of the Holocaust. (The Nazis had closed down the Frankfurt Institute of Social Research in March, and in April Horkheimer was formally dismissed by the University. The Frankfurt "school" already had its money abroad; it first moved to Switzerland, then wound up linked to Columbia University in New York City, and finally returned to Frankfurt after the war in 1949.) By the time of the official IPA report of the German Psychoanalytic Society in August 1934, which appeared in the *International Journal of Psychoanalysis*, twenty-four of the thirty-six full members had already left Germany. The teaching staff of the DPG's Institute had been reduced to two (Carl Müller-Braunschweig, a lay analyst, and Felix Boehm); and the number of people attending lectures had fallen from 164 (in 1932) to 34.[20]

The German Psychoanalytic Society was decimated in terms of its training abilities. Even before Hitler had come to power, Alexander (Chicago), Sandor Rado (New York), Horney (Chicago), and Sachs (Boston) had already resigned to go to the United States. Among the training-analysts who subsequently left Germany were Siegfried Bernfeld, Eitingon, Fenichel, Jenö Harnick, Reik, and Ernst Simmel. Of the old teaching staff that also departed were Steff Bornstein, Jeanne Lampl-de Groot, Wilhelm Reich, and Hugo Staub. The training-analysts who remained included, besides Boehm and Müller-Braunschweig, Therese Benedeck, Edith Jacobson, Werner Kemper, and Edith

Vowinckel-Weigert (who shortly left). But the two internationally most well-known figures of the German Society within the IPA were clearly Boehm (who became president and director of the Institute) and Müller-Braunschweig (who functioned as secretary, treasurer, as well as director of the Training Committee).

Eitingon had been among the first to decide to leave; he had officially proposed to resign as Abraham's successor as head of the Germany Society at a general meeting on May 6, 1933, although he did not finally immigrate to Palestine until the end of the year. Here the narrative of events gets obfuscated by Jones's characteristic narrative statecraft. He wrote, for example, of the spring of 1933 that "around that time a decree was passed that no foreigner was to function in the central executive committee of any medical society in Germany. Eitingon had Polish nationality...."[21] But the truth was more troubling. The Nazis had declared on April 7th that "non-Aryans" (Jews) were ineligible, and that was the decree precluding Eitingon's remaining on any governing board of the German Society (DPG). Jews had suddenly lost essential rights. (It should be notorious that a "non-Aryan" was defined as someone with one "non-Aryan" grandparent, and soon this was extended to anyone married to a "non-Aryan.")

Jones was following Freud's lead in describing Eitingon as now a "foreigner," except that Jones had left out Freud's pointed use of "etc." after the word "foreigner"; for Freud had sent the following advice to Eitingon on March 21, 1933:

> 1. Let us assume psychoanalysis is prohibited, the [training] Institute closed by the authorities. In that case there is least of all to be said or done about it. You will then have held out until the last moment before the ship is sunk.

> 2. Let us assume nothing happens to the Institute, but you, as a *foreigner etc.* [my italics] are removed from the directorship. But you stay in Berlin and can go on using your influence unofficially. In this case, I think, you cannot close the Institute. True, you founded it [Freud was referring to Eitingon's money] and stayed in charge the longest, but then you handed it over to the Berlin group, to which it now belongs. You cannot do it legally, but it is also in the general interest that it remain open, so that it may survive these unfavorable times. Meanwhile, someone like Boehm, who has no particular allegiance, can carry it on. Probably it will not be much attended, either by Germans or *foreigners* [my italics], as long as the restrictions continue.

> 3. Again, let us assume nothing happens to the Institute, but you leave Berlin, either voluntarily or under duress. This situation leads to the same considerations as the one I have just mentioned, except that your influence vanishes, and the risk grows that *opponents* [my italics] within such as Schultz-Hencke could take over the Institute and use it to further their plans. There is only one thing to be done about that: the Executive of the IPA disqualifies the Institute misused in this way, expelling it, as it were, until it can be absolved. But of course there must be a warning first.

What a miserable discussion![22]

As we shall see, Harald Schultz-Hencke (a Gentile, married to a Jewish woman) was an important "revisionist" thinker. Jones reported that in April 1933 Freud had again warned that "any concessions made to other forms of psychotherapy [such as Schultz-Hencke's] would be followed by exclusion of the Berlin Society from the International Association...." Jones added that that was "something that actually happened some years later," although there seems no evidence for that proposition.[23] At the May 6th General Meeting the Society would reject the proposal put forward by Boehm and Müller-Braunschweig that the Board of the Society be changed to exclude Jews. From Anna Freud's perspective, expressed in a June 1, 1933 letter to Jones, the problem was reduced to being a personal one: "Of course Boehm's ambition was at the bottom of that trouble in the Berlin Society!"

Eitingon was responsive to the Nazi decree against non-Aryans, and before he finally left Germany in late 1933, Eitingon (who had already, in 1929 and 1932, presided as president at two congresses of the IPA) proposed to innovate with a new category so that "direct membership" in the IPA be accorded to Clara Happel and "to any other ex-member of the German group who is for the time being unable to join any other existing group...."[24] Eitingon wrote that he did not think that this proposal needed "to be discussed at the Congress [scheduled for Lucerne in late August, 1934], although it does not appear in the statutes, because the question will have been settled by then. In my opinion such things can be decided by the Board itself in such unforeseen situations, in questions which because of their peculiarities do not need to become a precedent."[25] (Eitingon went on to found a Psychoanalytic Society in Palestine.)

* * *

Although Germans early on played a numerically important role in the IPA, both before Hitler as well as after World War II, the history of psychoanalysis in Germany is rather less studied than is the case in other countries. It is known that the original Berlin Psychoanalytic Institute became a model for the subsequent training institutes, even in Vienna, that were set up. Nevertheless, for Germans themselves it has been obviously terribly painful to have to look closely at what happened starting in the 1930s. But even for outsiders it is extremely difficult emotionally to follow the ins-and-outs of events that took place then. The Nazis publicly defamed psychoanalysis as an aspect of Jewish so-called parasitism within Christian culture. Freud, for example, was accused of having had a "filthy imagination," and his teachings were reduced to the "Asiatic ideology" of eat, drink, and be merry, for tomorrow we die.[26] Lamarck's conviction about the inheritance of acquired characteristics (which Freud happened to share) was associated with typically Jewish thinking. Supporters of homosexuality, and the destruction of the family, were also intimately linked in Nazi propaganda to psychoanalytic thinking.

In such a context Wilhelm Reich became an obvious liability to the German Psychoanalytic Society; he was a psychoanalytic psychiatrist originally trained in Vienna who had moved to Berlin. Reich had long been a leader in, among other things, bringing together Marxism and psychoanalysis. Fromm's early work had clearly benefited from some of Reich's ideas relating individual character to "bourgeois" social patterns. But Reich was also proposing to abolish the "patriarchal" middle-class family as a way of nipping neuroses in the bud, and he advocated the therapeutic significance of orgasmic sexual satisfaction. (Reich's important contributions to clinical technique and characterology were less obviously noteworthy, and are too often forgotten in today's psychoanalytic literature.) According to Harold Lasswell, after Reich's late 1920s lecturing in the Soviet Union the psychoanalytic movement seemed especially threatened there; Stalin was evidently then prompted to ban psychoanalysis. Freud had long been unhappy with some of the implications of Reich's ideas, and Freud's 1930 *Civilization and Its Discontents* was specifically directed against Reich's sort of thinking—sexual, clinical, and political. On January 17, 1932 Freud had written to Jeanne Lampl-de Groot, "I have begun the battle against the Bolshevistic aggressors Reich, Fenichel."[27] And "immediately after" the Nazis seized power, Eitingon had "informed Reich that he might no longer enter the premises" of the Psychoanalytic Institute, "so that in case he were arrested, this could not happen on our premises."[28]

Boehm had a personal meeting with Freud in April of 1933 (Paul Federn from the Vienna Psychoanalytic Society was also present). On the issue of the Nazis' determination to remove "non-Aryan's" from the Board of the German Society, Freud was pessimistic that there was any way of preventing psychoanalysis from being banned. But Freud did not think it made sense to give the government any "handle" for doing so, and therefore he agreed with changing the present Board as the government's decree required. This decision of Freud's would prove the beginning of a dangerously slippery slope; yet he had generally over-evaluated his Gentile supporters. (By Oct. 2, 1933, Jones could write Anna Freud that Boehm had "saved psychoanalysis.") According to Boehm, Freud had proposed Boehm as Eitingon's successor; Boehm's report of the interview also declared,

> Before we left, Freud expressed two wishes for the leadership of the Society: firstly, that Schultz-Hencke should never be elected to the Board of our Society. I gave my word that I would never sit on a Board together with Sch.-H. And secondly, he said: "Free me of Reich."[29]

Now Reich was a long-standing personal and ideological irritant to Freud. In 1932, Freud had been as blunt as he ever was in his old age about a "dissenter," without giving any of them any more publicity by mentioning their names. So he described what he called the "secessionist" movements in the history of psychoanalysis, which had seized hold of only a fragment of the truth; Freud then listed "selecting the instinct for mastery [meaning Adler], for instance, or ethical conflict [Jung], or the mother [Rank], or genitality [Reich]...."[30] By March 1933, Freud told Reich that the contract between Reich and Freud's publishing firm in Vienna for a book on character analysis had been cancelled.[31] In the summer of 1933, Ernst Simmel would propose that Reich no longer be listed as a member of the German Society. Evidently Eitingon agreed in principle, but wanted the decision for the "purge" of Reich to be postponed until after Eitingon had resigned from the Society.[32] Reich was practicing then in Copenhagen, but it would not have been unique to have analysts listed as members of more than one analytical group. In his *Sigmund Freud's Mission,* Fromm had italicized one word in a significant 1919 letter of Freud's to Jones: "Your intention to *purge* the London Society of the Jungian members is excellent."[33]

On August 1, 1934 Müller-Braunschweig, secretary of the German Society, accordingly wrote Reich,

> Circumstances seem to require the elimination of your name from the register of the German Psychoanalytic Society. I would greatly appreciate it if you would regard our request with understanding, relegating to the background any possible personal feelings in the interest of our psychoanalytic cause in Germany and expressing your agreement with this step. As a scholar and author you are too well known to the international world of psychoanalysis for this omission to cause you the slightest harm, as it might, for example, affect a newcomer in the field. Furthermore, the whole problem will be academic once the Scandinavian group is recognized at the Congress, thus assuring your inclusion in future membership lists of this new group.[34]

Reich was having serious professional and political troubles practicing in Denmark; although an analytic student of Reich's wrote to Freud for help, Freud "acknowledged Reich's stature as an analyst but stated that his political ideology interfered with his scientific work. He refused to join...[an] appeal to the Minister of Justice." Once Reich settled temporarily in Sweden, the police authorities were also suspicious of him; his permit to be there was revoked. Although someone like the great Polish anthropologist Bronislaw Malinowski, then living in England, sent a letter supporting Reich in his troubles, Freud himself remained negative, and wrote only, "I cannot join your protest in the affair of Dr. Wilhelm Reich."[35]

Reich protested to Anna Freud (then IPA secretary) against what became the engineering of his expulsion from the IPA; she in turn referred Reich to Jones, the incoming president. Behind the scenes, Jones had been campaigning against Reich; in May 1933 he had written Anna Freud, "My own opinion is that Reich should come to a definite conclusion about which is more important to him, psychoanalysis or politics." And the next month Reich was described by Jones in a letter as one of the troublemaking "madmen" in psychoanalysis.[36] Reich later bitterly recalled how Jones had told him "expressly, in London, that he would oppose my exclusion under all circumstances."[37] Reich (as a "guest") was allowed to present a paper at the Lucerne Congress on August 31, 1934, which was perfunctorily written up in the official proceedings, but Jones would not allow Reich to participate in the business meeting. Reich's name was never listed as either a member of the Danish-Norwegian Psychoanalytic Society nor the Finnish-Swedish Psychoanalytic Society; the two groups were "separated officially" in order to keep the Swedish group "out of Reich's hands."[38] Although the Norwegian group offered membership to Reich, "after long deliberation Reich decided to stay outside the psychoanalytic organizations entirely."[39] (Reich had unhappy experiences, around the same time, staying in Marxists groups too.)

Yet Jones only reported of the IPA Congress in Lucerne that this was the "occasion that Wilhelm Reich resigned from the Association. Freud had thought highly of him in his early days, but Reich's political fanaticism had led to both personal and scientific estrangement."[40] It is, however, fairer to conclude that at Lucerne Reich did not resign, but that he "had very definitely been in effect *expelled* from the International Psychoanalytic Association."[41]

* * *

This discussion about Reich may seem a digression, but it prefigures what would happen to Fromm later within the IPA; and I think it bears directly on Boehm's report of his meeting with Freud in Vienna in the spring of 1933 and how Müller-Braunschweig as well as Jones, and much later Ruth Eissler (in behalf of the IPA), would deal with Fromm. The reader will recall that in Vienna (1933) Freud had asked Boehm not only to "free him" of Reich, but to steer clear of Harald Schultz-Hencke within the DPG. Now Schultz-Hencke had been analyzed in Berlin (like Reich) by Rado, but had early on started to criticize Freud's libido theory. In 1927-28, he had taught at the German Psychoanalytic Society, but was "banned from teaching because of his criticism of the sexual theory and on account of his interest in making Adler's individual psychology and Jung's theories compatible with his concept of psychoanalysis."[42] Any sort of rapprochement with Adler and Jung was always seen by Freud as fundamentally impermissible, and those two names of pre-World War I "renegades" are still capable of sounding unacceptable within orthodox psychoanalytic circles. Groups can be held together by their so-called enemies, and Freud was insistent on the validity of the myths he built up about the danger of heretics in psychoanalysis.

Schultz-Hencke was a prolific author and successful as a speaker and orga-
nizer.[43] But in those days, Freud made it known that he was adamantly opposed to the idea of a psychoanalyst making what he saw as concessions
toward the ideas of Adler or Jung. In writing to Eitingon, Freud had referred to
Schultz-Hencke as an "opponent within" psychoanalysis, and threatened disqualifying and expelling the DPG if Schultz-Hencke were to play a governing role in the Institute. Otto Fenichel and Schultz-Hencke had led a
seminar at the DPG where Schultz-Hencke had supposedly "often presented
deviating views which led to vehement arguments."[44] "Deviation" was another word for heresy. When Freud met with Boehm, I believe Schultz-Hencke
was truly almost an equal danger (in his eyes) as Reich.

And then, as others also scrambled to come to terms with the Hitler regime,
in 1934 Schultz-Hencke would help found an organization that had the aim
of "teaching a psychotherapy in conformity with the National Socialist ideology."[45] He was nonetheless criticized in the Nazi period as an example of
"psychological gangsterism." Müller-Braunschweig had gone so far in 1933
as to publish an article in a Nazi weekly; instead of assisting weaklings,
psychoanalysis was supposed to be aimed at making productive members of
society. "In saying this…, when and where he said it, Müller-Braunschweig
was validating the same sort of language the Nazis used to describe the Jewish patients and practitioners of psychoanalysis." Müller-Braunschweig was
"to advertise psychoanalysis to the Nazis as a discipline dedicated to cultivating the strong and not indulging the weak." Schultz-Hencke did write an
essay (not in a Nazi Party publication) echoing Müller-Braunschweig, claiming that "the goal of psychotherapy was to free the powers of fitness and
proficiency within the individual…."[46]

One reliable observer has maintained of Schultz-Hencke that "in his political views he was no National Socialist, and did possess personal courage."
Like some others Schultz-Hencke was trying "to develop a universal, generally intelligible terminology,"[47] and this would also be in keeping with what
became Nazi objectives within Germany. Schultz-Hencke was evidently advocating shorter forms of treatment, and he has been criticized for "the rhetorical concession to Nazi aims" by an "opportunistic paen to the human
'fitness' produced by psychoanalytic treatment."[48] Yet it needs to be pointed
out how someone like Karen Horney in 1939 notably acknowledged "the
influence" on her "of Harald Schultz-Hencke and Wilhelm Reich, analysts
whom she knew from her days in Berlin."[49] In 1945, Horney wrote about the
significance of "a character neurosis":

> Actually, Freud's great pioneering work increasingly converged on this concept—
> though his genetic approach did not allow him to arrive at its explicit formulation.
> But others who have continued and developed Freud's work—notably Franz
> Alexander, Otto Rank, Wilhelm Reich, and Harald Schultz-Hencke—have defined it
> more clearly.[50]

Although differentiating her own ideas from those others who had "continued and developed Freud's work," at various points in her writings she referred with approval specifically to Schultz-Hencke's ideas.[51]

Horney knew how German analysts under Hitler were already moving toward being inclusive when it came to Adler and Jung, and that this could be viewed as the path of "saving" the practice of psychotherapy and psychoanalysis. (After World War II Schultz-Hencke would publish an article in Paris about having helped protect the survival of psychoanalysis in Germany.) Now even before Hitler, Schultz-Hencke had already been punished after 1927-28, within the DPG, for his beliefs about analytic doctrine; he was excluded from the pre-Nazi DPG teaching staff. But IPA bureaucratic concessions about organizational structures excluding Jews seem to me as striking as any possible ideological ones, for in the long run it might prove highly desirable to move away from phobias about the ideas of Adler and Jung; the exclusion of Jews from the Board of the German Society was, as we have seen, considered acceptable by Freud, although a direct and compromising response to immediate political pressure.

Jung's own role in Central Europe in the 1930s has tarred his own future historical standing, since he was outspoken after the Nazis came to power in identifying various flaws in Freud's thinking with his Jewish origins.[52] These public stands of Jung would justifiably be considered sins of his, whereas the behind-the-scenes maneuvering of someone like Jones (or Freud and the IPA itself) would remain harder to detect. Collaboration with totalitarianism, or authoritarianism, for that matter, can take place under many different guises. The lord-mayor of Hamburg was eloquent about the dangers of expediency in the face of Hitlerism when he addressed the 34th IPA Congress in 1985: "Every step rational and yet in a false direction. Here a compromise with individuals, there with substance; always in the vain hope of preserving the whole—which had ceased to exist.... In most cases freedom is lost in tiny steps."[53]

As we shall see, I do not think that the IPA comes out of this story looking heroic in contrast to Jung's behavior, and even a psychoanalytic liberal like Franz Alexander was being politically naïve in accusing Jung of somehow having "lacked Freud's uncompromising moral fortitude...."[54] Freud had to know more of what was going on than most have been willing to admit. (Jones's writing to Anna Freud about problems in the DPG sometimes gave Freud what is now known as plausible deniability.) For someone like Fromm and his colleagues in Frankfurt, emigration (never an easy lot) from Germany turned out to be more straightforward than the alternative of being a fellow traveler with the Nazis or committing domestic treason.

Starting in 1933, Jung had chosen a form of opportunism that someone like Reich was quick to denounce publicly; also Fromm's friend the analyst Gustav Bally in print criticized Jung then. For the German Society for Psychotherapy (founded in 1926) was reorganized under the Nazis, and Jung became president of the International General Medical Society for Psychotherapy, and editor of its journal. Jones wrote how "in June, 1933 the German Society for Psychotherapy had come under Nazi control" and he claimed that it "masqueraded under the aegis of an 'International German Medical Society for Psychotherapy,' which in turn was 'readjusted' in terms of the 'German National Revolution.'"[55] But in later years Jung defended what he had done on the grounds that he had been acting to protect the profession, and the Jews who practiced it, from needless suffering. As Jung argued, "the cast out Jewish doctors" were able "to become immediate members of the International Society...."[56] (Jones, following Eitingon's original idea, would work out a similar arrangement for Fromm and others within the IPA.) At the same time Jung— like Jones—was making these compromises within Germany, they both did help many Jewish refugees from Germany to establish themselves abroad.

To jump ahead a bit, in 1936 the Nazis then picked a psychiatrist distant cousin of Hermann Göring's, Dr. Matthias H. Göring, who had since 1933 headed the German Society for Psychotherapy, as Jung's co-editor. (Jung resigned in 1940). Matthias Göring had been analyzed by an Adlerian, Leonard Seif; Göring was to play a central part in the history of psychoanalysis under Hitler since in 1938 his new Institute would completely absorb the old German Psychoanalytic Society as a special subsection. (The DPG provided a building, library, and clinic.) In November 1933, Jung had written of Matthias Göring, whose notorious last name is likely today to close most reader's minds: he "is a very amiable and reasonable man, so I have the best hopes for our cooperation."[57]

On October 2, 1933, Jones had written to Anna Freud that he thought better of the actions of Boehm and Müller-Braunschweig now: "Schultz-Hencke, whom they do not regard as sufficiently reliable in his psychoanalytic work for this purpose, has unfortunately been given a permanent position as representing psychoanalysis" on a new commission of the government conducted by "a psychotherapist named Göring...who is a cousin of the famous addict." And later Jones wrote to Anna about Göring on July 20, 1936: "It was easy to get on excellent terms with Göring, who is a very sympathetic personality. We can easily bend him our way, but unfortunately so can other people."

Even more striking, I think, is Jones's 1957 judgment that he found Matthias Göring "a fairly amiable and amenable person...." Jones wrote with a qualification about Göring: "it turned out later [after 1936] that he was not in a position to fulfill the promises he made me about the degree of freedom that was to be allowed the psychoanalytic group [within Göring's Institute]." Jones (like Jung) was continuing to put psychoanalysis ahead of politics, and he wrote in 1957 of Göring's being disappointing: "No doubt in the meantime the Jewish origins of psychoanalysis had been fully explained to him."[58] But that explanation of Jones's was implausible; for not only was Matthias Göring a committed Nazi Party member, but he would make Hitler's *Mein Kampf* required reading at Göring's Institute. Matthias Göring went to his death in 1945 defending Berlin against the advance of the Allied forces.

* * *

To get finally to the specifics of what happened to Fromm in connection with the IPA, while he was already in the States, Müller-Braunschweig was on January 10, 1935 writing Fromm about the various dues he still owed to the German Psychoanalytic Society. (It was wholly tendentious for Jones to have maintained in his biography of Freud about the date 1934: "This year saw the flight of the remaining analysts from Germany and the 'liquidation' of psychoanalysis in Germany."[59] Consciously or not Jones knew there was plenty to be covered up after 1934.) It took awhile for the January 10, 1935 letter to get forwarded to Fromm's correct address in America. Müller-Braunschweig explained exactly what proportion of those dues of each member were owed in turn by the German Society to the IPA, and Müller-Braunschweig made it an "ultimatum" to Fromm to pay the accumulated dues of 211 marks before March 1.[60] Fromm offered, due to straightened circumstances, to pay by installments.

Then on March 3, 1936, Fromm sent Müller-Braunschweig a stiff letter:

> I am extremely sorry that I have up to now not been able to send you as promised the last installment of my debt. I am now in a position to do this, and would have sent the check within a few days had I not heard from various quarters that the German Psychoanalytic Society [DPG] had excluded its Jewish members. That you should have done this without even telling me about it (quite apart from the justification of this step, about which I do not want to speak here) seems to me so incredible that I am first asking you to enlighten me as to whether this rumor corresponds to the facts.[61]

Müller-Braunschweig wrote back to Fromm on March 21, explaining that the Jewish members of the German Society—at a meeting with Jones in the Chair—had voted to resign in the late fall of 1935. And on March 22 he also wrote to Jones rather helplessly,

> I am sorry to have to approach you over so unpleasant an affair. As far as I remember, when you kindly visited us in Berlin, you undertook to see that the Jewish members of the German Society [DPG] living abroad should be informed by the Central Executive [of the IPA] of the voluntary decision of the Jewish members living in Germany to resign from the Society, and that at the same time they should either be helped to transfer to another group or should be offered free-floating membership,
>
> A few days ago I had the enclosed letter from Dr. Fromm, which is very disturbing for us, as it raises the doubt whether you have informed all the Jewish members abroad and asked them to resign, as I recall we discussed.

It is so important for us here that everything should be clearly and unambiguously communicated to all concerned, and that everyone should know that nobody is excluded, but that it is expected that all Jewish members will resign; and that they will suffer no disadvantage if they transfer to other groups or take up free floating membership...[62]

Müller-Braunschweig was frustrated (but not helplessly) in trying to administer a scholarship fund that had originally been set up by wealthy Berlin analysts; it extended loans to students, like Fromm, in training. Once the Nazis took over it was going to prove hopeless to get Jewish beneficiaries to repay their loans. So Müller-Braunschweig finally proposed in 1937 transferring this fund to Jones and the IPA, for him to collect the debts—providing the DPG dues owed to the IPA could be first deducted from this supposed asset. The German attitude about this money was, to put it mildly, insensitive.[63]

Two outside events had taken place in the fall of 1935 that are directly relevant here. First, in September the infamous Nuremberg Laws were enacted by a special session of the Reichstag: Germans of Jewish blood lost rights, marriages between Germans and Jews were forbidden, and Jews could no longer employ "Aryan" servants. And entirely aside from this formal heightening of Nazi anti-Semitism, making it harder for Jews and "Aryans" to be in social contact, in October a Berlin training analyst, Edith Jacobson, was arrested by the Gestapo. She had belonged to some sort of underground resistance group, but had somehow tried to dump at the public Berlin Gruenewald Lake a trunk-full of anti-Nazi literature.[64] One would have thought that a pretty inept way of getting rid of subversive material, since a fireplace or a stove would have been more secure. Anyway, the international analysts were alarmed about the consequences for the woman as well as the German Society; Jones's efforts to help her stopped after an "urgent telegram"[65] from Boehm. (She was sentenced to two years in prison.) Already Jones had been also "quite critical of what he described as 'ultra-Jewish' attitudes on the part of some of the analysts."[66]

It is worth noting that earlier on July 28, 1934 Jones had written to Boehm before the Lucerne Congress:

I will ask you to keep this letter strictly confidential except to Dr. Müller-Braunschweig. It is to prepare you for difficulties you may have to encounter at the Congress.

You are not likely to know the strength of the storm of indignation and opposition which is at present agitating certain circles, especially among the exiles from Germany. This may easily take the form of a personal vote of censure against yourself or even a resolution to exclude the German Society [DPG] from the International Association.

You will know that I myself regard these emotions and ultra-Jewish attitude very unsympathetically, and it is plain to me that you and your colleagues are being made a dumping ground for much emotion and resentment which belongs elsewhere and has been displaced in your direction. My only concern is for the good of Psychoanalysis itself, and I shall defend the view, which I confidently hold, that your actions have been actuated only by the same motive.[67]

On November 21, 1935 Boehm telephoned Jones that the DPG was "in a serious crisis and its dissolution was imminent." Fenichel ineffectually protested on November 26, 1935 that the DPG was caving in to the Nazis, for example, replacing Freud's photograph with one of Hitler.[68] (Jones had written to Anna Freud on November 11: "I prefer Psychoanalysis to be practiced by Gentiles in Germany than not at all." Anna Freud had thought that "from a factual standpoint"[69] she thought Fenichel was correct.) After thinking about Boehm's November 21 telephone call, Jones sent a "brief telegram informing Boehm of a delay in his visit"; Jones had "sanctioned that the Jews voluntarily resign." Then Jones went himself to Berlin where he presided at the December 1 meeting of the DPG. Both Boehm and Edith Jacobson's supporters thought that the difficulties of the DPG came mainly from the new Nuremberg Laws.[70]

The issue arose of whether to dissolve the DPG, and/or to sever the affiliation with the IPA. Since 1933, there had been demands coming from the Nazis that the Jewish analysts resign, and by December 1935 "if the Jewish analysts did not resign, it was possible that the DPG would be dissolved" by the Nazis.[71] A new member like Eva Rosenfeld took what I consider an attractive position among the Jewish members themselves: "In her view the colleagues were in a predicament, which inwardly she could only reject, where they could not resign voluntarily because too high a degree of masochism would be involved, as though they had voluntarily to become their own executioners."[72] As the historian and analyst Peter Loewenberg has recently so well put it,

> Freud was clearly more interested in preserving the organization and presence of psychoanalysis in the Third Reich than he was in the dignity and self-esteem of his Jewish colleagues or in the conditions that are necessary for psychoanalysis to function as a clinical therapy....It is painful and mortifying to read the record of how the leaders of an honored institution, in order to save the organization and promote the careers of the new successors to leadership, humiliated and cast out a large majority of its members to accommodate to a totalitarian state. That a "scientific," or for that matter a "humanistic," society would exclude qualified members for ethnic, racial, religious, or other extrinsic grounds for the sake of the existence of the institution, defies the autonomy of science from political ideology and the morality of valuing individuals which is the humane liberal essence of psychoanalysis itself.[73]

Jones was to claim, in writing to Anna Freud on December 2, 1935, that he had been opposed to "expelling the Jews." Jones also told Anna in general what Jones thought: "Müller-Braunschweig is busy coquetting with the idea of combining a philosophy of Psychoanalysis with a quasi-theological conception of National-Socialist ideology, and you can imagine that this is a very busy occupation. No doubt he will proceed further along these lines, and he is definitely anti-semitic, which Boehm is certainly not."[74] (The Dutch IPA official van Ophuijsen had on September 21, 1933 written Jones that both Boehm and Müller-Braunschweig were confirmed Nazis.[75]) Jones thought that Schultz-Hencke "curiously enough, is often on the right side."[76] Boehm reported that Schultz-Hencke had proposed that "the Society [DPG] should leave the IPA and dissolve, while each one of us should secretly remain a member of the IPA, and carry on his or her psychoanalytic practice in secret."[77]

But Boehm, like Müller-Braunschweig and completely at odds with what Jones had written Anna Freud, insisted that Jones was in favor of the Jews leaving the Society; evidently Jones had also telegrammed Therese Benedeck, who had been a leader against the idea of having the Jews exclude themselves: "Urgently advise voluntary resignation."[78] (The Dutch analysts would later, under similar circumstances, choose instead to all resign in protest.) Still, Boehm was sufficiently in good graces within the IPA for him to spend three hours in 1937 describing the situation of psychoanalysis in Germany before a small group of Viennese analysts.

On March 26, 1936, Jones had written to Fromm, in response to the letter of Fromm's that Müller-Branschweig had sent:

> Dr. Müller-Braunschweig forwarded to me your letter of complaint considering the resignation of the Jewish members. It is not literally true that they have been excluded…, but after a considerable discussion in Berlin between them and their colleagues, a discussion at which I also was present, they subsequently decided it would be in everyone's interest for them to send in their resignation. It was plain to me that there was no alternative, and indeed I may tell you that I am daily expecting to hear the whole German-Society itself being dissolved.

The idea of any imminent dissolution might sound dramatic but was one of Jones's rhetorical fabrications; he went on to Fromm,

> As regards the question of communicating with you you will doubtless understand that it is far from easy to write from Berlin. There also appears to be a misunderstanding in the matter for which I am more to blame than Dr. Müller-Braunschweig. They assumed that I would notify the German members living abroad, whereas this was not-quite clear in my mind. I notified those in England and evidently thought this would suffice. You are the only other member in this category, and I had thought that you were now a member of the New York Society.

But A. A. Brill was in regular contact with Jones about any new members of the New York group from abroad, and Jones would have heard from Brill any such news. Jones certainly knew how lay analysts like Fromm were frowned upon all over American psychoanalysis. Nevertheless, Jones added: "If there is any difficulty in the way of your being accepted there [in New York], then I can offer you the direct 'Nansen' membership of the International Association. Will you be good enough to notify me about this."[79] ("The 'Nansen' membership was established similar to the 'Nansen' passport for political refugees that F. Nansen introduced for Russian refugees without citizenship."[80]

This would follow Eitingon's precedent with Clara Happel, and also Jung's procedure among his following of analytic psychologists.)

Because of a postal error, Fromm said he did not hear of Jones's March letter for a couple of months; Fromm then indicated,

> Since there is no alternative, I accept the fact of giving up my membership in the German Psychoanalytic Society. Though I am in close connection with the Washington-Baltimore Psychoanalytic Society where I gave a course of lectures last year, it would be against their principles to accept a non-physician as a member, and I would rather not press the matter. This being the case, I would prefer to become a "Nansen" member of the International Association and would be very grateful to you if you would take the necessary steps to arrange it.

(In April, Fromm had sent Müller-Braunschweig a check for fifty dollars, or 124 marks.) In June, Jones confirmed Fromm's standing as a direct member of the IPA, and hoped he would come to the forthcoming Congress in Marienbad. Fromm indicated he would not be able to attend the Congress, but was grateful for Jones's writing and wondered to whom he should send his membership fee. (No correspondence exists further on this point, and I am assuming that no agreed-upon fees for such direct members existed. In any event, it is striking that Fromm, who for the sake of privacy destroyed so much of his correspondence, still saved these letters between himself and Jones, Müller-Braunschweig, and, as we shall see, Ruth Eissler.)

The DPG went on existing; as a result of a July 1936 agreement between Jones, Brill, Boehm, Müller-Braunschweig, and M. H. Göring, the DPG (still part of the IPA) became part of the newly established so-called Göring Institute. The DPG celebrated Freud's eightieth birthday, but no Jews were allowed.[81] But the DPG, founded originally by Abraham in 1910, finally dissolved in November 1938; Jones first offered its members "direct membership" in the IPA, but Boehm rejected that proposal. The death knell of the DPG, as it had become "Working group A" of the Göring Institute, had really come only with Müller-Braunschweig's trip to Vienna after the Nazis marched in on March 12, 1938. (Working group B was Schultz-Hencke's neo-analysts, and Working group C meant the Jungians.)

Once the Nazis had seized the Vienna Psychoanalytic Association, its clinic, and Freud's press, his eldest son Martin—in charge then of Freud's finances – telegrammed for help to Müller-Braunschweig in Berlin. (Once again Jones disguised in his Freud biography the extent of the IPA's having initiated this cooperation by writing only that "Müller-Braunschweig, accompanied by a Nazi Commissar, arrived from Berlin with the purpose of liquidating the psychoanalytic situation.")[82] The idea evidently was to hand over to Müller-Braunschweig, and through him to the DPG, whatever assets that the analysts in Vienna then had. It seems to me scarcely self-respecting for Freud and the Vienna Psychoanalytic Association to be turning their official selves over to the Aryanized German Society, as they appealed to Müller-Braunschweig to come to Vienna.

But then all Freud's authoritarian political leanings in the last decade of his life in Vienna have gone generally unrecognized, although at the time it was heartbreaking to his politically idealistic followers from America who knew what was happening in Vienna. Ruth Mack Brunswick wept over Freud's politics, and Freud's analysis of her husband Mark was interrupted because of Freud's having "betrayed" the local socialists. "Chancellor Engelbert Dollfuss had already, in the early part of 1934, put down a Marxist revolt in Vienna by suspending Parliament and bombarding the huge socialist housing project in the city until it surrendered."[83] Yet Martin Freud strikingly hung a picture of Dollfuss in the office of Freud's psychoanalytic Press. Further, Freud's attempts to flatter Mussolini (who had been a protector of Austrian independence) and no doubt also to help psychoanalysis in Italy, does not withstand scrutiny.[84] Freud's decision to remain in Vienna so long got all sorts of people into hot water, since they felt they could not leave earlier without appearing to desert a sinking ship. (Four of his sisters later perished in Nazi concentration camps.)

Jones had come to the city right after the occupation of Austria, and he took part in the deliberations by which Müller-Braunschweig accepted becoming trustee for the Vienna Psychoanalytic Association in behalf of the DPG. There were too few non-Jewish analysts in Vienna for the project to succeed; therefore Jones had wanted the Gentile Richard Sterba to stay in Austria. Anna Freud was questioned about finances by the Gestapo after her brother Martin had left incriminating documentary evidence about money abroad; she then, to save herself, showed them a letter to her from Müller-Braunschweig, and the Gestapo consequently also questioned Müller-Braunschweig.[85] Evidently Müller-Braunschweig (along with many others who had acted to protect Freud) may have been some help to the Freuds in getting permission to leave Austria (Freud left Vienna on June 4, 1938.)

But the attempt at an Aryanized Vienna analytic group proved a fiasco, and the Press, the Psychoanalytic Association, and the clinic were liquidated on September 1, 1938. Meanwhile Müller-Braunschweig's reputation was tarnished back in Berlin; his letter to Anna Freud had consoled her, and advocated the future autonomy of the Vienna Institute from both National Socialism and the Göring Institute.[86] This was the occasion when the DPG also was dissolved. Not until the end of September 1938 did the Nazis revoke the licenses of all Jewish physicians and attorneys, almost three years after the Jewish analysts had themselves resigned from the DPG.

The activities of the Göring Institute, and what role the analysts there played, is an entirely separate story. We have been told that it could be "a refuge for most."[87] All the records of the Institute got destroyed in fighting at the end of the war. We do know now, however, that Müller-Braunschweig passed along to Fascist authorities, in code, the names of Jewish members of the Italian Psychoanalytic Society.[88] He declined to join the Nazi Party, which would have saved him from being prohibited from teaching and publishing; he was not allowed to enter the Göring Institute, yet his analyst wife taught there. Boehm could not conduct training analyses. But Müller-Braunschweig did remain "responsible for lecture organization even after 1938"[89]; he continued his private practice. And Boehm, who had earlier opposed the Nazi approach to homosexuality—"sterilization, hormone treatment, operations, prison, concentration camps and the death penalty"[90]—by December 1944 had come to agree with these practices. The issue of complicity in mass murder comes up, since soldiers with "battle fatigue" were to be exterminated too. It might go without saying that it was illegal to treat Jews at the Göring Institute; patients who were found to be untreatable were bound to wind up in the Nazi euthanasia program, and put to death. The fact that one German member of Working-group A—John Rittmeister, a communist who had once been a student of Jung's—was guillotined for treason in 1943 does not do much to brighten a terribly shabby episode in Western history.

According to a malignant irony, the Nazis were convinced that "mental disorder within the master race could not be genetic or essentially organic," and therefore thought applied depth psychology had a special role to play in the Third Reich.[91] I think that true psychotherapy itself was destroyed under the Nazis. The Göring Institute's success in giving help to the Luftwaffe and promoting the Nazi war effort itself besmirches the whole tradition of so-called German psychotherapy. All of us should be wary of the implications of any system of ideas which ever aims to "harmonize" the individual and the social order. Anyone who tries to argue that psychoanalysis was "preserved through the departure of the Jewish analysts and by the cover of the Göring name"[92] has missed the boat. Jones might have thought he had tried to "save" psychoanalysis in Germany, but by the end of the war he acknowledged the failure of such a project. (But his rationalizations in the form of the narrative he constructed in his Freud biography are harder to detect than Jung's own forms of apology.) To the extent that German culture once presented some of the best parts of the Western tradition, the tale of "psychotherapy" under the Third Reich has to be more ethically worrisome to me than the various abuses of psychiatry under the old Soviet regime.

* * *

Some of the worst aspects of this story remain to be told. For even though Jones had years earlier written to Anna Freud that Müller-Braunschweig was anti-Semitic, in the end Müller-Braunschweig (who went to a Jungian analyst after World War II) successfully led the post-World War II German group back into the IPA. Although Freud liked to castigate those who led "secessions" in the history of psychoanalysis, it has always been considered acceptable for a group to secede in the guise of psychoanalytic orthodoxy. Müller-Braunschweig was able to thrive as a leader within the IPA; orthodoxy was "one way of advertising one's dissociation from the Nazi past."[93] Freud, as we have seen, had been adamantly against Schultz-Hencke and the ideas he represented. (I suspect that Schultz-Hencke's use of the term "neo-analysis" may have later put Fromm off any such designation for his own point of view.) After the DPG with Müller-Braunschweig as president was reconstituted following the end of the war in 1945, the question then arose of its affiliation with the IPA.

Müller-Braunschweig was able to emphasize that Schultz-Hencke's view was that "the theories of psychoanalysis, particularly the libido theory, …[were] essentially antiquated and out of date."[94] By May 1946, Anna Freud would be writing Müller-Braunschweig, "I have always been very sorry that your visit to Vienna and your relationship with me in 1938 had such unhappy consequences for you. You know that was not my intention."[95] Psychoanalytic orthodoxy has always been blood thicker than political water. During the early 1930s a patient in training with Anna Freud, Esther Menaker, indicated that she was troubled by there being "'so many splinter movements: Jung, Adler, Rank. If you are all searching for the truth about human personality, why can't you work together?'" Anna Freud "replied without hesitation": "'Nothing is as important to us as the psychoanalytic movement.'"[96]

By December 1947, Anna Freud would be, as acting IPA treasurer, also writing to Müller-Braunschweig to "attend to the question of the payment of arrears of annual subscriptions since 1939…."[97] Implicitly, at least when it came to money, she was suggesting that the DPG had unofficially remained within the IPA. And that year, Anna Freud, as IPA secretary, listed the DPG's activities as of 1945-1947 within the *Bulletin* of the IPA.

When the DPG tried to be re-admitted to the IPA at the Zurich Congress in 1949, Jones in the Chair held that years of "amalgamating different forms of psychotherapy—Jung, Adler, Freud, Neo-Analysis" had had their ill effect, but that Müller-Braunschweig had remained one of the "true, real, genuine analysts."[98] Provisional acceptance of the Germans was therefore, he thought, in order. The English analyst John Rickman, although supposedly working in behalf of the British government, had turned over to the IPA analysts in London a report which described Müller-Braunschweig's "incompetence as an analyst and his Nazis leanings."[99]

Following the Zurich Congress there were some unpleasant exchanges between Müller-Braunschweig and Schultz-Hencke; Müller-Braunschweig thought that Schultz-Hencke was merely giving "the impression that you are a psychoanalyst." Schultz-Hencke protested that Müller-Braunschweig had misquoted him, giving the audience in Zurich "a catastrophic picture of my heresy." Schultz-Hencke maintained,

> You, and others from one side,...think that you can break the gentleman's agreement which has held up to now... If you go on asserting that I have abandoned 90% of psychoanalysis, I shall have to tell you most vehemently that younger psychoanalysts will find this opinion simply ridiculous...if we are going to talk numbers...my findings confirm 75% of the empirical discoveries of psychoanalysis, to which Freud attached decisive importance. I only criticize a metaphorical and theoretical superstructure which in addition, as Freud himself has explained, is partly hypothetical. I criticize the attempt, made in the spirit of the 90s, of naïve libido-energetic theory—again of a speculative nature. I think I am as completely justified in describing myself as a psychoanalyst as I ever was, at any rate exactly as the Americans in question call themselves Neo-Psychoanalysts.

Müller-Braunschweig found this letter of Schultz-Hencke's was "bristling with slanders, misrepresentations and insults." To Müller-Branschweig "your view of metapsychology as an unnecessary and outdated set of hypotheses" meant that Schultz-Hencke "held a different theory of the Unconscious from Freud's."[100] Müller-Braunschweig held a minority position within the DPG, and it will be remembered that Schultz-Hencke had been allowed to continue training candidates during the war. As a result of Müller-Braunschweig's tactical position as a minority within the DPG, he and five others (one now known to have been a Nazi Party member) organized a new German Psychoanalytic Association—(the "DPV"), which alone secured admission to the IPA at the Amsterdam Congress in 1951. As the Goggins have recently observed, "By supporting the admission of the DPV into the IPA, the leadership of the world psychoanalytic community had chosen to place theoretical orthodoxy as a more significant factor in readmission than the Nazification of the members being admitted."[101] "After a series of organizational maneuvers," Müller-Braunschweig "succeeded in having himself and a small group of colleagues accepted back into the IPA, leaving Schultz-Hencke out in the cold as not only the neo-Freudian—which he was—but also as the displacement object for their common guilt, the designated sole Nazi collaborator—which he was not."[102]

* * *

In the meantime Fromm, living in Mexico since 1950, discovered that he had somehow been dropped from being a direct member of the IPA. (Throughout the difficult conditions of World War II not even the general membership roster was maintained any longer in the *Bulletin* appearing in *The International Journal of Psychoanalysis*.) In 1952, the sole direct member listed was Dr.Werner Kemper, who had cooperated with Boehm in supporting the "extermination of both homosexuals and soldiers experiencing 'battle fatigue.'" Kemper was to be a significant source of disinformation about what had happened to psychoanalysis under the Nazis.[103] (He had also analyzed M. H. Göring's wife.) Further, Kemper had written on eugenics laws in Germany.

Jones had evidently encouraged Kemper to go to Brazil, where Kemper got involved, before returning to Germany, in accusations of distantly having sanctioning torture.[104] To recur to the question of analytic lineage and family tree matters, which we encountered at the outset of this paper; if analysts could proudly trace back their analytic parentage, then it seemed to some at least fair game to blame Kemper for what happened in the hands of his own pupils in Brazil.

On May 28, 1953 Fromm wrote to Ruth S. Eissler, IPA secretary, in care of the Institute of Psychoanalysis in London: Jones was by then honorary president of the IPA.

> I would greatly appreciate it if you would be kind enough to inform me on the following question: I have been a member-at-large of the International Psychoanalytic Association since about 1934, when I had to resign from the German Psychoanalytic Association [sic]. I find that my name does not appear any more on the [IPA] Association's list of members-at-large, although I never resigned, nor was I ever notified of a termination of my membership. Could you be kind enough to let me know what my status as a member is?

This letter bore an uncanny similarity to Fromm's equally poignant letter to Müller-Braunschweig in 1936.

Ruth Eissler replied from New York City on June 11, 1953:

> I have received your letter of May 28th.
> Since 1946, the American Psychoanalytic Association [APA] is the only component Society of the International Psychoanalytic Association in this country.

As of 1946 the earlier automatic membership in the APA of people in various branch groups was replaced by a special routine requiring APA acknowledgement before prescribed analysts of branch societies automatically became members of the APA; lay analysts had a special hurdle in America.

Ruth Eissler's letter went on,

> Membership in the I.P.A. depends on membership in a Component Society of the I.P.A. You are listed as a member of the Washington Psychoanalytic Society, which is not in itself a Component Society of the I.P.A. but is an Affiliate Society of the American.
> The old German Psychoanalytic Society no longer exists.

That was not true, and Ruth Eissler had to know it since the DPG's "provisional" 1949 IPA admission had not been extended in 1951. And the DPG (still outside the IPA) continues to function in the year 2003. Or was she also meaning to say that the DPG no longer existed as far the IPA was concerned? Such thinking would have been in keeping with the old prejudice that to be outside the IPA was to render one not an analyst. Eissler continued,

A new Society was organized under the Chairmanship of Dr. Carl Müller-Braunschweig [DPV]....

Membership-at-Large in the I.P.A. may be acquired in exceptional cases, by those who were previously members of a Component Society of the I.P.A. A number of lay analysts in this country, who are not members of the American Psychoanalytic Association but who reapplied for membership in the I.P.A. were willing to be screened by the Joint Screening Committee of the International and the American Associations. This Committee was established at the Congress at Amsterdam [1951] in order to help in the appraisal of foreign lay analysts for reinstatement of their membership in the I.P.A. It consists of three ex officio members: The President of the American Psychoanalytic Association; the Chairman of the Board on Professional Standards of the American Psychoanalytic Association; and a member of the Central Executive of the International Psychoanalytic Association who is a member of the American Psychoanalytic Association.

At present applications for reinstatement should be sent to me, as Chairman of the Joint Screening Committee, and should include a detailed curriculum vitae, including present activities.

I hope that this give you the information which you requested.

Fromm replied on June 29th:

Thank you very much for your answer to my letter.

I take it that if I want to continue my status as a member-at-large of the International Psychoanalytic Association, I would have to present the application for reinstatement. Before I make a decision, I would very much like to understand the situation a little better, and I would greatly appreciate it if you could enlighten me on the question of what is meant by a "screening" of previous members-at-large. Does it mean that it is considered that they lost their status as members-at-large, and that the screening amounts practically to a new application for membership? Or if not, according to what principles is such a screening carried out? Would, for instance, the fact that my psychoanalytic views do not correspond to the views of the majority be one of the factors to be taken into consideration at the screening, and a reason for denial of membership?

I have to confess even to an ignorance concerning the principles governing the American Psychoanalytic Association with regard to the acceptance of members. Is there any rule that as a matter of principle the American Association excludes all non-medical analysts?

Hoping that I am not imposing on your time too much by raising these questions, and thanking you for the trouble you might take in answering them,
Sincerely yours,

Ruth Eissler wrote back on July 27th, 1953; she had said as yet absolutely nothing about Fromm's many books, articles, or other well-known contributions to psychoanalysis. Nor could she possibly readily admit the truth that some lay analysts had been accepted as members of the American Psychoanalytic Association. The resolution at the Amsterdam Congress bearing on direct members had sounded like it was supposed to facilitate lay analysts, especially in America, becoming "direct" members of the IPA. Although "the status of Members-at-Large" was supposed to be granted after "careful evaluation of their qualifications," no hint was raised that this process could mean disqualifying people already accepted as direct members.[105]

Eissler continued in her earlier bureaucratic vein:

> I am sorry that my answer to your letter of June 29th was delayed; however, the preparations of the 18th International Psychoanalytic Congress kept me quite busy.
>
> In answer to your questions: At the 17th International Psychoanalytic Congress in Amsterdam, 1951 [where Müller-Braunschweig's new group—the DPV—won admittance], the Joint Screening Committee of the I.P.A. and the A.P.A. was established for the purpose of giving those lay analysts in North America who are not members of the A.P.A., and who had lost membership in the I.P.A. through the change of statutes of the International, the opportunity to be reinstated to membership. The American Psychoanalytic Association does not recognize lay analysts as members except those who had been members before 1939. All those lay analysts who used to be members at large in the I.P.A. and reside in North America have to reapply for membership through the Joint Screening Committee. Most of the former lay-members at large have done so. The reinstatement depends on the recommendation of the committee, which consists of three ex-officio members: the President of the American Psychoanalytic Association; the Chairman of the Board of Standards of the American Psychoanalytic Association, and a member of the Central Executive of the I.P.A., who is also a member of the A.P.A.

After repeating her earlier legalisms, Ruth Eissler then put in a zinger of a paragraph:

> I am, of course, not in the position of anticipating the recommendations of the Joint Screening Committee. Personally, though, I would assume that anyone who does not stand on the basic principles of psychoanalysis would anyway not be greatly interested in becoming a member of the International Psychoanalytic Association.

Fromm answered her one more time on August 26th, and evidently that was the end of their correspondence:

> Thank you very much for your informative letter of July 27th.
>
> I appreciate your comment that personally you assume that anyone who does not stand on the basic principles of psychoanalysis would not be interested in becoming a member of the International Psychoanalytic Association. I am sure you realize that the main issue is just what we mean by "basic principles" of psychoanalysis. I consider myself as sharing these principles, but the question is, how broadly or how narrowly the International Psychoanalytic Association interprets them. It is also not quite the question of wanting to become a member of the International Psychoanalytic Association, but rather, of the reasons for being dropped from membership.
>
> I shall give some more thought to he problem, and shall let you know in case I want to reopen the issue.

The logic of her argument might just as well imply that anyone who applied would automatically be accepted, but Fromm knew she was not saying that. Clearly he wanted to remain—not "become"—an IPA member. One might naively have thought she would be interested in bringing in his Mexican group to the IPA. But I doubt that Ruth Eissler would have responding the way she did entirely on her own hook; it remains to be seen, for example, whether the then IPA president, Heinz Hartmann, also living in New York City, or anyone in London, took part behind-the-scenes in this series of letters.

An examination of the files of Grete Bibring, Ruth Eissler's predecessor as IPA secretary, indicates IPA trouble about Fromm once he started practicing and training in Mexico. Austen Rigg's Robert Knight was, as of 1951, chairman of the board of professional standards of the American Psychoanalytic Association in addition to being president-elect of the American Psychoanalytic Association; when getting an inquiry about Fromm's standing, Knight wrote, after a long typed letter on the subject of Fromm, a handwritten P.S. for Bibring: "Is Dr. Fromm one of the people who wants status in the International as a member at large?" So, few people indeed can have understood the bureaucratic intricacies of the IPA. The Mexican who wrote to Knight in the first place was encouraged to inquire about Fromm's organizational qualifications by Karl Menninger. As of 1953 Menninger was still intensely irritated about Fromm. When the Information Service of the National Council of Churches of Christ referred to Fromm as "a noted psychoanalyst," Menninger objected that Fromm was

> noted all right, but not altogether in the good sense you infer. Dr. Fromm is a dissident from the psychoanalytic group and at present has gone to Mexico where he is instructing Mexican physicians his peculiar kind of psychoanalysis which the poor Mexican doctors will assume to be approved in America, which it is not.

Menninger compared Fromm in Mexico to how the National Council of Churches of Christ "would look upon a dissident in the Presbyterian Church, let us say, being a missionary in Mexico and preaching, for example, that Jesus was not a Jew, and really lived in North Africa, and thought that Muhammed was one of his prophets."[106] Grete Bibring's 1951 response to another inquiry about Fromm in Mexico was more tentative and smoothly politic than either Menninger or Ruth Eissler; Bibring said she was unsure "whether he plans to stay there long and it might be a better decision to wait and see how things shape up." A couple of years later, however, it would be clearer that Fromm's presence in Mexico was not going to be temporary.

* * *

Perhaps now it makes more sense how Fromm could legitimately defend himself against Marcuse-like charges that he was some sort of conformist. He had, for example, been risking his standing in the Washington Psychoanalytic Society by carrying on training not authorized by the APA. In 1971, he

wrote protesting to Martin Jay, a historian, the whole line of Marcuse's thinking that held that Fromm had given up essential Freudianism. Fromm argued
that he considered Jay's manuscript's thesis "a very drastic statement only
possible from the standpoint of orthodox Freudianism."[107] Fromm was also
unknowingly echoing Schultz-Hencke against Müller-Braunschweig, although politically Fromm was unlike them untarnished by any collaborative
politics. Like Lacan in France Fromm had to protest, "I have never wanted to
found a school of my own."

> I was removed by the International Psychoanalytic Association from membership in
> this Association to which I had belonged, and am still a member of the Washington
> Psychoanalytic Association, which is Freudian. I have always criticized the Freudian
> orthodoxy and the bureaucratic methods of the Freudian international organization,
> but my whole theoretical work is based on what I consider Freud's most important
> findings, with the exception of his metapsychological findings. (This, incidentally, is
> the reverse of Marcuse's position, who bases his thinking entirely on Freud's
> metapsychology and ignores completely his clinical findings, that is to say, the
> unconscious, character, resistance, etc.)[108]

Marcuse and his allies at the Frankfurt School had become unconsciously
authoritarian in identifying with the powers-that-be in orthodox psychoanalytic thinking.

Fromm had obviously been deeply hurt at his 1953 ostracism from the IPA,
and he would have been entitled to have been both resentful and offended in
his pride. (The IPA continues today to have "direct" members, but none has
ever matched Fromm's own singular contributions.) Fromm was unlike Reich
in that he did not publicize his being persecuted. If Fromm had been a better
bureaucratic infighter, he might have known the character of Müller-
Braunschweig's crew that had just been accepted as the DPV at the IPA, and
Fromm could have disputed Ruth Eissler's contention that the DPG no longer
existed.

Book writing was probably a better way of Fromm's proceeding. It would
be in the spirit of the ideals of the eighteenth-century Enlightenment to
believe that concepts are more important that analytic lineage, or a family
tree. Fromm had a genuinely radical spirit within psychoanalysis, which has
been ignored by the partisans in behalf of Marcuse's point of view.

It had to complicate Fromm's position that he did not share all aspects of
Schultz-Hencke's "neo-Freudianism," and Fromm distanced himself ideologically from Adler and Jung as well—they remain the arch-heretics in IPA reasoning, but Fromm was still somehow caught in that tradition of thought.
Fromm's own struggle was unlike theirs because it could not be considered in
any way as a personal problem that he had had with Freud. In 1961, after
Schultz-Hencke's death, Fromm would join with the DPG and other non-IPA
groups (like the White Institute) to set up the International Federation of
Psychoanalytic Societies.

Marcuse's idea that Fromm was a conformist is repudiated by this whole tale of the steps in his exclusion from the IPA. Fromm could readily acknowledge having given up his orthodox psychoanalytic views after about ten years of clinical practicing, and he was—unlike most others—willing to stand alone. That he sometimes had allies like Fromm-Reichmann, Horney, Clara Thompson, and Harry Stack Sullivan, as well as others, should not detract from the singularity of Fromm's achievement. (Part of Fromm's difficulties with Horney underline his uniqueness; although she herself had been the victim of orthodoxy, she succeeded in excluding Fromm as a training analyst in her own new institute on the grounds that he was not an M.D., leading to his resignation and joining the group associated with Sullivan. Fromm's short-run downfall here was at least in part due to the feelings of competitive rivalry that his own success generated.) But the special appeal of Fromm's books meant that he could reach over the heads of the IPA leaders. And in challenging Jones about Ferenczi (and Rank), as well as in writing *Sigmund Freud's Mission*, Fromm at least settled a score there. (According to Fromm's literary executor, Rainer Funk, Fromm felt uncomfortable enough about a critique he had published of Rank in the late 1930s so as not to want to have it reprinted.[109])

And then the future rewarded Fromm in an unexpected way. As we saw, he had been able to be cut out of the IPA because he was not, as a lay analyst, entitled to be a member of the American Psychoanalytic Association, at that time the only constituent body of the IPA in America. Yet for years he had been prominently associated with the White Institute, and it would be members from that group who in the 1980s would play a substantial role in successfully launching a restraint-of-trade anti-trust lawsuit against the training restrictions of the IPA and the American Psychoanalytic Institute.[110] Ironically, Ruth Eissler's husband Kurt had in 1965 written a long book defending non-medical analysis.[111] With all the examples of accommodation, adaptation, cowardice, and opportunism in the course of recounting how Fromm came to be dropped from the IPA, he himself comes across thoroughly self-respecting.

It is hard to see how Fromm could have done other in 1936 than to accept Jones's offer of becoming a "direct" IPA member; but having done so he was left, as a lay analyst in America, in an exposed position. In Britain, Glover had been savvy in the mid-1940s in insisting on becoming a member of the Swiss Society, having resigned from the British Society, rather than to settle for applying for the uncertain status of being a direct member.[112] In hindsight, it should be a truism that what an IPA president grants can just as easily be taken away, even by the secretary. Fromm was not, as when the DPG excluded its Jewish members in late 1935, even informed after the fact of what had happened to his standing as a direct member. Meanwhile it will be up to the reader to evaluate whether Ruth Eissler's edict was right that Fromm had become at odds with the "basic principles"of psychoanalysis.

A more important matter may be the general problem of how human beings accommodate themselves in social crises. For those of us who have never had to live through the experiences of such trying times as in Central Europe during the 1930s and the war itself, it is tempting to suppose that human beings might have behaved with more honor in the face of Nazi tyranny, rather than to engage in so many varieties of Machiavellianism. After all, analysts were almost uniquely equipped to practice their profession abroad. On the other hand, all of us are inevitably enmeshed in the life of the ideologies of our times. We today merely have to deal with charges associated with "political correctness," as opposed to the question of whether neo-Freudianism could be considered fascistic. Still, as clear-sighted a view of the past as possible still seems to me desirable, and in keeping with Fromm's teachings.

It has to be striking that the story of Fromm's exclusion from the IPA, with all its ramifications, has so far remained untold. It is not easy to follow things when someone as talented as Jones was capable of getting narrative rabbits out of a hat. For example, as late as at the Paris IPA Congress in 1938 he had maintained,

> The German Society continues to live a somewhat delicate existence. The new German Institute for Psychological Research and Psychotherapy [the Göring Institute], of which the Psychoanalytic Society is a separate department, was founded in May, 1936. The department has enjoyed considerable autonomy, many candidates have been trained and the total membership list increased.

And Jones reported that as of November 1938 the German Psychoanalytic Society, transformed into Working Group A, had resigned its membership of the IPA.[113] Unless one had followed the whole story with closest scrutiny, it would be impossible to understand what had actually happened. By 1957 Jones could, as we have seen, make the somersault of authoritatively writing in his Freud biography that psychoanalysis in German had been "liquidated" as of 1934. And it has taken almost fifty years Jones since wrote those words to untangle the complexities behind his reasoning. Freud distrusted Jones, who had been the author of a famous early paper on rationalization, in part because of how difficult it could be to keep track of Jones's duplicities.

Freud was himself a great writer, and enduringly important enough as a thinker for us to be able to understand how his own flaws could be partly those of the times and culture. When he died in London in 1939, he was eighty-three years old; I believe that he partly stayed in Vienna because of the doctors familiar with his case, and in London his health went downhill rapidly. He does not need any more of our mythologizing, and his life can sustain the closest scrutiny. We have been told of a meeting that Freud had with Boehm in November 1936; Freud had ended the meeting with an admonition to Boehm that was "in a reality a tactful indirect condemnation. He said: 'You may make all kinds of sacrifices, but you are not to make any concessions.'"[114]

Old World charm should not ever take us in; Freud and the IPA had already made abundant concessions, and would continue to do so, even though we in the New World can be gullible in mistaking hypocrisy for the truth. A central theme in Henry James's novels was how European manners and American sincerity keep colliding with one another.

Even when we try to admit all the faults we are apt to have in North America, it does not mean that one need turn a blind eye to the dubious means it took, under the guidance of Freud, Jones, and others, for the IPA to become the powerful institution it was to turn out. Luckily Fromm's own form of resistance did not have to take the tragic shape of Rittmeister's in Germany during the war. The choice is not, as Jones would have had it, between psychoanalysis and politics, but what the proper relationship should be between those inevitably different sorts of inquiries.

Notes

1. Paul Roazen, *Oedipus in Britain: Edward Glover and the Struggle Over Klein* (New York: Other Press, 2000).
2. Paul Roazen, "The Problem of Silence: Training Analyses," *International Forum of Psychoanalysis*, Vol. 11 (2002), pp. 73-77.
3. Ernst Falzeder, "Family Tree Matters," *Journal of Analytical Psychology*, Vol. 43 (1998), pp. 127-54, and Ernst Falzeder, "The Threads of Psychoanalytic Filiations or Psychoanalysis Taking Effect," in *100 Years of Psychoanalysis, Contributions to the History of Psychoanalysis*, ed. Andre Haynal and Ernst Falzeder (Geneva: Cahiers Psychiatriques Genevois, Special Issue, 1994), pp. 169-94.
4. See, for example, Erich Fromm, "The Method and Function of an Analytic Social Psychology" and "Psychoanalytic Characterology and Its Relevance for Social Psychology," in *The Crisis of Psychoanalysis* (New York: Holt Rinehart & Winston, 1947), Erich Fromm, "The Social Background of Psychoanalytic Therapy," translated by Caroline Newton (New York Public Library); Erich Fromm, *Escape From Freedom* (New York: Holt, Rinehart & Winston, 1941). See Paul Roazen, "Fromm's *Escape From Freedom* and His Standing Today," *International Forum of Psychoanalysis*, Vol. 9 (2000), pp. 239-40.
5. Erich Fromm, *Man For Himself: An Inquiry into the Psychology of Ethics* (New York: Holt, Rinehart & Winston, 1947), Erich Fromm, *Psychoanalysis and Religion* (New Haven, CT: Yale University Press, 1950), Erich Fromm, *The Forgotten Language: An Introduction to the Understanding of Dreams, Fairy Tales and Myths* (New York: Grove Press, 1957), Erich Fromm, *The Sane Society* (London: Routledge & Kegan Paul, 1956).
6. Erich Fromm and Michael Maccoby, *Social Character in a Mexican Village: A Sociopsychoanalytic Study* (Englewood Cliffs, NJ: Prentice Hall, 1970; new edition, with an introduction by Michael Maccoby, New Brunswick, NJ, Transaction Publishers, 1996).
7. Erich Fromm, *The Art of Loving* (London: George Allen & Unwin, 1957), Erich Fromm, *To Have Or To Be?* (New York: Harper & Row, 1976), and Erich Fromm, *The Anatomy of Human Destructiveness* (New York: Holt, Rinehart & Winston, 1973).

8.   Ernest Jones, *The Life and Work of Sigmund Freud*, Vols. 1-3 (New York: Basic Books, 1953-57), Erich Fromm, *Sigmund Freud's Mission: An Analysis of His Personality and Influence* (New York: Harper & Brothers, 1959).

9.   Fromm, *Sigmund Freud's Mission*, pp. 105-06.

10. Erich Fromm, "Psychoanalysis – Science or Party Line," reprinted in *The Dogma of Christ and Other Essays on Religion, Psychology and Culture* (New York: Holt, Rinehart & Winston, 1963), pp. 131-44.

11. Neil McLaughlin, "How To Become a Forgotten Intellectual: Intellectual Movements and the Rise and Fall of Erich Fromm," *Sociological Forum*, Vol. 13 (1998), pp. 215-48; Neil McLaughlin, "Why Do Schools of Thought Fail? Neo-Freudianism as a Case Study in the Sociology of Knowledge," *Journal of the History of the Behavioral Sciences*, Vol. 34 (1998), pp. 113-34. See also Daniel Burston, *The Legacy of Erich Fromm* (Cambridge, MA, Harvard University Press, 1991).

12. See Erich Fromm, "The Dogma of Christ," in *The Dogma of Christ*.

13. Lawrence J. Friedman, *Identity's Architect: A Biography of Erik H. Erikson* (New York: Charles Scribner's Sons, 1999), p. 162. Erik H. Erikson, *Childhood and Society* (New York: W. W. Norton, 1950).

14. See Paul Roazen, *Erik H. Erikson: The Power and Limits of a Vision* (New York: The Free Press, 1976; Northvale, NJ, Aronson, 1997).

15. Erik H. Erikson, *Young Man Luther: A Study in Psychoanalysis and History* (New York: W. W. Norton, 1958), p. 239.

16. Karl Menninger, "Loneliness in the Modern World," *Nation*, Vol. 154 (March 14, 1942), p. 317.

17. Otto Fenichel, "Psychoanalytic Remarks on Fromm's Book *Escape From Freedom*," in *The Collected Papers of Otto Fenichel*, second series (New York: W. W. Norton, 1954), ch. 19, pp. 260-77; so also Otto Fenichel, *119 Rundbriefe*, Vol. 2 (Frankfurt, Stroemfeld, 1998), ed. Elke Mühleitner and Johannes Reichmayr, pp. 1559-89.

18. Paul Roazen, "Book Review of *Ideas and Identities: The Life and Work of Erik H. Erikson*, ed. Wallerstein & Goldberger," *Psychoanalytic Psychology*, Vol. 17 (Summer 2000), pp. 437-42.

19. Rainer Funk, *Erich Fromm: His Life and Ideas*, translated by Ian Portman and Manuela Kunkel (New York: Continuum, 2000), pp. 74-77.

20. Karen Brecht, Volker Friedrich, Ludger Hermanns, Isidor Kaminer, Dierk Juelich, editors, *"Here Life Goes On In A Most Peculiar Way...,"* translated by Christine Trollope (London: Kellner-Goethe Institute, 1993), p. 72.

21. Jones, *The Life and Work of Sigmund Freud*, Vol. 3, p. 182.

22. Brecht et al., *"Here Life Goes On,"* p. 112.

23. Jones, *The Life and Work of Sigmund Freud*, Vol. 3, *op. cit.*, p. 183.

24. Brecht et al., *"Here Life Goes On,"* p. 83.

25. Ibid.

26. Ibid., p. 101.

27. I am indebted here to Hans Israels.

28. Brecht et al., *"Here Life Goes On,"* p. 118.

29. Ibid., p. 119.

30. "New Introductory Lectures on Psychoanalysis," *Standard Edition*, Vol. 22, p. 144.

31. *Reich Speaks of Freud: Wilhelm Reich Discusses His Work and His Relationship with Sigmund Freud* (New York: Noonday Press, 1968), p. 159.

32. Brecht et al., *"Here Life Goes On,"* p. 121.

33. Fromm, *Sigmund Freud's Mission, op. cit.*, p. 65. See also *The Complete Correspondence of Sigmund Freud and Ernest Jones 1908-1939*, ed. R. Andrew Paskauskas (Cambridge, MA, Harvard University Press, 1993), p. 335.
34. *Reich Speaks of Freud*, p. 189.
35. Myron Sharaf, *Fury on Earth: A Biography of Wilhelm Reich* (New York: St. Martin's Press, 1983), p. 185.
36. Paul Roazen, *Freud and His Followers* (New York: Alfred A. Knopf, 1975; reprinted, New York: Da Capo, 1992), pp. 370, 503-06.
37. Wilhelm Reich, *People in Trouble*, translated by P. Schmitz (New York: Farrar Straus & Giroux), pp. 246, 210.
38. Ilse Ollendorf Reich, *Wilhelm Reich: A Personal Biography* (New York: St. Martin's, 1969), p. 31.
39. Ibid.
40. Jones, *The Life and Work of Sigmund Freud*, Vol. 3, p. 191.
41. Ilse Reich, *Wilhelm Reich.*, p. 31.
42. Brecht et al., *"Here Life Goes On,"* p. 172.
43. See Henri F. Ellenberger, *The Discovery of the Unconscious* (New York: Basic Books, 1970), pp. 640-41.
44. Quoted in James E. Goggin and Eileen Brockman Goggin, *Death of a "Jewish Science": Psychoanalysis in the Third Reich* (West Lafayette, IN: Purdue University Press, 2001), p. 60.
45. Brecht et al., *"Here Life Goes On,"* p. 172.
46. Geoffrey Cocks, *Psychotherapy in the Third Reich: The Göring Institute*, 2nd ed., rev. & expanded (New Brunswick, NJ, Transaction Publications, 1997), pp. 61, 86-87, 91.
47. Käthe Drager, "Psychoanalysis in Hitler's Germany," *American Imago*, Vol. 29 (1972), pp. 199-214.
48. Geoffrey Cocks, "Book Review," *Psychohistory Review*, Vol. 24 (1996), p. 211.
49. Bernard J. Paris, *Karen Horney: A Psychoanalyst's Search for Self-Understanding* (New Haven, CT: Yale University Press, 1994), p. 118.
50. Karen Horney, *Our Inner Conflicts: A Constructive Theory of Neurosis* (New York: W. W. Norton, 1945), p. 11.
51. Karen Horney, *The Neurotic Personality of Our Time* (London: Routledge & Kegan Paul, 1937), p. 38; Karen Horney, *New Ways in Psychoanalysis* (London: Routledge & Kegan Paul, 1939), p. 95; Karen Horney, *Self-Analysis* (London: Routledge & Kegan Paul, 1942), p. 60; Karen Horney, *Neurosis and Human Growth: The Struggle Toward Self-Realization* (New York: W. W. Norton, 1950), p. 369; Karen Horney, *Feminine Psychology*, ed. Harold Kelman (New York: W. W. Norton, 1967), p. 228.
52. Paul Roazen, "Jung and Anti-Semitism," in *Lingering Shadows*, ed. Aryah Maidenbaum (Boston: Shambahla, 1991), pp. 211-21.
53. Fritz Stern, "Fink Shrinks," *New York Review of Books* (Dec. 19, 1985), p. 48, n.3.
54. Franz Alexander and Samuel Selesnick, *The History of Psychiatry* (New York: Harper & Row, 1966), p. 407.
55. Jones, *The Life and Work of Sigmund Freud*, Vol. 3, p. 186.
56. Roazen, *Freud and His Followers*, p. 293.
57. Geoffrey Cocks, *Psychotherapy in the Third Reich* (New York: Oxford University Press, 1985), p. 127.
58. Jones, *The Life and Work of Sigmund Freud*, Vol. 3, p. 187.
59. Ibid., p. 185.

60. Rainer Funk, "Erich Fromm's Role in the Foundation of the IFPS," *Fromm Forum* (International Erich Fromm Society), Vol. 3 (1999), p. 22.
61. Brecht et al., *"Here Life Goes On,"* 139.
62. Ibid.
63. Ibid., p. 79.
64. Ibid., p. 126; Goggin and Goggin, *Death of a "Jewish Science,"* p. 98.
65. Brecht et al., *"Here Life Goes On,"* p. 126.
66. Goggin and Goggin, *Death of a "Jewish Science,"* p. 61.
67. Brecht et al., *"Here Life Goes On,"* p. 78.
68. Ibid., pp. 126, 181.
69. Goggin and Goggin, *Death of a "Jewish Science,"* p. 99.
70. Brecht et al., *"Here Life Goes On,"* p. 129.
71. Goggin and Goggin, *Death of a "Jewish Science,"* p. 88.
72. Brecht et al., *"Here Life Goes On,"* p. 137.
73. Peter J. Loewenberg, "Foreward," Geoffrey Cocks, *Treating Mind and Body: Essays in the History of Science, Professions, and Society Under Extreme Conditions* (New Brunswick, NJ, Transaction Publishers, 1998), pp. ix-x.
74. Brecht et al., *"Here Life Goes On,"* p. 134.
75. Goggin and Goggin, *Death of a "Jewish Science,"* p. 97.
76. Brecht et al., *"Here Life Goes On,",* pp. 130-31.
77. Ibid., p. 134.
78. Ibid., p. 136.
79. Ibid., p. 138. I am indebted to Rainer Funk for having allowed me to make copies from his Fromm Archives of the correspondence between Müller-Braunschweig and Fromm, the letters between Jones and Fromm, and the later exchanges between Ruth Eissler and Fromm.
80. Funk, *Erich Fromm*, p. 23.
81. Goggin and Goggin, *Death of a "Jewish Science,"* p. 105.
82. Jones, *The Life and Work of Sigmund Freud*, Vol. 3, p. 221.
83. Goggin and Goggin, *Death of a "Jewish Science,"* p. 41.
84. See Paul Roazen, "Psychoanalytic Ethics: Freud, Mussolini, and Edoardo Weiss," *Journal of the History of the Behavioral Sciences*, Vol. 27, October 1991.
85. Goggin and Goggin, *Death of a "Jewish Science,"* p. 139.
86. Ibid., p. 130.
87. Drager, "Psychoanalysis in Hitler's Germany," p. 212; See also, Rose Spiegel, "Survival, Psychoanalysis, and the Third Reich," *Journal of the American Academy of Psychoanalysis*, Vol. 13 (1985), pp. 521-536; Rose Spiegel, Gerard Chrzanowski, Arthur Feiner, "On Psychoanalysis in the Third Reich," *Contemporary Psychoanalysis*, Vol. 11 (1975), pp. 477-510; Arthur Feiner, "Psychoanalysis During the Nazis," *Journal of the American Academy of Psychoanalysis*, Vol. 13 (1985), pp. 521-36.
88. Goggin and Goggin, *Death of a "Jewish Science,"* p. 144.
89. Brecht et al., *"Here Life Goes On,"* p. 154.
90. Ibid., p. 168.
91. Cocks, *Psychotherapy in the Third Reich*, p. 12. See Paul Roazen, *Encountering Freud: The Politics and Histories of Psychoanalysis* (New Brunswick, NJ, Transaction Publishers, 1990), pp. 34-37.
92. Cocks, *Psychotherapy in the Third Reich.*, p. 9.
93. Goggin and Goggin, *Death of a "Jewish Science,"* p. 145.
94. Brecht et al., *"Here Life Goes On,"* p. 199.
95. Ibid., p. 201.

96. Esther Menaker, *Appointment in Vienna* (New York: St. Martin's Press, 1989), p. 40. Reprinted as *Misplaced Loyalties* (New Brunswick, NJ, Transaction Publishers, 1995).
97. Brecht et al., *"Here Life Goes On,"* p. 217.
98. Ibid., p. 202.
99. Goggin and Goggin, *Death of a "Jewish Science,"* p. 172.
100. Brecht et al., *"Here Life Goes On,"* p. 204-07.
101. Goggin and Goggin, *Death of a "Jewish Science,",* p. 173.
102. Anna Antonovsky, "Aryan Analysts in Nazi Germany," *Psychoanalysis and Contemporary Thought*, Vol. 11 (1988), pp. 213-31.
103. Goggin and Goggin, *Death of a "Jewish Science,"* pp. 122, 198.
104. Helena Besserman Vianna, *Politique de la Psychanalyse Face à la Dictature et à la Torture* (Paris: Harmattan, 1999).
105. *International Journal of Psychoanalysis*, Vol. 33 (1952), p. 256.
106. Karl Menninger, *The Selected Correspondence of Karl A. Menninger, 1946-65*, ed. Faulkner & Pruitt (Columbia: University of Missouri Press, 1995), pp. 123-24.
107. Erich Fromm, in Michael Kessler/Rainer Funk, *Erich Fromm und die Frankfurter Schule* (Tubingen: Francke Verlag, 1991), p. 251. See Martin Jay, *The Dialectical Imagination: A History of the Frankfurt School and the Institute of Social Research, 1923-1950* (Boston: Little Brown, 1973).
108. Fromm, Ibid., p. 251.
109. Erich Fromm, "The Social Philosophy of 'Will Therapy,'" *Psychiatry*, Vol. 2 (1939), pp. 229-237.
110. Robert S. Wallerstein, *Lay Analysis: Life Inside the Controversy* (New York: The Analytic Press, 1998).
111. Kurt R. Eissler, *Medical Orthodoxy and the Future of Psychoanalysis* (New York: International Universities Press, 1965).
112. Roazen, *Oedipus in Britain*.
113. *International Journal of Psychoanalysis*, Vol. 20 (1939), p. 123.
114. Richard F. Sterba, *Reminiscences of a Viennese Psychoanalyst* (Detroit: Wayne State University Press, 1982), p. 157.

2

The Strange Case of Alger Hiss
and Whittaker Chambers

The Hiss-Chambers case has haunted American liberalism for over fifty years now, and yet I wonder whether future generations are going to be able to understand just what has been at issue. In 1999 Hiss's son Tony published his second book on the subject, *The View From Alger's Window: A Son's Memoir*.[1] Alger Hiss died in November 1996, at the age of ninety-two, and at his memorial service in New York City more than 800 people attended. Tony Hiss now lives with his wife and son in the same apartment that his parents once occupied, and the twenty-five hundred letters and post-cards his father exchanged with his now deceased first wife Priscilla and to Tony, while Alger was imprisoned for forty-four months after being convicted of perjury, make up the substance of this latest piece of the puzzling Hiss-Chambers tale. As we shall see, the contours of the controversy would seem to have expanded as the years have passed.

The heart of the old political war over Hiss between the Left and the Right still continues as heatedly as ever. Victor S. Navasky, the distinguished author of *Naming Names* (1980) and editor of the *Nation*, in reviewing Tony Hiss's new book pointed out a numerical balance in new evidence: Alger Hiss's family writings from federal prison almost match in number the almost three thousand decryptions of the early 1940s cables (known as the Venona Project) between Soviet agents working in the States and the authorities in Moscow.[2] Hiss was incapable of being tried for espionage because the statute of limitations had expired. It seems striking to me that Navasky is so ready to compare as fresh bits of "Cold War archives" Hiss's family missives and the newly released transcriptions connected with the old Soviet Union's spies. In exchange for money donated to the KGB retirement fund, once-secret records have been released by the Russians; and experts have concluded that the Venona cables help document Hiss's participation in Soviet espionage.[3]

Tony Hiss seems to me a far better writer than his father, and it looks like—until definitive documentation appears from the files of the Soviet military intelligence (separate from the KGB)—that the Hiss-Chambers saga is going to continue to attract fresh debate. Tony Hiss puts what he calls "the core of Alger's problem" this way: "he was not a person who had been blighted by the kind of mental dissociation that would lead him to act dishonorably, and then hide his actions, but he was a person who suffered from an unwariness and a detachment that would cripple his attempts to defend himself effectively against invented charges...."[4] But I think Tony Hiss has put the case for his father disingenuously: for there can be little doubt that however dishonorable many of us might think Hiss's actions, at the time he could, like so many others, think of them as undertaken in behalf of the beleaguered cause of the embattled "progressive" Soviets. But Tony Hiss has come close to the core of the matter when he invokes the concept of "dissociation." Spies seem capable of an extraordinary amount of what is now commonly known as the capacity for compartmentalization. Klaus Fuchs, who stole important atom bomb secrets and then defected behind the Iron Curtain, looked back on his spying life as "a controlled schizophrenia."[5] The frightening-seeming loneliness of the spy can be alleviated by the ideological satisfactions of supposedly high-minded purpose. In Hiss's mind his treason could be justified and honorable. He surely was not alone in how he rationalized the betrayal of his native country.

What is unusual was his studied denial, into extreme old age, of ever having committed the acts which the testimony of people like Chambers, and an accumulation of documentation from the files of the Soviet Union which Hiss could never have thought would become available, have made appear more certain than ever. (Julius and Ethel Rosenberg, right up to their 1953 executions, also protested their innocence, but the Venona material seems to have settled the question of at least Julius's guilt.[6]) Hiss always continued to stonewall about every one of Chambers's central charges. While others, such as Fuchs, confessed and moved to their ideological homeland, Hiss hung tough. It seems almost certain that his wife Priscilla knew and shared in the truth; but Hiss continued to lie to his friends, his son, and the world. (It now appears that Hiss and his underground group had evidently succeeded in winning Soviet military decorations.) Once Hiss had been steadfast in his loyalty to the Soviets, and lied to his son, there might have been no way for Hiss to have altered course. But given the path Hiss chose to take, he would seem to have allowed his son's life to be built upon that original lie.

Tony Hiss's earlier book, *Laughing Last: Alger Hiss*[7] (1977), was livelier than *The View from Alger's Window*. But Tony's prose (he has worked as a staff writer for the *New Yorker*) continues to be more interesting than his father's. Still even in *Laughing Last* Tony could utter a wholly improbable-sounding declaration like: "Al [Alger] didn't know any, or at least didn't know anyone who ever claimed to be a Commie."[8] The loyalty of a son to a father is admirable, but allows Tony to express a politically untenable position. Alger Hiss was a prominent New Dealer, and it is simply impossible in the Great Depression that he failed to know communists, including those who readily admitted their affiliations. I think that anyone familiar with the commonplaceness of communism among American intellectuals of the 1930s would scoff at Tony's retrospective credulity.

But I have to admit that when I first read Alger Hiss's *Recollections of a Life*[9] (1988) I temporarily had my doubts. The memoir was so touchingly eloquent, in a quietly understated way, that I felt it was impossible to put it down without at least conscientiously asking myself, could Hiss, after all, have been framed at the height of the Cold War hysteria? Was it possible that Whittaker Chambers, working in cahoots with the FBI's J. Edgar Hoover and the young Richard Nixon, had railroaded an innocent Hiss? The controversy over Hiss has been compared to France's celebrated Dreyfus case. Dreyfus, however, was exonerated after a relatively short time, while the Hiss case has been going on now for over half a century.

The known facts are as follows. In 1948 Chambers accused Hiss (then head of the Carnegie Endowment for International Peace) of having once been a communist; Chambers admitted having been a courier for the Soviet Union, and alleged that while working at the State Department in the 1930s Hiss had passed classified documents to Chambers for transmission to the Russians. At first Chambers, who appeared to have emerged from the political gutter, looked implausible as an accuser; Hiss himself was a secure member of the Establishment, a New Dealer who had won the trust and respect of people such as Dean Acheson, Justice Felix Frankfurter, Walter Lippmann, and Eleanor Roosevelt, among others.

Hiss sued Chambers for libel, but then was indicted and tried on charges of perjuring himself in testimony before the House Committee on Un-American Activities. Although the first trial resulted in a hung jury, the second one convicted him. Chambers went on to write his best-selling *Witness* (1952), while Hiss was disbarred and ruined. Congress even deprived Hiss of a small federal pension, although in 1973 the Supreme Court declared that congressional act unconstitutional. And the state of Massachusetts allowed Hiss to practice law once again. But Hiss never succeeded in overturning the verdict against him or in winning a new trial. President Ronald Reagan awarded a posthumous Medal of Freedom to Chambers in 1984, and in 1988 Chambers's Maryland farm became a national historic monument. Hiss remained out in the cold, and his few remaining defenders are apt to seem eccentrics, a rare form of political vegetarian. Yet Tony Hiss has found prominent publishers willing to bring out his defenses of his father; and there were all those people present at Hiss's funeral in 1996. (Bard College has established an Alger Hiss professorial chair.)

A recent close inspection of Hiss's own *In the Court of Public Opinion*[10] (1957), written after his release from prison, made it seem to me strikingly unpersuasive. Tony Hiss in his *Laughing Last* reported that *In the Court of Public Opinion* was said by "a lot of people" to have had "'no feeling.'"[11] Alger himself referred to it as "a legal brief." But it is incredible to me that Hiss, given that the central accusation against him was that he had been an undercover communist, did nothing whatever to rebut Chambers's main charge. One would have thought that Hiss would have tried to explain how it was impossible for him to have been such a communist, or a spy. Instead, we got a rehearsal of all the once-celebrated and now mind-numbing details – the car, the rug, the typewriter, the warbler. (These were the specific means by which Chambers was able to establish his intimacy with Hiss, and the transmission of government documents.) Hiss was right in thinking that originally "the only real issue" was "Chambers's veracity against mine."[12] Long before now, however, material confirming Chambers's unlikely sounding story has proliferated, and one might have thought that a heartfelt confession was more in order rather than Hiss's continual blank denial of wrongdoing. He must have considered himself basically innocent, in the context of the times, which then allowed him license so arrogantly to repudiate even having once known Chambers, not to mention other communists. Out of all the 800 pages of Chambers's *Witness* what stood out in my mind most—over forty-five years after first reading it—was the transcript of Hiss's encounter with Chambers before the House Un-American Activities Committee. (Hiss specifically asked to see Chambers with his mouth open, so that he could view his teeth.) Hiss did not seem to realize that his legalisms made him seem evasive, his own worst enemy. At one of his trials the courtroom broke out in laughter when Hiss pedantically expressed his enduring puzzlement about how Chambers could have gotten into Hiss's house to type documents on Hiss's typewriter.

Hiss's *Recollections of a Life* contained what I thought was a powerful chapter based on Hiss's experiences as a private secretary to Justice Oliver Wendell Holmes, Jr. (Felix Frankfurter had made the selection for Holmes, and Hiss's brother Donald—also named as a communist—was Holmes's secretary as well.) Hiss's admiration for Holmes was so convincingly expressed that in itself it made one wonder how Hiss could ever have been believed to have done anything illegal, not to mention having been guilty of the terrible crimes Chambers alleged. Yet in *In the Court of Public Opinion* Hiss seemed to drag Holmes's name in by the hair, alleging that if Chambers had really been such a friend, and spent time in Hiss's library, he would have spotted the facsimile edition of the book of Holmes's readings.[13] At this point I now felt that Hiss should have been ashamed of abusing Holmes's memory. Hiss had originally had to deny Chambers's charges, to keep his position at the Carnegie Endowment for International Peace. (The Republican John Foster Dulles was then chairman of its board.) Hiss also had to sue Chambers for libel, which then provoked Chambers's espionage evidence; and Hiss would have had to testify before the grand jury, which then indicted him, because otherwise no one would have believed his declarations of complete innocence. Tony has commented that "Al's demeanor as defendant and witness seemed curiously detached,"[14] without it sinking in that such detachment might have been part and parcel of the kind of dissociation that Tony has tried to protect his father from.

In this whole curious story of Chambers and Hiss it has been hard to keep the issue of psychopathology out. During a Hiss trial two eminent psychoanalysts testified in his behalf: Dr. Carl Binger and Professor Henry A. Murray. (Binger's wife was a college classmate of Priscilla Hiss.) It was doubtless a sign of the times, at the height of the Freudian wave of influence in the U.S., that the judge allowed any such allegedly expert testimony from people who had never known or interviewed Chambers. Both Binger and Murray thought they could convince people, on the basis of his courtroom behavior and what he had published, that Chambers was some sort of psychopath, at any rate sick or disturbed enough to be disbelieved. The prosecution, even according to Tony, made "mincemeat" out of such testimony.

In *Laughing Last* Tony provided evidence for the Hiss family's involvement with psychoanalysis. Priscilla Hiss had been analyzed "by a student of Freud's" for a year in the 1920s. After her separation from Hiss in early 1959 she went to another analyst. Hiss himself had an analyst in New York City whom he cited by name. He was quoted as having maintained, "I was very much interested in psychoanalysis...because of Prossy [his wife]...."[15] There was a least one psychiatrist friend of the family who helped Tony out, and he later was sent as a child to someone for a couple of therapeutic sessions a week. One does wonder about the nature of the Hisses commitment to psychoanalysis, and to what extent they thought of it as a science; given the accusation of communism, and the efforts made by others to relate psychoanalysis and Marxism, it is hard at least for me not to be curious about the Hiss involvement with psychoanalysis. Chambers's own *Witness* provided rich psychological material about the motives behind his having become a communist, and then a renegade, but, in contrast to Hiss's icy intellectualism, Chambers recorded no specific indebtedness to psychoanalysis.

Something beyond this general background seems needed to help explain a curious long book authored in 1967 by a psychoanalyst, Meyer Zeligs: *Friendship and Fratricide: An Analysis of Whittaker Chambers and Alger Hiss.*[16] Zeligs reported that he had started out with "no political ax to grind," and that he thought that the Hiss-Chambers case presented "a fascinating riddle in human behavior." Although only Hiss, and not Chambers, agreed to cooperate with Zeligs, the psychoanalyst undertook, he tells us, "to maintain careful analytic neutrality toward them."[17] Freud himself had a more cynical conception of biography-writing, at least when someone was proposing to write about himself; as he once wrote in 1936,

> Anyone who writes a biography is committed to lies, concealments, hypocrisy, flattery and even to hiding his own lack of understanding, for biographical truth does not exist, and if it did we could not use it. Truth is unobtainable, mankind does not deserve it, and in any case is not our Prince Hamlet right when he asks who would escape whipping were he used after his desert?[18]

Zeligs, armed with zealous psychoanalytic convictions about scientific neutrality, proceeded to write profiles of Hiss and Chambers which were unquestionably partisan, besmirching the character of Chambers while exonerating the personal qualities of Hiss. Freud could be far less damning about biography writing when he did not feel himself threatened, and could even engage in it himself when it came to Woodrow Wilson[19]; but assuming that the inspiration of Freud's ideas is employed with sophistication, his kinds of concepts can best be used relevantly at certain points in anyone's life history.[20] Almost all of psychoanalytic theory should be put to one side, I think, in biography-writing; modern psychology, if it is going to help, should have already left a sediment in one's bones. No biographical study should ever be constructed in order to prove a theoretical point, because such an enterprise is bound to distort the complexities of a human life. And psychological terms should not become substitutes for political judgments. One would have expected a psychoanalyst, in a situation where one party was cooperative and the other not, to proceed cautiously. Zeligs however came up with psychological profiles of Hiss and Chambers which temporarily became notorious for its bias.[21]

In reality the Hiss-Chambers case represented a subtle confrontation in which the American Establishment was at odds with itself. For Chambers had friends in the best literary and intellectual life almost as well placed as Hiss's high-level political associates. Chambers had gone to Columbia and became an intimate friend of Meyer Schapiro, who went on to be a great art historian; Chambers had notably studied under the literary critic Mark Van Doren, and retained his friendship. A classmate of Chambers's, Lionel Trilling, became the first to write about Chambers in the course of constructing a 1947 novel *The Middle of the Journey*.[22] For many, Trilling's fictionalized portrait of the apocalyptic-sounding ex-communist Chambers would stick in their minds almost as securely as what they came across in political life subsequently.

Chambers's *Witness*[23] was beautifully written and powerfully persuasive. It ranks, I think, as an account of the psychology of a former communist with Arthur Koestler's *Darkness at Noon* or with the contributions to *The God That Failed*.[24] Chambers succeeded in making himself come across as a driven Dostoevsky-like character, determined to convert others as his own experience had led him away from the materialism of Marxism. *Witness* was not only passionately pro-Christianity but almost anti-intellectual in tenor. After surfacing from the communist underground, Chambers had gone to work in the late 1930s for Henry Luce at *Time*, and he ended up in a friendly alliance with

William F. Buckley and his *National Review*. Chambers told of making sui-
cide attempts and he had heart problems; he died prematurely in 1961.
Chambers's name remains permanently associated with the post-World War II
Red Scare; Richard Nixon had been the member of the House Committee on
Un-American Activities who believed in Chambers, and Nixon's career flour-
ished on Hiss's fall. The worst of Senator Joseph McCarthy's assaults on
American freedoms got their start once Hiss had been indicted. In effect, the
whole New Deal intelligentsia stood accused of having been complicit in
Hiss's own betrayal of America. Hiss had been with Franklin Roosevelt at the
Yalta conference, and Hiss had also presided at a founding session of the
United Nations. It is hard not to hold one's head at how politically far up Hiss
had gone. Even after his conviction (by which time President Truman was
convinced of Hiss's guilt) Secretary of State Acheson publicly said he would
not turn his back on Hiss.

So Zeligs was addressing himself to a genuine psychological riddle by
means of writing *Friendship and Fratricide*. Either Chambers or Hiss had to
have been lying, or perhaps both Hiss and Chambers were similarly guilty of
twisting the truth. Wherever there are such grave distortions of events, it is
easy to think of what might have possibly motivated men. But just because
Freud taught us to believe in the importance of unconscious motives does not
mean that all irrationalities are equally plausible; discrimination and tact are
still needed in order to differentiate between different possibilities. When I
taught a large undergraduate course on "Psychology and Politics" at Harvard
from 1966 until 1971, I used to lecture on Zeligs's book; and when I complained in class that Zeligs had made Hiss appear to be a saint, almost every
year there would be a student who would come up to me after class to tell me
that "Hiss *is* a saint." Hiss's great charm (which did not come through at all in
his *In The Court of Public Opinion*) was such that people were still swearing
by his innocence.

Hiss had had the Ivy League credentials that gave him all the "class" that
someone like Nixon lacked. I have never forgotten how Nixon was made
initially suspicious by Hiss's testimony having appeared to Nixon to be
"mouthy." Hiss had been a Phi Beta Kappa at Johns Hopkins before going on
to Harvard Law School, where he first attracted the attention of Felix Frankfurter. American liberals could never forgive Nixon for his role in having
successfully brought Hiss down. It was during a period when Americans had
just lost their nuclear monopoly to the Russians, and China had also recently
"fallen" to the communists. Furthermore, Hiss could appeal to the American
gullibility about spies; it is hard for Americans to accept the inevitability of
espionage, and America was still relatively new to its role as a world power.
Also Hiss could profit from America's generosity about even those convicted
of high crimes; for Hiss to have been innocent would have appealed to the
characteristic American respect for the underdog. But it is doubtful that the

post-World War II Red Scare would ever have been as bad without Hiss's indictment and conviction. Hiss's treason as an underground communist may have turned out to have done less damage than what happened politically when Chambers first exposed him, and Hiss chose to fight the charges.

The contrast between Chambers and Hiss helped in itself to make for high political drama. Chambers had throughout his years in the communist underground led an isolated and secretive existence. He invented various aliases for himself, and was conspiratorial in every aspect of his existence; he kept dossiers on people as part of maintaining what he called future "life-lines" to outside reality. All political informers are bound to seem like "stoolies," which helps account for why Chambers struck so many as a distasteful character.

Hiss, on the other hand, was detached and meticulous in his attention to detail, seemingly oblivious "to the spirit of the moment."[25] Chambers, in contrast, was unusually skillful in dramatizing himself and his claims. Chambers's hiding microfilm inside a pumpkin (the material becoming known as "The Pumpkin Papers"), which he made public only after Hiss went ahead with the libel charge, would be hard to match as a political sensation. Zeligs was able to establish the unlikelihood of Chambers's story about being fourteen inches across the shoulders at birth, and that it had not been snowing, as Chambers had claimed in *Witness*, on the night of his birth. But otherwise Zeligs's book amounted to a sophisticated form of name-calling.

Zeligs interpreted Chambers as "a desperate young man, searching for meaning and direction in life."[26] Zeligs was quick to spot signs of Chambers reacting to "a homosexual temptation from which he panicked and fled."[27] The whole issue of homosexuality was a long-standing undercurrent to the Hiss-Chambers story. Hiss's stepson had been involved in a homosexual episode while in the military, which supposedly accounted for Hiss's unwillingness to allow him to testify at the perjury trials.

And Chambers admitted to the FBI, once Chambers feared the Hiss camp would bring the issue up, that Chambers had engaged in brief homosexual episodes before leaving the Communist Party. Outside observers had wondered whether there could ever have been a liaison between Hiss and Chambers, and Hiss finally endorsed the theory that Hiss had unknowingly repudiated Chambers's sexual advances, which supposedly helped account for the revenge motivation behind Chambers's determination to destroy Hiss's career.

But essentially Zeligs took a partisan psychological view of everything in Chambers's life. For example, Chambers had once reported

> Two impressions sum up my earliest childhood world. I am lying in bed. I have been told sternly to go to sleep. I do not want to. Then I become conscious of an extreme silence which the fog always folds over the land. On the branches of the trees the mist has turned to moisture, and, as I listen to its irregular drip, drip pause drip pause, I pass into the mist of sleep.

Zeligs gets this following speculation out of that short passage:

> This "earliest childhood world" suggests the pattern and quality of Laha's mothering by revealing her son's feelings of impoverishment and intense loneliness. The poignant sensibilities of his childhood suffering are sharply remembered. In his metaphoric way Chambers describes how he tried to alleviate his hunger and to fall asleep by drawing into himself all possible external sounds or stimuli. Thus he strove to incorporate whatever sensory "nutriment" his surroundings could supply. In his nocturnal wakefulness Vivian reached out with elongated auditory antennae to absorb the sound of the moist drippings from the tree branches outside the house, and by drinking in the repetitive sounds he enables himself to pass "into the mist of sleep." From this memory one gets an important glimpse into an area of his earliest infantile strivings, his shift of attention away from his "sad" mother onto her surrogate, Mother Nature, the only other available source of supply.[28]

Zeligs not only over-interprets this brief childhood reminiscence of Chambers, but does so in behalf of hypothesizing Chambers's inner "impoverishment" and "emptiness."[29] In Chambers's youthful running away from home, Zeligs found "the clinical features of a serious mental break."[30] (Elsewhere Zeligs wrote, "there is no doubt about the severity of this psychotic break."[31]) Zeligs maintained that for Chambers "excitement and escapades provided external fulfillment for his inner emptiness."[32] One has to remember that Chambers was on a first-name basis with Mark Van Doren, and a close friend of Meyer Schapiro. Zeligs misunderstood Chambers's poetic extravagances, and instead found evidence of "hallucinations."[33]

Zeligs felt licensed to proceed in "decoding"[34] Chambers's fantasy life. Chambers's brother committed suicide, and Zeligs would have it that Chambers was "harassed, thereafter, with an intractable persecution complex."[35] Zeligs attributed to Chambers "delusional and paranoid symptoms."[36] We are told about "Chambers' inner emptiness, his tragic incapacity to feel, suffer, or love any human object...."[37] Zeligs was really attributing to Chambers mental illness, even though Chambers had not been hospitalized, and had a devoted wife and two children. Nonetheless Zeligs found "the chronic retaliatory quality of Chambers' paranoia, an ambulatory illness that harassed him throughout his life."[38]

This sort of diagnostic overkill about Chambers contrasts with how gingerly Zeligs approached Hiss's life. Hiss's father and a sister had also killed themselves, but Zeligs found no such malignant consequences for Hiss as Zeligs had conjectured in connection with Chambers's brother's death. (Zeligs does however woodenly consider Hiss's father's death as "the nuclear trauma of his life."[39]) Hiss's "compulsive style" was only linked to his becoming "a model of good manners."[40] Instead of seeing in Hiss Chambers's sorts of self-destructive vicious cycles, Zeligs described Hiss's growth as one in which he was capable of adding "an important measure of security to his sense of self."[41] It has to be striking that in reconstructing "Hiss's activities during the

years 1934-35," Zeligs was "impressed with the fullness rather than the loneliness of Hiss's life."[42] Yet those were the years, assuming Chambers were
telling the truth, when Hiss was also successfully functioning as an underground communist. Zeligs did acknowledge that before the House Un-American Activities Committee Hiss's "painstaking manner" had "succeeded in
giving the appearance of evasiveness and pettifoggery," and that Hiss's "quasi-
virtues of perfectionism, deliberateness, and ultra-caution were self-defeat-
ing...."[43] When Alger and Priscilla came to separate, Zeligs could not even
allow them to have a normal-sounding divorce; instead we are told that "The
belated recognition of this marital breach came neither as surprise nor shock.
It was the ultimate emergence of a subliminal fact...."[44]

   Zeligs's big book, inadequate though it is, still has something important
to teach. It has to stand as one of the testimonies to the passion of the enduring Hiss-backers. When Chambers himself once referred to the "pro-Hiss psy-
chosis,"[45] he was invoking the same psychopathological school as Zeligs
although obviously from an opposite standpoint. And yet when all is said and
done, there does seem to be a perplexing psychological side to the Hiss-
Chambers confrontation. This cannot have been a tale of misperceptions or
the failure to communicate; somebody was clearly not telling the truth. And
yet it is not easy to explain the motivation behind such lying. Chambers had
staked a successful journalistic career on his claims; essentially his being an
editor at *Time* was over once this celebrated case got underway. And Hiss
became one of the greatest disgraces in twentieth century American history. If
he was victimized by Chambers, what can account for it? On the other hand,
if as seems far more likely Hiss was continuing to fulfill what he took to be his
obligations to the Soviet Union, do we really yet understand how someone
could find in communism so much appeal as to betray family, friends, and
country? Those 800 people who attended Hiss's memorial service in New
York are a permanent testimony to Hiss's long-standing appeal to part of the
American Left.

   In this whole tortured tale one has to suspect some sort of Jekyll and Hyde
psychology. Something beyond purely rationalistic behavior would seem to
have been at work. If Chambers had been the one guilty of fabricating the
evidence against Hiss, then his own psychopathology would have to be understood, even if not along the partisan lines that Zeligs laid out. (Zeligs did
allude to "the shiftings of Chambers' 'dissociated mind.'"[46]) And if instead
Hiss were the one to have lived a double life, then we have so far had an
inadequate psychological picture of what might have driven him to persist in
his duplicity. And then of course the link between Chambers and Hiss is in
itself fascinating. Two such different men, from contrasting spheres of American life, seem destined to remain locked together as figures in American
history. It remains still an open question just what can account for why they

became such close friends, assuming as I do, that Chambers's essential story will be proven true.

As soon as the beginning of the 1950s writers like Murray Kempton and Leslie Fiedler[47] were both articulately convinced of Hiss's having been guilty of treason. Yet fifty years later the story has only expanded in its complexity. We have had the various defenses by both Hiss and his son Tony. And now the Soviet archives are unburdening themselves, just as the Venona transcripts have become available. Assuming that Hiss was the criminal, then his crimes include not only almost incredible stubbornness but the basest sort of family disloyalty. (Then again his responsibility to Priscilla and his brother Donald might have conflicted with that to his son Tony.) It is hard to believe that anyone could be so convinced in his own rectitude and invulnerability as to have risked so much. At least in great literature the worst villains are rarely so cold-blooded as never to have sought the relief of confession. If Hiss was willing to sacrifice his life, his marriage, and his son, then at some point one might have expected him to have questioned whether the cause had been worth it. So that when the final documentation appears, presumably from Soviet military intelligence archives, it is still going to be a psychological puzzle to explain Hiss's behavior. Perhaps American liberalism's particular psychology is inadequate to account for the special fanaticism of dedicated communists. Nothing yet to come can fail to color the confrontation between Hiss and Chambers in anything but the most dramatic sorts of terms.

Notes

1. Tony Hiss, *The View from Alger's Window: A Son's Memoir* (New York: Alfred A. Knopf, 1999).
2. Victor Navasky, "Alger, Ales, Tony, and Time," *Tikkun*, Vol. 14 (Sept.-Oct. 1999), pp. 66-68.
3. Allen Weinstein and Alexander Vassiliev, *The Haunted Wood: Soviet Espionage in America—the Stalin Era* (New York: Random House, 1999). See also Allen Weinstein, *Perjury: The Hiss-Chambers Case*, 2nd edition (New York: Random House, 1997), and Sam Tanenhaus, *Whittaker Chambers: A Biography* (New York: The Modern Library, 1998).
4. Hiss, *The View from Alger's Window*, p. 82.
5. Weinstein and Vassiliev, *The Haunted Wood*, p. 324.
6. Ronald Radosh and Joyce Milton, *The Rosenberg File*, second edition (New Haven, CT: Yale University Press, 1997), and Weinstein and Vassiliev, *The Haunted Wood.*.
7. Tony Hiss, *Laughing Last: Alger Hiss* (Boston: Houghton Mifflin, 1977).
8. Ibid., p. 86.
9. Alger Hiss, *Recollections of a Life* (New York: Henry Holt, 1988).
10. Alger Hiss, *In the Court of Public Opinion* (New York: Alfred A. Knopf, 1957).
11. Tony Hiss, *Laughing Last*, p. 72.
12. Hiss, *In the Court of Public Opinion*, p. 214.
13. Ibid., p. 153.

14. Tony Hiss, *Laughing Last*, p. 135.
15. Ibid., p. 133.
16. Meyer A. Zeligs, *Friendship and Fratricide: An Analysis of Whittaker Chambers and Alger Hiss* (New York: The Viking Press, 1967).
17. Ibid., pp. ix, xiv.
18. *The Letters of Sigmund Freud and Arnold Zweig*, ed. Ernst L. Freud, translated by Prof. and Mrs. W. D. Robson-Scott (London: The Hogarth Press, 1970), p. 127.
19. Paul Roazen, *Freud: Political and Social Thought* (New Brunswick, NJ: Transaction Publishers, 1999), 3rd edition, "Epilogue: Woodrow Wilson."
20. Paul Roazen, *Canada's King: An Essay in Political Psychology* (Oakville: Mosaic Press, 1998), "Introduction: How Psychology Relates to Politics."
21. Meyer Schapiro, "Review of Zeligs's *Friendship and Fratricide*," *New York Review of Books*, Feb. 23, 1967, pp. 5-9.
22. Lionel Trilling, *The Middle of the Journey* (New York: Doubleday Anchor Books, 1957); Lionel Trilling, "Whittaker Chambers and 'The Middle of the Journey,'" *New York Review of Books*, April 17, 1975, pp.18-24; Irving Howe, "On 'The Middle of the Journey,'" *New York Times Book Review*, Aug. 22, 1976, p. 31.
23. Whittaker Chambers, *Witness* (New York: Random House, 1952).
24. Arthur Koestler, *Darkness At Noon* (New York: Bantam Books, 1966), Richard Crossman, ed., *The God That Failed* (New York: Bantam Books, 1954).
25. Zeligs, *Friendship and Fratricide*, p.8.
26. Ibid., p. 59.
27. Ibid., p. 60.
28. Ibid., p. 33
29. Ibid., p. 60.
30. Ibid., p. 49.
31. Ibid., p. 290.
32. Ibid., p. 291.
33. Ibid., p. 65.
34. Ibid., p. 81.
35. Ibid., p. 93.
36. Ibid., p. 323.
37. Ibid., p. 105.
38. Ibid., p. 260.
39. Ibid., p. 182.
40. Ibid., p. 154.
41. Ibid., p. 160.
42. Ibid., p. 206.
43. Ibid., p. 276.
44. Ibid., p. 411.
45. Ibid., p. 213.
46. Ibid., p. 385.
47. Murray Kempton, *Part of Our Time: Some Ruins and Monuments of the Thirties* (New York: The Modern Library, 1998), Ch. 1 "The Sheltered Life: Alger Hiss and Whittaker Chambers," and Leslie Fiedler, *An End to Innocence: Essays on Culture and Politics* (Boston, Beacon Press, 1955), ch. 1 "Hiss, Chambers, and the Age of Innocence."

3

Notes on Leonard and Virginia Woolf

Even though Virginia Woolf has been long established as a central figure in the early twentieth-century flowering of the British intelligentsia known as the Bloomsbury group, I only came to her work by a circuitous route. The first member of that set that I read was John Maynard Keynes; when a paperback edition combining his *Essays in Biography* and *Two Memoirs* first attracted me in 1959 it was partly because Keynes was such a central figure in modern economics. I can still recall how scintillating I found his "My Early Beliefs." And Keynes seemed as breathtaking a writer when talking about Robert Malthus, Lloyd George, Winston Churchill, the mysterious Dr. Melchior, Trotsky, the makers of the Versailles Treaty, or Newton.

It was only at Oxford, during my next year of graduate study, that I had the leisure actually to read Keynes's *The General Theory of Employment, Interest, and Money* (1936); by that time I was well aware of Keynes's talents as a writer as well as an economist. His *The Economic Consequences of the Peace* (1919) was an unforgettable experience, as much for its powerful sketches of the statesmen involved at the conclusion of World War I as for its prophecies of what would follow for Europe from the provisions of the peace treaty. I had initially started off to read then for a degree in Politics, Philosophy, and Economics, and I suppose it was because of the unusual vitality of philosophy at Oxford at that time, the central place it played in the intellectual life there, that I also then read much of G. E. Moore's *Principia Ethica* (1903). Moore's argument was rather more intensive than I, as a student of political philosophy, absolutely needed to understand, but I felt I was encountering the thinker Keynes, as well as others, considered the main philosophical figure for Bloomsbury. I had already acquired my interest in Freud, none of whose books were then available at my Magdalen College library. Over the next few years I read almost everything by E. M. Forster, a close friend of Keynes's and also Virginia Woolf's. As Leonard Woolf's autobiographical volumes started to come out in 1960, I found they provided a memorable account of a Cambridge intellectual's life; and it was hard as an American not to envy the way Britain's restricted geography, as opposed to the vastness of the New World, meant that old friends could so easily keep in touch.

By the summer of 1965 I had completed my Ph.D. thesis on "Freud and Political Theory," been promoted to a full-time teaching position at Harvard College, and undertaken to interview (also while doing research in London) all those I could find who had known Freud personally. In 1917 Leonard Woolf had, with Virginia, founded the Hogarth Press, then still functioning as a publishing entity; since the Hogarth Press had become Freud's English-language publisher in 1924, it made sense for me to try to interview Leonard. (Kurt Eissler's interview with Leonard Woolf is still locked up at the Library of Congress until 2013.) Although I took careful notes during and after my interview, it now seems to me that I overlooked marking down perhaps the two most memorable aspects of that encounter. First, the whole ambience at the Hogarth Press, located in 40 William IV Street in W2, was all that one could hope for an old-fashioned British publisher who loved books to be like; the musty building seemed to have a wonderfully ramshackle appearance, and one climbed up narrow rickety stairs to reach Woolf's small office. There was no sign of the uniformity, modern chrome or technology that was to become ever more dominant in commercial publishing firms. But secondly, in the midst of our conversation, Leonard happened to glance over at something of Virginia's he was overseeing for posthumous publication; I think it was one of the volumes of her essays, which he edited, but it could also have been part of her diary. His whole face seemed momentarily transformed as he slightly turned towards the manuscript, and I have always thought that the way he at that instant so memorably glowed expressed something of what her genius had brought to his life. Leonard was then close to turning eighty-five, and his hands (which struck me as enormous) shook a bit, but his mind still seemed as good as ever; his lined face had immense character. I remarked in my notes that he must have once been a very sturdy person. (He only lived another four years.)

It had been Leonard's old friend James Strachey, a younger brother of Lytton's, who had initially brought the proposal that the Hogarth Press become Freud's publisher. Unwin had been the psychoanalysts' British distributor at first, but Leonard thought that "such arrangements are never satisfactory." Freud had his own publishing house in Vienna, and they had printed up some of his books in English there. According to Leonard the analysts were "incompetent" as businessmen, and—out of a kind of megalomania—could produce 10,000 copies of a book that would be lucky to sell 300 or 400 copies in a year. (When Woolf took over as Freud's publisher, he inherited the books which had been printed first in Vienna; often they had gotten soiled, because of the way in which they had been kept abroad, and "for years" Leonard had gotten complaints from London booksellers.) A Publications Committee had been set up at the British Psychoanalytic Institute, and it consisted of Ernest

Jones, John Rickman, and James Strachey. Originally Leonard had dealt on publication matters with Freud's eldest son Martin in Vienna, and then in London with Martin's youngest brother Ernst.

Leonard had exchanged a few letters with Freud himself. In Leonard's view Freud was "not a good businessman." For he had sold outright to Jones's Institute, for fifty pounds each, the rights for the *Collected Papers*, which appeared in four volumes. It was not long before the Hogarth Press had made that all back, at which point Leonard wrote Freud offering him the normal terms on royalties amounting to 10 percent of the receipts.

When Freud emigrated to London in 1938, Leonard and Virginia had gone to see him for tea at Maresfield Gardens. Freud's daughter Anna showed them into the consulting room-library. Leonard had brought along a clipping from a newspaper about a London trial at which someone was convicted of having stolen among other things one of Freud's books from a big bookstore, Foyle's, such theft being a common enough event at the time. The judge, in sentencing the thief to three months in jail, added, "I only wish I could sentence you to read all of Freud's books." I thought it was a very funny story, and wondered how Freud had reacted; yes, Leonard reported, Freud had laughed.

Leonard later put this story into the fourth volume of his autobiography, *Downhill All the Way* (1967):

> Nearly all famous men are disappointing or bores, or both. Freud was neither; he had an aura, not of fame, but of greatness. The terrible cancer of the mouth which killed him only eight months later had already attacked him. It was not an easy interview. He was extraordinarily courteous in a formal, old-fashioned way—for instance, almost ceremoniously he presented Virginia with a flower. There was something about him as of a half-extinct volcano, something sombre, suppressed, reserved. He gave me the feeling which only a very few people whom I have met gave me, a feeling of great gentleness, but behind the gentleness, great strength. The room in which he sat seemed very light, shining, clean, with a pleasant, open view through the windows into a garden. His study was almost a museum, for there were all round him a number of Egyptian antiquities which he had collected. He spoke about the Nazis. When Virginia said that we felt some guilt, that perhaps if we had not won the 1914 war there would have been no Nazis and no Hitler, he said, no, that was wrong; Hitler and the Nazis would have come and would have been much worse if Germany had won the war.

Leonard told Freud the Foyle's story, and Freud was "amused and, in a queer way, also deprecatory about it. His books, he said, had made him infamous, not famous. A formidable man."[1] Virginia Woolf's own account in her diary, which appeared only in 1984, is also interesting:

> Dr. Freud gave me a narcissus. Was sitting in a great library with little statues at a large scrupulously tidy shiny table. We like patients on chairs. A screwed up shrunk very old man; with a monkeys light eyes, paralysed spasmodic movements, inarticulate: but alert. On Hitler. Generation before the poison will be worked out. About his

books. Fame? I was infamous rather than famous. Didn't make 50 pounds by his first book. Difficult talk. An interview. Daughter & Martin helped. Immense potential, I mean an old fire now flickering. When we left he took up the stand What are *you* going to do? The English—war.

The next day she continued to recount the interview:

> Freud said It would have been worse if you had not won the war. I said we often felt guilty—if we had failed, perhaps Hitler would have not been. No, he said with great emphasis; he would have been infinitely worse. They considered leaving for 3 months; made up their minds in 24 hours. Very alert at L.'s mention of the case when the Judge decreed that the criminal should read 20 of Freud's books. Adrian [Stephen, Virginia's analyst brother] says the Pss Bonaparte [Princess Marie Bonaparte] gave him this great silent solid Hampstead mansion. "But we don't like it as well as our flat in Vienna" said Anna. A certain strain: all refugees are like gulls with their beaks out for possible crumbs. Martin & his novel; she on her book. The strain on us of being benefactors.[2]

Curiously enough Virginia seems to have been either a genius lacking in a sense of humor (her "Am I a Snob?"[3] struck me as wonderfully funny), or one who missed Freud's own ironic way of having fun. When Freud evidently said to her, after she and Leonard had come in, "We like patients on chairs," they both seemed to have missed the backhanded reference to his own preferred customary way of seeing analysands on the couch; sitting up in a chair was definitely not what Freud's psychoanalysis had recommended for its clients, and Virginia seems not to have noticed Freud's attempt at being playful. (Alternatively Virginia meant that she and Leonard had been sitting like patients on chairs, but she still would have missed Freud's preference for the use of the couch, part of the furniture of the room.) And, unlike Leonard's autobiographical memory, she had not mentioned his laughing in any way over the magistrate's comments in sentencing the thief. (Freud had written to Leonard after their tea, somehow thinking that the judge had been Norwegian: "Handicapped in the use of your language I think I could not give full expression to my satisfaction of having met you and your lady. The condemnation delivered by the Norwegian judge I take to be a misrepresentation or a bad joke by a malicious journalist."[4] This letter makes me wonder just how amused Freud had been by the Foyle's story.)

Leonard also told me something about his own early favorable book reviewing response to Freud's *The Psychopathology of Everyday Life*. The American writer Walter Lippmann had also been early on receptive to Freud's work; Leonard and Lippmann had talked together before World War I about Freud's significance. I asked whether Lippmann had known a lot about psychoanalysis, and Leonard hesitated before modestly answering, "about as much as I did." Leonard had later worked some of Freud's ideas into his political theoretical works (which Lippmann also did within his own writings), though Virginia seems to have read rather less of Freud than Leonard.[5] (Evidently it was only a few months after meeting Freud that she began to read him at last.) Leonard had notably never taken Virginia, with all her recurrent mental troubles, to any psychoanalyst. (James Strachey told me that perhaps Leonard had never read the Freud books he had published. James's wife Alix thought that probably Virginia feared that analysis might interfere with her creativity.) In those days, Leonard said, very few people were interested in Freud. When I asked about Leonard's friends, he mentioned as exceptions the Stracheys and the Stephenses (Virginia's brother Adrian, and his wife Karin, had both become analysts). "T. S. Eliot talked a good deal about psychoanalysis; and Roger Fry seemed exceptional in his hostility." (I regret not asking about Keynes and Forster; I already suspected that the customary youthful homosexuality among the English literati complicated the British response to psychoanalysis, with its own rather grim-sounding views on "perversion.")

Leonard had been in touch with Martin Freud about publishing matters, and in her diary Virginia was alluding to his then unpublished novel. (Anna Freud's book that Virginia mentioned might well have been her first book on child analysis that Jones had, out of his allegiance to Anna's rival Melanie Klein, not allowed in print.) Leonard told me that he and Virginia had had Martin to dinner, and were rather friendly with him. (In 1940 Leonard, a socialist, had written to Clement Atlee, Lord Privy Seal in Churchill's war cabinet, to protest Martin's having been interned as a dangerous alien; his son had been shipped to Australia.[6]) It was "most mysterious" to Leonard what Martin ever did for a living in London. Leonard thought that Martin was "rather" an intellectual, when I asked about it. Martin had offered the Hogarth Press his novel, but Leonard had not thought it was very good—a judgment that, now that I have read it, seems to me charitable.

My main reason for seeing Leonard had been to find out something about the sales figures of Freud's books. Leonard replied that such information was not confidential, but he feared it might have gotten lost because of their moving about during the war; rain came in after they had been bombed. It appeared that the Hogarth Press had made quite a bit of money out of Freud's *Collected Papers*. That project had been one of the "most profitable ventures" they ever made, and the books had been "reprinted and reprinted." In America, he said, Macmillan would know their own sales figures since they were Hogarth's distributors there; of course in the States they had also had A. A. Brill's translations of Freud, which were "awful." *The Collected Papers* may have been Jones's idea of putting them together in the first place; by 1965 James Strachey was advocating a new arrangement to come out, with his revised translations and elaborate editorial notes. (It had been quite a feat to straighten out the snarled American copyrights before Strachey's twenty-four-volume *Standard Edition* could appear; that set was sold in America as produced by the Hogarth Press.)

Leonard rather teased me, with a big smile on his face, as he asked whether I was going to write about the controversies Freud had had with his former students Alfred Adler and Carl Jung. At that stage of my work I doubt I could have been certain in my answer, but I know I asked whether Adler and Jung had ever been considered on a par with Freud among English intellectuals. Leonard's answer was a decisive "no." He also was curious about whether in Vienna by 1965 there were any outstanding analysts. (At that time the Viennese Psychoanalytic Society was exceptional in being one of the few such groups that did not flourish.)

The day after I saw Leonard, he sent me a letter about the sales figures I had inquired about. (I had felt no anti-Americanism in Leonard, but neither he nor Virginia ever went to the States for their careers.) The Hogarth Press had started out with publishing Volumes 7-10 in the Psychoanalytic Institute's Library series; these were the four volumes of Freud's *Collected Papers*, which each sold about 300 copies in the first twelve months.

The next Freud book was *The Ego and the Id* and we sold 404 in the first 12 months. The way in which Freud's reputation rose is shown by the following figures:

	Published in	Copies sold in 1st 12 months months
Future of An Illusion	1928	899
Civilisation and Its Discontents	1930	929
New Introductory Lectures	1932	1211
Autobiographical Study	1935	1697

These compare with the following by other authors:

Ferenczi: Further Contributions	1927	302
Flugel: Psychology of Clothes	1930	406
Klein: Psychology of Children	1932	343[7]

(I do not know how Leonard came up with these figures so quickly, but they only roughly conform to a more comprehensive list compiled by J. H. Willis for his account of the Hogarth Press in 1992.[8])

Although my seeing Leonard Woolf was because of my interest in the history of psychoanalysis, I kept up with my general reading; and my interest in Bloomsbury was accelerated by Michael Holroyd's wonderful books about Lytton Strachey that first appeared in 1967.[9] I even once published a little piece about a curious-seeming link between Lytton Strachey and Freud.[10] In various of my books the Bloomsbury circle had come up, but it was only in the course of writing a recent book of mine that I had to deal with Virginia Woolf's brother Adrian's place in the British Psychoanalytic Society.[11]

An interesting biography of him had appeared, and curiously enough, since he had been the little boy who had pleaded to go for the trip to the lighthouse, that drove me finally to finish reading, for the first time, Virginia's *To the Lighthouse*. (I had, however, already read her nephew Quentin Bell's two-volume biography of her[12].)

Although I came to Virginia Woolf's writings so late, I have found that my contact with Leonard Woolf was a help to understanding some of the recent literature about their marriage. Hermione Lee's new biography *Virginia Woolf* seems the best, most comprehensive work to have appeared. It did however, strike me as odd that in her opening pages about this self-absorbed writer Lee commented, "Not for nothing did Freud, on the only occasion when they met, in 1939, give her a narcissus."[13] Does Lee think that at that great age, and in ill health, Freud had prepared for the Woolfs's visit by going out in the garden to select which flower might be most suitable for Virginia? The overwhelming odds seem to me that someone else in the household had picked whatever flowers were in the consulting room-library, from which Freud made his no doubt limited choice.

More substantially, though, it seems to me that Lee's biography misses key elements to the relationship between Leonard and Virginia. Leonard, who had just returned from being a colonial civil servant in Ceylon before marrying Virginia in 1912, was bound to have seemed to both Virginia's friends and family as someone who could suitably take care of her. (She was almost immediately ill for three years after the wedding.) She had had her first mental breakdown after her mother's death in 1895. Virginia was then thirteen. According to Lee "the most distressing aspect" of Virginia reaction to her mother's dying was her inability to "feel anything." Lee remarks that "this troubling feeling of dissociation often recurs in her adult life."[14] This "embarrassed inhibition about grieving" could have been related to what the psychoanalyst Helene Deutsch described in her famous paper on the subject of "Absence of Grief," and how delayed mourning can be a powerful source of empathy and intuition.[15] To Lee this incident connected with Virginia's mother's death "presaged a life-long embarrassment about expressions of emotions,"[16] whereas one might instead have thought it also fed her unusual delicacy of feeling.

Leonard had been to Cambridge with Virginia's brothers Thoby and Adrian, but Leonard was unusual in both being a Jew and in having relatively few financial means. As late as 1930 Virginia could write in a letter, "How I hated marrying a Jew—how I hated their nasal voices, and their oriental jewellery, and their noses and their wattles—what a snob I was." Lee is undoubtedly correct in observing of Virginia, "her racial and class prejudice were indistinguishable."[17] The whole of Bloomsbury shared a characteristic elitist anti-Semitism. Nobody could have anticipated, one would expect, just how much of an invalid Virginia would prove to be. Financially Leonard had for himself only a small fraction of Virginia's own money. But it is also likely that there was a shared conviction about Virginia's instability that made Leonard seem a good bet as a husband. Little in the way of sexuality, it seems generally agreed, ever went on between Leonard and Virginia. A famous British psycho-analyst once speculated that the Woolf marriage might have been an unconsummated one; if this were not literally the case, it was essentially an accurate rendition of the long-standing situation.

Lee observes that "witnesses to the marriage had been quick to deduce that it was sexually inadequate."[18] A son of Harold Nicolson and Vita Sackville-West concluded, for example, that Virginia had been "sexually frigid."[19] From early on in the marriage Leonard and Virginia had separate bedrooms, but he customarily used to bring her breakfast in bed. Lee finds "the standard image of Leonard Woolf as a full-blooded heterosexual sacrificing himself on the altar of her genius" as "simplistic."[20] The idea of children, it is agreed, would have been out-of-the-question for someone in as precarious shape as Virginia. But somehow Lee tries to maintain that "This was not an a-sexual marriage, but one which thrives on affectionate cuddling and play."[21] I would have thought the Woolfs had as asexual a relationship as one could imagine. Leonard always had to be anxious about Virginia's health. Lee quotes Virginia writing to a friend in 1912: "Leonard made me into a comatose invalid"[22] without pointing out how self-indulgently spoilt Virginia was sounding. Lee is undoubtedly correct in observing that "there is a narrow line between this careful watchfulness and a desire for control," and Leonard was no doubt "more of a guardian than a lover."[23] Lee does say of Leonard that he "was a person of deep, articulate, excitable feelings, controlled by fierce self-training."[24]

Yet Lee never asks whether Virginia could ever have become a great novelist without Leonard. She had still, at the time of their marriage, not published her first fiction. Her great talents as a writer are evident even in some of her first letters. But Lee never credits Leonard with providing the essential structure for her literary achievements. Yes, he could be misanthropic, controlling, and financially tight. But such carping really misses just what he did for her—as well as what she brought to him. How easy it would have been, with someone as fragile as Virginia, who despite all Leonard's care had a number of serious breakdowns and ended up killing herself, for her genius to have failed to find expression in the works she accomplished.

Without Leonard, Virginia's life could have gone in a catastrophic direction much earlier. What I missed in Lee's account of the marriage was more of what Virginia and Leonard gave to each other; the intellectual and emotional communication they had between them made for something that is critical in other marriages as well, though usually not so starkly divorced from sexuality. Although I find it difficult to put my finger on what is missing in Lee's account of the marriage, one hint comes up in connection with a passage in a letter written by Virginia's half-sister Stella about a suitor: "I cannot think of him without a shudder and yet he is much to be pitied—it is awful." Lee comments obtrusively: "What can he have done?"[25] But why need he have done anything at all? Stella's feelings had changed, even though she still thought he was "much to be pitied." Throughout *Virginia Woolf* I felt a touch of modish respect for feminist victimologizing. It might be in keeping with Virginia's respect for androgyny to ask: What if Virginia had been a man, and Leonard the woman? In that case I suspect that today's biographers would likely be in no doubt about the self-sacrificing spouse. And yet even with Leonard I came away from meeting him convinced of how much Virginia had brought to him. Freud thought that all truly civilized people are also partly masochistic, and ideally an account of a marriage should encompass both what each elicited in the other as well as what they paid for in frustration or blockage.

Inevitably accounts of Leonard and Virginia reflect prevailing moods about the relations between the sexes. Whatever the defects in Lee's *Virginia Woolf* nothing matches the sensationalism of Phyllis Grosskurth's 1980 *Times Literary Supplement* review of Vol. VI of Virginia Woolf's letters.[26] Grosskurth tried to advance the unfounded idea that after Virginia's suicide "rumors circulated in the village that Leonard Woolf had done away with her and hidden the body." Grosskurth proposed to find in one of Virginia's last novels that an unattractive account of a Jew might have been Virginia's "describing her own grievances against the Hogarth Press." Both Leonard and Virginia found being publishers burdensome, and Leonard may have thought that it was particularly therapeutic for Virginia to have such a realistic aspect to her life, but nothing supports the idea that Virginia could have been so crass as to criticize Leonard via a scene in a novel. Grosskurth even proposed that "after the artistic failure" of *The Years* (which became a bestseller in North America), "Leonard made a concerted attempt to undermine Virginia's confidence in herself." Such speculations really seem wicked to me. Grosskurth claimed that Leonard, who not unnaturally for someone politically sophisticated might have found the pacifist antiwar objective in the brilliantly written *Three Guineas* naive, suggested that Leonard might have been "oppressed by the weight of its facts and arguments" because supposedly Virginia was becoming "a financial liability." According to Grosskurth, Leonard "told her not to labor over the tedious Roger" Fry biography she had undertaken. Grosskurth found in Virginia's last published novel *Between the Acts* the model in Leonard and Virginia of "two beings locked in eternal warfare."

John Lehmann, who had known both the Woolfs and worked as a partner in the Hogarth Press, immediately wrote in to repudiate the Grosskurth account of Leonard and Virginia: "I feel I must protest vehemently against the innuendoes about Leonard Woolf which run right through Phyllis Grosskurth's review." In opposing Grosskurth's "insinuations," Lehmann maintained what was the obvious: "one of the central concerns of his life was the well-being of his wife...."[27] (Essentially Leonard's multi-volume autobiography came to an end with Virginia's suicide.) Grosskurth was undaunted by Lehmann, and replied the next week: "The burden of my review was an attempt to question the widespread belief that Leonard was a devoted husband. Indeed I go further: is it possible, I have suggested, that Leonard Woolf's treatment of Virginia could actually have hastened her death?"[28] Two weeks later Quentin Bell wrote in to the *TLS* also objecting to Grosskurth's central thesis in the course of her dealing with "the volume of correspondence which she was ostensibly reviewing."[29] Nigel Nicolson then made plain that there was no documentary basis whatever for the alleged village gossip that Grosskurth claimed to be relying on.[30] Lee mentions in one of her final notes to her long book that "some critics of LW [Leonard Woolf]" implied "that he may have been in some way responsible for her death,"[31] citing the Grosskurth review and an earlier article, without any reference to the published objections to that whole line of reasoning. In 2001 a book called *Who's Afraid of Leonard Woolf?*[32] proposed among other allegations that he killed her.

The way academics could transform Leonard's devotion into something so different from what anybody who knew them might have imagined has led me to question Lee's account (and that of others too) of the nature of Virginia's mental difficulties. A whole chapter has, within quotation marks, the title of "Madness"; the quotation marks are, presumably, meant to qualify the term, or put it in some perspective. But Lee's chapter begins in a way which I find most unsatisfactory: "Virginia Woolf was a sane woman who had an illness."[33] But it should be evident that Virginia's medical problems were not like having allergies or arthritis. Virginia's illnesses threatened to overthrow her mind, and frequently did; Lee's use of a recent term like "bipolar disorder"[34] does not satisfactorily account for the way this sickness could feed as well as overwhelm her creativity. To describe her as a "sane woman who had an illness" assumes that the so-called sanity could always count on all Leonard's faithful ministrations. Her suicide attempts, the hallucinations, headaches, loss of appetite, and so on amounted to enough for Leonard, in Lee's words, to have "made Virginia's illness into one of his life's works."[35]

Virginia responded especially badly to "the stress of finishing a book," but somehow Lee does not relate that to Virginia's general sensitivity to loss. Nor does she connect those recurrent crises to how she fell apart after the death of her mother. Leonard also seemed, in his autobiography, strikingly un-psychological about Virginia's collapses. But it seems to me nonsense for Lee to agree in any way with how Leonard has been "implicated with the oppressive procedures of Virginia Woolf's doctors."[36] The real mystery may be how Leonard's handling of his wife's problems, with whatever medical help he managed to get, succeeded as well as it did. Of course, any such conjectures have to be in hindsight, but under all the circumstances it does seem to me woefully inadequate to describe her only as "a sane woman who had an

illness." Virginia was quite right to be wary, like Leonard, of what psychoanalytic treatment might have been able to do for her. Her critique of Freudianism
in understanding fiction had some acute points, as for example when she
objected to "all the characters" becoming "cases," and above all perhaps that
the new system of thought "simplifies rather than complicates, detracts rather
than enriches."[37] Virginia and Leonard may have been shrewder about who
could help her than many observers have supposed. A first-class analyst even
then would have been suspicious of resorting to psychoanalytic treatment
with someone as potentially unbalanced as Virginia.

One whole chapter is devoted to what Lee calls "Abuses," except here she
uses no quotation marks around the title. And it seems to me that while Lee
has been unduly skeptical on the question of "madness," she has been too
credulous on the issue of so-called abuse. The problem here seems to have
started with Quentin Bell. In writing about Virginia's half-brother George,
Bell reported,

> Vanessa came to believe that George himself was more than half unaware of the fact
> that what had started with pure sympathy ended by becoming a nasty erotic skirmish.
> There were fondlings and fumblings in public when Virginia was at her lessons and
> these were carried to greater lengths—indeed I know not to what lengths—when,
> with the easy assurance of a fond and privileged brother, George carried his affec-
> tions from the school room into the night nursery.[38]

But this line of reasoning is, I think, highly suspect. Looking at the primary
evidence, we find that Virginia had written Vanessa in 1911 about a mutual
friend:

> She has a calm interest in copulation...and this led us to the revelation of all George's
> malefactions. To my surprise, she has always had an intense dislike of him; and used
> to say "hew—you nasty creature," when he came in and began fondling me over my
> Greek. When I got to the bedroom scenes, she dropped her lace, and gasped like a
> benevolent gudgeon. By bedtime she said she was feeling quite sick, and did go to
> the W.C., which, needless to say, had no water in it.

The letter goes on with other apparently sexual references, and ends with the
likelihood of their friend Duncan Grant having by now "seduced" their brother
Adrian: "I imagine a great orgy on the river tonight."[39]   Unless one understands the way Bloomsbury people were stylized in their exaggerations, it is
impossible to follow what was going on. They delighted in using the term
"copulation" as a way of shocking themselves and others; it did not necessarily mean what we might think of as intercourse. When Virginia wrote about
George's having come in and "fondled" her in public, it may have meant no
more than he was being demonstratively warm and/or friendly. Virginia was
not suggesting that their intimate friend Duncan had been guilty of abusing Adrian through any real seduction, nor was she actually proposing

that anything like what we would think of as a "great orgy" had ever taken place. Lee maintains that "the whole document makes a show of sexual frankness for Vanessa's approval and amusement,"[40] but I think everything has to be put in the perspective of the hyperbolic language they used then. All their words have to be translated for our own times. If George is to be considered "an incestuous seducer" then what about Duncan Grant? The truth is that neither of them may have been seducers in any modern sense. Both Virginia and her sister remained fond of George (who with Vanessa was a witness at her wedding, and became the first publisher of Virginia's fiction), and at his death in 1934 they both sound positive about him. In a 1904 letter of Vanessa's to Virginia, she had written that "George embraced and fondled me in front of the company, but that was only to be expected."[41] The word "fondled" has to be treated as circumspectly as the term "copulation"; Vanessa was not suggesting any incestuous move on George's part toward her, and nobody in the literature seems to have expressed surprise that Vanessa did not grow up with Virginia's mental difficulties. When Virginia in 1920 presented her autobiographical memoir "Hyde Park Gate" before the Memoir Club, I do not believe anybody present believed that she was literalistically accusing George of having been the "lover" of herself and Vanessa.[42] It seems to me that Lee has been exceptionally clumsy in handling this material: "There is no way of knowing whether the teenage Virginia Stephen was fucked or forced to have oral sex or buggered."[43]

Others have been even more extreme than Lee on the issue of her half-brothers. She quotes from a passage at the beginning of Virginia's 1939 "Sketches of the Past" in which her half-brother Gerald had indulged in what Lee calls "a sexual assault...in very early childhood."[44] (Gerald was twelve years older than Virginia, George fourteen years older.):

> There was a slab outside the dining room door for standing dishes upon. Once when I was very small Gerald Duckworth lifted me onto this, and as I sat there he began to explore my body. I can remember the feel of his hand going firmly and steadily lower and lower. I remember how I hoped that he would stop; how I stiffened and wriggled as his hand approached my private parts. But it did not stop. His hand explored my private parts too. I remember resenting, disliking it—what is the word for so dumb and mixed a feeling? It must have been strong, since I still recall it. This seems to show that a feeling about certain parts of the body; how they must not be touched; how it is wrong to allow them to be touched; must be instinctive.[45]

This passage should, I think, be approached cautiously. What she meant by Gerald's "exploring" her "private parts" might also need to be put into some sort of linguistic context, which Lee never does. She does however quote John Maynard Keynes's 1921 reaction to an early memoir of hers. Keynes told her that her best writing was "your memoir on George. You should pretend to write about real people & make it all up."[46] Lee does show some skepticism about how the incident with Gerald should be understood, when she tells us it "has been described as a 'life-threatening' act of extreme sadism which froze Virginia Stephen's sexuality and ignited her madness," making Virginia an "incest survivor."[47]

Lee describes Gerald's touching Virginia as a small child as "it seems, a sexual assault."[48] Somehow Lee thinks the "story of George's sexual activities" is "much more damaging."[49] Quentin Bell had been bold enough to maintain that "Virginia felt that George had spoilt her life before it had fairly begun. Naturally shy in sexual matters, she was from this time terrified back into a posture of frozen and defensive panic."[50] Nigel Nicolson, however, dissented, claiming that Virginia had been "exaggerating in recollection."[51]

The biographer of E. M. Forster, who was only a few years older than Virginia, reports a real sexual encounter Forster had as a small boy with a male stranger; P. N. Furbank cautiously comments: "It is an interesting story and has some significance, I think, for his later development."[52] That is not the same as going on to attribute some causal meaning to an early trauma; one would have thought it accepted by now that adults retrospectively dwell on events in early childhood that they find for one reason or another significant. And presumably it is not new that we repress memories which do not serve later needs.

Lee's huge biography was so interesting that it held me stationary reading it for days on end; once I started it I found myself hooked until I finished it. And ever since then I have been busily reading Woolf's writings, as I once had reacted to Holroyd's biography of Strachey and then undertook to read everything by him I could lay my hands on. Nonetheless, my brief contact with Leonard Woolf gave me a certain skepticism towards Lee's account of the Woolf marriage, and has emboldened me to be critical of what seems to have entered the commonplace of literary criticism about Virginia. Her illnesses, and the presumed "abuse" by her siblings, need to be re-considered more carefully. But if a biography promotes reading an author's work, maybe that it is the best a biographer can hope for. It is inevitable that our version of the past reflects our own contemporary understanding of the relations between the sexes, but such presentism can go too far. And I propose that it may be well to step back a bit and reflect on how today's clichés—about victimization, and the baleful effect of brothers and husbands—may have gone too far.

Every great life becomes a contemporary standard for us. But the ancient battle between the sexes needs little more trashing of husbands and brothers. Virginia Woolf suffered as every genius must, if only because her sensitivities were on so much greater a scale than those of everyday life. I feel most firm in defending Leonard, but in thinking about that marriage I have been emboldened to reflect about her half-brothers. Today's literature shows, I think, too little skepticism about the biases of the leading spokespersons for the trade union of womankind, who have been tempted to make Virginia into an abused heroine. I confess that my own immediate reaction to Virginia's *To the Lighthouse* was that she had been too harshly unfair in picturing her father, but then there are signs that she must have known how much of him she shared in her own makeup; it sounds disturbingly credible when Vanessa said of Virginia, more than once, that she "never gave but always took."[53] Clive Bell, Vanessa's husband, had reacted to an early draft of *The Voyage Out* by saying that the male characters had been especially unattractive:

> Our views about men & women are doubtless quite different, and the difference doesn't matter much; but to draw such sharp & marked contrasts between the subtle, sensitive, tactful, gracious, delicately perceptive, & perspicacious women, & the obtuse, vulgar, blind, florid, rude, tactless, emphatic, indelicate, vain, tyrannical, stupid men, is not only rather absurd, but rather bad art, I think.[54]

My suspicion is that Virginia learned from Clive's critique, which may be why she once credited Clive with having been "the first person who ever thought I'd write well."[55] The limitations I have found in Lee's excellent biography, and in other Woolf literature, may reflect some imbalance within Woolf's writings itself. The greatest artists, like Tolstoy in *Anna Karenina*, have been fully able sympathetically to portray the opposite sex. Dickens may have sometimes engaged in his century's tendency to idealize women, which was a weakness, but he triumphed in spite of his flaws because of the universality of what he proposed in the magic of his use of words. Woolf may have inadvertently set a tone about men which also went beyond her conscious intentions. But all my remarks about Leonard and Virginia Woolf are merely intended as "Notes," tentative cautions to what has already appeared so prominently in print.

Virginia Woolf's hyperboles were to be misunderstood by a later generation, so that this brilliant and subtle writer succeeded in becoming the prototype of the crude Freudianism she had so long disdained. The author of such superb polemics as *A Room of One's Own* and *Three Guineas* willy-nilly lent support to social movements that could threaten her artistic achievements; her political naiveté left her open to the exploitation of those craving models for the narrow cause of social protest. She killed herself fearing a recurrence of her madness, but her biographer puts madness into quotation marks, and instead makes so-called abuse central. If not a despotic husband as the villain, then half-brothers, a father, or perhaps society. Her fate would be worthy of one of her own cynical essays, but that would have to be comic, while to me her story marks high tragedy, ours as well as hers.

Notes

1. Leonard Woolf, *Downhill All The Way: An Autobiography of the Years 1919 to 1939* (New York: Harcourt Brace Jovanovich, 1969), pp. 168-69.
2. *The Diary of Virginia Woolf,* Vol. 5, ed. Anne Olivier Bell (New York: Harcourt Brace, 1984), p. 202.
3. Virginia Woolf, *Moments of Being*, second edition, ed. Jeanne Schulkind (New York: Harcourt Brace, 1985), pp. 204-20.
4. *Letters of Leonard Woolf*, ed. Frederic Spotts (London: Weidenfeld and Nicolson, 1989), p. 244.
5. Jan Ellen Goldstein, "The Woolfs's Response to Freud," *Psychoanalytic Quarterly*, Vol. 43 (1974), pp. 438-76.
6. *Letters of Leonard Woolf*, pp. 425-26.
7. Leonard Woolf to Paul Roazen, August 18, 1965.
8. J. H. Willis, Jr., *Leonard and Virginia Woolf As Publishers: The Hogarth Press 1917-41* (Charlottesville: University Press of Virginia, 1992), Appendix C.
9. Michael Holroyd, *Lytton Strachey: A Biography* (London: Penguin Books, 1971) and Michael Holroyd, *Lytton Strachey and the Bloomsbury Group: His Work, Their Influence* (London: Penguin Books, 1971).
10. Paul Roazen, "Freud and Lytton Strachey: An Uncanny Parallel," *Psychologist/ Psychoanalyst*, Summer 1991, pp. 43-44. (Also in Paul Roazen, *The Historiography of Psychoanalysis* [New Brunswick, NJ, Transaction Publishers, 2001, pp. 346-49]).
11. Paul Roazen, *Oedipus in Britain: Edward Glover and the Struggle Over Klein* (New York: Other Press, 2000).
12. Quentin Bell, *Virginia Woolf: A Biography, 1882-1912,* Vol. I (London: The Hogarth Press, 1973) and *Virginia Woolf: A Biography, 1912-1941* Vol. II (London: The Hogarth Press, 1973).
13. Hermione Lee, *Virginia Woolf* (New York: Alfred A. Knopf, 1998), pp. 5, & 701.
14. Ibid., pp. 129, 131.
15. Ibid., p. 131; Helene Deutsch, "Absence of Grief," in *Neuroses and Character Types: Clinical Psychoanalytic Studies* (New York: International Universities Press, 1965), pp. 226-36.
16. Lee, *Virginia Woolf*, p. 131.
17. Ibid., p. 308.
18. Ibid., p. 326.
19. Ibid.
20. Ibid., p. 327.
21. Ibid., p. 328.
22. Ibid., p. 331.
23. Ibid.
24. Ibid., p. 334.
25. Ibid., p. 122.
26. Phyllis Grosskurth, "Between Eros and Thanatos," *Times Literary Supplement*, Oct. 31, 1980, pp. 1225-26.
27. John Lehmann, *Times Literary Supplement*, Nov. 7, 1980. If the reader needs a professional psychiatrist's judgment, see Peter Dally, *The Marriage of Heaven and Hell: Manic Depression and the Life of Virginia Woolf* (New York: St. Martin's Press, 1999).
28. Phyllis Grosskurth, *Times Literary Supplement*, Nov. 14, 1980.
29. Quentin Bell, *Times Literary Supplement*, Nov. 28, 1980.

30. Nigel Nicolson, *Times Literary Supplement*, Jan. 23, 1981.
31. Lee, *Virginia Woolf*, p. 861.
32. Irene Coates, *Who's Afraid of Leonard Woolf?* (New York: Soho Press, 2001). An interested reader should also consult Natalie Rosenfeld, *Outsiders Together: Virginia and Leonard Woolf* (New York: Princeton University Press, 2000).
33. Lee, *Virginia Woolf*, p. 171.
34. Ibid., p. 172.
35. Ibid., p. 174.
36. Ibid., p. 185.
37. Ibid., p. 193.
38. Bell, *Virginia Woolf*, Vol. I, p. 43.
39. Lee, *Virginia Woolf*, pp. 153-54.
40. Ibid., p. 154.
41. Ibid., p. 155.
42. Virginia Woolf, *Moments of Being*, p. 177.
43. Lee, *Virginia Woolf*, p. 156.
44. Ibid., p. 123.
45. Virginia Woolf, *Moments of Being*, p. 69. Cf. also Lee, *Virginia Woolf*, p. 123.
46. Lee, *Virginia Woolf*, p. 153.
47. Ibid., p. 124, 123.
48. Ibid., p. 123.
49. Ibid., p. 124.
50. Bell, *Virginia Woolf*, Vol. I, p. 44.
51. Lee, *Virginia Woolf*, p. 777.
52. P. N. Furbank, *E. M. Forster: A Life*, Vol. I (New York: Harcourt Brace, 1977), p. 37.
53. Lee, *Virginia Woolf*, p. 214.
54. Bell, *Virginia Woolf*, Vol. I, p. 209.
55. Ibid., p. 212.

4

Tragedy in America

National cultures are more powerful than one might like to think. In the late nineteenth century, discussions of national character were closely associated with racist thinkers. By the 1930s and 1940s cultural anthropologists (like Margaret Mead and Ruth Benedict) were popularizing the notion of the importance of dominant national traits in behalf of their promoting progressive social purposes. Whether reasoning about the importance of national character gets endorsed by the right or the left, societies do tend to exhibit powerful dominant values and beliefs which underlie formal political systems. And America is sufficiently old to have acquired social characteristics that are deeply rooted enough to be remarked on.

Thirty-five years ago, I thought it one of the tasks of scholarship to point out all the savage comments Freud had once made about America, and which had been expurgated from his published letters on behalf of forwarding the psychoanalytic movement in the New World. It seemed incongruous to me then that Freud had such dreadful things to say about the one country where his work had been received with more favorable recognition than anywhere else in the world. Yet now, when developments in psychopharmacology have so captured the American imagination that psychoanalytic thinking is being popularly relegated to a dustbin of old-fashioned speculation, I am wondering whether there might not have been more truth to Freud's suspicions about the New World reaction to his work.

There is no doubt that Freud had an immense impact on American culture as a whole. The Freud Exhibit that the Library of Congress has mounted, and now is sending around to different cities in the world, may not have much to add to the life of the mind, but it does demonstrate the success psychoanalysis had at the level of popular culture such as cartoons and television series. Alfred Hitchcock's *Spellbound* had a famous story-line about an amnesia induced by a traumatic crime reawakening early guilt feelings; spectacular dream sequences became a key to unraveling the hidden secret, which, when discovered, freed the hero to go off with his psychiatrist, Ingrid Bergman.

This glamorized Hollywood version of detective work as psychoanalytic treatment was an expression of the kind of therapy that Americans could feel at home with. But this superficial picture of Freud's work was more in tune with traditional American utopianism than with any intent that the founder of psychoanalysis had had in mind. Even as early as the 1890s Freud had proposed, in famous words coming at the end of his *Studies on Hysteria*, to succeed in "transforming…hysterical misery into common unhappiness."[1] It is worth pointing out that he was holding such relatively limited aims at the outset of his therapeutic career; by the 1930s, as in "Analysis Terminable and Interminable," he was even more cautious about what might be accomplished therapeutically. America's own reaction to Freud was in terms of its tradition of meliorism and hopefulness about the possibilities of change.

From the outset American ideals have been at cross-purposes with the realities of its history. Thomas Jefferson's Declaration of Independence pledged the country to the objectives of "life, liberty, and the pursuit of happiness." As historians have emphasized, however, late eighteenth-century America was not simply the product of a set of rational aims set out by the Founding Fathers; the America that decided to break with the British Crown in Parliament had had over a century and a half to develop its special institutions. The colonists then were trying to reassert the legitimacy of the long-standing institutions that had grown up in America. So the American Revolution was partly a conservative rebellion against the attempted novel intrusions by the British. When the Americans did turn to Jefferson to express their ideal purposes, he put it in terms of that glorious trinity of "life, liberty, and the pursuit of happiness." America may have been basing its resistance to the British on a tangle of legalistic objections to how George III had become tyrannical, but the ideals themselves were expressed as a coherent and consistent set of moral purposes.

I believe that such idealism is historically important. If one contrasts, for example, the Declaration of Independence's three bold aspirations with those of the British North America Act, Canada's original founding document, one finds there a nation conceived with the aim of attaining "peace, order, and good government." The contrast between those goals and the ones that Jefferson articulated goes far to illustrate some of the central characteristic differences, even today, between Canada and America as political systems. Canadians have for example never enjoyed anything like the civil liberties that Americans have grown used to; as a matter of fact writs of assistance, which were one of the American colonists reproaches against the British, were legal in Canada until the relatively recent repatriation of the Canadian Constitution. Prime Minister Trudeau's invocation of the War Measures Act against a few violent Quebec separatists should seem a nightmare to all civil libertarians. America has every reason to be proud of the relatively stable liberties enshrined by its Founding Fathers.

But the standard of "life, liberty, and the pursuit of happiness" still leaves something to be desired. For implicit in the Jeffersonian agenda is a questionable outlook on the way values can be made to fit together. America has had the conviction that all good things can be sought at the same time, and that the valuable parts of life can be achieved together. America has, to put it in a nutshell, not had to accept the inevitability of tragedy and the way values can conflict with one another. Freud had something to teach on this score, since he was a superb representative of Old World culture that insisted on the incompatibility of ideals with one another. His *Civilization and Its Discontents* is a lasting testimony to his faith that mankind cannot have its cake and eat it too. His message there is so grim that many do not want to absorb what he was trying to say. He thought that human sexuality was inherently at odds with itself, so even the sexual act had to be intrinsically unsatisfactory.

Now America is a country that has still never lost a war; and we have not known the experience of being occupied by a foreign power. And therefore the presence of evil seems largely a consequence of bad planning. Our liberal tradition has been built on the idea that it is possible to have social and political institutions so constructed that they check and balance each other in a way that neutralizes wickedness. James Madison, for example, thought that ambition can be made to counteract ambition in such a clever political way as to allow constructive social forces to do their good works. Ingenuity can supposedly succeed in engineering a system that allows for the unimpeded flowering of human individuality, which is supposed to take place in a harmonious way. This set of beliefs is so deep rooted that Americans have even transposed it onto their international ventures; World War I was a war supposedly fought to end all wars. And the establishment of the United Nations can seem a universalistic substitute for old balance of power foreign policy. America has innocently believed that ideals, rather than just national self-interest, can decisively govern its foreign policies. I do not think any other great power has ever moralistically used the policy of non-recognition of foreign regimes in order to promote its policies. For many years the House Un-American Activities Committee sought to uncover domestic subversives who were working in behalf of foreign governments. The old seventeenth-century Puritan aim of creating in America a beacon on a hill has continued to dominate our relations with the rest of the world.

It is true that the American South suffered decisive defeat in its defense of its particular way of life. Slavery was the central flaw in the work of the Founding Fathers, and an attempt to finesse the issue through compromise led in the end to the terrible failure of the Civil War. Yet even after that bloody conflict, the worst of the nineteenth century, America immediately managed to make national heroes out of the generals who fought on both sides of the war. It should be no surprise that Southern writers have been the most eloquent dissenters from some of the more dominant values of American life.

William Faulkner for example knew the power of the past, and the whole tragic view of life can be found in other Southern thinkers as well. They knew the reality of failure; trapped in an ideology of their own which enshrined the legitimacy of conservatism, when at their roots they had Jefferson himself as well as the reality of slavery, the South knew at first hand the way ideals could be at cross-purposes.

Other American writers, besides Southerners, knew the power of everything that challenged what William Dean Howells once called the "smiling" sides of life. Melville felt the power of blackness, and although his best work went unrecognized in the nineteenth century he tried to write about the most painful sides of life. Hawthorne too recognized how deceptive the surface of American life could be. Even Mark Twain, that great exemplar of American comic imagination, knew something enduring about the darkest sides of life. He became a prophet of the dangerous course of American imperialism in the twentieth century. Dreiser would be another who defied the yea-saying side of American political and social expectations. Hemingway too wrote about the centrality of defeat. Any great artist appreciates the tragic side of life. But the incredible abundance on our continent has encouraged a kind of Pollyannaism that seems so strange to the rest of the world.

It seems to me that it is entirely in keeping with American life that Freud was received in the one-dimensional way he was. Americans latched onto psychoanalysis because of its optimism; they sought in Freud a new means of overcoming the disabilities of infantilism. So they welcomed Freudian thinking as a new way of reconstructing human fallibilities. The tyranny of childhood was supposedly transitory; the past could be bettered, and humanity could be successfully freed from the shackles of the unconscious. (I think I know the name of the American patient Freud is supposed to have dismissed on the grounds that he "had no unconscious.")

Some of the characteristic distortions of American culture can be detected in our typical ways of responding to Freud's teachings. American feminists are surprised that in France, for example, feminists tend to ignore American contributions. Yet the American reading of what Freud had to say about women is typically one-sided. Freud gets denounced as a misogynist. Yet before World War I he was arguing in behalf of admitting women to the Vienna Psychoanalytic Society. Despite Freud's stated position, a large proportion of his younger supporters voted against allowing women to hold first-class status. After allowing everybody to have their say, Freud typically ignored his opposition and went ahead and allowed women in. I do not think there was any profession in the twentieth century in which women went further than they did in psychoanalysis; as a matter of fact I think that it may well be that during Freud's lifetime women became more prominent within psychoanalysis than they are today. Progress was another American ideal that Freud did not share.

The American feminist misunderstandings of Freud are instructive. Not only did they unfairly blame him for many of their problems in attaining equality, but they could not follow the more subtle courses of psychoanalytic reasoning about women. When someone like Helene Deutsch wrote about the intrinsic conflict between motherhood and sexuality, as a special problem for feminine psychology, feminists denounced her for pessimism. Americans, after all, are not eager to acknowledge the inevitability of suffering, since our heritage teaches us that our ideals are capable of being reconciled harmoniously with one another. Freud dared to say that the superego of women was different than that of men; in fact I think he was also trying to say something about what he considered the inherent superiorities of feminine intuition and tact. But Americans balked at the essential idea in Freud that people have bodies, and that our biological nature says something essential about ourselves. Differences do not necessarily entail inequalities. With all the criticism Freud has undergone for his proposal of feminine castration anxiety (penis envy), virtually none of the feminist critics have understood that Freud's theory of femininity was designed to put the development of women on a standing of theoretical equality with that of men. If Freud was wrong about penis envy in women, might he not have been also mistaken about the role of castration anxiety in men? Freud has been unfairly criticized for being too exclusively in error about women. But then a Freudian view on men might strike Americans as being excessively cynical; I am thinking of the classic movie *The Captain's Paradise* starring Alec Guinness, in which his ideal plan for having two wholly different types of women in his life gets fouled up in a wonderfully comic mix-up.

Freud was saying something about the inevitability of suffering that Americans have never wanted to hear. When he wrote about masochism, or distinguished between male and female varieties, readers have not desired to absorb his point. Freud believed that being civilized entailed a degree of masochism; an Oedipus complex was to him a sign of cultural achievement. Only the good-for-nothings of this world failed to develop oedipal feelings. Americans have difficulty not only accepting the permanence of conflict, but also Freud's assumption of inequality. We do not readily buy into the idea that there can be, as Freud had thought, "worthless" people as well as worthy ones. Freud was laying down a fundamental challenge to Christian ethics, so that for him there was no necessity of universalizing egalitarianism. Americans do not even like to accept the reality of social hierarchies. We still imagine that talent is the only criterion for success.

A good part of the history of American psychoanalysis in the twentieth century was associated with the mid-century growth of ego psychology. I think this was in its origins a perfectly legitimate development from within Freud's system. Psychoanalysis as Freud had left it was inherently negativistic, and something needed to be done to inject a more positive note into the theoretical system as it was at his death. But correcting the imbalances in psychoanalysis could go so far as to extract from the word tragedy its essential meaning. For example, there is one point at which Erik H. Erikson says that tragedy is a kind of developmental lag. It should be possible to be humane without wearing rose-colored spectacles. Freud meant the concept of the Oedipus complex to say that each of us is inevitably trapped in a situation not our making, one that implies a set of limits to what we can achieve. The whole concept of the unconscious was designed to insist on how little we can know ourselves consciously.

The American orientation has on the contrary been one that puts a premium on how much rationality can accomplish. Psychoanalysis itself was accepted as a new way of fixing things. But Freud's intention had been that his psychological system teach how necessary it is to make compromises between ideal possibilities, choices that entail giving up certain chances. The American tendency has been to scapegoat authors or problems as the source of our troubles; the underlying assumption is that differences between people have only transitory cultural roots, and that these patterns can be adjusted and changed in a superior direction. But Freud once, when informed about the Nazi's burning his books, reflected on what progress we had made; once he would have been burnt, and now only his books were being destroyed. That sort of mordancy appeals more to Old World culture. And yet although one might have thought that the success of psychoanalysis in America meant something in the way of Europe's changing how we think, by and large American national culture has continued going on in its own way without benefit of what the Old World had to teach.

Americans value self-expression and spontaneity, and are put off by what seems like the duplicity of European manners. Almost everything that Henry James once wrote about the conflict between America and Europe is still valid. Freud could write shocking things from an American perspective; he could send letters about the same subject which contradict each other, and he could praise one person publicly while damning him in private to another. When he approvingly cites someone like Melanie Klein it should be taken with a grain of salt, and an eye on his British followers he did not want to lose. The whole European world Freud came from is one that still remains alien to America. And I think that there is a real sense in which Jacques Lacan accomplished a genuine "return" to Freud in that he picked up an accurate reflection of Freud's commitment to a tragic view of life. The intrinsic inevitability of conflict would not, I think, seem surprising to Lacan. Both Freud and Lacan shared a European perspective that remains at odds with the characteristically American one.

Shakespeare's whole outlook is one that at bottom Americans find it difficult to accept. The problems of King Lear are not the result of bad social policy toward the aging. Romeo and Juliet do not get into such a fix because of some local family rivalries; they are "star-crossed" lovers. *Macbeth* is not only an account of a nightmare of perverted political ambition. And Anthony and Cleopatra are not deluded by their respective mid-life crises. Shakespearean tragedy should teach us about an essential and unalterable level of failure that is at the same time a tribute to the capacity of the human spirit to triumph over adversity. I doubt that Freud knew about Japanese kabuki theater, but those plays would confirm his belief in the existence of some universal human dilemmas beyond mere cultural differences.

Freud once singled out, with contempt, the American reliance on Prohibition, not because he took any special pleasure in wine or liquor but because it seemed like such a simplistic social solution to intractable human propensities. We tend to think that evil is something that we can somehow banish. If it is difficult for couples to get on with each other, then invent "no-fault" divorces to solve the problem. Divorce is seemingly no bigger a problem than traffic accidents, and to some it seems expedient and wise not to assign blame. Freud came from a world in which commitments were more serious, and the relations between the sexes more layered; prostitution, and infidelity, were more structured into the expectations of civilized life. The same sorts of problems reappear on the public level; a great American secretary of war once supposedly disbanded a decoding unit on the grounds that gentlemen do not read other people's mail. Espionage is something heinous that other people, from Benedict Arnold to Alger Hiss, do to us; Americans do not engage in spying, rather we are concerned with intelligence gathering. Words can disguise from us the realities of what we do.

If one thinks of life in what used to be the old Soviet Union, it seems to me a miracle that human beings have been able to cope with the circumstances they have lived through. Boris Pasternak's *Doctor Zhivago* is such a great novel because he is dealing with the issue of how it is possible for the human spirit to endure despite revolution, civil war, and Stalinism. People in Russia over this past century have had to endure a range of social conflicts that are mind-boggling. Children have grown up in a world where betrayal, deception, and heroism are everyday facts of life. If masks and duplicity of manners are necessary to cope there, then I think that it is more typical of human experience in general than what Americans have come to expect. We are the fortunate inheritors of a rich continent without the kinds of painful choices imposed on people in most other cultures. Our experience is such that we are ill equipped to deal with the everyday tragedies others know so intimately. We talk on endlessly about the crime of the Holocaust while being able to do little to deal, for example, with the horrors of the disintegration of the old Yugoslavia, or of African tribalism.

And so we remain "God's Own Country." Our great good luck, socially and economically, leaves us ill prepared to sympathize with the troubles that others less lucky than ourselves have had. As the war in Vietnam recedes from our memory, some may want to think of it as somehow merely an aberration in American policymaking. But a great novelist like Graham Greene, in *The Quiet American*, could capture in a short book that combination of innocence and naiveté that could lead to such a calamity for South East Asia. We erect a monument for the Vietnam war which turns out to be a memorial to ourselves, rather than those who suffered from our policies. I suppose President Lyndon Johnson did have New Dealish objectives about bringing American technology and know-how to that far-off part of the world, but without any understanding of the objections that the Vietnamese might have had. Had America started from a position of the acceptance of the inevitability of sin, Graham Greene argued, we would not have inflicted that kind of suffering on people who live in a world so different from our own. But Americans have not been accustomed to accepting self-limitations. When I was a graduate student the most common clinical problem of those undergoing psychoanalyses with candidates in training in Boston was the inability to complete a Ph.D. dissertation; I think one can be skeptical of how much savvy the young physicians conducting those analyses had about academic life, or the reality of the so-called symptom they were attempting to treat.

Within psychoanalysis Americans have not even found it easy to acknowledge the boundaries to any possibilities of self-development. The latest idea is that by taking pills one can solve problems without paying any sorts of human price; it is only a rare commentator like Peter Kramer[2] who deals with a few of the pros and cons involved in relying on some of the new medication. Aldous Huxley's *Brave New World* predicted some of what would happen with human reliance on medication. But there is almost no literature on what is actually going on within biological psychiatry today, or follows the latest abuses that a technological approach can take. One suspects that it is once again proving to be the case that Lord Acton was right that power corrupts, and that absolute power tends to corrupt absolutely. But then we have scarcely ever acknowledged that there is a power element in all forms of psychotherapy.

Nor do Americans find it easy to accept the inevitability of politics in all psychology. B. F. Skinner's *Walden Two*[3], and behavioral psychology in general, can be seen as an effort to substitute engineering for ethical choices. This sort of psychology can be attractive to Americans precisely because it proposed to substitute science for moral decision-making.

Yet in this area Freud has not left us with a useful legacy. For he tended to think that he had solved the problems of philosophy by substituting a neutral sort of science. He pretended that decency was the only standard he needed, and that moral values were ultimately self-evident. And so he proposed to divorce psychology from philosophizing, separating off an understanding of what we ought to do from what in fact happens. The more one explores the world of depth psychology, however, the more it should become clear that many of the rival points of view are really quarrels over how life might best be lived.[4] And in the vacuum of philosophy that Freud espoused psychoanalysis itself became an unacknowledged moral end. It is no wonder that some of the quarrels between different schools have been so bitter.

In some sense Freud was correct, in that it is not easy to see how one can succeed in persuading anyone to another moral point of view. So ethics have to be in some sense self-validating. Justice Holmes used to talk about his "can't helps,"[5] ethical commitments which he felt were rock-bottom; but then Holmes had served in the Civil War's northern army, and for the rest of his long life felt the painful moral consequences of having soldiered in a cause, sometimes against former classmates, which he little understood but still believed in. His sort of skepticism has brought down on his head moralistic denunciations for his lack of belief in what now seems politically correct. But then Holmes's intellectual orientation was cosmopolitan and European, which introduced an element of detachment towards more commonly accepted American beliefs.

Psychoanalysis can serve as a powerful check on certain typically American tendencies. Freud's system of thought is used in so many different national traditions today that just following what is going on contributes an element of universalism to one's thinking. DSM-III and DSM-IV seem laughable to some educated European analysts, but those handbooks of so-called abnormal "disorders" have attracted little skeptical criticism in America. We still find rare discussion of what it might mean to be "normal." It sometimes seems to me that we are roughly back where we were at the turn of the twentieth century, when the central issue was considered heredity and diagnostic classification. (Jung once challengingly proposed that a diagnosis could only be made after the completion of treatment.) Freud used to like to quote Hamlet's having said: "There are more things in heaven and earth, Horatio, Than are dreamt of in your philosophy." Maybe now that psychoanalysis in America has run into heavy weather, it will attract practitioners more interested in some of the central European themes that inspired the early analysts. Clinical work is bound to be enhanced, I believe, by a greater appreciation, on the part of both patients and analysts, of the tragic sides of existence.

Notes

1. "Studies on Hysteria," *Standard Edition of the Complete Psychological Works of Sigmund Freud,* ed. James Strachey (London, Hogarth Press, 1953-1974), Vol. 2, p. 305.
2. See, for example, Peter D. Kramer, *Listening to Prozac* (New York: Viking Penguin, 1993).
3. B. F. Skinner, *Walden Two* (New York: Macmillan, 1948).
4. See Paul Roazen, *The Trauma of Freud: Controversies in Psychoanalysis, op. cit.*
5. *The Mind and Faith of Mr. Justice Holmes,* ed. Max Lerner (New York: The Modern Library, 1943). See also Albert W. Alschuler, *Law Without Values: The Life, Work, and Legacy of Justice Holmes* (Chicago, University of Chicago, 2000).

5

The Old *Encounter*

Intellectual history is an academic orphan. The study of past ideas is too amorphous to appeal to most university administrators. Colleges, at least in North America, tend to respond instead to the latest fashions, which often means studying topics that are apparently useful. In the midst of all the pressures now to be politically correct, I find myself nostalgic about that year I spent as a graduate student at Magdalen College, Oxford in 1959-60. It was customary there only to study history or literature that could be dated before the outbreak of the First World War, although I have heard that by now it is considered proper to extend attention up until the start of World War II. At the time I chafed at what seemed to me old-fogeyism, especially since Oxford philosophy could be so self-confident as to pride itself on examining the writing of contemporary dons. Yet as I look back now that educational experience seems to me blissfully detached and monastically isolated from the outside world.

As far as I am concerned the history of ideas is a legitimate way of describing an effort to comprehend the life of the mind in the past. But establishing what constitutes an "idea" can be an uncertain endeavor. If one sets out to study the course of business cycles, patterns of social stratification, or monetary policy, these topics are likely to seem concrete and discussable, whereas ideas are apt to appear so intangible as to appear airy.

If intellectual history has not been more celebrated as an essential enterprise, part of the explanation may be that it seems too subjective to qualify as a unique discipline. To study ideas means that one has to cut across many academic fiefdoms, without respecting the boundaries surrounding fields that have established themselves as respectable. Political scientists, sociologists, and historians, for instance, cultivate their own special turfs. It is well known that one gets ahead professionally by writing for a narrow audience of one's peers.

I want here to offer an example of what I consider a highlight in mid-twentieth century intellectual life. It is of course too soon to know how later

generations are going to look back on us. But I would like to call attention to
how there once existed, starting in 1953, an exceptional monthly coming
from London, England known as *Encounter*. Its circulation seems to have
risen remarkably in a short period of time. In 1959, 16,000 copies of each
issue were printed; that figure rose another 4,000 the next year. By October
1961 the print order was up again—7,000 more than the year before. In the
fall of 1966 *Encounter* was producing around 40,000 copies of each issue.
When *Encounter* ceased to exist in early 1991, I saw only one obituary notice, written by Ferdinand Mount, then the editor of the *Times Literary Supplement*. Mount's short piece alluded to other notices of the demise of *Encounter*,
which unfortunately escaped me since evidently they all appeared in Britain.
Yet once *Encounter* had been central for all intellectuals. I am referring to the
old *Encounter* of my youth.

Despite more moves in my life than I care to remember, up to the early
1990s I had retained all my back copies of *Encounter*. At that time I luxuriated in going back over my old issues, cannibalizing specific articles, tearing
them out to file away under various separate categories of mine. I re-exam-
ined every issue in my possession before allowing myself to do away with the
whole collection.

An institutional high point came for *Encounter* when it published its hundredth number in January 1962. Various writers in other publications took
note of the event, but none of them, in a characteristically low-key advertisement on the back jacket of a later issue of *Encounter*, were identified by
name. According to someone in the *Guardian*, "when a British intellectual
monthly sells close on thirty thousand copies something is happening which
we thought had gone out with the decline of the great Victorian reviews.... It
has discussed ideas and current affairs with great vigour." A writer in the
Observer remarked: "I can remember no equivalent of *Encounter's* present
blend of world politics, sociology, and the arts.... It is easily the most successful magazine of its scope and type, and for my part the most compulsively
readable." The *Times Literary Supplement* had observed: "*Encounter* has
now established itself as one of the most stimulating and wide-awake of all
our monthly reviews." *New Statesman* was also quoted: "Its list of bomb-
shells is impressive.... It must have provoked more cocktail-party conversation than any other comparable magazine of our time." From North America
only the *Toronto Daily Star* was quoted: "Of all the magazines I see, *Encounter* is the most engaging and the most useful. It combines broadmindedness,
seriousness and journalistic professionalism in a way that is not matched on
either side of the Atlantic. It is now probably the one indispensable intellectual magazine."

Within the January 1962 issue itself Stephen Spender allowed himself, as
editor, a pronouncement about *Encounter's* "achievements and goals." He
said that *Encounter* had been more successful than anticipated, since he had

originally hoped to maintain a circulation of 10,000 readers. He sought to relate the kind of magazine *Encounter* was to two vanished predecessors, *Criterion* and *Horizon*, and he quoted Cyril Connolly's remarks in the hundredth number of *Horizon*. Spender went on to remark that in *Encounter*:

> We have always been concerned with the conditions that affect the kind of culture we live in. What our wide angle view tries to take in is those circumstances in the surrounding world which are changing our values. It is, on the whole, their relevance to these changes which determines our interest in the tension between East and West, between the "advanced" and the "emerging" nations, the law and obscenity, the two cultures, the conflicts of ideas in the Labour Party, the divergence of critical standards in Anglo-American and French criticism, the impact of Asia and Africa on America and Europe, and a dozen other subjects we have touched on.

Politically, *Encounter* had tried "to provide a platform for the greatest possible amount of disagreement within a broad area of agreement."

> We are agreed that in the present state of the world, democracy provides the basis for individual freedom that is denied under communist and other dictatorships; and that therefore this freedom should be exercised, maintained, and defended....Broadly speaking, we are pro-American as we are pro-British—because we support democracy. But we are critical of many things in America, as in England.

Conor Cruise O'Brien was exceptional in publicly distrusting the particular political slant to *Encounter*. Writing for the *New Statesman* in December 1963, he singled out *Encounter*'s anti-communism; he claimed the magazine was too soft on America, and at the same time excessively severe about the Soviet Union. But even though O'Brien minded what he saw as *Encounter*'s "pro-capitalist propaganda," he also commented: "It has been ably edited and never less than interesting; almost every issue contains some work of real merit, almost always non-political."

O'Brien's piece was occasioned by the publication of a book made up of selections from *Encounter*. This was a tenth-anniversary anthology, and Sir Denis Brogan wrote the introduction, which appeared in the November 1963 *Encounter*, an issue devoted to the role of intellectual reviews in general. Brogan classed *Encounter* as a periodical of "opinion." Such publications had played "a great part in the intellectual history of Europe for nearly two hundred years." Although Brogan cited a handful of celebrated examples, it seems that he had one main precursor in mind: "The first great modern review of the type to which *Encounter* belongs was the *Edinburgh Review*...." *Encounter* was part of a tradition of "the old-fashioned review, a vehicle of exposition and controversy." Brogan described *Encounter* as an organ of protest against the betrayal of the intellectuals, which is precisely what gave O'Brien an opening for accusing *Encounter* of being guilty of that specific form of treason.[1] O'Brien reprinted his *New Statesman* review in a 1966 collection of essays. But by then the *New York Review of Books* was already secure, and a new forum for the intellectual establishment existed; *Encounter* had necessarily lost its unique standing from the old period.

The earliest issue that I had on hand was from July 1957; I bought it for some 75 cents during the summer of my junior year at Harvard. When I belatedly looked at the names of the editors, I was surprised to find out that Spender was joined then by Irving Kristol. In those naïve days for me it was the articles themselves that mattered, and I paid no attention to the editors. Spender was a man of letters and a poet, but I had failed then to associate Spender's name with the novelists and publicists who participated with him in writing *The God That Failed*[2], a work that had an immense impact on me.

According to a notice in the November 1958 issue of *Encounter*, Kristol resigned then to return to New York City as editor of the *Reporter*, to be succeeded as co-editor of *Encounter* by Melvin J. Lasky. Kristol has maintained his social and political visibility, even though the *Reporter* has long since ceased to exist. The *Reporter*, a bi-weekly, was more tied to current events than *Encounter*, and its articles were less spacious.

At the time I first got hooked on *Encounter*, the reviews and articles in the *Times Literary Supplement* were still unsigned. Like others I did not trust the anonymous reviewer's sense of responsibility to succeed in protecting books from the natural proclivity of writers, especially in Britain, to settle old scores. Whereas reviewing in North America has tended to become an extension of advertising copy, the British can be almost frighteningly awful to one another.

Looking through an index in the July 1957 issue reminds me what one could expect of *Encounter* then. W. H. Auden had a poem and a book review; James Baldwin published an article; there was a piece by Albert Camus, and also one by Herbert Butterfield. Stuart Hampshire and Morton White had written on British and American philosophy. There was an essay by Mary McCarthy, "The Arthur Miller Case," and one by Lionel Trilling about *Emma*. Politically the authors were diverse. Dwight Macdonald seemed to have something in almost every issue, while David Riesman and A. J. P. Taylor also represented the Left. Hugh Trevor-Roper published an article called "Arnold Toynbee's Millennium" in the June issue, and it may have been that famous polemical assault on Toynbee (which did not keep him out of future issues of *Encounter*) that first brought the magazine to my attention. The July issue had a letter to the editor by Philip Toynbee in defense of his father. The correspondence in *Encounter* was always one of the most fascinating parts; the letters had a vigor and bite that stand out even now.

I noticed only later at the back of this, my first issue of *Encounter*, a statement that it was being published then by Martin Secker and Warburg Limited in London, for the Congress of Cultural Freedom in Paris. Readers were told that "the views expressed in the pages of the *Encounter* are to be attributed to the writers, not to the sponsors." I did not know anything whatever then about either the London publisher or the Paris organization, whose president was listed as Denis de Rougemont and whose secretary general was Nicolas Nabokov. (Nabokov's cousin Vladimir was not yet famous as a writer.) Only years afterwards did I find out that the Congress for Cultural Freedom had been founded in June 1950 at a conference held just before the outbreak of the Korean War; the participants included Ignazio Silone, Andre Malraux, Arthur Koestler, John Dos Passos, Arthur Schlesinger, Jr., James T. Farrell, Carson McCullers, Tennessee Williams, Sidney Hook, and James Burnham. Its honorary presidents were to be such luminaries as Benedetto Croce, John Dewey, Karl Jaspers, Jacques Maritain, and Bertrand Russell.

By 1958 I was so absorbed by *Encounter* that I saved almost every issue from that year. In the fall of 1959 when I was at Oxford, I recall *Encounter* coming up in conversation with an exceptionally bright young English undergraduate. He, although only around eighteen years old, reeled off a version of the differences between the early, middle, and late Ludwig Wittgenstein. This young man, whose father had been in a Labor Cabinet, held a contrasting set of political convictions from my own, and we disagreed on many points. Eisenhower was at the end of his presidency, and I felt suitably disaffected by the state of American politics. But I was mildly shocked to be told by this young Englishman that the monthly I had come to admire was a front for the Central Intelligence Agency. My friend had so many odd-seeming political beliefs that I thought I could safely dismiss this accusation about *Encounter*, which was by then a sacred part of my intellectual life.

Anyone now looking at those issues of the old *Encounter* has to be impressed by the extraordinary quality of the pieces. Stravinsky was interviewed in July 1957; *Encounter* in 1958 contained work by Leslie Fieldler, James Agee, Bertolt Brecht, Michael Oakeshott, George Steiner, and Raymond Aron. In the following year *Encounter* could boast of contributors like John Kenneth Galbraith, Richard Hofstadter, Vladimir Nabokov, George Kennan, Edmund Wilson, C. P. Snow, Ted Hughes, Leonard Woolf, and C. V. Wedgewood. Someone else would select a different set of celebrities from the pages of *Encounter*. But there seemed no editorial principle of selection about authors, either Right or Left, other than a commitment to the life of the mind. (If I paid less attention to the poetry and fiction than I should have, that choice reflected my own limitations rather than those of *Encounter*.)

Or so I naively reasoned about the ideology behind *Encounter*. I would not have seen O'Brien's blast against *Encounter* when it first appeared in the *New Statesman*. Wherever one lives is bound to have its parochialisms, and no one I knew on this side of the Atlantic regularly got the *New Statesman*. The limitations of geography help explain why it was such a joy to get one's hands on each issue of *Encounter*. The splendid way it was bound made it seem like an eclectic paperback, with an appropriate kind of book-like ink on the pages.

A formal "postscript" appeared at the back of the July 1964 issue:

> The British press, as well as many newspapers in Europe and the United States, has published the recent news of an announcement by the Editors of *Encounter* and Mr. Cecil King, Chairman of the International Publishing Corporation. For the record, and for the benefit of those readers who may have missed it, we print it here below. On occasion, too, we should like to restate our heartfelt gratitude to the Congress for Cultural Freedom in Paris. Its grants over the years made it possible to establish and sustain this journal. No committee of sponsors was ever at once so generous and so enlightened, for it understood that magazines aren't produced by committees (only camels are) and that editors could only go their own way, beholden to nobody but themselves (and their passions, prejudices, and philosophy). In that spirit of independence we intend to go on.

Henceforth *Encounter* would be published by the *Daily Mirror*, which would make possible the magazine's "additional expansion." *Encounter* was no longer a "little magazine" but "an international journal with forty thousand circulation." According to this formal press release, up to then *Encounter* had been supported "by the Congress for Cultural Freedom in Paris, whose grants have come from private foundations, mostly American...." Spender and Lasky wrote:

> We are deeply grateful to Mr. King for the generous terms of support he has offered us in response to our request for publishing assistance. The prospects are now good that with more effective distribution and management *Encounter* may well become the first "high-brow review" to be self-sustaining. No editorial changes are involved and we will continue to produce as independent and controversial a review of literature and politics as we know how.

This shift in *Encounter's* backing was of no consequence to me as a subscriber. But over the years of my readership I had come across various appeals and protests put forward by the Congress for Cultural Freedom. In the December 1958 issue a collective telegram was printed that had been sent on behalf of Boris Pasternak, whose fate in the Soviet Union then seemed uncertain. It would be hard to imagine a more catholic list of distinguished signers – Maurice Bowra, Kenneth Clark, T. S. Eliot, E. M. Forster, Graham Greene, Aldous Huxley, Julian Huxley, Rose Macauley, Somerset Maugham, J. B. Priestley, Alan Pryce-Jones, Herbert Read, Bertrand Russell, C. P. Snow, Stephen Spender, Rebecca West, and Angus Wilson. Although that telegram in Pasternak's behalf was not specifically identified with the Congress for Cultural Freedom, the December 1960 *Encounter* contained a formal protest by the organization against the French government's having taken steps, without any trials, in forbidding certain artists and intellectuals from "all activity in State-supported theatre, cinema, radio, and television...." Some French teachers, too, had arbitrarily "been deprived of the right to exercise their profession." *Encounter's* original benefactors seemed squarely on the side of the angels, and stood up for the ideals of democracy:

The Congress for Cultural Freedom…must protest against those recent measures of the French government, the object of which is clearly to deprive artists and intellectuals of the normal right to exercise their professions. The Congress feels that these measures cannot but lead to the regimentation and servitude of art and thought. Their approval would place all public liberties in jeopardy.

Then again, in the October 1961 issue of *Encounter*, a special insert appeared, a letter to Mayor Willy Brandt. He had "recently appealed to the Congress for Cultural Freedom to bring to the attention of world opinion the gravity with which its friends and associates regarded the violation of human rights involved in the closing of the Berlin border to east German refugees." In reply to Brandt's request for help, "thirty intellectuals and civil leaders from Europe, Asia, Africa and the Americas" published an appeal they sent in behalf of Brandt's struggle against the erection of the Berlin Wall. No forum comparable to *Encounter* existed when, for example, the world later witnessed the barbarities that took place in what once was Yugoslavia.

Encounter was out front on a variety of political issues. For example, Theodore Draper kept an eye on Castro's Cuba, and he took the position that the nature of Castro's regime was indigenously determined and not just the result of American opposition. In 1961 Spender and Lasky defended *Encounter* against "sneering journalism that appeared in *Time and Tide* because of Draper's coverage of Cuba. In particular, they insisted that:

The Ford Foundation is not in any sense of the phrase our "discreet all-American parent organization." It has, over the years in which it has given financial support (all publicly announced) to schools, universities, research institutes, etc., been generous enough to help support a series of international conferences which the Conference of Cultural Freedom has organized in Oxford, Paris, Berlin, Cairo, Bombay, and Tokyo. *Encounter* has, from time to time, published accounts of the debates which took place on those occasions.

Spender and Lasky went on in their letter to *Time and Tide*:

What would be slanderous if it were not so absurd is the suggestion that we have been "adopting straight Cold-War positions; no word of structural criticism of their sponsor country or the West generally, day-in-day-out onslaught on the East." *Encounter* is an independent review, "Anglo-American" if you will in its co-editorship, and we do not believe it would be able to command either the attention or the circulation that it does if it were the propaganda sheet which your writer insinuates. *Encounter* is a critical review, and no culture, East or West, and no governmental politics, Left-wing or Right-wing, has been immune from criticism in our pages. It can hardly have escaped your attention that in our last number we published from the pen of P. M. S. Blackett the most serious and formidable criticism of U.S. defence thinking that has yet appeared.

The April 1961 *Encounter* had contained not only Blackett's "Nuclear Stalemate," but James Baldwin's "Richard Wright," A. J. Ayer's "John Paul

Sartre," Cyril Connolly's "Beyond Believing," Frank Kermode's "Graham Greene," and Claude Levi-Strauss's "Tristes Tropiques."

Although the *Daily Mirror*, not the Congress for Cultural Freedom was *Encounter*'s backer as of July 1964, a series of charges about its funding were yet to be aired. By August 1966 the issue of *Encounter*'s integrity had taken a serious turn for the worse, meriting a column in *Encounter* signed by "R," which evidently stood for Goronwy Rees. O'Brien had not only republished his original review of the *Encounter* anthology, but he returned to the problem in the *Washington Post Book Week* and a lecture at New York University. And the *New York Times*, in a series of articles on the CIA, had on April 27, 1966 mentioned *Encounter* as one of the agency's projects. By then the furtive escalation of American military involvement in Southeast Asia had rendered the CIA, to me at least, an odious source of financial support.

So the apparently wild charges of my well-connected British friend at Oxford seemed true. *Encounter*'s August 1966 column was mainly directed against O'Brien. He had thought that *Encounter* held "such a central position in the English speaking world in the second half of the 20th century and such a mediating role between the writer and the capitalist power structure that it deserves...our particular attention...." The *New York Times* accusation of secret CIA financing was picked up by O'Brien; according to him, "the beauty of the operation was that other writers of first rank, who had no interest in serving the power structure, were induced to do so unwittingly."

The August 1966 "R" column ridiculed the CIA allegation. It were "as if J. Edgar Hoover had taken to what Mr. O'Brien calls 'politico-cultural criticism.'" *Encounter* had sent a letter of correction and denial to the *New York Times*. Prominent contributors wrote in defense of the editorial independence *Encounter* had achieved. The August 1966 *Encounter* column took the position that O'Brien had been indulging in a version of the tactics of the late Senator Joseph McCarthy, "hunting for CIA agents beneath the beds of Stephen Spender, Irving Kristol, Melvin Lasky, and Frank Kermode," all editors of the monthly.

At the time the CIA story first surfaced, I reflected on the April 1963 issue of *Encounter*, "New Voices in Russian writing," which was dominated by contemporary Soviet writers. I had originally thought only crackpots could believe the story of CIA funding, until the *New York Times* first lent support to the idea. All of the dissident Soviet writers featured in *Encounter* had been risking at home the charge of betraying their country by publishing at all in the West. Literature and politics had been closely intertwined throughout Russian history in the nineteenth and twentieth centuries; *Doctor Zhivago* had only appeared in 1959, and Pasternak was particularly pleased with the reception his book had received in *Encounter*.

The CIA support for *Encounter*, no matter how indirectly through the Congress for Cultural Freedom it had been arranged, fulfilled the worst fears of Russian writers who had published abroad. For it had turned out that they had allowed themselves to be used as pawns within the Cold War. Without knowing it they had put themselves in the service of their country's enemy. As of the July 1964 declaration, *Encounter* had supposedly cut itself loose from the Congress for Cultural Freedom, and therefore liberated itself from the tainted source of CIA money. Any link between *Encounter* and the CIA seemed intrinsically objectionable, and was specifically denied in the August 1966 column.

I wonder now whether the advertising in *Encounter* should have been any kind of ideological tip-off. My eyes at the time had focused on the book ads, but who would have thought that quarterlies that took out space were also beneficiaries of the Congress for Cultural Freedom? Perhaps it should have been striking that the British Iron and Steel Federation, or Olivetti and Ford, had placed ads, but I can still see no reason why private industry would not support something as meritorious as *Encounter*. The Olympia Press in Paris also took out a full-page advertisement; in my time the only way to get one's hands on Henry Miller's controversial novels was to smuggle them in from Olympia Press, which had originally published Nabokov's *Lolita* in 1955. *Lady Chatterley's Lover*, once also available only in France, came out in Britain while I was at Oxford, but the main bookseller there, Blackwell's, would not display it; one had to ask for it, and then it would be brought out from under the counter. (The head of All Soul's College had an arresting piece in *Encounter* on the allegedly homosexual nature of Lawrence's depiction of love.) How was one to suspect *Encounter* of betraying the cause of enlightenment and free thought, and lying as well? The connection of people like J. Robert Oppenheimer, George Kennan, or Bertrand Russell, not to mention all the others associated with *Encounter*, seemed reassuring.

At least one person I knew said she had cancelled her *Encounter* subscription the moment the news was first out about CIA money. I myself continued to keep on getting *Encounter* throughout the 1960s, despite my disappointment about what had happened. Nevertheless I had the definite impression, which I cannot verify, that there was a watershed between the old *Encounter* and what appeared after 1966. At least certain writers would have steered clear of it now. Perhaps there was not really such a shift in the list of contributors; maybe I was simply not taking *Encounter* as seriously as I once had. But cynics have been able to argue that, paradoxically, during the period of CIA funding *Encounter* achieved its most remarkable publications.

The story about CIA financing did not evaporate, and after about a year Lasky acknowledged his regret about having been insufficiently "frank." In the interim, *Ramparts*, an American New Left publication, had published another article on *Encounter* in March. And worst of all was a May piece, in the low-brow *Saturday Evening Post* of all places, in defense of the CIA. No one could object to the proposition that "cultural achievement and political freedom were interdependent." But the author, who had joined the CIA in 1950, penned sentences that were to be the last straw: "We had placed one agent in a Europe-based organization of intellectuals called the Congress for Cultural Freedom. Another agent became an editor of *Encounter*."

The "trustees" of *Encounter* published a "statement" in the July 1967 issue. It sounds now almost Vatican-like in its aloofness and self-importance. "The Trustees of *Encounter* deeply regret the serious differences of view-point that have caused two of the Editors, Mr. Stephen Spender and Professor Frank Kermode, who had rendered services of the highest value to the maga-zine, to resign. The views and opinions of all concerned have been amply ventilated in the public press." No apology or explanation was offered; the tone of the "statement" implied that there was no need for the readers to be informed further about the matter. The trustees were announcing that "in order to ensure continuity Mr. Melvin J. Lasky, who has made over the past nine years a notable contribution to the success of *Encounter*, has agreed to remain as co-editor. Mr. Nigel Dennis has been appointed as the other co-editor." According to this statement,

> The main point is that *Encounter*, since it was established in 1953, enjoyed complete independence in its editorial policy. The Editors alone have always been responsible for what they published. This was so before 1964, when the magazine was finan-cially supported by the Congress for Cultural Freedom, and subsequently when the financial sponsorship has been provided—as it is at the present—by the Interna-tional Publishing Corporation....The Trustees are confident that the same editorial independence will be maintained by *Encounter* in the future.

The trustees who signed the statement were Sir William Hayter, Arthur Schlesinger, Jr., Edward Shils, and Andrew Shonfield. Yet they had done noth-ing to enlighten posterity about the nature of the problem leading to the resignations of Spender and Kermode. It still makes me squirm to read in Mount's *TLS* obituary notice for *Encounter*: "The intellectual defeat of com-munism was certainly the cause for which it was started in 1953 and the reason why the CIA so notoriously channeled money into it through the Congress for Cultural Freedom."

I can remember heated debates about which of the *Encounter* editors must have known about the CIA connection. Lasky had been in on the creation of the Congress for Cultural Freedom in 1950, although he joined *Encounter* only in 1958; he was still in charge of *Encounter* at its end in 1991. Yet I would still stand up for the special intellectual status that the old *Encounter* had attained. I know nothing further about *Encounter's* circulation figures, but I presume the CIA scandal and how it was handled had a damaging effect. *Encounter* continued to be a remarkable magazine, but increasingly it had other competitors, for instance, the *New York Review of Books*, which became more central to intellectual life.

In 1969 I had a piece of my own appear in *Encounter*.[3] I did not kid myself that this bit of success was anything near as momentous as having something published in the old *Encounter*. In addition, there was some disagreeable back-and-forth between Lasky and myself in connection with the article, and afterwards I let my subscription lapse. Over the next years, on occasion, I would buy a copy of *Encounter* at the newsstands. But for me the glorious days of my commitment to *Encounter* were something from the distant past.

A good book, the *Liberal Conspiracy: The Congress for Cultural Freedom and the Struggle for the Mind of Postwar Europe*[4], appeared in 1989. The author, Peter Coleman, not only examined the private files of the organization, but interviewed the surviving participants. *Encounter* was considered by the CIA to be the Congress's "greatest asset." I am indebted to Coleman's story, which has details not to be found elsewhere. But I wonder whether he has not confused the forest with the trees. For he tells his readers, after a blow-by-blow recital of the 1966-67 period, that following "much anguish and heartbreak the magazine survived and subsequently flourished." Such a sentence makes me wonder whether, with all his scrupulous and interesting attention to private correspondence among the editors, Coleman actually bothered to read *Encounter* itself. Although Coleman is informative about how the CIA revelations came out, he omits the bootless attempt of *Encounter* to defend itself.

Here I feel in a quandary. *Encounter* was guilty not just of lies by omission, but had deliberately misled us. According to Coleman the editors already knew in 1964 of the *New York Times* investigation of the CIA's cultural activities, which I think might explain the effort of *Encounter* to get itself into the hands of the *Daily Mirror*. Yet, according to Coleman, the Congress for Cultural Freedom was still giving *Encounter* $30,000 as late as 1966. The denial about the Ford Foundation looks like a shell game. (After 1966-67, when the CIA ceased funding the Congress for Cultural Freedom, the Ford Foundation picked up the tab.)

I appreciate today, as I could not at the time, the fix *Encounter* found itself in by 1967. The creation of the Congress for Cultural Freedom, in 1950, has to be one of the best ways the CIA ever spent money. Stalinism was a real threat, and Western intellectuals had been notoriously naïve about Soviet tyranny; the Russians invaded Hungary as late as 1956, and India remained neutral until its military difficulties with China. *Encounter* was never simply a propaganda organ. But whatever occasional warnings might have appeared in *Encounter*, I do not remember any special political role *Encounter* played in alerting us to the dangers of a Vietnam debacle. The *New York Review of Books* did take a part in that story, but by then some of the old *Encounter* writers were appearing in the *NYR*.

Jason Epstein, a founder of the *NYR* who denounced the CIA's "secret gravy train" had himself taken part in the American Committee for Cultural

Freedom. Could anyone of stature involved with it have been exempt from what looks like corruption? One has to suppose that at least Spender should have known what was going on at *Encounter*. Before the appearance of the *Saturday Evening Post* story, it had been possible for Sir Isaiah Berlin (another of Epstein's later authors) to advise Lasky: "The proper role of *Encounter* is simply to say that they acted as they did in ignorance...Men of sense and goodwill will understand this; those who lack it will continue to snipe away."

As late as November 1967 George Kennan was writing to the new president of the Congress for Cultural Freedom:

> I was delighted to see that you have taken the presidency....It is an institution of great value, which should have a permanent place, it seems to me, in the life of our western world. The flap about C.I.A. money was quite unwarranted, and caused far more anguish than it should have been permitted to cause. I never felt the slightest pangs of conscience about it, from the standpoint of the organization. This country has no ministry of culture, and the C.I.A. was obliged to do what it could to try to fill the gap. It is unfair that it should be so bitterly condemned for its failures, and should then go unpraised when it does something constructive and sensible. And the Congress would itself have been remiss if it had failed to take money which came to it from good intent and wholly without strings or conditions.

I am no longer, as I was in 1966-67, so sure of my moral judgment, and I now think Kennan's position deserves a respectful hearing. What sustains and promotes intellectual life remains a mystery; universities can only do so much, and an institution like the old *Encounter* added something all its own. Perhaps that is why the betrayal in connection with the CIA funding seems so serious.

As of early 1991 *Encounter* had ceased to be published. According to the editor of the *TLS*, "Britain seems to have lost, more or less irrevocably, what must have been its only memorable journal of ideas since the great quarterlies of the nineteenth century." Apparently the other post-mortems about the demise of *Encounter* pointed out the irony of an anti-communist journal failing once communism itself had ceased to be an operative political and military threat. "Yet for the generation which grew up in the mid-1950s, the anti-communism was not *Encounter*'s main attraction...." Mount's impression exactly matches my own: "What the magazine offered to us was the excitement of an intellectual abroad. Every month, those block-shaped grainy pages offered a kind of adventure which the timorous British newspapers and weeklies of the late 1950s and early 1960s would not have dreamed of essaying." That is the same period I remember as being so particularly remarkable about what I have called the old *Encounter*. According to Mount, then writing as editor of the *TLS*, later issues of *Encounter* were also remarkable, which I do not doubt. But however great a contribution *Encounter* continued to make to intellectual life, it is that period of the late 1950s and early 1960s, which happened to mean so much to me personally, that I think most important.

There was a leisureliness about *Encounter*'s monthly appearance that made one think there was no hurry about perusing the whole thing before the next issue threatened to appear. I am also thinking now of the controversy in its pages about the seventeenth-century English gentry, and whether it was rising or falling; however this problem may have echoed anti-Marxist concerns, it was admirable how such an esoteric subject could command the attention of such embattled and literate contestants. And it is unforgettable how Edmund Wilson and Vladimir Nabokov, former friends, could bitterly argue over issues of Russian translation both in the *NYR* and *Encounter*.

I would insist that the central objective of intellectual history involves putting oneself back into the shoes of the past, and even painstakingly conscientious research, such as Coleman's on the Congress for Cultural Freedom, can manage to miss the boat about the old *Encounter*. To wave the flag of anti-Stalinism cannot exhaust the achievements of that magazine. Yet after the CIA revelations of 1966-67 its best period was gone; whatever the undoubted merits of *Encounter* after the resignations of Spender and Kermode, it played a wholly different role. Historians of ideas are notoriously wary about the issue of influence, but I would contend that the old *Encounter* had a special impact, and it would be unfortunate to forget this. In contrast to interesting quarterlies like the *American Scholar*, the *Yale Review*, or the *Virginia Quarterly Review*, there was always something electrifying about the appearance of an issue of the old *Encounter*. Worthy weeklies like the *New Republic* or the *Spectator* cannot hope to compete with the spaciousness of a monthly.

Goethe once warned young men to beware of their aspirations, for when they are middle-aged they will have achieved them. Looking over those back issues of the old *Encounter* reminded me how my friends once agonized over the French involvement in Algeria. And in retrospect, our whole generation was misled about how monolithic so-called totalitarianism was; except for Kennan, I cannot think of anyone else who even hinted that communism could collapse like a house of cards. (He readily admitted later to having underestimated the damage Stalin did to the old Soviet society.) The only part of those issues of *Encounter* I had so loyally saved that struck me as boring were interminable discussions of struggles within the British Labor Party.

Aside from specific political and social matters, I found it curiously reassuring to look at the old *Encounter*. How nice to discover A. S. Byatt there, even though I never read her until *Possession* was brought to my attention. How comforting to find that the vitality of the old *Encounter* still reached me, and that despite the passage of time I still retained traces of the same boy who picked up that copy of *Encounter* as long ago as 1957.

Notes

1. See most recently Mark Lilla, *The Reckless Mind: Intellectuals in Politics* (New York: New York Review of Books, 2001).
2. *The God That Failed*, ed. Richard Crossman (New York: Bantam, 1952).
3. Paul Roazen, "Sigmund Freud, Lou Andreas-Salomé, and Victor Tausk: A Curious Triangle," *Encounter*, October 1969. (Also in Paul Roazen, *The Historiography of Psychoanalysis* [New Brunswick, N.J., Transaction Publications, 2001], pp. 195-204.)
4. Peter Coleman, *The Liberal Conspiracy: The Congress for Cultural Freedom and the Struggle for the Mind of Postwar Europe* (New York: The Free Press, 1989).

6

Three Philosophers Analyze Freud: Wittgenstein, Althusser, and Buber

In libraries across North America, Freud's works are catalogued under the designation "Philosophy," and therefore writings in the tradition of thought he succeeded in inspiring—which means a lot of books by now—have accordingly been similarly categorized. The librarians who made the original choice about where to place Freud's texts have seemed confirmed in their judgment. At any rate, and as a matter of historical inquiry, we now know that Freud was more philosophically well read and sophisticated than he ever liked to acknowledge in public. At the time he was getting his medical qualification he also toyed with taking a simultaneous degree in humanities.

Reading books like Ray Monk's superb biography, *Ludwig Wittgenstein: The Duty of Genius*[1] and Louis Althusser's engrossing memoir, *The Future Lasts Forever*[2] is a reminder of just how important a figure Freud has been throughout the twentieth-century history of ideas as well as psychiatry. One might suppose that Wittgenstein's legacy—both his earlier positivistic phase as well as his engagements with the epistemology of ordinary language—would be immune to the reach of psychoanalysis. And, within the rather hermetic tradition of French Marxist thinking, it could appear that Althusser was also outside the scope of Freud's impact. But, as we shall see, in wholly different ways Freud's psychoanalysis becomes central to understanding what such different thinkers as Wittgenstein and Althusser were up to.

Monk has provided an account of Wittgenstein's life that is thoroughly compelling, interweaving his subject's ideas with the world in which he moved. He may have become one of the most strikingly original figures within British empirical philosophy, but Wittgenstein was born (1889) into one of the richest families in Hapsburg Vienna. Monk, by training a philosopher, is marvelous at recreating the cultural ambience of old Viennese society. For example, Wittgenstein's upper middle-class father was once offered the chance to join the aristocracy, but refused the possibility of adding the aristocratic "von" to his name on the grounds that "such a gesture would be seen as the mark of the parvenu." In the last days of the Austro-Hungarian Empire no one with self-respect wanted to appear patriotic, and in everything Monk writes about Wittgenstein's early life one can also see something of the world in which Freud was then living as well. Pre-World War I Vienna, which rightly thought of itself as poised on the precipice of extinction, was at the same time a great showplace for many of the best elements of Western culture. In music and art, not to mention philosophy and psychology, Vienna was an outstanding representative of the achievements of the West. The most creative of Vienna's writers and artists all knew one another, and the story becomes the more staggering as one realizes that the spiritual birthplace of Nazism was also that of Zionism.

Wittgenstein's own family seems to have been both talented and torn by self-divisions; three of his brothers committed suicide, and one of his sisters was an early advocate of Freud's views and evidently personally analyzed by him. Monk persuasively argues that Otto Weininger's *Sex and Character* can be a central means for understanding the conflicts with which Wittgenstein found himself confronted. Weininger's book was a special source of inspiration to Wittgenstein, and many of its views are reflected in his own later philosophical writings.

Once Wittgenstein had been advised to go to Cambridge for the sake of studying with Bertrand Russell, we start to understand something of how formidable, if not terrifying, Wittgenstein could be to encounter. Although the friendship between the two men lasted only a few years, it is impressive how Wittgenstein's demanding character was temporarily matched by Russell's ability to put up with his protégé. Wittgenstein appeared as painfully tortured as anyone in the history of philosophy; although he was never committed to an asylum by civil authorities (as Althusser would be) for having violated basic legal commandments, he possessed a temperament that required his acquaintances to devote the most trying sort of attentiveness to his wild mood swings and argumentative nature. His colleagues and friends ascribed this all-or-nothing attitude to a set of nervous sensibilities that was both his greatest potential source of strength as well as his Achilles' heel. Wittgenstein had a capacity to transform even the most abstract-seeming lines of thought into concrete life-and-death struggles, which makes him as compelling to read about as it must have made it difficult to deal with him in person.

Throughout Wittgenstein's adult life he would be passionately concerned with how a moral and decent person ought to live, and he repeatedly felt forced to retreat from human contact in order to achieve his own personal equilibrium. Although many of the later students of Wittgenstein's work did not recognize this side of him, Monk shows how at every stage of Wittgenstein's career he was obsessed with essentially religious questions of belief. If ever there was a God-ridden man, it was this one; unable either to believe or disbelieve, Monk's version of Wittgenstein comes as close to being a character out of a Dostoevsky novel as anyone else in the history of Western thought.

Right from the outset of Monk's book one is reminded of Jean-Jacques Rousseau. According to Monk, the subject of Wittgenstein's earliest recorded philosophical reflections repeats a central theme from Rousseau's *Confessions*: "Why should one tell the truth if it's to one's advantage to tell a lie?" Rousseau put the issue of truth-telling slightly differently, as he agonized over his first falsehood; but the quest for spiritual purification in Wittgenstein is reminiscent of Rousseau, as is Wittgenstein's recurrent conviction that he was surrounded by people who hated him. It seems remarkable, given Wittgenstein's sensitivities, that he was able to fight as a member of the Austrian army during World War I, and later served on Britain's Home Front in World War II. In whatever Wittgenstein did, he always remained a tormented thinker, agonizing over conscience as the voice of God and self-critically examining his soul for the sake of discovering whether he had been able to overcome his "lack of decency." It should not be surprising to discover that, during the frustrating search for a publisher for his first book, he was in a "suicidal state during the autumn of 1919."

According to Monk, Wittgenstein always lived "a devoutly religious life," surely in contrast to the serene way Freud claimed to be able to take morality for granted, on the premise that he could securely count on his own decent impulses. But despite all the differences in temperament and philosophical outlook, there are some striking similarities between Wittgenstein and Freud as well. Freud, although he succeeded in living a conventional middle-class existence surrounded by a large family, was afflicted by the fear that professional rivals might succeed in stealing his ideas, a tormenting anxiety Wittgenstein knew well. And both thinkers, by somewhat different means, managed to collect their own fervid bands of devoted disciples.

When Wittgenstein returned to Cambridge in 1929, John Maynard Keynes wrote to his beloved wife Lydia Lopokova, "Well, God has arrived. I met him on the 5:15 train." Like Freud, Wittgenstein looked on himself as someone of extraordinary stature. One of Wittgenstein's sisters wrote about him: "it is not easy having a saint for a brother." Wittgenstein had renounced his family fortune and was full of an intense kind of earnestness; he thought it better to be good than clever, and found that the best aspect of mysticism was its power to make him stop thinking.

Inevitably one wonders about the possibility of there having been more direct links between Wittgenstein and Freud. One of Wittgenstein's younger friends, the brilliant logician Frank Ramsey, went to Vienna to be analyzed but suffered from an untimely death in 1930 at only twenty-six years of age. Wittgenstein once considered studying psychiatry himself and was particularly interested in psychoanalysis, going so far as to describe himself as "a disciple of Freud," and he seems to have been extraordinarily prescient about

Freud's central achievement. "It's all excellent similes," he proclaimed of Freud's work in a lecture; and Wittgenstein saw his own contribution to philosophy along identical lines: "What I invent are new *similes*."

Monk's wonderful biography of Wittgenstein can be linked to the equally absorbing Althusser autobiography by virtue of the centrality of Freud, although psychoanalysis in France means something altogether different from how Wittgenstein understood it. As a cultured Viennese, Wittgenstein saw Freud within the ambience of the dark days of the old Austrian Empire; when Wittgenstein talks about Freud, I have the firm conviction that he knows whereof he speaks. But with Althusser one is dealing with the rarefied air of the Parisian intelligentsia; although a committed Marxist theoretician, he takes Freud almost woodenly for granted. Althusser's account of his own tragic life is almost impossible to put down, and the root of much of this tragedy may be that although he was in analysis for decades he did not seem to realize, even up to the time of his death in 1990, that he might have been medically mistreated. (Friends of his signed an unpublished letter to *Le Monde* protesting the conduct of Althusser's analyst.) At a time when psychoanalytic treatment was reduced to the psychiatric margins in North American medicine, Althusser remained incredibly naïve about the efficacy of Freud's method; Althusser thought psychoanalysis "could cure neuroses and even psychoses," which was at odds with Freud's own skepticism.

In 1980, while massaging his wife's neck, Althusser discovered that he had somehow strangled her to death. He was under the influence of a variety of drugs at the time, but he never seems to have realized the damage they might have done to his reasoning or memory. Although Althusser treats psychiatrists as a new priesthood, "bound to silence," as a man of the left it does not dawn on this otherwise well-educated Parisian to question any of the key postulates to the Freudian framework he chooses to take as an ideological given. He does take note of some of his own limitations: "Alas, I am no Rousseau." (I am reminded of a subtle letter Freud wrote to the mother of a patient he had diagnosed as suffering from schizophrenia; Freud tried to reassure the woman that her son was merely of the type of Jean-Jacques Rousseau.) Althusser's memoir is intended as a concrete lesson in his self-torture, but he appears to me appallingly uncritical of Freudian terminology and beliefs.

So we find Althusser writing about "screen memories" from his childhood, as if no one, such as Carl Jung, had exposed the way all such early recollections necessarily serve defensive functions of self-deception. While Monk's book makes a leisurely read, as one slowly absorbs the extensiveness of Wittgenstein's self-lacerations, Althusser's memoirs have all the hallucinatory force of a vivid nightmare. Reading Althusser is rather like seeing *Macbeth*; the horror is quick moving and unique. When one puts down *The Future Lasts Forever* it almost seems as if nothing in it could ever have happened.

But what I find most incredible is the way in which Althusser—like all too many Parisians even today—takes such a formulistic, deadpan version of psychoanalysis, exactly the outlook that Wittgenstein was able to see through. Compared to Althusser, Woody Allen has been a great skeptic. Even with the death of his wife long past, Althusser tells us with a straight face that what he knows about his mother's love he understands thanks to "the light of my analysis."

Wittgenstein never went for analytic treatment, and ended up with an admirable degree of detachment toward Freud. But Althusser was so enamored of Freud's abstractions that he lost his critical faculties – again, this is a weakness shared by many French philosophers to this day. Even after the deadly catastrophe of 1980 he does not seem to realize that he may have had a right to blame the way he had been treated by his analyst.

Instead Althusser presents us with an almost stereotypical account of how, after his terrible crime, he was confined to an insane asylum, thereby losing all his normal legal rights; we are told of "the ill-effects of confinement," and that "Foucault himself" came to see him twice. Although the tale Althusser tells is wholly riveting, still it is hard to believe that anybody so brilliant could remain utterly childlike about psychoanalysis and psychiatry. Yet Althusser remained convinced that just as his work had succeeded in getting back to Marx, so had his understanding of psychoanalysis been a part of Lacan's return to Freud. Nonetheless Althusser admitted,

> As a matter of curiosity I was never able to penetrate a single text by Freud or his commentators (which is doubtless highly significant, though the significance escapes me and perhaps always will), despite all my psychoanalytic samples and personal experience (as analysand)! He remained a closed book to me.

Althusser reassured himself that there was nothing to worry about, on the grounds that "What matters in analysis is not the theory but the *practice* (a fundamentally materialist Marxist principle)." It is hard to imagine a mind more doctrinaire, and one can only hope that this is not typical of philosophers. Raymond Aron, we are told, once accused Althusser of "an imaginary version of Marxism," which I think applies also to his Freudianism; yet one suspects that Althusser was hardly alone in his ideological commitments.

Althusser may take his version of Freud for granted, but he tells us of his self-doubt about having remained in the Communist Party. Supposedly "the stupidest mistake" of Althusser's life came when he failed to accept the invitation to an interview with Mao. Althusser sounds proud of his tolerance for Trotsky, despite Trotsky's "curious practice of never being on the spot at key moments in Soviet history." If this reasoning makes any sense to others, it does not to me. Nor can I understand how Althusser can inform us how "an analyst friend of long-standing" explained, to Althusser's "great surprise," that strangling his wife was a manifestation of his unconscious desire to kill his analyst. One would have thought any such dime-store interpretations beneath the level of French intellectuals.

It looks like the more brilliant the French philosopher, the less contact with common-sense psychoanalytic reality. Wittgenstein's wry skepticism about Freud ("hold onto your brains!") seems to me preferable to Althusser's dogmatism. While Trotsky is reproached for "never being on the spot," Althusser does not see fit to condemn Stalin for having his exiled and perse-cuted rival murdered in Mexico City. And Althusser swallows the argument that his wife made no effort to defend herself. He tells us how, after all sorts of powerful drugs and shock treatments had been administered to him, "one day, to cap it all, she simply asked me to kill her myself...." That suggestion, "unthinkable and unbearably awful," made him "tremble convulsively for a long time. It still makes me shudder."

I find it frightening that ideas are capable of being so addictive. The Viennese Karl Kraus's most memorable aphorism may have been that "psy-choanalysis is that mental illness of which it believes itself to be the cure." Had Kraus leveled his irony at anyone but Freud, I would have expected the creator of psychoanalysis to share his sense of the absurdity of the situation. The philosophies of both Wittgenstein and Althusser show how impossible it would be now to think about how we think without the categories Freud gave us. At the same time, I suspect philosophers will continue to try to come to terms with the intellectual revolution Freud initiated. And even the grossest misuse of psychoanalysis need not imply that the answers all lie in some biochemical cure-all. Wittgenstein and Althusser may have been exposed to more than their fair share of suffering, but we must remember that philoso-phers always have been apt to be sensitive enough that they react immoder-ately to the most central moral dilemmas of their times. In the end, Freud may have succeeded in fundamentally transforming our conception of human nature, which he knew was a bigger objective than any near-term therapeutic achievement.

Therefore I think that when one looks back over the intellectual history of the twentieth century, there can be little doubt that Freud stands out as the most prominent single psychologist. The stature of the founder of psycho-analysis partly comes from his extraordinary abilities in founding a school that carried on his work well after his death. But a central part of Freud's power came also from his literary talents; he was such a great writer that people started saving his letters even while he was a young man, and when all his correspondences finally appear in print they will over-shadow in size the works that Freud actually published.

Acknowledging Freud's pre-eminence does not mean that it is necessary to ignore where he went wrong, and often badly so. He proposed sweeping theories and also had concrete practical recommendations; a central source of

Freud's commanding presence has been the extent to which his concepts not only formed a consistent body of ideas, but led directly to clinical consequences. In practice we now know that Freud could set aside his theories, and violate some of his most famous therapeutic principles. For example, he was in reality by no means as uninvolved in the lives of his patients as he usually liked to pretend. Freud captured his personal adherents by a variety of means, and these disciples, beneficiaries of Freud's flexibility, often disguised from the outside world his idiosyncratic actual practices. The impact of psychoanalysis became so great because Freud had constructed a system of thinking that was integrated enough to be a self-sustaining inspiration, as we saw with the example of Althusser.

Freud's success in the history of ideas has been such that it can take a special effort to recall that right from the outset of his work he had critics of his who respectfully disputed his central contentions. These pioneering skeptics have rarely been given an adequate hearing. Sometimes those who rejected psychoanalysis had no personal familiarity with it, but opposed Freud on a variety of theoretical grounds. Although Freud had great success with organizing a personal following, he also ran into pupils who disagreed enough with him that they were deemed "deviators" who had to be expelled from the psychoanalytic "movement." All these ideological squabbles were in themselves a tip-off to many that in spite of Freud's position within medicine he had in fact created a secular religion. Psychoanalysis became a "cause" that demanded intense loyalty as well as the scapegoating of occasional "dissenters."

Recently in the English-speaking world, the pendulum has swung so far that seemingly unremitting Freud-bashing has achieved novel heights, and it has become fashionable to think of psychoanalysis solely as involving either unprovable hypotheses or else notions that have long since been falsified. Within medicine, Freud's reputation is about as low now as it has ever been; in a few countries analysts are once again, as at the beginning of the twentieth century, outsiders at odds with the conventional status quo of the professional universe.

As a philosopher, however, Freud's reputation is more substantial than ever, so the confrontation between Martin Buber and Freudian thinking becomes a special and largely unknown aspect of the history of ideas. Both Freud and Buber were Austrians and Jews; it would be impossible to understand either of them apart from their cultural and religious backgrounds. Out of the remarkably cosmopolitan maelstrom of Old World civilization they went in startlingly opposite directions. Although Buber never undertook the full-scale reconsideration of Freud that he is reported to have contemplated, there is plenty of evidence about the divergent ways of their respective thinking and how they bear on one another.[3] We know that in the spring of 1908 Buber had visited Freud and asked, unsuccessfully, that he write a book for a series Buber was editing.[4] At a time shortly thereafter, when Buber thought of writing a critical book about psychoanalysis, he allowed himself to be dissuaded by Lou Andreas-Salomé, Nietzsche's old friend who came to Freud's circle before World War I; apparently Lou argued that psychoanalysis was still a young doctrine in need of getting established, and this seems to have convinced Buber.[5]

Although intellectual historians today are unlikely to challenge Freud's stature, his specific therapeutic recommendations are not apt to be highly recommended now. Even a disciple like Lou Andreas-Salomé took a different tack from Freud himself, and he allowed her a great deal of latitude if only because of her special talents as well as the Central European historical tradition she had come to represent. Despite all the controversies associated with Freud, Buber ranks as one of the most prescient skeptics who expressed the enduring suspicion that Freud's real intentions went far beyond modest-sounding psychology itself.

At times Freud claimed to be merely a ploddingly neutral scientific investigator. Although Buber rarely specifically took Freud on, Freud's old "crown prince" Jung, who became a psychoanalytic "renegade," replied to Buber's criticisms of what Jung had called his own "analytical psychology." Jung, despite all his other differences with Freud, alleged like Freud that he was just a dispassionate scientific investigator, and Jung protested that Buber was ignoring Jung's so-called findings. Despite all the deep cleavages between Freud and Jung, they continued to have much in common: they took a similar outlook on the methodology of science, and neither Freud nor Jung was readily able to acknowledge the extent to which their respective psychologies were enmeshed in implicit worldviews.

It may seem ironic that Buber should have tangled with Jung, and not Freud, in that Freud had been the one to have been especially savage about religious belief. Part of the falling out between Freud and Jung came over the question of religion, and how to approach it psychologically. Jung, a pastor's son, was from Freud's point of view far too tolerant of what could be learned from comparative religious beliefs, and Christianity itself seemed to Freud a great rival. Buber was remarkably open to Christian teachings, but he suspected something in Jung's reasoning that was at odds with the promotion of genuine faith. Jung and Buber argued partly because they were on something of the same wavelength, whereas Freud steered as clear of Buber as Buber did Freud. The outlooks that Freud and Buber represented were so at odds with one another that they could not share enough common ground to make a genuine dispute feasible.

Freud's prophetic pronouncements, against religion for example, prove that he had not succeeded in detaching psychology from philosophy. By now it should be clear that everything he wrote has to be understood in the light of certain central values and beliefs that Freud was trying to promote. Buber intuitively knew that Freud was a moral theorist, and one with whom Buber felt he had too little in common to make possible a genuine dialogue.

Oddly enough, it is the most abstract side to Freud's thought, linking him to Nietzsche and all other previous writers who have sought to inquire about how the good life ought to be lived, that has helped keep his work alive and relevant. For despite what has happened within American medicine, where psychoanalysis now plays a minor role, psychoanalysis is more central today throughout European and Latin American circles than at any previous time. Freud's theories, and those of his followers, have become part of university higher education, where the subject of psychoanalysis is being studied as part of normal academic life and not by people who only want to go on to be therapists themselves.

Although Freud might have writhed at his current preeminence as a philosopher, he also would have especially disdained Buber's sort of critique. Freud might not have been surprised at the quarrel between Buber and Jung, even though to Freud they both appeared to be too close to mysticism. Jung was at least ready to acknowledge his own genuine links to philosophizing, and in particular to theology, while Freud was trying to withdraw with quiet contempt from precisely those issues that would turn out in the long run to have been paradoxically responsible for ensuring the contemporary vitality of psychoanalysis's contribution.

It will be necessary to tease out from the individual slivers offered by a great system builder like Buber the exact relevance now for what he had to say, not just about the practice of psychotherapy but about the moral direction in which he was proposing that humanity move. Freud could have agreed, for instance, with the conceptual contrast Buber drew between guilt and guilt "feelings." Freud steered clear of any romantic-sounding association with theories of self-enhancement, unlike Jung's own interest in what he called "individuation." Freud himself took a rather dim view of such theories of self-development and stood on the side of therapy that entailed a stoical compromise between known evils.

As hard-working a clinical practitioner as Freud was, he did not pitch his teachings on his success as a therapeutic helper. Nor did he think of himself as in any way on the same moral level as those he treated. Psychoanalytic patients could learn to become superior, and Freud thought that out of his treatment setting a new set of moral standards might arise; but inequality and hierarchy were both taken for granted by Freud as he proceeded to work with neurotic clients.

Buber's whole orientation, implying that the therapist has as much to learn as the patient, would have made no sense at all to Freud. Psychoanalysis was not designed to be a kind of level playing field. But then the scope of Buber's interests sought out the existential problems of people far more disturbed than the garden-variety neurotics Freud wanted to specialize in. Buber, paradoxically, probably had more formal psychiatric experience, as a young student just starting out in his studies, than had Freud, who was trained as a neurologist and had little familiarity with psychiatry.

Buber came to play a role in the development of so-called third force psychology, and Buber's contact with Carl Rogers was an aspect of Buber's significance for psychotherapeutic matters. In an exchange between Buber and Rogers one can see how far they both were from the world of Freud, which presumes an omniscient analyst dealing with curiously foolish neurotics. Freud's aloofness might have been self-deceptive, but he never advocated anything like the mutual give-and-take that Buber and Rogers had in mind. Even Jung, unknown to Buber, was critical of the power implications built into the orthodox Freudian analytic situation.

Buber did become aware of some of the humanistic strands within psycho-analysis, and in particular the proposals of Harry Stack Sullivan, who had worked with psychotics and made self-esteem a central part of what the thera-pist must concentrate on maintaining. Others within psychotherapy chal-lenged the kinds of goals Freud had in mind. Freud claimed he had limited objectives, centering on enabling the patient to make autonomous choices. Ideals like authenticity and health were not ones with which Freud felt com-fortable, yet since his death most analysts have more or less conceded the necessity of coming to terms with areas Freud had wanted to bypass with silence.

Although the idealism behind a contrast between a "true" as opposed to a "false" self would have seemed alien to Freud, it has not prevented his school from being prominently concerned with exactly that distinction. The whole notion of selfhood became one of prime importance within modern psycho-therapy. As one reads essays by Buber, and comes across a concept like that of "confirmation," it is hard not to think that he succeeded in having more of an impact on the profession of psychotherapy than most have been willing to acknowledge. Key concepts like anxiety, transference, and the unconscious itself need to be reexamined in the light of Buber's teachings. Much has recently been written about the necessary reciprocity in the relationship be-tween therapist and patient, although once again Freud himself never made any such concession from the point of view of orthodox theorizing. But his former apostle Otto Rank would come to use Buber-like language: in 1928, Rank maintained that "in contrast to I-psychology…one might designate ethics as Thou-psychology."[6] R. D. Laing also acknowledged Buber.[7]

Within Freud's thinking he missed out on the significance of the social and human context in which people exist. He even frowned on talking about national characteristics, as if cultural differences were superficial and not of true scientific interest. Freud reacted to his own Jewish background by an insistent yearning to universalize each of his insights, and he struggled to get beyond the confines of his own social beginnings. Acquiring Jung as a stu-dent had meant for Freud a breakthrough into the world of the Gentiles, and, in allying with a Christian, Freud could imagine that he was now securely able to challenge Christian teachings. Jung shared some of Freud's discontent with inherited religious doctrine, and although in the end religion was one of the fatal sources of their falling out, it had at the outset helped to bring them together.

Buber's mind was in another world from that of early psychoanalysis, and the passage of time has shown how relevant his thinking can be to how we approach the healing professions. Freud liked to think of himself as undermining some of the highest ideals of the West; each time he quotes Goethe's Mephistopheles we should remember with whom he took pride in allying himself. Humanitarianism, however, need not be the enemy of modern psychotherapy, and because of Buber's attempts to keep the Judeo-Christian tradition alive his thoughts on psychology remain keenly pertinent.

Freud never made any public reference to Buber's writings, but he certainly knew what kind of standing he had attained. (Both failed to win Nobel prizes.) It turns out that in his consulting room Freud could compare himself with a Hasidic rabbi, and recount Hasidic tales in the course of clinical practice.[8] Freud once specifically mentioned Buber in a letter concerned with the possible reactions to the appearance of Freud's *Moses and Monotheism*. In the last year of his life while in exile in England, he wrote to a loyal disciple who lived in Palestine: "Martin Buber's pious phrases won't do much harm to *The Interpretation of Dreams*. The Moses is more vulnerable, and I am prepared for an onslaught by the Jews on it."[9] The whole interrelation between Buber, Jung, Freud, and modern psychology in general, besides the issues posed by Wittgenstein and Althusser, make a fascinating addition to our understanding of social and political thought.

Notes

1. Ray Monk, *Ludwig Wittgenstein: The Duty of Genius* (London: Jonathan Cape, 1990).
2. Louis Althusser, *The Future Lasts Forever* (New York: The New Press, 1993).
3. *Martin Buber on Psychology and Psychotherapy: Essays, Letters, and Dialogue*, ed. Judith Buber Agassi (Syracuse, NY: Syracuse University Press, 1999).
4. Ernst Falzeder and Eva Brabant, with the collaboration of Patrizia Giampieri-Deutsch, eds., *The Correspondence of Sigmund Freud and Sandor Ferenczi*, Vol. 2 (Cambridge, MA: Harvard University Press, 1996), p. 179.
5. Maurice Friedman, *Martin Buber's Life and Work: The Early Years, 1878-1923* (Detroit, MI: Wayne State University Press, 1988), p. 172.
6. Otto Rank, *A Psychology of Difference: The American Lectures*, ed. Robert Kramer (Princeton, NJ: Princeton University Press, 1996), p. 231.
7. Bob Mullan, *Mad To Be Normal: Conversations with R. D. Laing* (London, Free Association Books, 1995), pp. 112, 115, 136.
8. Paul Roazen, *Freud and His Followers* (New York: Alfred A. Knopf, 1975; New York: Da Capo, 1992), p. 408.
9. Quoted in Yosef H. Yerushalmi, *Freud's Moses* (New Haven, CT: Yale University Press, 1991), p. 115.

7

Theorists

Although there is a risk that I will sound like an old codger, it does seem to me that the subject of political theory has fallen on hard times. I was therefore greatly heartened to read Roger Masters's lively book on a curious (and doomed) project in Renaissance Italy. Forty or fifty years ago political philosophy was distinctly the most prestigious part of political science, the main area with established standards of scholarly excellence: the rest of the field seemed tainted by being associated with current events, and the subject of international relations was considered the bottom-of-the-barrel. Every academic department then prided itself on the prestige of its political theorists, and no halfway decent university could be without at least one or two such practitioners. I can even remember when the Harvard Government Department felt remiss in never having replaced the great Charles McIlwain with a suitable medievalist.

Today, alas, political science has come in line with the proposal to become, short-sightedly, more relevant. Departments seem swept up with competing in housing former politicians, or practicing journalists; they provide step-ups on the ladder of power to aspiring political leaders; and they engage also in dry-as-dust model building about supposed rational political behavior. Policy issues take precedence in America over intellectual history, although the traditional pursuit of political philosophy is still undertaken in Britain and on the continent. Here, however, the study of constitutional law has been by and large handed over to law schools, while it was once a required aspect of the field for undergraduate political science majors. The old idea of ivory tower scholars pursuing the history of ideas has pretty much disappeared. World War II drew many academics into temporary government service to fight the Axis powers, but the Vietnam War, when soft State Department money for instance was made available to fund junior academic appointments, further eroded the autonomy of political science. The example of Henry Kissinger, and other advisers to governmental policymaking, has helped transform the nature of the academic curriculum and the ambitions of young faculty.

To further compound matters, ideological sectarianism has afflicted the ranks of those who pursue the study of political theory. A variety of different sects have had turf-battles over the shrinking pie that is allowed to political theory. Conservatives like the followers of Leo Strauss have continued to promote their teachings, methodological as well as substantive; while the liberal contingent has been apt to be attracted by what departments of philosophy happen to be interested in, which means that the history of thought itself, not to mention the social bases to political philosophizing, have taken a back seat. Marxists from different schools of thought have pursued their special agendas, and social radicals have carved out their own take on political thought. The upshot has been that while students in college are as interested in political theory as ever, departments seem able to get away with sponsoring relatively fewer theorists. The center of the discipline has shifted away from history to concerns that are at least apparently more practical.

It is in this context that Roger Masters's recent *Fortune is a River: Leonardo da Vinci and Niccolo Machiavelli's Magnificent Dream to Change the Course of Florentine History*[1] comes as a distinct and welcome surprise. A few of Masters's early comments touch on the need for secrecy in the Renaissance; heresy was still a dangerous crime, and Machiavelli was once arrested and tortured for allegedly having conspired to plot against the Medici in Florence. The importance of secret intentions of political theorists has long been a contention on the part of Strauss and his disciples, so I suppose Masters belongs to that camp. Unfortunately, the Straussians have been so high-handed about the alleged intellectual inferiority of biographical inquiry that no biography of Strauss has yet been published, and we are the poorer for it. Accounts of Strauss's school, with its different wings, have been mainly written by Strauss's opponents, concerned that he has largely encouraged neo-conservatives.[2]

While all the attractions of Strauss's teachings have largely escaped me, I must say that Masters's new book has an appeal that is far from being scholastic. *Fortune is a River* got adopted by the Book of the Month Club, the History Book Club, as well as the Quality Paperback Book Club. So it is not speculative to think that this book had a wide readership, even though that would be at odds with the generalizations I have made about the state of political theory today. The thrust of the book is not any hothouse enterprise, although as we shall see some of its central contentions seem questionable. It has already occurred to me that the students of Leo Strauss, whatever I may have thought of their politics, have done more to keep political philosophy alive than I would ever have anticipated, and if Masters can be correctly associated with Strauss it would add to the luster of his legacy.

The thesis of *Fortune is a River* concerns a new link that Masters has hypothesized between Machiavelli and Leonardo da Vinci. The traditional Machiavelli literature ignores his possible relationship with Leonardo, although it would seem that art historians have known at least a bit about the political thinker's association with the artist. In any event, despite the absence of documentation that will satisfy everyone, Masters explores an effort on the part of the Florentines in the early sixteenth century to divert the Arno River in such a way that not only would Florence become a seaport, but the city of Pisa would have been deprived of its water supply. Even today Florentine children are raised to believe that the Pisans are a good deal less than human, almost five centuries after the rivalry between the cities that was the concern of Machiavelli as a high civil servant of the government of Florence. Italian unification is relatively recent, and the ancient conflicts between cities and regions are still very much a fact of contemporary political life. But I take it that today's Florentine enmity toward Pisa reflects in a pale way the immensity of what the animosity was at the beginning of the sixteenth century.

Masters calls the tie between Machiavelli and Leonardo "a mysterious friendship," when in fact there is no reason to think that they were in reality friends. Masters argues that they "probably first met" during 1502, when their paths crossed at Cesare Borgia's court. Later that same year they were both in Florence working on the project to divert the Arno, which ultimately proved a failure. Ten years earlier, Leonardo had hoped to make the Arno navigable, which would have meant that Florence would become a seaport and the Arno valley irrigated. Machiavelli's interests were in Florentine military and foreign policy, and Leonardo's proposal would have been seen as an instrument in trying to win the war against Pisa that had been a source of intense frustration for a decade.

Aside from the Arno project, Leonardo did in 1503 also get a commission from Florence to paint a huge fresco. One of Machiavelli's assistants described the battle scene to be painted, and it has been found in Leonardo's *Notebooks*. The same assistant of Machiavelli helped Leonardo in a Florentine legal claim over an inheritance.

Unfortunately for what Masters calls the "magnificent dream to change the course of Florentine history" the ditches to divert the Arno collapsed due both to engineering incompetence and genuine misfortune. The project was finally abandoned, although there was unpleasantness about how much money had been wasted. Even the fresco Leonardo did for Florence proved a failure, since his experimental paint did not prove reliable, and the drawing was given up. Masters thinks that these "setbacks" can "probably" explain why neither Leonardo or Machiavelli wrote of their work together. Since their judgment and competence were called into question by the "disaster" of the collaboration Masters has reconstructed, he thinks it can account for why neither of them wanted to call attention to that which did not pan out.

Masters's evidence for how Leonardo and Machiavelli worked together is at best fragmentary, but I think the specifics of his thesis are less important than the general cultural impact of *Fortune is a River*. For the book can become a vehicle for learning about the parallel careers of Leonardo and Machiavelli, however fragile the basis in historical fact for their collaboration in 1503-06. Those familiar with Machiavelli's career are unlikely to be as at home with Leonardo's life story, and art historians cannot be expected to be knowledgeable about the ins-and-outs of Machiavelli's political fortunes. Although Leonardo, perhaps as important to science and technology as art, had a worldly career that went on to flourish, that of Machiavelli did not; but the writings that ensured Machiavelli's enduring reputation were made possible by the enforced leisure he had once he was rusticated from the power he had earlier exercised.

Fortune is a River successfully revives the world of the Renaissance; one of the immortal images of Machiavelli's *The Prince* turns on how fortune can be a river, either rampaging or possibly tamed. Reports of Columbus's first voyage had been published in Florence by 1493, but it took almost a decade for it to be established that he had found a new continent instead of the mainland of Asia he supposed. For merchants the implications were that the earth's being so much larger enhanced the possibilities of commerce. And the attractions of Florence becoming a seaport were also increased. Interestingly, Masters points out that the background to Leonardo's Mona Lisa, painted during the period of the Arno project, contains not only a river but a fort outside Pisa.

So in spite of what I think of as the poor state of contemporary political theory, so often marked mainly by writers addressing themselves for the benefit of each other, Masters has revived the older tradition of political philosophers who took as their responsibility to help educate the general public. I am thinking, for example, of how Carl Becker once wrote about the Declaration of Independence, and the Enlightenment; and also how Harold Laski in England addressed himself to pressing difficulties using the most abstract categories. Dangers can be inherent in public intellectuals who mix scholarship and daily life, and the names of Becker or Laski are apt to evoke groans from fashionably up-to-date academics. I worry that Masters himself may go too far in treating Leonardo and Machiavelli as our contemporaries, thereby making anachronistic assumptions about the past and failing in the historian's central task of showing us a world unlike our own. In practice, though, *Fortune is a River* illustrates a universe distinctive to its time. Masters has implicitly picked up the old ambition of making political theory central to our understanding of politics. The pursuit of intellectual history, untangling the intricacies of what might or might not have gone on between Machiavelli and Leonardo, may seem in one sense divorced from everyday life. But I share the faith that an informed citizenry is a critical basis for democracy enduring, and that therefore nothing is more ultimately relevant than having a good general education.

*   *   *

Ever since Jean-Jacques Rousseau's first essay in 1750, "A Discourse on the Arts and Sciences," which denounced the corruption of modern civilization, he has been justly considered a giant in Western culture. It did not take long, however, before he became notorious.

Rousseau's rationalist contemporaries in the French Enlightenment were distraught over the direction his ideas had taken. Denis Diderot, once Rousseau's friend, wrote on the evening of their last meeting: "He makes me uneasy, and I feel as if a damned soul stood beside me....I never want to see that man again; he could make me believe in devils and hell." When, in 1776, two years before Rousseau actually died, a rumor circulated about his death, Voltaire bitingly wrote, "Jean-Jacques really did the right thing by dying." And once Rousseau was quoted by the French revolutionaries on behalf of their cause, his reputation assumed an altogether more dangerous and sinister connotation.

Rousseau's work has given rise to a dual tradition of both defenders and detractors. On the one hand he has been portrayed as the true pioneer of modern individualism, a man who championed the unfettered liberty of feeling and the rights of the human heart. And in terms of the distinctly social and political implications of his writings, some consider him a great democrat, one who wanted the maximum degree of public participation in decisionmaking.

Conversely, Rousseau's detractors charge that he so loosely conceived of the emancipation of mankind that he completely abandoned every ethical obligation and all precepts of duty. In addition, since the rise of totalitarianism in the twentieth century, Rousseau has been blamed for having recklessly proposed the sacrificing of the individual to the group, allowing neither freedom of action nor liberty of conscience.

Such a dichotomy of opinions has prompted vast writings about Rousseau. Still, Starobinski's *Jean-Jacques Rousseau: Transparency and Obstruction,*[3] which first appeared in France in 1957 (and was later enlarged in a 1971 edition), was only translated into English in 1988, though it has long been acknowledged as a critical masterpiece. More than a biography, the book is enriched by Starobinski's meticulous attention to Rousseau's ideas as well as his life. Starobinski succeeded in writing one of the truly great books on modern political theory.

Starobinski's special contribution to current studies of Rousseau was in highlighting the extent to which Rousseau was "haunted by the idea that human communication is impossible," and how this often left him in temporal reverie. Such fear began at an early age when Rousseau experienced the trauma of false accusation. He had been mistakenly accused of lying about a trivial misdeed, a broken comb. The injustice of this incident meant for Rousseau that paradise, which for him was always defined by the possibility of transparent communication between people, was lost. Subsequently,

Rousseau became obsessed with, and appalled at, how people could fail to connect and often would hide from one another.

The crux of Rousseau's challenge, according to Starobinski, is that we live in an opaque hell. Rousseau's belief that people must regain the transparency they had lost appealed to many of his contemporaries. Rousseau was a revolutionary in the defense of the ideal of an eternal human nature forced to endure in the stultifying air of established culture. He attempted to make his life an example of unsullied innocence by distancing himself from his former friends, whose philosophies he considered parasitic on a society in disintegration.

Rousseau chose to exile himself from a universe he viewed as alienated, a world he sought to make ashamed of itself. He reasoned that if transparency could be achieved by the general will, then society should be deferred to, even at the expense of individual happiness. But, if transparency could only be embodied in solitary life, then withdrawal from the corruptions of communal existence was the only answer.

Rousseau's theoretical position made him unpopular with his fellow philosophers. Still, even without their disapproval, he had harbored ideas about being slandered and persecuted. Starobinski is gentle when he invokes diagnostic categories, but he cannot avoid referring to Rousseau's paranoid delusions. The paranoia was intrinsic to Rousseau's whole philosophic enterprise. Combating all obstacles to the utmost expression of human sincerity, he sought to be an educator of humanity who could awaken the dormant possibilities of goodness. He felt his adversaries could only imagine impersonal forces and were merely "mechanical objects" moved by "blind necessity."

In Rousseau, Starobinski finds a man in quest of personal salvation. And yet many of the eighteenth century's major thinkers were preoccupied with secularizing basically religious concepts. In his autobiographical introspection, Rousseau followed the model of St. Augustine. But the picture he presented of himself was so startlingly disharmonious that Starobinski rightly observes "it took Freud to 'think' Rousseau's feelings." Psychoanalysis should be able to understand Rousseau's fondness for tolerating all the tortured extremities of his convictions.

That his ideas would lead to misunderstandings should have been obvious to Rousseau. He loved to formulate paradoxes. However, for those interested in the history of conceptions of liberty, Rousseau will be remembered as someone who fervently insisted that inner turmoil interferes with self-fulfillment. Acutely conscious of how obstructive our own "lower selves" can be, he argued, "I have never believed that man's freedom consists in doing what he wants, but rather in never doing what he does not want to do." For some narrow libertarians, Rousseau seems to have been engaging in monstrous double-talk. But for many of us he is heroic for the way he permanently redefined the stature of freedom in a psychologically realistic manner.

This edition of Starobinski's original text is enriched by the inclusion of seven additional essays by him, written between 1962 and 1970, that cover various key themes and problems in understanding Rousseau's thought. And while no single text can settle the debate about the stature of Rousseau's ideas, I can think of no other book about Rousseau that is so convincingly original while being so thoroughly fair-minded.

* * *

As I have already intimated, I think that the current state of the study of political theory is pretty dismal. Yet Michael Walzer recently reported in *Dissent* that "more people are working at political theory in the academic world than ever before." Somehow he thinks that such numbers are evidence that "the field is thriving," and Walzer went on to claim that this is "perhaps because there is so little serious thinking and arguing about politics outside the academy."

As far as I can see the real story is a different one. Scholasticism in the university pursuit of political theory has never been worse than now. If one opens a volume of the *American Political Science Review* from forty-five years ago, there will be articles on political theory that are literate, leisurely, and intellectual spacious, interesting to a general reader; with increased numbers of practitioners has come not progress but, I think, decline. Nobody seriously interested in current political life is likely to benefit from the narrow, sectarian way academics now approach the study of political theory. A series of self-admiring and complacent groups exist within the academy, each of which approaches political theory in its own idiosyncratic way; advancement in university life depends on pleasing a very few rather than appealing to an educated reading audience. There are, of course, broad-minded as well as parochial Marxists, tolerant Straussians as well as embattled ones, serious philosophers as well as logic-choppers, genuine historians as well as pedants; but out of the welter of rival sects, each of which is capable of rewarding its members in worldly academic advancement, has come a field which even drives interested university students away. The vitality of political argument outside the academy persists despite the irrelevance of so much academic ideology peddling.

My impression is that the situation in both England and France is superior to what we have in North America. At any rate, Stanley Ayling's *Edmund Burke*[4] is a fine biography that will interest anyone concerned with intellectual history. An Englishman like Ayling has remained aware, despite the mounting trivia of the worst of our smug academics, that biographies remain absolutely essential to our understanding of past political thought. The London School of Economics' Maurice Cranston was another holdout against the more recent academic fashions; we owe him not only for a wonderful 1957 biography of John Locke, but in 1983 he started publishing a fascinating three-volume biography of Rousseau. Biography does not suit the demands of what William James termed the Ph.D. Octopus, yet biographers are still thriving in literary circles even if political theorists somehow feel entitled to look down their noses at them.

Ayling is not interesting in the academic gamesmanship that mars so much of today's study of political theory. His life of Burke is the first to follow the completion of the publication of Burke's collected correspondence, which appeared between 1958 and 1978 in a ten-volume edition. (Despite what the publisher misleadingly claims on the jacket, Ayling's *Edmund Burke* is not "the first biography of Burke to appear for fifty years.") Ayling's book is relatively short and sparse, a little under 300 pages long; my main complaint is that with a figure as large and fascinating as Burke I would have liked a longer, more sprawling work. It is hard to think how anyone concerned with the English language could fail to be attracted to Burke's greatness as a writer.

The chapters on Burke's childhood and youth are, for my taste, all too brief. As Conor Cruise O'Brien has so persuasively established, Burke's Irish origins play a key part in understanding his later politics; for Burke was a Protestant son of a Catholic mother. (It has even been suggested that his father converted from Catholicism, but only for opportune motives.) Burke's apparently wild defense of the *ancien régime* in France has to be understood in the light of how hard he also tried, having emigrated to London at the age of tweny-one, to protect Catholics in Ireland. (Burke's wife and sister were both Catholic.) Burke was, in Irish terms, a troublemaker who was resolutely opposed to the English status quo that deprived Catholics of rights and liberties. Ireland was after all a conquered country, and therefore Burke had a controlled sympathy for revolution. Even in Burke's role within British politics he was pretty much an outsider; although he is justly famed as a great theorist of conservatism, in his lifetime he appeared eccentric in his thinking and even sometimes unbalanced. If Ayling does not do much, in his examination of Burke's earliest years, to prepare us for this adult radicalism of Burke, at least he does not indulge in any bizarre biographical speculations by dragging in supposed psychoanalytic tenets.

As a young man in London, Burke won the admiration of Samuel Johnson; later, when Boswell's *Life of Johnson* was first completed, Boswell was careful to show it to Burke (among others) in order to win his approval. Burke was also a close friend of Oliver Goldsmith and Sir Joshua Reynolds. In the context of his time, however, Burke and his relatives seemed like Irish adventurers bent on establishing themselves as gentlemen. Burke early on established an alliance with one wing of the Whig party that took its leadership from Lord Rockingham, a wealthy and influential magnate. With the support of his patron, and in behalf of a recognized faction that was highly critical of King

George III, Burke served as a member of the House of Commons for twenty-nine years.

Burke's conciliatory position toward the American colonies at the time of the War of Independence is legendary; it is noteworthy that when Burke took his stand against what he, and the colonists, saw as the innovative intrusions of the British government in American affairs, his own constituents were unhappy with his position since it was at odds with their own temporary self-interest. This occasioned his famous speech defending the autonomy of a representative's deliberations; he repudiated the idea that as an M.P. he was merely an agent for the will of those he represented. His politics were unpopular enough that subsequently he had to find himself another seat. Burke believed in the old idea about the desirability of property qualifications for voters; his confidence in the rationality of the electorate was so limited that by the end of his life he thought that only a small fraction of the total population had a legitimate claim to vote.

Although Burke is now best known for his early opposition to the French Revolution, and his extraordinary prescience about the bloody consequences of uprooting a society through radical change, he himself as an old man was most proud of his sustained critique of Warren Hastings's abuses of power in India. Burke relentlessly pursued the impeachment of Hastings who had been governor general of the East India Company. As much as Burke held that subordination is a social necessity and that leaders must be insulated from the demands of the mass, in practice, Burke sympathized with the oppressed Indians whom he saw as victimized by a system embodied by Hastings. The language of Burke's speeches was so vehement that they provoked what he called "a run" against him. Ayling takes Burke's views on India, as on America, completely seriously, in contrast to those like Tom Paine who have always sneered at the fanciness of Burke's talk camouflaging base self-interest. (Burke's brother had speculated unhappily in India.)

Burke's rhetoric repays the closest professional scrutiny, but in his own day the extremity of his language meant that he was never seriously considered for the highest public offices. Rockingham's death in 1782 was the beginning of the end of Burke's wing of the party, and the Whigs as a whole were to be decimated by internal divisions over the proper reaction to the French Revolution. Amidst the collapse of the political bases of his support Burke accepted his unpopularity with the public and his loneliness in his party.

Burke saw himself as a stalwart defender of the constitutional principles of Britain's Glorious Revolution, the settlement of 1688. Unfortunately he did not feel the need to inquire into the social bases of the French Revolution, or its idealistic aspirations; to Burke it was enough to attribute such an upheaval in France to the consequences of irresponsible scribblers, as he sought to distinguish the French situation from what had happened in late seventeenth-century England.

Contemporary academic students of Burke are too apt to seek a false kind of consistency in him. Although he was in no sense a technical philosopher, Burke expounded some remarkable ideas in unforgettable language. For example, he agreed that the French were "deserving" of "liberty," but he worried (like Rousseau) about "the worst of all slavery, that is the despotism of...blind and brutal passions."

> Of all the loose terms in the world liberty is the most indefinite...it is not solitary, unconnected, individual, selfish liberty....The liberty I mean is *social* freedom. It is that state of things in which liberty is secured by the equality of restraint....This kind of liberty is but another name for justice, ascertained by wise laws, and secured by well constructed institutions.

Burke perceived the French Revolution to be a danger not just to England but to many parts of Europe; his *Reflections* sold 19,000 copies in the first six months and also did well in France. Since other Whigs saw Louis XVI as a French version of the mistrusted George III, Burke regarded himself as now "excommunicated" by his party. While isolated at home, Burke now received European recognition; even George III appreciated Burke's special capacities.

Burke's last years (he died in 1797) were harrowed by grief over the abrupt death of his only, beloved son. Yet Burke's powers as a writer remained undiminished. His *Letter to a Nobel Lord* (1795) was a remarkably eloquent piece of invective. His final phase was marked by physical decline. It is unfortunately not clear from Ayling's fine biography whether Burke knew by then that he was one of the immortals in intellectual history. Nevertheless it seems to me that Ayling has thoroughly succeeded in getting the proper center of gravity for Burke's work, and skillfully woven together the private and public aspects of his story. Professional students of political theory, with any disdain for all thought "outside the academy," ought to note that Ayling, who has also written lives of John Wesley, George III, the Elder Pitt, and Richard Brinsley Sheridan, has held no university appointment.

* * *

Political theory is an area of knowledge in which it is exceptionally hard to be original, since the secondary literature is both vast and sophisticated. Although people who like to engage in logical games find it relatively easy to construct novel-seeming arguments, playfully batting about alternative possibilities, few would be apt to confuse that sort of exercise in mental gymnastics with a genuine contribution to scholarship. When it comes to studying any of the truly great figures in the history of political philosophy, Burke ranks in the company with those authors who are responsible for creating what Matthew Arnold called culture: "the best that has been thought or known in the world." Burke belongs among the greatest figures in the history of social thought, and therefore to come up with a fresh interpretation of him poses a daunting challenge.

In the context of how unusual new directions are in this field, I can report that when in the early 1970s I first read Conor Cruise O'Brien's introduction to the Pelican Classics edition of Burke's *Reflections on the Revolution in France* it seemed like a revelation. I had grown up thinking of Burke as a great conservative, and in my youth he was often approvingly cited by leading anti-communist proponents. Yet here was Conor Cruise O'Brien, well known as a man of the left, bringing to bear all his sympathetic understanding to Burke as a fellow Irishman. O'Brien strikingly reinterpreted Burke's opposition to the French Revolution in terms of Burke's special Irish background. O'Brien saw Burke as obsessed with the fate of Ireland, and the anti-Catholicism of the French revolutionaries seemed to O'Brien a threat to Burke's hope to emancipate his oppressed Irish Catholic compatriots. The British support for the Revolution was, in O'Brien's view of Burke, seen as part of virulent anti-Popery. Whereas once there had been a debate over whether Burke was consistent in having supported the American revolutionaries while opposing those in France, to my mind O'Brien shifted the whole center of gravity in the understanding of Burke. In O'Brien's interpretation Burke as an Irishman had retained a close emotional tie to those who had been conquered there, and he was filled with hatred toward the ascendancy of the Protestants that the Glorious Revolution of 1688 had imposed on the people of his home country.

O'Brien's Burke was a new one. In the course of Burke's having opposed the French Revolution, he had appealed back to the righteousness of the principles of the settlement of 1688, which in O'Brien's view had to be a conflicted basis on which Burke took a stand. But O'Brien was presenting a far more complex Burke than one had ever imagined. Burke grew so frenzied about the French Revolution precisely because he himself harbored seditious aspirations in Ireland. Burke in 1790 was as prophetic about the future behavior of the Jacobins as Winston Churchill was in the late 1930s about the Nazis, and O'Brien searches for the possible motives for Burke's extraordinary insights. According to O'Brien, Burke felt forced to disguise his sympathies for the oppressed Irish Catholics; and Burke explained in correspondence, for example, why he felt that he could not defend publicly an accused Irish papist.

Over the years I had learned that O'Brien was working on a more extensive study of Burke. He published an introduction to a reissue of Matthew Arnold's collection of Burke letters, speeches, and tracts on Ireland. And O'Brien also brought out an article concerned with Burke's endless-seeming attack on

Warren Hastings for his conduct in behalf of the East India Company; Burke saw to it that Hastings was impeached by the House of Commons because of his oppressive behavior toward the Indians, but in the end the House of Lords failed to convict Hastings. O'Brien showed Burke to have been an anti-imperialist, rather in keeping with O'Brien's own 20th century politics. The upshot was a far more interesting Burke than anything received conventional wisdom had prepared one for.

Finally in 1992 we got O'Brien's long awaited *The Great Melody: A Thematic Biography of Edmund Burke.*[5] The title comes from W.B. Yeats's poem "The Seven Sages":

> American colonies, Ireland, France and India
> Harried, and Burke's great melody against it.

O'Brien tells us here that an earlier attempt to produce a traditional biography of Burke came to naught. After a series of frustrated attempts to complete it, that project was abandoned; and O'Brien returned to Burke with the idea of writing a "thematic" biography. And there is in fact something distinctly musical, if not Wagnerian, about O'Brien's long book. For he takes up subjects like Ireland, the American colonies, India, and then France, going over some of the same chronological ground in each section, but building up, sometimes through repetition, a swelling understanding of Burke's deepest if often unspoken commitments. By the time that O'Brien gets to a late chapter, "France, Ireland, India 1791-1797," we feel the inner harmony between Burke's apparently disparate convictions.

The introduction lays a splendid groundwork for what follows in that O'Brien traces how the historiography of eighteenth-century England, led in particular by Sir Lewis Namier, systematically sought to describe Burke as an opportunist and an adventurer, a man without serious convictions. Oddly enough the Namierite attack on Burke had been heralded by Karl Marx's own disdain for Burke. But the work of the Namierite school was not as ideologically easy to spot as that of the Marxists, and Namierites proceeded to disparage Burke largely by innuendo and cutting asides.

After beginning *The Great Melody* with the central features to the Burke literature over the last 200 years, O'Brien starts off with Burke's relationship to Ireland. As we have touched on, O'Brien reminded us that Burke's mother, wife, and sister were all practicing Catholics, but O'Brien begins with examining the evidence that Burke's father may have left the Catholic Church out of convenience. The Irish Penal Laws were in full force, and Catholics could neither vote nor sit in the Irish Parliament; even converts, when married to Catholics, had in principle difficulties in the practice of law, Burke's father's profession. O'Brien sounds right when he refers to "the depths of horror that the Irish Penal Laws inspired in the mature Burke." O'Brien's central thesis in

The Great Melody is that although as a young man Burke moved to England, "Ireland continued to preoccupy Burke—to haunt him, would not be too much to say—throughout his life."

Burke was for almost thirty years a member of the British House of Commons, and O'Brien believes that he not only was constant to the cause of Ireland, but that "at serious cost to his own political career" Burke rendered important political "services to the Irish Catholic people." Although the tale of Burke's relationship to Ireland has to be considered O'Brien's central concern, he also provides fresh insight into Burke's outlook on the American colonists. Burke saw the British position toward the Americans as another example of the abuse of power. I had not realized just how influential Burke was within the Whig party. *The Great Melody* is filled with such copious quotations from Burke that one comes away from it with the conviction that one has been reading him as well as O'Brien. Although I had still naively thought of Burke in the old-fashioned pigeonhole of his being a great conservative thinker, O'Brien demonstrates the extent to which the key to his career was his opposition to political authoritarianism.

From the point of view of an outsider, Irish politics seems an unusually topsy-turvy situation; for example, in connection with the rebellion of the American colonists, support in Ireland for the American Revolution was mainly a Protestant affair. Throughout *The Great Melody* we find Burke in a series of difficult alliances. Burke is forced to dissimulate about his true convictions, and in the period of the American Revolution there was a special gulf between Burke's outward beliefs and his real feelings about Ireland. Independence for Ireland would have meant the ascendancy of an exclusively Protestant Irish Parliament, so Burke had to be on his guard against that possible eventuality. Burke committed himself to supporting American freedom at the same time that he opposed the independence of Ireland. Although I had known of Burke's long years in the British House of Commons, I had not realized how experienced, astute, and energetic a parliamentarian of the opposition he was.

Although Burke never held the highest public office, he exerted enormous influence as a confidential adviser to Lord Rockingham. After the unexpected death of Burke's patron in 1782, Burke's party-political career went into decline. But he increasingly moved into the role of being a prophet over India, France, and Ireland. Burke was rather slow to get going about the wrongdoings of the East India Company, but O'Brien thinks that only contributed to "the concentrated, compulsive venom" of Burke's final attack on Warren Hastings. To O'Brien, Burke's concern for the suffering people of India "clearly has something to do with his concern for his own suffering people: the Catholics of Ireland under the Penal Laws." O'Brien does not hesitate to expand on what he takes to have been Burke's unconscious motivation: "by defending the independence of the East India Company up to

1772, he had betrayed the oppressed people of India, just as his father had betrayed the oppressed people of Ireland, by abjuring their religion."

Although Burke's pursuit of Hastings lasted for so many years that it came to seem a marked eccentricity on his part, when the French Revolution broke out he was so far ahead of events as to appear almost clairvoyant. By the end of 1789 Burke had already thought through how mistaken were the defenders of the French upheaval. To Burke, it was an example of sorcerer's apprentices, infatuated by ideology, who were unleashing forces they little understood. Although for years Burke had been a critic of King George III, now he saw all monarchy, indeed civilization itself, as threatened. And he foresaw that the outcome would be military despotism in France.

Charles James Fox, and most other Whig leaders, defended the French Revolution, so Burke was temporarily left in an isolated position. Years ahead of time Burke warned about the intensification of the revolution, and the threats to the lives of the king and queen. And Burke centrally blamed the abstractions of Rousseau for the social calamity in France.

Yet O'Brien seems curiously unaware of the extent to which Burke's philosophy bore similarities to that of Rousseau. Both thinkers argued that human freedom required the presence of social sources of support, and that liberty was only conceivable with the help of outside assistance. But O'Brien is so intent on pursuing his reevaluation of Burke in the light of the Irish question that he has little interest in pursuing such niceties of intellectual history as how Burke and Rousseau resembled each other.

O'Brien, as a masterful writer himself, appreciates Burke's capacities in rhetoric. But the readers should not come to *The Great Melody* expecting a balanced appreciation of Burke within the history of ideas. Burke may have been a close friend of Sir Joshua Reynolds, but he plays no role whatever in *The Great Melody*. Even people like James Boswell, Oliver Goldsmith, and Samuel Johnson take the most minor parts in O'Brien's "thematic biography." If O'Brien has made it impossible now for anyone to forget Burke's tortured relationship to Ireland, it will still be necessary to supplement his interpretation with those more traditional accounts that see Burke in the context of the leading figures who were his contemporaries.

* * *

Alexis de Tocqueville has still not been accorded the stature he deserves as a political theorist. It is of course widely acknowledged that he wrote the greatest study ever made about America; but the two-volume *Democracy in America* remains unclassifiable and therefore hard to assign in universities. It is also generally thought that *The Old Regime and the French Revolution* is a masterpiece, yet it is not readily comparable to other works of nineteenth-century political thought since it does not directly address the most abstract problems. It almost seems that those figures who are the greatest writers, like Tocqueville himself, are among the last to earn full recognition, on the grounds that their lucidity makes them suspect; more abstract writers, who demand exegesis, readily attract scholars. In any event one would have thought that Tocqueville's *Recollections*, one of the most extraordinary political memoirs I have ever read, would have been enough by itself to be convincing about his genius; yet that book has up till now attracted relatively little interest.

It turns out that even after more than 140 years since his death in 1859 abundant archival material has remained to be tapped. The Tocqueville family archives comprise some 110 cartons, twenty-three of them consisting of his correspondence. Some of this historical evidence has been used in the definitive edition of Tocqueville's work that has been coming out in Paris, and which is nearing completion. In addition, a collection at Yale consists not only of the travel diaries of Tocqueville and his friend Gustave de Beaumont but a large part of their American correspondence and their manuscripts, including rough drafts at various stages of the completion of *Democracy in America*.

The plenitude of Tocqueville materials does raise some interesting methodological questions. For it is still an unsettled matter how one weighs, for example, a writer's letters to friends, associates, and family, as opposed to a thinker's published texts; private communications can be at least as telling about a writer's intentions, and sometimes more so, than works published in a theorists' lifetime. Tocqueville's magnificent *Recollections* came out posthumously. Yet at the same time one hesitates to detract from the status ordinarily accorded to a work like *Democracy in America* or *The Old Regime*. It seems to me a perplexity what standing should be accorded to early drafts of the published texts. With other, older figures, a similar problem does not as often arise, usually for lack of the available private evidence. On the whole, political theorists have not paid as much attention as they should have to the significance of documents other than public works. (It seems to me to have been a long-standing scandal that it took so long to have readily available Thomas Hobbes's letters, even though he is generally acknowledged the greatest political philosopher in the English language; such so-called private material still deserves to be fully integrated into our accounts of Hobbes's more formal writings.)

André Jardin's *Tocqueville: A Biography*[6] is the first comprehensive one ever to appear, and it is masterly. Only the first page or two make for hard reading; I found that it took a few difficult minutes for the book to transport one imaginatively into French culture, and that after one had made the appropriate mental adjustment the rest was easy.

Although Tocqueville's aristocratic lineage is hardly news, Jardin spells his ancestry out with details that are unforgettable. A comrade of William the Conqueror belonged to Tocqueville's family; the great writer had noble ancestors on both his father's and his mother's side. His father was a prefect under Louis XVIII. Tocqueville was part of the best aristocratic tradition for whom "morality consisted of serving the State, defending the liberty of all, hating tyranny." And the "center of interest" of Tocqueville's intellectual life was the historic movement that constituted the transition from aristocratic society to a democratic one. For Tocqueville, nations were like people in that, as he put it, "circumstances of birth and growth affect all the rest of their careers." And a key insight of his about the United States was that it had been able to avoid a European-style revolution: "The great advantage of the American is that he has arrived at a state of democracy without having to endure a democratic revolution; and that he is born equal without having to become so."

Although some of Tocqueville's most significant ideas are by now well known, Jardin fills out his life with new biographical material. Tocqueville married at the age of thirty an Englishwoman who came from a middle-class family; she was years older than he, but the marriage, which caused family scandal, regularized a liaison that had already lasted for some time. The couple had no children; but their relationship succeeded in giving Tocqueville the security he needed. Evidently his wife complemented his "unstable" nature, and her maternal side was able to cope with Tocqueville's characteristics as a "spoiled child." Among the many fascinating details to be learned from Jardin's biography is that the language of the household was English.

If he stood up to his family with his marriage, professionally he had been more compliant; in accord with their wishes he had studied law from 1823 to 1826. He evidently expected to spend a lifetime in the judiciary. Then in 1831 Tocqueville undertook, with his good friend Gustave de Beaumont, their famous trip to America, that was to involve their spending a little over nine months in North America. Their pretext for the journey was to study how to reform the French system of penal incarceration. Their willingness to pay for the trip themselves had facilitated the formal leave of absences they secured. But their intention to study the American penitentiary system was an excuse; for "what Tocqueville sought knowledge of…was the way of life in a democracy, a prototype for the future for France."

As Frenchmen they were exempt from being the objects of scorn that the Americans then felt for the British. Their letters back to France vividly complement what later appeared in print. Their travels brought them in contact with many levels of American society; and they managed to meet Daniel Webster, John Quincy Adams, as well as President Jackson. The first volume of *Democracy*, written in less than a year, was published early in 1835, and immediately became "the book of the year" in Paris. It was widely recognized to be a classic. The writing of volume two of *Democracy* took some four years; this more complex work, published in 1840, did not win the same immediate applause. Throughout both books Tocqueville sought to inquire whether it was possible to establish human freedom in an egalitarian society. His audience was French; he aimed "to awaken France's conscience and continue her civic education."

Tocqueville got elected to the Chamber of Deputies in 1839, and always took his political career seriously. He chose his ideological place to be on the "left center" of the political spectrum; he was, however, a poor orator and quickly became an isolated figure. He soon realized that he "absolutely" lacked "the talent for extemporizing," without appreciating how damaging that was bound to be to his political aspirations. He served briefly (for five months) and relatively unsuccessfully as minister of foreign affairs. Ill health, from a slowly developing tuberculosis, combined with the coming to power of Napoleon III to put an end to Tocqueville's political life; he refused to serve under the authoritarian Empire. In his retirement he went back to his writing, and his *Recollections* and *The Old Regime* date from this final period of his internal exile.

Jardin's biography is such a pleasure to read that it seemed almost impossible to put down. Jean-Claude Lamberti's *Tocqueville and the Two Democracies*[7] is, by contrast, labored and requires effort to read one's way through; yet Lamberti's book is in its own way almost as rewarding as Jardin's. Lamberti is a professional sociologist in Paris, and unlike so many of his country's intellectuals he has not disdained keeping abreast of academic developments in North America. As a matter of fact, because of the abundant interest in Tocqueville on this side of the Atlantic, the French are a bit fearful that they are in danger of losing control of the Tocqueville secondary literature.

Even though *Tocqueville and the Two Democracies* does make for a hard read, at least alongside Jardin's biography that is written without any academese, I nevertheless think I learned an immense amount from Lamberti. Although I found it unfortunate that he chose to isolate *Democracy* from Tocqueville's other texts, he does establish (along with other commentators) that Volume I was primarily written as a study of American society, whereas Volume II was more an examination of democracy in general. Lamberti considers *Democracy* as "the greatest political work of the nineteenth century," and emphasizes Tocqueville's love of liberty and hatred of revolution. Notably Lamberti makes extensive use of the Tocqueville material at the Yale archives. Assuming Lamberti is correct that *Democracy* ranks as "among the master-works of political philosophy," his conscientiousness about early drafts, notes, revisions, marginalia, and letters all seems warranted.

Then, two-thirds through the book, I suddenly sat upright when Lamberti quotes from Tocqueville's published text itself:

> I see an innumerable multitude of men, alike and equal, constantly circling around in pursuit of the petty and banal pleasures with which they glut their souls. Each one of them, withdrawn into himself, is almost unaware of the fate of the rest. Mankind, for

him, consists of his children and his personal friends. As for the rest of his fellow citizens, they are near enough, but he does not notice them. He touches them but feels nothing. He exists in and for himself, and though he still may have a family, one can at least say that he has not got a fatherland.

Over this kind of men stands an immense, protective power which is alone responsible for securing their enjoyment and watching over their fate. That power is absolute, thoughtful of detail, orderly, provident, and gentle. It would resemble paternal authority if, fatherlike, it tried to prepare its charges for a man's life; but, on the contrary, it only tries to keep them in perpetual childhood. It likes to see the citizens enjoy themselves, provided that they think of nothing but enjoyment. It gladly works for their happiness but wants to be sole agent and judge of it. It provides for their security, foresees and supplies their necessities, facilitates their pleasures, manages their principal concerns, directs their industry, makes rules for their testaments, and divides their inheritances. Why should it not entirely relieve them from the trouble of thinking and from all the cares of living?

This electrifying (and famous passage) stands out in Lamberti's book in such sharp contrast to the rest of the quotations from Tocqueville's early drafts, etc. that despite my respect for Lamberti's scholarly achievement the words from *Democracy* itself make me wonder whether it does not after all make more sense to pay fuller attention to the great work itself. I think it a tribute to Jardin's biography that the same passage, in the midst of his well-written book, appears to flow inconspicuously with the rest of the elegant narrative that he has constructed.

It is an old problem in historiography how one should balance the life and work of a great writer. While I would not expect anyone to better Jardin's biography at least for another generation, Lamberti's book is only one among many possible approaches to his texts; yet Lamberti's discussion of *Democracy* will be a permanent part of the scholarly literature, and certainly combined with reading Jardin's book helps to bring Tocqueville alive in a way that was hardly possible before.

Tocqueville stands as a great figure in the history of modern liberalism, for he fought to defend individualism without confusing it either with egoism or conformity. And as Lamberti put it, Tocqueville accepted the principles of 1789 "but rejects the revolutionary spirit." It still remains true for ourselves that we confront the dilemma of reconciling the contradictions Tocqueville struggled with, which is why he remains such a vividly contemporary figure.

* * *

For reasons that I have continued to fail to understand, Freud remains outside the traditional canon of the study of political theory. The creator of psychoanalysis is most apt to be dismissed as the author of daffy ideas, and despite the fact that such a wide range of social theorists in this past century have been influenced by him, his work remains in a kind of limbo so that students of political theory are rarely expected to be knowledgeable about it. The problem cannot be just a question of how short a period has passed since his death in 1939, since a variety of lesser continental thinkers have attracted a good deal of scholarship connected with twentieth-century political thought.

It is in this context that *Freud and the Politics of Psychoanalysis,*[8] a book by Jose Brunner, an Israeli political theorist who has studied abroad, seems to me so outstanding. The reader will find no ideological partisanship here, as Brunner starts out by placing Freud within his proper social setting. If I may question one point, Brunner is surprisingly accepting of Freud's own argument that he had been "brought up without religion" and therefore Brunner minimizes the characteristically Jewish elements to Freud's thinking. For my taste Brunner is too credulous about Freud's having succeeded in creating "a universal science of the Mind," instead of seeing Freud's need for universalism as a defense against the relative narrowness of Freud's own religious beginnings.

It is not necessary to propagandize on behalf of any part of psychoanalysis to see it as a doctrine in the history of ideas that demands scholarly scrutiny. Freud is generally acknowledged to have been the greatest psychologist of this past century, and whatever his many mistakes he will remain outstanding as a writer. His volumes of correspondence are going to dwarf in size, for example, the *Standard Edition* edited by James Strachey. If somewhere around 25,000 letters of Freud's have survived the upheavals of two world wars, that is testimony to his capacities as a stylist who cannot be legitimately ignored.

An immense secondary literature surrounding Freud has arisen, and even though professional legitimization among political theorists is lacking Brunner does not deal with this material as an amateur. He moves deftly among the various authorities, and yet also has his own point of view to present. *Freud and the Politics of Psychoanalysis* is a welcome addition, and hopefully will be followed in the future by political philosophers who dare risk ridicule for taking Freud and his followers seriously.

* * *

Political science treats psychoanalytic thinking as an annoying stepchild. Although Harold Lasswell first broke the professional ice over seventy years ago, as I alluded to in the preface it is still today not the case that one can be interested in psychoanalysis without raising eyebrows. Among political theorists, who have long thought of themselves as the intellectual aristocrats of the profession, anything to do with a branch of the Freudian school of thought will earn less professional advancement than a treatise on almost any thoroughly well-studied thinker from the canon. For example, anything that interests philosophy departments will automatically play well within political science.

C. Fred Alford seems to me outstanding in that he has been bucking the received conventional wisdom. Previously he has authored *Narcissism: Socrates, the Frankfurt School, and Psychoanalytic Theory* and *Melanie Klein and Critical Theory: An Account of Politics, Arts and Reason Based on Her Psychoanalytic Theory.*[9] It happens that I cannot agree with much, if not most, of what Alford argues. But I do want to say at the outset that he is remarkable as a serious political theorist with a good background in modern psychoanalytic thinking.

In the latest of Alford's books, *The Self in Social Theory: A Psychoanalytic Account of Its Construction in Plato, Hobbes, Locke, Rawls, and Rousseau,*[10] he is concerned, as the title suggests, with shifting concepts of the self, and the light that psychoanalytic theory can throw on them. Unlike his last book, where he demonstrated his familiarity with Melanie Klein's thought, this book examines the concepts of Jacques Lacan and Heinz Kohut. Lacan has had an immense impact on current French intellectual life, and Kohut has created a whole movement known as "self psychology." Political theory has yet to absorb the different challenges Lacan and Kohut posed.

Reading *The Self in Social Theory* one comes across some remarkable observations, and the ambitiousness of the author's endeavor should be an occasion for admiration. The two chapters on Plato seemed to me particularly strong and well sustained by the secondary literature. But the problem with the book as a whole is its lack of an adequate conceptual unity.

For why Plato, Hobbes, Locke, Rawls and Rousseau in that precise ahistorical order? Alford makes no effort to justify the choice of the particular authors he has decided to examine. I would have thought that if Alford wanted to demonstrate his undoubtedly sound point—that conceptions of the self held by previous political thinkers can be explored by means of a psychoanalytically informed psychological perspective—then he would have been advised to stick to one writer and pursue the matter in depth. As it is, we have a series of disconnected essays, linked largely by Alford's interest in Lacan and Kohut. And instead of Alford working within the texts of the classic authors themselves, using contemporary psychoanalytic thinking where it becomes relevant, too often he places the cart before the horse; it seems that what really mattered to Alford was Lacan and Kohut.

Alford deserves to be congratulated for the vein of thought he has been examining. I just wish he would slow down a bit, and use his learning about political theory, as well as his sophistication on psychoanalytic matters, to investigate with more care and so that his readers in political theory can easily follow, explaining why he thinks that this is a fruitful line of inquiry. As it is, *The Self in Social Theory* contains too much jumping around to enable the neophyte to make sense of what he has been up to. It is precisely because I share so many of Alford's own conceptual interests that I wish him well and hope he will succeed in the long-standing enterprise of increasing our profession's receptivity to the significance that the Freudian revolution in the history of ideas holds for our understanding of the whole tradition of political theory.

* * *

D. Steven Blum's *Walter Lippmann: Cosmopolitanism in the Century of Total War*[11] is a good solid book on an important subject. Lippmann's reputation is now under a cloud. Partly this is due to his retirement from journalism even before his death in 1974; many writers suffer a decline in their standing once they are deceased, as memories of their writings begin to fade. But in Lippmann's case the more general problem was compounded by the appearance in 1980 of an authorized biography by Ronald Steel, *Walter Lippmann and the American Century*. Although Lippmann had entrusted Steel with writing his life, after Lippmann had failed to work successfully with Richard Rovere, Steel's dislike of his subject took many forms in the book that ultimately appeared.

Any official biographer is bound to be conflicted, as he is influenced by both the demands of objectivity and those of loyalty. But with Steel one suspects that, being himself a journalist who writes on foreign policy, he lacked the imagination to appreciate the seriousness of Lippmann's books. As Blum carefully notes, Lippmann himself, although he believed that his books and journalism were obviously interrelated, was most proud of the former and thought them the more important. Blum tells us he considers Steel's book "a distinguished biography," thinks that Steel has provided the "finest analysis of Lippmann's international affairs writing," and yet knows that "perhaps the most serious weakness of the biography...is Steel's judgment that Lippmann is hardly worth discussing as a political philosopher...."

A relatively recent collection of Lippmann's letters, *Public Philosopher: Selected Letters of Walter Lippmann*, edited by John Morton Blum (not a relative of D. Steven Blum) has implicitly sought to correct the unbalanced impression left by Steel about Lippmann. But in selecting from among the twenty-odd thousand letters of Lippmann, Blum tended to pick that correspondence which was primarily political rather than of strictly intellectual interest. Yet D. Steven Blum cites in his *Walter Lippmann* an exchange of letters between Lippmann and the political economist Friedrich von Hayek: that is exactly the kind of material that tends to get excluded from John Morton Blum's excellently edited *Public Philosopher*, and which D. Steven Blum got hold of because he did library research among Lippmann's papers at Yale University. D. Steven Blum has by no means exhaustively gone through the extensive Lippmann archives, which will evidently have to be left to other students of intellectual history. But his book does confirm the conviction that Lippmann's full standing as a thinker has yet to be established.

The point is not that Lippmann was a bookish writer. My own examination of his library indicates that, as far as one can tell, after his excellent education and his personal encounters with men like William James, Graham Wallas, and George Santayana, Lippmann ceased to rely on books and instead found himself able to think for himself. Other figures in the history of ideas have also felt entitled to dispense with keeping up with theoretical literature. Lippmann had deliberately rejected the academic life of political science as a professional career.

The central merit of D. Steven Blum's study of Lippmann is that he takes Lippmann's books thoroughly seriously, and yet does not examine them pedantically. Many works on Lippmann's ideas have already appeared, although none are as good as this one. Steel's biography did turn up an enormous amount of invaluable information about Lippmann's private life as well as his journalism, and this book by Blum is the first to reconsider Lippmann's major writings in the light of this new material.

At least one wonderful book of Lippmann's, *Men of Destiny*, could have been recalled for today's readers and Blum might have discussed it, but on the whole he did an admirable job of recreating for a new generation what a pivotal figure Lippmann once was. It is a pleasure to have had the chance to reread here some of Lippmann's unusually lucid sentences, and yet Blum has not weighted down the book with too many quotations.

As an interpreter of Lippmann Blum makes a real contribution in stressing continuities and consistencies in all Lippmann's work. He had started publishing books in 1913, and it has not been hard to find different stages in his thinking, if not outright incompatibilities in his many contentions. But Blum knows that he was centrally concerned with the problem of the viability of democratic theory; it is remarkable how many common threads he is able to find in all Lippmann's books.

A note of Blum's about Louis Auchincloss's novel *The House of the Prophet* confirms for me that he is essentially on the right track. Blum observes that "Auchincloss not only is a distinguished novelist but also was Lippmann's attorney—a combination put to great advantage. No one seriously interested in Lippmann should overlook this novel, arguably the most searching portrait of the man behind the words." This book by Blum admirably enhances our understanding of a thinker I would rank as the most important American political theorist of the twentieth century.

* * *

A central silence in the official story of the history and development of psychoanalytic thought has to do with Erich Fromm's contributions. The whole movement that was once known as "neo-Freudianism" has been almost forgotten now. Individual leaders in that once well-recognized and powerful strain of thought—like Harry Stack Sullivan and Karen Horney—have by one means or another now won substantial recognition within the so-called mainstream of psychoanalysis. But for a variety of different reasons Fromm has himself largely remained left out in the cold.[12]

In spite of how I think Fromm has been neglected as a matter of intellectual history, a topic I was touching on in chapter 1, I would argue that no book by a psychoanalyst—with the exception of Freud's own *Civilization and Its Discontents*—has had as big an effect on my own field of political science as Fromm's 1941 *Escape From Freedom*. That text not only became central to the professional education of my own generation studying politics, but it also once had an immense influence within fields like sociology, anthropology, and clinical psychology. Yet by now it is easy for beginning students to be unaware of how momentous an impact that one book was capable of having had throughout the social sciences.

When I was first assigned *Escape Fromm Freedom* to read in 1955 as an undergraduate in the Government Department at Harvard, it seemed to fit into a preexisting tradition of social thought. Fromm had proposed a specific twist to our thinking about freedom—not just as a negative release from external constraints, but also as a positive emancipation from inner passions. Jean-Jacques Rousseau had meant something similar, I think, with his notion of "forcing" people to be free. Not long after I first absorbed the meaning of *Escape From Freedom* Sir Isaiah Berlin would in 1958 deliver his famous Oxford inaugural lecture "Two Concept of Liberty," which can be taken to be an indictment of the position that Fromm had advanced.[13] But Berlin's skepticism about so-called positive freedom at least accorded Fromm's sort of reasoning a prominent place within political thought.

By the time I had embarked on my own graduate work, I became aware that Fromm had acquired ideological enemies not just within non-Marxist political theory, but Fromm had, starting with *Escape From Freedom*, aroused the most intense sorts of belligerence from within psychoanalysis. People like Karl Menninger and Otto Fenichel had been blistering about Fromm. To repeat a couple of lines from Menninger's critique in the *Nation*: "Erich Fromm was in Germany a distinguished sociologist. His book is written as if he considered himself a psychoanalyst."[14] Fenichel linked his own indictment to Fenichel's distaste for the ideas of Karen Horney.[15]

Oddly enough it was in the so-called radical decade of the 1960s that Fromm's reputation, at least in North America, ran into its heaviest weather. Fromm's own political commitments—on nuclear disarmament for example – tended to overshadow his early contributions to problems basic to social science, such as his powerful appendix "Character and the Social Process" in *Escape From Freedom*. Fromm's commitments as a "peacenik" became more notable (at least in political science) than his trenchant books like *Man For Himself* (1947) or *The Sane Society* (1956). Fromm's *The Art of Loving* (1957) was commercially so immensely successful as to have made many intellectuals suspicious of Fromm's seriousness. Fromm seemed too like a secular preacher, akin to Norman Vincent Peale. The most tough-minded socialists (Adorno thought Fromm needed to read more Lenin) had had as little use for

Fromm as the orthodox Freudians, and Fromm's reputation started on what became a precipitous slide from what it had once been in the mid-1950s. To give only one illustration: when a 1973 anthology of mine of ten essays about Freud (including only one piece by Fromm) got reviewed in the *International Journal of Psychoanalysis*, almost the whole review got taken up with an indictment of Fromm.[16] A fine sociologist has recently been accurately describing the decline and fall of Fromm's standing.[17] Herbert Marcuse, who once did so much damage to Fromm, had himself little interest in clinical psychoanalysis, but his indictment of Fromm was taken up anyway, and Marcuse's works remain alive in universities and are still coming out in a collected edition.

From the perspective of the history of ideas, which is my own special interest, there is something seriously amiss with how Fromm is being treated today. It is true that his books seem to translate well; and in some parts of the world, Italy and Germany for example, Fromm's books may still be more readily available at airport bookstands than the work of any other psychoanalyst. But it would seem that Fromm's early courage[18] in pointing out flaws in Freud's approach have helped cost Fromm the support he deserves from within clinical circles. A book like Fromm's *The Forgotten Language* (1951) rarely gets cited. Many intellectuals today do not even realize Fromm was a practicing analyst whose theories have important implications for clinical work; feminists for example usually ignore how he pioneered in behalf of revising Freud's theories of femininity. And no matter how the whole field of the historiography of psychoanalysis has been flourishing lately, Fromm's critique of Ernest Jones's official biography of Freud, *Sigmund Freud's Mission* (1959), has received too little recognition.

Outside North America Fromm's standing probably never rose as high as it did here, nor has it now fallen so low. But in general I think it remains true that Fromm today ranks as one of the neglected forefathers in the history of psychoanalysis. This current neglect is so even though *Escape From Freedom* was initially "reviewed enthusiastically by such prominent public intellectual figures as Margaret Mead, Ashley Montagu, and Dwight Macdonald."[19] It should not require ill-considered zealotry in behalf of Fromm to accord him the standing that he deserves. Of course there were inadequacies – political, social, as well as psychological—to how Fromm constructed his point of view. But he did produce a structured way of looking at things, and that perspective once exerted an immensely influential impact. Fromm succeeded in changing the way people thought, and perhaps that helps account for why he was so well hated. I think a volume of Fromm's surviving letters would help awaken people nowadays to the genuine power of his mind. In any event, Fromm deserves recognition for what he managed to add to the body of work that consists in what psychoanalysis has amounted to.

* * *

Michael Ignatieff's fine biography of Isaiah Berlin, who died in 1997 at the venerable age of eighty-eight, has been written by a political theorist who interviewed Berlin over the last decade of his life.[20] A lesser biographer might have puffed-up this slim text into twice its length. As it is, Ignatieff's narrative is moving and the reader becomes acquainted with new links between Berlin's life and works. One of the most touching aspects of the book comes toward the end, when Berlin is about to be hospitalized for the last time; he met with his biographer to be sure that the book, which it had been agreed would not appear in Berlin's lifetime, not become a betrayal. Berlin was savvy enough to know how often authorized biographies can, even if unintentionally, turn on their subject. But Berlin had chosen wisely in his biographer, and it is a little sad to think that he could at the end be self-doubting about his prior judgment.

Over forty years ago, when I first starting reading Berlin, his writings were only available in scattered and often obscure publications. Berlin had the good fortune that a philosopher, Henry Hardy, who had done graduate work at a new Oxford college that Berlin had founded, pulled together Berlin's essays into a sequence of easily available collections. An endnote in Ignatieff's biography indicated that a new book of Berlin's lectures on romanticism, edited by Hardy, would be appearing; other texts have also now come out, and several volumes of correspondence are in the works, so it would seem that Berlin is going to have a remarkable afterlife of published works.

Ignatieff has become an accomplished journalist, and he starts off the biography with a splendid word-snapshot of what it was like to meet Berlin at his rooms in his club in London. From beginning to end this book succeeds in awakening the memory of what Berlin was like at his best. The essay of Berlin's that probably remains most well known is his study of Tolstoy's philosophy of history, first published in book form as *The Hedgehog and The Fox*. But I am not sure that Ignatieff is correct in supposing, as one purpose of this book, that though "the range of his work may make him seem like a fox, who knows many things; in reality, he was a hedgehog, who knows one big thing." For Ignatieff cannot, I think, succeed in elaborating what "this one big thing was," even though he succeeds in showing examples of what Berlin's talents were like as a fox in the history of ideas.

The book is peopled by the great and the famous that Berlin had relished encountering—Virginia Woolf, Freud, Wittgenstein, Keynes, Weizmann, Stravinsky, Picasso, not to mention President Kennedy and British prime ministers. Berlin is worth paying attention to on all these people, and his pithy sayings are telling. Berlin was bubbling over with talk and conversation, and his writings, in his late years regularly dictated, are an expression of the free flow of his mind. He had a musical capacity to hear the central melodic themes in past thinkers, which is what distinguished his work from contemporaries of his who could get lost in their own cleverness.

For me the most moving chapters in the biography have to do with Berlin's 1945 visits to Moscow and Leningrad. My guess would be that one reason Berlin picked Ignatieff as a biographer was because they both shared a Russian background. Berlin was born in Riga, Latvia, but his family fled from Petrograd in 1920 for exile in England. The four essays of Berlin's on the birth of the Russian intelligentsia in the 1830s and 1840s, which first appeared in *Encounter* in the 1950s as "A Marvellous Decade," established Berlin's credentials as a historian of Russian intellectual history. When Berlin went back after World War II, he not only encountered his own roots but met the great survivors of the tradition of the nineteenth century, Boris Pasternak and Anna Akhmatova. Pasternak, whose relatives in Oxford knew Berlin, had not yet written *Doctor Zhivago*, but Akhmatova (whose poetry Berlin had then scarcely read) was already a symbol of the unconquerable Russian spirit, and wrote poems on him after their memorable meetings.

The weak chapters in Ignatieff's book touch on Berlin's private life. Only in his forties did he fall in love with a married woman with children, and they became a happy couple for over forty years. Berlin has been dead for so short a time that it would have been unseemly for Ignatieff to have probed more deeply. Someone like Berlin who wrote so eloquently about the painfulness and inevitability of human tragedy had surely made some hard choices in his own life. Yet although we read of occasional nervous collapses, Ignatieff does not pursue such points. Ignatieff recognizes the oddness of Berlin's "lifelong dislike of Freud," and brings this up in the context of those who wondered whether Berlin "actually read the books he cited so effortlessly." But I would have thought that Berlin was deeply offended by Freud's theory of perversion, and the implications this had for Oxonians of Berlin's time.

Ignatieff is right to highlight how thrilling Berlin's lectures could be, which is why he became such an exciting teacher at Oxford. In 1959 he gave a lecture in the dining room of my college on Marx's great enemy Bakunin, and I rushed out to buy and read E. H. Carr's big book on Bakunin. There was less in what Carr (an enemy of Berlin's) had written than in the immediacy of Berlin's presentation, which got largely lost when Berlin finally wrote it up for publication. But when Ignatieff tells us how bored by individual tutorials Berlin could be, the reader might miss the implication this had for those who tried to study with him. This "Paganini of the platform" could be a disaster in face-to-face encounters, and it was only years after I had had him as a tutor that I was fortunate enough to be able, a couple of years before he died, to meet Berlin finally on some sort of footing of adult mutuality.

Ignatieff is balanced and persuasive on the strengths of Berlin's special brand of anti-utopian liberalism, and how he valued pluralism in the tradition of John Stuart Mill. And Ignatieff is correct in drawing a sharp line between Berlin and the ideas of Herbert Marcuse as well as Hannah Arendt. Marcuse was, in Berlin's eyes, contemptible for his Hegelian sleights-of-hand, which could lead to whitewashing some of the greatest crimes of twentieth-century politics. In Arendt's case they differed in their approaches to Zionism; while she suspected (rightly or wrongly) that Berlin had helped orchestrate the attack on her *Eichmann in Jerusalem* (1962), he lived to single her out after her death as an over-rated thinker. He maintained that her liaison with Heidegger succeeded as well as preceded World War II. (No one has pursued the implications of this possibility.) One of his own last public acts was a plea in behalf of the "Peace Now" movement in Israel. How Arendt and Berlin differed in their allegiances to Judaism would be a subject for an entirely separate treatise.

Berlin was insistent that the most monstrous crimes of this past century have been committed on behalf of ideals that might sound most attractive, which is why he distinguished so sharply between what he called negative as opposed to positive liberty. Marx, like Freud, was too eager to champion a version of what Rousseau had once said was "forcing" people "to be free." Berlin stood for calling a spade a spade, and he distinguished liberty from other possible values, such as justice or equality. Intellectuals who recklessly play around with ideas could end up, like Heidegger, proponents of Hitler, and Stalin had his own group of well-educated apologists. Berlin came to symbolize the best in the British tradition, which he had linked up to the most humane Western stream of thought. Ignatieff has ably brought to life Berlin's work, and the biography outshines previous attempts to synthesize his special contribution to social and political thought.

Notes

1. Roger Masters, *Fortune Is A River: Leonardo Da Vinci and Niccolo Machiavelli's Magnificent Dream To Change the Course of Florentine History* (New York: The Free Press, 1998).
2. Shadia Drury, *Leo Strauss and the American Right* (New York: St. Martin's Press, 1999).
3. Jean Starobinski, *Jean-Jacques Rousseau: Transparency and Obstruction*, translated by Arthur Goldhammer (Chicago, University of Chicago Press, 1988).
4. Stanley Ayling, *Edmund Burke: His Life and Opinions* (New York: St. Martin's Press, 1988).
5. Conor Cruise O'Brien, *The Great Melody: A Thematic Biography of Edmund Burke* (Chicago, University of Chicago Press, 1992).
6. Andre Jardin, *Tocqueville: A Biography*, translated by Lydia Davis with Robert Hemenway (New York: Farrar Straus & Giroux, 1988).
7. Jean-Claude Lamberti, *Tocqueville and the Two Democracies*, translated by Arthur Goldhammer (Cambridge, Mass., Harvard University Press, 1989).
8. Jose Brunner, *Freud and the Politics of Psychoanalysis* (Blackwell, Oxford, 1995).
9. C. Fred Alford: *Narcissism: Socrates, the Frankfurt School, and Psychoanalytic Theory* (New Haven, Yale University Press, 1988) and *Melanie Klein and Critical Theory: An Account of Politics, Arts and Reason Based on Her Psychoanalytic Theory* (New Haven, Yale University Press, 1989).

10. C. Fred Alford, *The Self in Social Theory: A Psychoanalytic Account of Its Construction in Plato, Hobbes, Locke, Rawls, and Rousseau* (New Haven, Yale University Press, 1991).
11. D. Steven Blum, *Walter Lippmann: Cosmopolitanism in the Century of Total War* (Ithaca, Cornell University Press, 1984).
12. But see Daniel Burston, *The Legacy of Erich Fromm, op. cit.*
13. Isaiah Berlin, *Four Essays on Liberty* (London, Oxford University Press, 1969), pp. 118-172.
14. Karl Menninger, "Loneliness in the Modern World," *The Nation*, Vol. 154 (March 14, 1942), p. 317.
15. Otto Fenichel, "Psychoanalytic Remarks on Fromm's Book *Escape From Freedom*," in *The Collected Papers of Otto Fenichel*, Second Series (New York: W. W. Norton, 1954), Ch. 19, p. 271.
16. Frederick Wyatt, "Review of *Sigmund Freud*, ed. Paul Roazen," *International Journal of Psychoanalysis*, Vol. 54 (1976), pp. 488-91.
17. Neil McLaughlin, "How To Become a Forgotten Intellectual: Intellectual Movements and the Rise and Fall of Erich Fromm," *op. cit.*; Neil McLaughlin, "Why Do Schools of Thought Fail? Neo-Freudianism as a Case Study in the Sociology of Knowledge," *op. cit.*; and Neil McLaughlin, "Nazism, Nationalism, and the Sociology of Emotions: *Escape From Freedom* Revisited," *Sociological Theory*, Vol. 14 (1996), pp. 241-61.
18. Paul Roazen, "Fromm's Courage," in *Fromm*, ed. Mauricio Cortina (Northvale, N.J., Aronson, 1996). This essay of mine also appears in my *Psychology and the Psychology of the Unconscious* (London, Open Gate Press, in 2000).
19. McLaughlin, "Nazism, Nationalism, and the Sociology of Emotions," *op. cit.*, p. 243.
20. Michael Ignatieff, *Isaiah Berlin: A Life* (New York: Metropolitan Books, 1998).

8

Vietnam and the Cold War

The Vietnam War remains the worst moral crisis in my life as an observer of politics. I can still remember as a boy when the French were holding out at Dienbienphu; the failure of that garrison to survive against domestic insurgents seemed largely a French matter. But then in the early days of Kennedy's presidency somehow the names of certain Laotian princes, curiously similar to one another, kept cropping up in the news. It was only in the first half of 1965 that Vietnam became front and center of my political consciousness. After President Lyndon Johnson had decisively beaten Senator Barry Goldwater in 1964, America surreptitiously entered into a war. I can remember what it was like to travel then at airports, where one saw for the first time in my adult experience soldiers suddenly travelling to and fro. We were already at war without the general public knowing it. Those first months of 1965 are indelibly etched in my mind because I felt then that this was a terrible mistake, immoral and perhaps criminal; but it would take some ten years for America to be extricated from what Johnson had started. (As time went on the War in Southeast Asia became a more accurate label than just the Vietnam War but the shorter version has stuck.) The first time I saw the Vietnam Memorial in Washington I was irritated rather than moved by it; for like so much in connection with that war the Memorial was dedicated to the Americans who had lost their lives there, not the Vietnamese. (One of the worst arguments I heard advanced against the war was that it was tearing America apart; national selfishness could hardly be more nakedly invoked.)

My whole interest in the Vietnam War was heightened by the fact that I had spent so many years in the Government Department at Harvard. Professors in my department had a history of participating in foreign policy matters in Washington, for even before the Cold War began academics put themselves in at least part-time public service. Starting under President Franklin Roosevelt talented lawyers, for example, following the model of Felix Frankfurter's commitment to public affairs, went into government work; and during World War II patriotic duty called for professorial participation in organizations like the OSS, precursor to today's CIA, and the State Department. But then Kennedy invited people like Arthur Schlesinger, Jr. from our History Department, and also McGeorge Bundy from the Government Department. (The university was therefore, in my view, "politicized" before the student protest movement had begun.)

I had once taken an excellent foreign policy course from Bundy, and like everybody else could not but admire his unusual brilliance and articulateness. (How he functioned as Dean of the College was beyond my competence.) It would be awhile until Henry Kissinger joined Nixon's team in 1968, but by then the pattern was clear; the Department of my youth was not only intimately connected with the making of the highest kinds of public policy, but the atmosphere was one in which it seemed I was surrounded by ambitious young people who had their eyes not on library work and scholarship so much as on getting ahead in American national politics or the media. It seemed to me then that I had lived through a transformation in the nature of the university life that I was most intimately acquainted with. Political opportunism replaced the ideal goal of scholarship that at least I thought had characterized the world in which I had lived. One of the reasons I was happy to move to Canada in 1971 was that York University was wholly out of the loop of engineering high political decisions; I felt I was going back to the world of my origins, when universities were concerned with teaching and books.

So when a study about the Bundy brothers appeared, although at first I avoided reading it, when I finally held it in my hands it seemed almost as if it were alive. The one play of Shakespeare's that comes to my mind in connection with Kai Bird's *The Color of Truth*[1] is *Macbeth*. Thunder and lightning in the air, and witches conspiring in an open place about when they will meet again, seem the appropriate place for the tale about Vietnam to start. Foul, filthy air should fill the opening of the story. It still seems to me a matter of murder, and also betrayal. One of the personally painful aspects of the Vietnam War was the way old friends essentially had to stop speaking to one another. This should seem small potatoes compared to the real destruction of lives that actually took place in Southeast Asia. But if I am writing about what it was like as a conscientious American then, the bitter feelings seem one of the worst aspects of it. I do not happen to find it easy to read books about the Vietnam War. The Pentagon Papers are a huge mass of documents that others are more expertly able to evaluate; someone like Robert McNamara was never part of my world. But McGeorge (known as "Mac") Bundy, if not his brother "Bill," was most certainly someone whose career I watched.

The Vietnam War meant an upheaval in my life in more than one sense. I was easily able to evade the problem of the draft because of my age and the deferments that it was then possible to get throughout graduate school work. But as the student protests against the war escalated, and young people not unreasonably thought that Harvard was heavily implicated in the war effort, the functioning of the university actually broke down at one point in 1969.

It may be hard to believe today, but riot police once had to cordon off Harvard Square; tear-gas rising in the sky above the Square could be seen for miles around. Store-windows were smashed, and protesters hurt by the police. Whatever dogmatic slumbers my thinking had allowed me up until then, the Vietnam War seemed to challenge everything. I wonder whether, with the exception of the Civil War, in its over three hundred year history the university has been as torn apart. I may have been isolated from some precious former friends by the intensity of the political debate; but I never went so far as to believe that we had to rethink the whole origins of the Cold War, for example, as a subsequent generation of "revisionist" historians were to do. (In that tale Stalinism remained for me the central culprit.) And to put all my old-fashioned cards on the table, I had been reliably taught as an undergraduate that the Japanese cabinet, even after the dropping of two atomic bombs, was still so deadlocked that it required the personal intervention of the emperor for Japan to surrender in 1945. As we shall see, all these issues are relevant to evaluating Kai Bird's *The Color of Truth*. (The title comes from McGeorge Bundy's having said in a 1967 speech: "Gray is the color of truth.")

Although to me the whole American involvement in Vietnam seems like a terrible nightmare, and the participation by people like McGeorge Bundy an appalling twist of fate, Kai Bird's account is remarkably sunny. He tells us at the outset of his introduction of how in 1972 he first heard in person Bundy, who had once been the national security adviser to both Presidents Kennedy and Johnson, speak at his college in Minnesota. Bird was only twenty-one then, but he had already been arrested two-and-a-half years earlier for having blocked the entrance to a draft-induction center. Bird was far more heroic than anything I did, which mainly consisted in gnashing my teeth and voting at Harvard faculty meetings in ways that were at odds with most senior members of my Department. There have been times over the last thirty-five years when I have pondered whether I had been right to take the positions that I once did; although it is true that I came to distrust the motives of many of those who helped lead the anti-war cause at Harvard, since it seems they were as opportunistically trying to get academic power as anyone, basically I have remained content with where I once stood politically.

It was hard for me even to start reading Kai Bird's book, since the name Bundy is in my mind such an inevitably distasteful one. Bird tells us in his introduction that when he first interviewed McGeorge Bundy for *The Color of Truth*, he had said that his mother would not have approved of his cooperating in the project. Bundy had a one word explanation for what he took to be his mother's disapproval—"Halberstam." It is true that in a famous 1969 piece in *Harper's*, and then in a 1972 bestseller *The Best and the Brightest*,[2] David Halberstam had journalistically destroyed Bundy's reputation. It did not mean that when Bundy left the White House in 1966, he was not perfectly capable of landing on his feet as president of the Ford Foundation. But Halberstam, especially in his *Harper's* article, had described Bundy's career in ways that were then unthinkable at Harvard. I remember one senior professor, like Bundy pro-war, whose eyes widened as he mentioned as we passed in a hallway the *Harper's* piece; if Bundy, at the time still an untouchable, could be so taken apart, then no one was safe, and there but for the grace of God went he himself.

Bird's book has nothing of the devilish flair of Halberstam. Instead Bird has given us an informative, even-tempered, if sometimes a bit flat, account of the lives of McGeorge Bundy and his brother William. (William Bundy was a more politically reclusive figure than McGeorge, and stayed on in government far longer.) It all starts with the father, Harvey Hollister Bundy, who had once worked for the great American secretary of war, Henry Stimson. McGeorge Bundy helped Stimson with his writing, and was officially co-author of Stimson's memoirs. (It does sound like Bundy did all the real writing work.) Again and again, we are told by Bird that it was the Stimsonian world view which pervaded the later thinking of the Bundys. Stimson might have been a Republican, but he fiercely opposed isolationism and the appeasement policies that led to Neville Chamberlain's bringing back his notorious "peace in our time" agreement from Munich. Supposedly the Bundys were driven to support the Vietnam War lest they cooperate in another Munich. But Bird does not mention that at the time of the Munich agreement there were those who resigned from politics rather than to participate in a fatally unwise policy. It would seem that Americans, unlike the British, have no such established tradition of people sacrificing public life for moral reasons. (Bird tells us, "if his president had decided to send in the troops without any fanfare, he felt he had no choice but to go along." But the issue was not just one of "fanfare," but democratic accountability, which might have been heightened by a major resignation. And it amounts to a cop-out for Bundy's defenders today to claim he was merely a cog-wheel in the making of policy that he always defended; that amounts nearly to the Eichmann defense.)

Harvey Bundy had attended an eastern prep school, and then Yale; later he went to Harvard Law School, and clerked for Mr. Justice Holmes. In marrying into a famous Boston Brahmin family Harvey Bundy was immediately a part of the American establishment. His sons went to Groton before enrolling in Yale. Bird gives a straightforward account of the educational background of "Mac" and "Bill" Bundy. And although Bill inevitably seems less colorful than the remarkably tart Mac, we do get an idea how early on Mac had become the audacious man who would later so self-confidently play his role on the world stage. Bill married the daughter of Dean Acheson, and became a specialist in cryptology during the war; Mac was assigned to be a personal aid to a rear admiral who was married to Mac's mother's best friend. Bill graduated from Harvard Law School, before pursuing his career in the CIA and later the State Department. But Mac went to teach Government at Harvard, where he met and married a young admissions officer at Radcliffe who was also a family friend.

In almost no time Mac had become by 1953, under the new president of Harvard Nathan M. Pusey, dean of the College. Bird spends a good deal of time on what Bundy did or did not do about the place of Communist Party members or sympathizers on the faculty. This was a bit before my time at Harvard, but there is something about Bird's account that does not read like the work of a seasoned insider. Eccentric judgments about Bundy's deanship are quoted alongside those of more middle-of-the-road observers. But perhaps my main uneasiness about Bird's choice of Harvard sources comes from what he has to say about 1965. By then Bundy had been presidential national security adviser since the beginning of Kennedy's term. (It is no doubt wicked of me, but I have taken a certain malicious pleasure in informally hearing about how Johnson was capable of mistreating Bundy.)

Everyone is in agreement that the year 1965 was to prove a watershed in the American involvement in Vietnam. For example, I remember with absolute clarity how in June 1965, when Bundy came back to Cambridge to deliver the Phi Beta Kappa oration, he was grilled by a panel of students before a large group of interested faculty in the New Lecture Hall. I can never forget the incident, because when one audacious student demanded to know just exactly how many troops would be involved in the war, and gave alternative figures, when he got to numbers like 75,000 or 100,000 and perhaps more, Bundy shook his head negatively, indicating that the war was not going to be anything like on that sort of scale. Since by the fall those numbers had been reached or exceeded, I have long felt that Bundy had deliberately misled us. Perhaps, more charitably, he did not himself know how ineluctably things were going to escalate, but then he should not have been reassuring us that there was nothing to worry about. I mention this incident because, although it had special meaning for me since I felt betrayed by a former teacher, others too recall the meeting at New Lecture Hall. Yet it does not appear at all in *The Color of Truth*, except in a sentence that relies on a *Time* magazine report. Just as disquieting is that Bird seems to have naively relied on interviews with only a relative handful of faculty, and in particular one anti-war professor whom Bundy (along with others) considered a snake-in-the-grass. Bird should certainly have talked to plenty of others on the faculty, and old-fashioned spadework ought to have gone into background digging rather than rely on a few illustrious-sounding Harvard names.

Early in 1966 Mac Bundy moved to the Ford Foundation, while leaving "behind a brother who would fight the war for another three years." (Bill was also for some time editor of the establishmentarian *Foreign Affairs*.) Mac Bundy seems to have thrown himself into the problem of race relations with the same self-assuredness that he once brought to Southeast Asia. But no set of domestic good works, even assuming that they were merited, make up to my mind for the calamity of what happened in Vietnam. It becomes a wry footnote that both Bundys became involved in "a running feud" with Kissinger over Nixon-Ford decisions. Kissinger was in an altogether different stratosphere of deviousness than the Bundys, and has written enough in the way of serpentine memoirs to keep historians occupied in tracking down what actually happened until few are likely to be interested in the truth.

Mac Bundy died in 1996, at the age of seventy-seven, and Bill (older by two years) was reported to be in ill health until his death in 2000. But although the word "tragedy" comes up in the last sentence of the book— "theirs was indeed a peculiarly American tragedy"—I wonder whether Bird has not really exemplified in his book what he is writing about. A tragedy does not mean, except in America, only a mistake that did not need to happen. Only a merely pragmatically oriented outlook can reduce the meaning of tragedy to such a mundane level. Evidently Mac Bundy could, in his last years, habitually drink too much; not a word about that here appears here. Bird has instead given a safely sanitized version of events. Mac Bundy's career was, in the eyes of those who watched him, a failure, and he seems to have shared something of that judgment; he must have felt his defeat more keenly than those with fewer abilities, or less ambitious intentions.

Bird's *The Color of Truth* contrasts with Graham Greene's *The Quiet American*, a novel which Halberstam refers to but which Bird does not cite. Greene understood how American naiveté and innocence meant that the best of intentions could lead to horrible social and political results. Pyle, the quiet American, lacked the sense of evil and sin that Greene held to be essential to mature human existence. I suppose Lyndon Johnson did, at his best, believe that he could bring a giant Tennessee Valley Authority to Southeast Asia. But this was an Asian world wholly beyond the ken of those who sought to fix things by some sort of ideal New Deal solution.

Macbeth is only one example of the varieties of possible tragedy. The problem, as I see it, is that Bird is too much like Greene's Pyle. If the White House had not been full of self-confident operatives convinced that they knew how to run the world, Vietnam would never have happened. It was not a classical tragedy. Nor is the failure of Mac Bundy's career of tragic proportions; how he dealt with what looks like his misspent White House years is another matter. Bird, who seems to think that the whole Cold War was an unnecessary error, and the decision to drop the atomic bombs wrong, has not with *The Color of Truth* at least changed my mind. Telford Taylor's argument that the Americans, by the standards of the Nuremberg trials, had through the Vietnam War committed war crimes of their own deserved some discussion by Bird. As it is, Bird's own gentle approach illustrates to me the soundness of Graham Greene's suspicion that Americans lack the sense of limits which would enable them to govern properly the Empire that they have been running. Pyle is too shallow and restricted to become a genuinely tragic figure. Both Bundys sound no match for Kissinger, which may be telling about some of the central flaws in the characteristically American approach to world politics.

* * *

Perhaps the Vietnam War remains so agonizing a moral conflict for me because evading the draft was so easy. I was getting deferments as a graduate student until I was old enough to be considered militarily over-the-hill. But the frustrations connected with that war seemed maddening. As I have said, it was clear to me in the spring of 1965 that the American involvement in Southeast Asia was escalating surreptitiously. And then, even after President Johnson in 1968 withdrew as a candidate for reelection, as many lives continued to be lost as ever. Richard Nixon became president, and a war that I considered incapable of being won kept dragging on. In 1969 the war intruded directly on my life, since that spring over a hundred students at Harvard took over a central university building, and the university president (Nathan Pusey) called on the Cambridge police to get them out. It now became a town-gown matter. A strike was called, and it quickly became apparent that the university community had fallen apart. One beloved teacher of mine, who had known me for a dozen years, stopped speaking to me because I was too sympathetic to the students; he was so upset over the university mess that he had a fatal heart attack. I have often worried whether I was right during that crisis. In 1997 Roger Rosenblatt, through a gripping narrative of the events that spring, entitled *Coming Apart,*[3] brought it all back to life for me.

At the time Rosenblatt was, like myself, a junior faculty member, but we did not know each other. He considers himself to have been a relative outsider, since he had come to Harvard only as a graduate student; yet he acknowledges that he was a "fair-haired boy" who held an administrative position in one of the undergraduate residences and served on the disciplinary committee which was elected to cope with any punishments to be meted out to the students involved.

Rosenblatt does not sound tortured by the dilemmas posed by these students. He tells us that he usually did not read newspapers in those days, and was as opposed to the war as most people he knew. In the end, sixteen people were dismissed or suspended for taking part in the civil disobedience, and as a result Rosenblatt found himself less popular with many students. Like most of us, he failed to achieve tenure at Harvard, but left academic life to become a freelance journalist. Thirty years later he contacted many of the people he worked with during those turbulent times and reports that "their passions seemed as alive as they were originally." This remains true for me too.

Still, there are problems with Rosenblatt's memoir. For he makes an inadequate effort to put these university troubles in military or political context. He does describe the momentous-seeming struggle in the winter of 1969 over ROTC courses, which culminated in the faculty voting to deny credit to them. They were anyway intellectually miserable, and took up a fourth of a student's academic time. ROTC was singled out as a symbol of the university's involvement in the war. The links between the federal government and Harvard had grown so complicated that students might well believe that by paralyzing the university they were accomplishing something politically.

At the time I was horrified by the idea of students occupying a building and rifling through confidential files. But I felt that if there was a question of the local police being called in, it should be a faculty-wide decision, not an administrative one. What happened was grim: Cambridge cops not only cleared the building, but chased and beat the kids. It was impossible for me to see the physical harm to the students without feeling paternally protective. Rosenblatt would not be surprised by my reaction, which was shared by others. But he entirely leaves out a key detail. Immediately after the sit-in was forcibly broken up, the students posted copies of an arresting letter on the trees in Harvard Yard. It had been composed by the dean (historian Franklin Ford) after the faculty's ROTC decision and was addressed to President Pusey. The dean said that the faculty was out of control, and he suggested that the dean of the law school might be able to figure out a way to circumvent the faculty decision. This was our dean undermining our decision as a faculty. It seemed incredible that he could have written such a letter, leaving it around for the students to find.

The faculty split in half, and a liberal caucus was at odds with a conservative one. (A tiny radical caucus also existed.) In meetings we voted by standing up, so commitments were public. Rosenblatt thinks of himself as a member of the liberal group, but in *Coming Apart* he now sounds like a conservative. It is demeaning to be told that "each group was made up of people who simply did not like some people in the other group." For Rosenblatt seemed little troubled by ethical quandaries, and he describes these events too much as a blip in his career. Also, he has unnecessarily filled the book with the names of people then involved (such as roommates Al Gore and Tommy Lee Jones) who later went on to worldly fame. To his credit, though, he discusses another important area of controversy; black studies also had their start at Harvard in 1969, and for those who would like the background to the growth of political correctness in universities, *Coming Apart* would be an excellent place to start.

I would contest some of the things Rosenblatt reports individuals having said at faculty meetings, and would challenge his appraisal of a few of the key people. At other points I honestly cannot remember some of what he recounts, and am inclined to give him the benefit of doubt. Once I started reading

Coming Part I could not put it down until I had finished. Sometimes when I go back to Harvard Square now, I can visualize the broken shop windows and the tear gas (that I have already mentioned) rising over the whole area—a great cloud that could be seen from neighboring towns. If Rosenblatt had not written this compelling story, one might wonder sometimes whether it had just been a private nightmare.

* * *

A fascinating and highly readable book, *The Cultural Cold War: The CIA and the World of Arts and Letters*[4], by Frances Stonor Saunders, came out first in Britain under the more provocative title: *Who Paid the Piper?* The reader ought not to be put off by the book's extravagant, almost McCarthyite opening pronouncement: "During the height of the Cold War, the US government committed vast resources to a secret program of cultural propaganda in western Europe." The author never attempts to calculate just how much money the CIA put up to back an organization like the Congress for Cultural Freedom, or any of the CIA's other efforts to sustain "the cultural cold war," all of which must have been, however vast-seeming, a drop in the bucket compared to the Pentagon's own expenditures. Saunders's way of beginning the book is a pretty good tip-off to what is the underlying slant to her narrative. The CIA, we are reminded in the Introduction,

> masterminded the overthrow of Premier Mossadegh in Iran in 1953, the ousting of the Arbenz government in Guatemala in 1954, the disastrous Bay of Pigs operation in 1961, the notorious Phoenix Program in Vietnam. It spied on tens of thousands of Americans, harassed democratically elected leaders abroad, plotted assassinations, denied these activities to Congress and, in the process, elevated the art of lying to new heights.

The concluding paragraph of the book reminds us again of CIA sins:

> the same people who read Dante and went to Yale and were educated in civic virtue recruited Nazis, manipulated the outcome of democratic elections, gave LSD to unwitting subjects, opened the mail of thousands of American citizens, overthrew governments, supported dictatorships, plotted assassinations, and engineered the Bay of Pigs disaster.

Now the Bay of Pigs was politically embarrassing, an almost comic foul-up, but I wonder on what grounds it can deserve to be singled out as a "disaster." And I cannot understand how Saunders lists the Cuban missile crisis as one among other American "imperial blunders." It remains unclear how an independent observer should be expected to judge the Soviets' 1956 march into Hungary, the British-French invasion of Suez, the French rule in post-World War II Algeria, or any other non-American misdeed. As a matter of fact,

I would contend that any great power that aspires to govern an empire is bound, without justifying them, to commit atrocities which look terrible in isolation. The Americans after World War II undertook a challenge of almost unprecedented scope in world history; a country with only limited experience in world affairs, and virtually no career civil service, undertook to withstand the aggressive intent of one of the world's most inhumane dictatorships. Now that Josef Stalin's Soviet Union is receding in memory, it may be harder for the present generation to appreciate what a terrible threat the Americans once sought to head off. I will not itemize all the successes of American policy in saving Western Europe from imminent collapse after World War II ended, but it would be a poor show for anybody now to take for granted what once seemed very much at issue.

I think I should put more of my cards on the table before beginning to consider this otherwise excellent book. The author has constructed an altogether engrossing narrative of how the CIA undertook to secretly fund various cultural organizations, including sending the Boston Symphony Orchestra abroad for a tour in the 1950s. The one institution that Saunders rightly concentrates on is the Congress for Cultural Freedom, and especially its creation of the monthly *Encounter* which first started coming out in 1953. But one might never guess from the step-by-step narrative that she constructs how magically wonderful a publication *Encounter* once was. The scandals associated with the revelations in 1966-67 of the way the CIA had been financially supporting *Encounter* meant, as we have seen, the effective end of that monthly's central role in the intellectual life of the West, but Saunders neglects to report, even in the context of some rather piously moralistic comments from one of the founders of *The New York Review of Books*, how many of *Encounters* own authors went on to publish later in that same presumably ethically superior bi-weekly.

Saunders does start off her book with a reminder of just what a mess Europe was in at the conclusion of World War II, and for instance how dicey a situation Germany's greatest musical performers posed, since so many of the most famous of them had politically compromised pasts: Wilhelm Furtwängler, Elisabeth Schwarzkopf, and Herbert von Karajan all had highly distasteful political involvements with Hitler's Third Reich. Melvin Lasky, who ended up the longest-serving editor of *Encounter*, first made his mark on the public stage of postwar Germany.

Stalin's Cominform was his instrument for political warfare, which replaced the perhaps more well-known Comintern. The American OSS had attracted during World War II to its intelligence work some of the brightest and most idealistic American intellectuals, and it was not surprising that although many of the most famous future leaders of academic life got their starts there, more than a few of them also stayed on in government service. The OSS was succeeded by the CIA, which was created by 1949 congressional legislation.

Although Saunders seems to take a dim view of George Kennan, who initiated the rationale for the containment policy, I think he deserves to stand as one of the great heroes of the Cold War. His firm belief that if the Soviets were checked from expanding their power outwardly they would eventually collapse from within was in my youth in political science scoffed at by hard-nosed Kremlinologists as an aspect of Kennan's alleged religious mysticism. And he went on to be one of the greatest historians of twentieth-century diplomatic relations with the Soviets. Saunders, doubtless starting out from an awareness of Kennan's retrospective justification of the CIA's funding of *Encounter*, on the grounds that Kennan felt that the absence of a ministry of culture in the U.S. left it few other avenues of matching the Soviets own efforts at cultural war, pokes at Kennan for having "introduced the concept of 'the necessary lie' as a vital constituent of American post-war diplomacy." I wonder whether Saunders thinks that Kennan, with a high position in State Department policymaking, should have been thinking like a proverbial saintly Pope. I would think it bootless to have to explain the unfortunate inevitability of "necessary" lies in great power politics. If Saunders were Swiss, rather than British, she might call upon a heritage of virtuous neutrality; but then even the Swiss, at least during World War II, turned out to prove how unsavory neutrals can sometimes be. Small states can sometimes enjoy the luxury of ethical high-mindedness impossible for the greatest world powers.

The CIA cultural endeavors require going back a bit in memory: an astonishingly large group of intellectuals have been attracted by the appeals of Marxism, and by the end of the 1940s it appeared that the Soviets, who exploded their first atomic bomb in the summer of 1949, were going to be relatively unchecked in the battle for the minds and hearts of the western world. The writers (like Arthur Koestler, Ignazio Silone, Richard Wright, Andre Gide, Louis Fischer, and Stephen Spender) who put their sour experiences with communism into *The God That Failed* (1949) seemed then relatively in the minority among the intelligentsia. These ex-communists could be too easily written off for their fanatical loss of faith in a set of Marxist dogmas that other more politically balanced people would have had the good sense not to succumb to in the first place. But freedom is a precarious entity, and democracy all too rare even now; some overall strategy to combat the Soviets was in order. South Korea's invasion from the north, not to mention the revelations about Soviet atomic spying that had proved successful both in Britain and America, seemed to mandate some public crusading response. Saunders quotes Arthur Schlesinger, Jr. as having maintained that "It seemed not unreasonable to help the people on our side. Of all the CIA's expenditures, the Congress for Cultural Freedom seemed its most worthwhile and successful." In those days around 1950 the Soviet Union was spending more on cultural propaganda in France by itself than the U.S. did in the entire world.

The means that the Americans chose to combat the Soviets were some dummy foundations that channeled money in the direction that the CIA ordained. The routes seem in hindsight almost palpably obvious. People like Arthur Schlesinger, Jr., or Isaiah Berlin for that matter, surely knew—without publicizing it—that the CIA had funded many of the cultural events that they and their friends participated in. Officially the leaders of the Congress for Cultural Freedom, of which *Encounter* was an offshoot, knew nothing about the sources of the money.

Saunders paints a graphic picture of someone like the high-living impresario Nicolas Nabokov, with his five successive wives, and the more monastic, wire-pulling Michael Josselson who went from being a cultural affairs officer for the American Military Government in Germany to be recruited into the CIA. Tom Braden, Irving Kristol, Melvin Lasky, Dwight Macdonald, and Raymond Aron are only some of the most well known of the leading figures in the tale that Saunders has so artfully reconstructed. Spender (who remained one of the editors of *Encounter* until the scandal about the secret CIA funding broke) turned out to be a somewhat hapless-seeming front-man, who should have known all along what was going on, but could put up a fuss afterwards about having been taken-for-granted, gulled and misled. (Although Saunders seems to share too many British anti-American prejudices—it is wrong to think that in America owning a Paul Robeson record "could be considered an act of subversiveness," or that Dashiell Hammett, with the help of his rich lover Lillian Hellman, can be said to have "died in poverty"—she does point out how British intelligence money also got passed on to *Encounter*.)

Saunders's *The Cultural Cold War* is filled with fascinating details, such as the 1977 *New York Times* story that the CIA had been involved in the publication of at least a thousand books. Some of these were unusually worthy, such as Milovan Djilas's *The New Class*. There is of course the serious issue of how this was secretly done; but I think that we should be driven to examine the more general problem of the role of secrets in a democratic society, and how they can be either justified or criticized. I think that minimizing secrecy ought to be an important political objective, but too often Saunders seems to imply that all democratic secrets are illegitimate. Painters (often left-wing), musicians, as well as thinkers, were the beneficiaries of American governmental largesse.

Saunders does come up with a couple of disturbing examples of how the powers-that-be were able twice to kill articles submitted to *Encounter*. But like others who have written about that monthly, with all their interest in the behind-the-scenes maneuvering, she does not seem to have read *Encounter* itself, which was capable of publishing serious critiques of American foreign policy. CIA money went to other publications as well—including *Partisan Review*, *Kenyon Review*, *Hudson Review*, *Sewanee Review*, the *Journal of the History of Ideas*, and *Daedalus*. Students of the Cold War period, which lasted after all for over forty years, will want to check Saunders's text to see just which intellectuals were the beneficiaries of the central political conflict of that era.

Paul Goodman and Conor Cruise O'Brien were the ones who most notably charged in public that *Encounter* had been the recipient of CIA funds, and then a 1966 *New York Times* article reinforced those claims. As we have discussed earlier, *Encounter* had been busy trying to find more savory sources of support, but it was already too late; Spender, Kristol, and Lasky did their best to defend their reputation for independence in the face of the first CIA news story. And a published letter signed by John Kenneth Galbraith, Kennan, Robert Oppenheimer, and Arthur Schlesinger, Jr. tried to proclaim the autonomy of the Congress for Cultural Freedom, without explicitly denying the CIA link. A 1967 article in the West Coast *Ramparts* was the straw the broke the camel's back; everything that O'Brien had once said seemed confirmed, and Lasky alone remained in place as an editor of *Encounter*. Spender (along with Frank Kermode) had resigned. When Spender's wife went to collect his belongings from *Encounter*'s office, she found that his "locked cupboard had been broken into." Such shenanigans were obviously not up to the best standards of British fairplay, but still small potatoes compared to the deadly characteristic struggles that took place behind the Iron Curtain.

Saunders does a good job of assessing the list of those people within the Congress for Cultural Freedom who knew, or should have known, about the CIA funding. Many innocents were compromised, including people in the "Third World" as well as some within the realm of the Soviets who had thought they were reaching out to impartial authorities in the West. One CIA operative even published an article, titled "I'm Glad the CIA is 'Immoral,'" that spring of 1967, sensationally maintaining that they had put an "agent" into being an editor of *Encounter*. In explaining such an apparent indiscretion on the part of a CIA employee Saunders persuasively proposes that someone within the CIA had wanted to use the occasion to break with the non-communist left.

There were real victims of what had happened, and intellectuals could be as corrupted by money and power as anybody else. If there were those who were suckers, hypocrisy also cropped up, as the *Partisan Review* (hardly possessing clean hands) published a moralistic disclaimer about the wrongs of such hidden governmental subvention of magazines. Spender never bought or read another issue of *Encounter* (which lasted until 1991, not 1990, as Saunders would have it), and was knighted in 1983. Saunders ends *The Cultural Cold War* on a somewhat journalistic note, as she tries to make out that the "proponents of the Cold War…were also in some measure its victims." For most of the people whose careers I have followed, the *Encounter* episode was merely an intermediate way station to further successes. And the proper relation between public money and private culture remains an issue that has rarely been examined. (Although Canada has had its Canada Council and Public Lending Right Commission, America has never had its equivalents. Thanks to the umbrella of the American military Canada's defense budget has been proportionately among the lowest in Nato.) Polemicizing about the admittedly long list of wicked deeds perpetrated by the CIA does not by any means solve the dilemmas that we ought to be facing up to. In my view Saunders's *The Cultural Cold War* should be considered a beginning in the exploration of how we should proceed in the future.

Notes

1. Kai Bird, *The Color of Truth: McGeorge Bundy and William Bundy – Brothers in Arms* (New York: Simon & Schuster, 1998).
2. David Halberstam, *The Best and the Brightest* (New York: Random House, 1972).
3. Roger Rosenblatt, *Coming Apart: A Memoir of the Harvard Wars of 1969* (Boston: Little Brown, 1997).
4. Frances Stonor Saunders, *The Cultural Cold War: The CIA and the World of Arts and Letters* (New York: The New Press, 1999).

9

On Intellectuals and Exile

I cannot imagine most of the greatest figures in modern social philosophy functioning at all well in any university setting. Machiavelli, Hobbes, Rousseau, John Stuart Mill, and Marx all did nicely without university affiliations. And Sigmund Freud, the thinker whose career I know best, never got beyond a marginal position at the University of Vienna, and devised other means for exerting the influence of his teachings. So I see no sound reason why we should expect that really important and original work should necessarily arise within an academic context.

If one confines attention to the most recent period and discusses what has happened over the last generation to alter the gulf between the educated public and university intellectuals, it seems far too early to make any secure judgments. The appearance of Allan Bloom's best-selling *The Closing of the American Mind* in 1987 can hardly be taken to mean that the so-called decline of the public intellectual has been reversed. Yet it would surely be wrong to think that only left-wing writers are entitled to have their popular successes applauded. John Kenneth Galbraith was widely known within academic life before he published *The Affluent Society*, but only immediately thereafter did he succeed on a genuinely broad public stage.

It is notoriously hard to generalize about anything as unexpected and mysterious as the flowering of talent. For myself, I see no reason why anyone should expect that social prophecy, for example, will emanate from a university context. James Baldwin's *The Fire Next Time* was read as avidly among my friends in graduate school as I like to imagine Tom Paine's *Common Sense* was in the late eighteenth century. Yet Baldwin and Paine would both have been out of place within an academic setting.

I believe that there should be a gap between what goes on in universities and in the general society as a whole. I see no reason why our higher learning should be watered down to the lowest common denominator. We do our students a great disservice when we transform our universities into training centers for life. Secondary education in the high schools has fallen down on its educational job precisely because of too great an eagerness to satisfy the immediate and practical demands of so-called relevance. The upshot has been that we have cheated people out of a unique opportunity to detach themselves from their parochial cultural backgrounds. A university should ideally give a precious breathing space, a time when, for a few short years, it becomes possible to come in contact with the best that has been said and thought in at least Western culture. So I am in favor of the old ideal of the ivory tower.

Under today's circumstances, such a project is not easily viable, but still I think that we have to do the best we can. In Canada, where I once taught, university admissions policies, whatever the changing (but essentially meaningless) grade-averages required, amounted to a policy of open enrolment. So Canadian colleges were not so much attaching students to the great traditions of Western thought as they were socializing them into contemporary North American society. New immigrant groups are eager to send their children to such universities; and although the professors may have been trained in tackling some of the greatest issues of human thought, they end up in practice teaching the elementary rules of reading and writing.

The overall functions of universities have been transformed in the course of this past century, and the results are by no means automatically for the better. My hunch would be that seventy or eighty years ago the students who graduated from a few of the best high schools were better educated than most of today's university graduates. As institutions, universities nowadays provide democratic services that before they never were expected to fulfill; but the often intellectually demoralizing university milieu is not especially conducive to preparing us as writers to reach out to the largest problems of society as a whole.

Universities still do offer their faculties both salaries and abundant free time, and for that we should be immensely grateful. It is also a challenge to try to reconstruct the essential ingredients of a general education for students who are so ill prepared for contemplating the life of the mind. However niggardly the public funding for universities may have recently become in Canada, they do have both immense numbers of students and a large variety of campuses. I think that throughout North America university education has reached out to staggering quantities of young people; whether we are truly succeeding in the ancient task of higher education is, I am afraid, altogether another story.

I hope that my reflections do not sound like a lament of their own, an account of decline and fall. But, given our special social tasks, I see no special reason why genuinely creative people should exclusively seek a life within academic walls, except for the critical security that universities continue to provide. It is nonsense, I think, to suppose that a generation of intellectuals somehow migrated to universities, and withdrew elsewhere. We have more than our share of unfortunates within the academy, and some of the smartest people I know, with the broadest range of public concerns, can be found in publishing, law, public service, and elsewhere.

A genuine university intellectual is, in my experience, too rare a bird. We do far too little to encourage intellectuality within university life. Unfortunately, much of our modern mass higher education works at cross purposes with the goals of creativity and research; I shudder at the thought of the depressing experience of almost all university committee work.

I suspect that a good deal of the indictment of the state of our culture in Russell Jacoby's *The Last Intellectuals*[1] comes from his taking a narrower view of creative activity than I myself would be inclined to adopt. For example, it is striking to me that he makes no mention of Gary Wills. I think that Wills, who does have an adjunct teaching appointment at Northwestern, is not only a great success at the most popular level but has been determined to make his mark in the strict world of scholarship as well. I have seen him on occasion upset the apple carts of some of our most learned scholars; and yet Wills has no trouble turning out bestsellers that are also serious contributions to public thinking. Jacoby does mention the name of Walter Lippmann once as the kind of generalist figure he admires from the past, but I would have thought that Wills was a worthy, even if wholly distinct, successor. A writer such as Jonathan Schell, much of whose politics I cannot share, would serve to answer Jacoby's quest for independent and publicly oriented intellectuals. Novelists like Toni Morrison and D. M. Thomas may not qualify as "young," but they are intellectuals whose inspiration has come from outside academic life. Furthermore, to look for a youthful C. Vann Woodward—also not mentioned by Jacoby—would be a contradiction in terms, for Woodward became partly revered for his years of past excellences.

Much as I genuinely admire how challenging Jacoby has been in all his books, too much of his argument in *The Last Intellectuals* arises from within the confines of the sectarianism of the left. What he seems to be bemoaning amounts largely to the failure of Marxist criticism to fulfill its large-scale social purposes. Nothing seems to me surprising or notable in devotees of a secular religion becoming ingrown and irrelevant.

But it is odd to complain about the loss of publicly accessible university writers at a time when universities are more democratically ambitious than at almost any time in the past. Now that Edmund Wilson is dead he has been canonized; even his journals are publicly studied. But while he was alive this sort of standing was hardly secure. I remember that when he taught one year at Harvard almost nobody took his graduate course, and certainly none of his texts were touted in the way we (probably rightly) only do those by deceased authors. Can one imagine Lytton Strachey coping with our first-year students and also writing his delicious prose? As far as I am concerned, we cannot have our cake and eat it too; we have undertaken the task of providing extraordinary numbers of people with what passes for higher education. And some of the people who do it creditably are by no measure of things capable of being creative intellectuals in their own right.

Originality arises in the interstices of society; creative work makes itself known in unexpected ways. It is surprising to me that we have as much aliveness in universities as we do. But I do not think one should expect to find the sole home of creativity in academic life. Nevertheless, Stephen Jay Gould wa not that old, taught full-time at a university, and yet reached as broad a public as any of the older figures about whom it is possible to become more nostalgic.

Canada has had some special problems of its own. It seems to me a national scandal, for example, that in the whole country there are only a tiny handful of regular newspaper book reviewers. It is impossible to conceive of a culture in which people write books without needing a responsive echo; yet no author in Canada can count on any regular body of reviewing opinion. With all the ink that has been spilt over the state of Canadian national culture, no one has yet devised a simple expedient of getting the better newspapers to hire a staff of full and part-time people who specialize in book-reviewing.

On this score Canada is worse off than the United States, where books are more apt to get a serious hearing from reviewers. And this is not just a matter of population, for Great Britain is, in turn, vastly more literate than America. Not long ago, and it is probably still true, as many books were published each year in England as in the whole of the United States. It has happened to me that when books of mine have come out in England they have been immediately reviewed in a batch of Sunday newspapers and weeklies, and by a reliably predictable group of reviewers. England still has a cohesive national culture, much more so than America or Canada, and the success of literacy in Britain derives, I think, in large part from the class structure that the universities have done little to challenge.

Old World culture was more secure and established—also elitist. In order to write successfully for a public audience one has to know something of who is out there reading. But as we have democratized education on this continent, and tried to make it more broadly available, we have simultaneously made it mean a good deal less. So we have university graduates who are barely literate, certainly not especially worth writing for.

We also have a society that is more open, and less constricted in social movement, than would be the case on the European continent or in Mrs. Thatcher's England. In contrast, our children, from a wide variety of walks of life, are being raised pretty much in response to the same social stimuli. We probably will continue to expect too little of them culturally, and not encourage youngsters enough to go off in any deviant or "elitist" directions. But then they are less likely to suffer the agonies of isolation and misunderstanding that go with creative work; they will, of course, miss out on the ecstasies of originality as well, but then our society, on this side of the North Atlantic, has always been committed to the advantages of uniformity.

Being different is traditionally a problem, and I see no change within the last generation. No genuine intellectual can be successfully "professionalized," or distracted from his unique calling, whatever the democratic pressures from within our society, nor can creativity be engineered through planned social policy. But one can do the best one can to think without preconceptions. It is therefore still possible to offer our students a model of thoughtfulness and learning. And, despite the rubbish that any culture is bound to surround us with, it is conceivable that one write as directly and openly as possible.

* * *

Socrates could have fled Athens rather than drink from the cup of hemlock, but chose otherwise. James Joyce, living away from his native Ireland, kept hearing the note of banishment in Shakespeare's plays. When the citizens in *Coriolanus* first chime in with the judgment that he be exiled, Coriolanus retorts:

> You common cry of curs, whose breath I hate
> As reek o' th' rotten fens, whose loves I prize
> As the dead carcasses of unburied men
> That do corrupt my air, I banish you!
> And here remain with your uncertainty.
> Let every feeble rumour shake your hearts!
> Your enemies, with nodding of their plumes,
> Fan you into despair! Have the power still
> To banish your defenders, till at length
> Your ignorance – which finds not till it feels,
> Making but reservation of yourselves,
> Still your own foes – deliver you as most
> Ablated captives to some nation
> That won without blows! Despising,
> For you, the city, thus I turn my back,
> There is a world elsewhere.[2]

Such powerful sentiments make a kind of sense that is only partly under-stood by the time of the twentieth century. In an earlier time it once did seem plausible for political theorists to propose a state of nature. That concept of a pre-social existence implied that either human beings had deteriorated from a golden age, as in Rousseau's thinking, or else that civilized community was threatened by an eruption of barbarism, as in Hobbes's system. Locke's own version of the state of nature was the one to be treasured by liberalism; the founders of American democracy, for example, proposed that they were with-drawing their allegiance from George III and instead setting up their own new community. "In the beginning," Locke had argued, "all the world was America."

The idea was that if a political community felt tyrannized over, the people can pull out, dissolve the social contract, and then re-establish a new system with a different set of rules. If leaders ever violate the trust of their followers, then a peaceful transition can make way for a different system altogether.

Some such mythology underlies modern democracies. Yet one of the most frightening features of twentieth-century history was the very disappearance of the social luxuries of all preceding times. Statelessness is a uniquely modern phenomenon, one that forces us to rethink all prior notions of exile. For when the Nazis withdrew citizenship from native German Jews, and then expelled them from the nation's borders, that meant exile in a wholly novel sense. For no state can now be expected to admit citizens without proper papers. Yet Hitler taught us a lesson that we might not like to hear. Under the conditions of contemporary life, the Lockean state of nature has vanished. If the state withdraws citizenship, there may now be no place to go. It turns out that we are more dependent on the state for our liberties than any of us might like to think. We ought not to forget the plight of displaced peoples, boatloads of human beings refused landing rights. Refugees and detention camps have changed our image of exile. To be forced out from a country can entail something different from old-fashioned concepts of exile. Modern technology means that the empty spaces that once existed politically are apt to be no longer there.

Spiritually, circumstances have changed as well. It is true that all intellectual activity involves some version of inner exile, withdrawal from the surrounding community. People who are at one with their fellow creatures do not feel the necessity of coming to terms with the need to challenge other beings. England's seventeenth century, for example, is usually considered the greatest single period of political philosophy in the English language; the fundamental social conflicts that resulted in a civil war prompted thinkers to get beyond the usual banalities of existence, and promoted fundamental reconsiderations of social life. If North America has been relatively impoverished in social and political thinking, at least compared to Western Europe, it may be because all the good fortune of this continent has meant that people could evade reconsidering the exceptional circumstances that permitted them to be relatively lazy intellectually.

At the same time there is something different in the kind of detachment creative thinkers are apt to have in our own time. Machiavelli, for example, was a high civil servant for some years, and it was only after he was put out to pasture that he wrote his masterpieces. When he felt able to throw down a gauntlet to all previous political thought, insisting on the radical divorce between Christian morality and the public necessity of reason of state, he could call upon years of practical political experience. He dedicated *The Prince* to a living political leader, and yet proposed ideas that would remain notoriously like the devil's advice even now, almost 500 years later. One of the marks of his break with contemporary political thought was that he wrote in Italian, as a Renaissance man, rather than in Latin. He was both at one with his time and yet opposed to it—a phenomenon we rarely see in our own time.

It has to be puzzling what sort of audience contemporary social philosophers can be expected to have in mind. Someone like Hannah Arendt has to be considered an exception; herself an exile from Germany and its cultural traditions, she insisted on chastising her native land at the same time that she tried to renew its kind of philosophic thinking. Her contempt for what her book on Eichmann called "the banality of evil" was directed toward the low level of thinking characteristic not just of the bureaucratic mind but of the corrupted state of mass society in general.

The conditions of modern life have insidiously undermined the possibilities of composing fundamental social insights, so that commentators have been tempted to think that the great tradition of political philosophy, that started in ancient Greece, has come to its end. The death of political thought has been repeatedly proposed in the last half-century, especially by those most responsible for promoting its demise. Academic trade-unionism has divided up sociology, philosophy, psychology, history, and politics into narrow compartments so that social thinking would be unrecognizable to our predecessors.

Too much recent political thought has had a hothouse quality to it, as writers think they are working in the great tradition when in reality they are simply writing for one another, commenting not even on the leading figures of past centuries but instead elaborating on the most recent outpourings from university life. If one protests that in the guise of being loyal to academic trade unions the great questions of the past are being neglected, one risks being accused of the supposedly dread crime of elitism. Hobbes never ran any such risk by allowing his work to pander to the demands of everyday life. His complicated reasoning was correctly perceived as a threat to the powers-that-be, and he high-tailed it to France for the composition of *The Leviathan*. He, like Machiavelli before him, would be denounced as a disturber of the intellectual peace, and both of them have had to endure a rather unsavory reputation ever since.

But until the last century such people could expect at least the support that comes from being critically examined. Creativity requires social supports, and contemporary society makes it hard to imagine how old-line social and political thought can be successfully undertaken. It can be painful to be different, and the lures of being conditioned to conformity undermine the possibilities of detachment. Thorstein Veblen, perhaps the one North American thinker sure to be known abroad, once wrote a piece on the special position of the Jew as a natural outsider, and Veblen, who himself had one of the most wretched academic careers imaginable, knew at first-hand how detachment can be both painful as well as desirable. To complicate matters, Veblen has been understood as writing on behalf of the intellectual pre-eminence of Jews in response to the Balfour Declaration. A Jewish state, Veblen feared, would wipe out the marginality that, he held, was a key to Jewish originality. Such an idea would hardly be considered politically correct, but then Veblen scorned the idea of being socially acceptable.

Internal exile may be harder to achieve than it once was. Efforts to educate a larger proportion of society than ever have been accompanied by an unprecedented degree of semi-literacy. We have succeeded in producing more than one generation of students who would not dream of reading a morning newspaper. We know of civilized Germans who remained at home despite their inner opposition to Nazism; that such people could survive at all is testimony to their participation in traditions of thought that provided them a sustenance from the past that I doubt would be possible today. (Pasternak's *Doctor Zhivago* seemed such a miracle because it demonstrated the survival of humane Russian high culture despite years of Stalinism.) As Madame de Staël declared after the French Revolution, "liberty is ancient, despotism is modern." Any such aphorism is bound to be at odds with today's conventional wisdom implying that history moves in a progressive direction, ensuring as a matter of course greater harmony and enlightenment. The impact of television and Hollywood can amount to the watering down of ideas to the lowest common denominator. It is disturbing to travel in Europe and find the same movies playing as back at home. The impossibility of escaping from a common culture does not seem to me a happy prospect.

I am more hesitant to speak about what exile can mean for strictly literary writers. Someone like Vladimir Nabokov, for example, managed to flourish in more than one language. Thanks probably to his aristocratic past he succeeded in coping with life outside his native land, but it can hardly be an accident, or just a tribute to excessive taxes for writers here, that shortly after the success of *Lolita* he went to live in Switzerland.

Edmund Wilson is another example of someone who drew strength from inner traditions at odds with his surroundings. He kept appealing back to an older America, less commercially driven and more committed to the enduring significance of great books. His good friend F. Scott Fitzgerald concluded *The Great Gatsby* with a lyrical testimony to a lost world.

Nostalgia, it might be thought, can be comparatively easy and come too cheaply. But an opposition between the old and the new can itself be a source of creativity. Nabokov did not have to spell out concretely what he felt confronted with on this continent, although he did write an autobiographical *Speak Memory!* And Joseph Conrad did not have to recur explicitly to his Polish roots in order to alert us to at least one source of the depths of his insights. It seems almost unbelievable that in a second language Conrad could achieve the simplicity and grandeur of his English. Yet it would not be far-fetched to be reminded with *Lord Jim*, and the theme of betrayal, of Conrad's own feelings connected with the abandonment of the long-suffering Poland he had left behind.

Exile is a tragic inevitability, and such a disability seems to be an essential constituent of strength. André Gide seems out of style now, in a way that was not true in my youth; but in his *Philoctetes* he described how an invalid hermit devotes himself to something above the gods. As Edmund Wilson put it in *The Wound and the Bow*, the misfortune of Philoctetes's island exile enabled him to perfect himself. It is, I think, a relatively recent idea that genius and disease are inevitably linked with one another. The notion that one cannot have insight without suffering was shared by Thomas Mann as well as Sigmund Freud, each of whom came to know exile.

Tradition has it that when Mann was asked, on arriving in California before World War II, how he would manage without German culture, he retorted: "I *am* German culture." Yet after the war he went back to Europe. In the case of Freud, this pioneer of modern thought wrote again and again about how alienated he felt in Vienna, and it was true that his reputation abroad was always far ahead of any deference he was granted in the city to which he was brought as a small child. Yet despite Freud's expressed distaste for Vienna, he stayed there long after it had ceased to be safe, and only because of his foreign contacts was he able to get away in 1938 to the safety of England, as he put it: "to die in freedom."

Political exile is not identical to being a spiritual outcast. And neither form of being an outsider is any kind of insurance for being creative. Much of human experience leaves sensitive people feeling estranged. It used to be the self-proclaimed function of university education to promote estrangement. The whole concept of an ivory tower was that education be in principle not relevant to everyday life: in the precious breathing space of higher education there was an opportunity to help detach students from their inevitably limited backgrounds. Any such intention of bringing students in contact with the best that has been said and thought, at odds with life as they know it, is not apt to be popular today. The loss of that particular kind of exile may be at the expense of future generations.

Notes

1. Russell Jacoby, *The Last Intellectuals: American Culture in the Age of Academe* (New York, Basic Books, 1987).
2. III, iii.

10

Methodology

One of the most fascinating intellectual issues of our day concerns the uses of modern psychology in the study of history. How can ideas drawn primarily from clinical work with more or less disturbed patients be of help in our understanding of political and social life, past as well as present? And to what extent are such psychiatric ideas sufficiently humanistic, yet at the same time scientifically disciplined enough, to be of importance for all students of society?

Dr. Robert J. Lifton, first a professor of psychiatry at Yale, then at John Jay College in New York and finally at Cambridge City Hospital, has spent decades exploring the frontiers between psychoanalytic psychology and history. As he rightly maintains in the introduction to a collection of his essays, *History and Human Survival*, "The boundaries set by traditional academic disciplines, and even by traditional intellectual callings, have less and less to do these days with real concerns or with affinities of one mind for another."[1] Thoroughly steeped in the best of contemporary psychoanalysis as well as modern social science, Lifton has succeeded in overcoming formidable barriers to interdisciplinary communication.

Lifton earlier published an important and influential book on thought reform in China, another volume on the survivors of Hiroshima (which won a National Book award), and a book on Mao Tse-tung and the Chinese cultural revolution. Along with a study on the role of death symbolism in an age of nuclear weapons, Lifton has become one of the most prolific writers in this new field where human inner psychodynamics are studied in relation to the external world.

The book's most memorable single essay is an unforgettable account of the minds and hearts of the survivors of the Hiroshima bomb. Working within the intellectual tradition of Freud as an observer of human affairs, Lifton went to Japan and interviewed the survivors of that catastrophe. In addition to his interpretation of the psychological reactions of these people, Lifton has some provocative ideas about how the mere existence of nuclear arms now impairs our relationship to death and symbolic immortality, and therefore interferes with the possibilities of our successfully handling these new weapons.

Lifton's activities as a "psychohistorian" carry him in many directions in this book. It has, for example, an engrossing section on Japanese youth, who have played a notable part in the whole youth rebellion that at one time seemed to be sweeping the industrialized world. Since Japan has had claims to having the most militant students and some of the most conflict-ridden universities, the efforts of a broad-gauged psychiatrist in understanding the youth of that country are welcome.

At this stage of the game little doubt should exist that modern psychology has to be considered relevant to political and social life. Whether one is writing about the effects of nuclear holocausts or the motivation behind youth rebellions, on racism or biography, witchcraft in the seventeenth century or indoctrination in our own day, the issue is not so much *if* one needs to rely on psychological principles, but rather *how* one does so, and which approaches are most likely to be successful. Lifton has emerged from within the Freudian tradition, aware of individual psychodynamics and yet sophisticated about social life, and as such he surely stands as one of the most notable workers in the area of psychology and history.

Many people have praised the merits of interdisciplinary collaboration, and certainly one would expect to find that workers in fields like psychoanalysis and history would have much in common. For instance, both analysts and historians seek to reconstruct the past on the basis of fragmentary evidence, yet in as scientific a spirit as is compatible with the frequently subjective nature of the material they have at hand. In the earlier part of the twentieth century, professional historians were rather standoffish about what seemed to them the somewhat grandiose social speculations of Freud and his early followers, yet more recently, partly due to the influence of Erik H. Erikson but also traceable to the growing understanding of the significance of unconscious motivation for all the social sciences, historians have shown an exceptional receptivity to the possibilities inherent in a depth psychological perspective.

If such interdisciplinary work is to accomplish some of its objectives, however, the relationship between psychoanalysis and history must be a two-way street. As each of us can hope that through the study of another professional discipline we can be partially freed from the parochialism of our own educational background, then the analytically oriented worker must expect to change and broaden his scope through contact with the historian every bit as much as the latter has had to adapt his own earlier preconceptions in the light of psychoanalytic insights.

The Psychoanalytic Interpretation of History[2] illustrates some of the key problems involved in any of this work. The title leads one to expect far more than any collection of essays by different authors can ever succeed in accomplishing, and one of the difficulties all along with using psychodynamic ideas in the social sciences has been the magical expectations with which people have undertaken this work. In his foreword to this volume, the historian William Langer cautiously points out, "One can probe the personality of men of the past only if they have left behind them a generous amount of correspondence, autobiographical material, and kindred records." Even though the clinician is used to working with patients able to limit and correct the analyst's interpretations, whereas the historian has no such living check (save for colleagues and his own professional conscience), the student of history has one paradoxical advantage. Contemporaries of our own are all too apt to be so familiar with psychological terminology that when they deceive themselves, they do so within this new framework, whereas at least past figures are apt to have been defensive in terms of religious and metaphysical concepts. As Langer points out, where useful historical records exist "they are apt to be of special value because they were set down not with an eye to the analyst, but for very mundane, practical purposes."

Essays brought together like these are bound to leave an uneven impression. Perhaps because of his lack of concentration on Anglo-American trends and his knowledge of continental developments, Ronald Grimsley's "Psychoanalysis and Literary Criticism in Historical Perspective" seemed to me outstanding. Robert G. L. Waite's "Adolf Hitler's Anti-Semitism" is a fascinating study of how the dictator's personality affected his political convictions and style. And Peter Loewenberg's examination of Theodor Herzl is an excellent example of how an author's wise initial choice of a biographical subject may go far to explain the successful use of psychological concepts in understanding a political leader.

Throughout almost all the essays, however, runs one defect: the relative lack of distance toward contemporary moral values. Too often psychoanalysis tends to get used, sometimes unintentionally, for the sake of explaining the exceptional and the deviant, whereas conformism and lack of individuality would seem equally worthy of psychodynamic inquiry. Is it really correct to brand Hitler and Stalin with psychopathological labels, instead of the more old-fashioned and straightforward terms for evil and depravity? Is power-seeking in democracies any more psychologically "normal," or are ordinary Western politicians not every bit as capable of being described by pathological labels as those figures who seem extraordinarily political noxious to our standards of ethics? If psychoanalysis and history cannot take us to any intellectual millennium, they can at least help to stretch our imaginations, provided we do not use another professional discipline simply to reaffirm with new terminology what we think we already know to be true.

* * *

"A new type of man is taking over leadership of the most technically advanced companies in America. In contrast to the jungle-fighter industrialists of the past, he is driven not to build or to preside over empires, but to organize winning teams. Unlike the security-seeking organization man, he is excited by the chance to cut deals and to gamble....And he is troubled by it: the new industrial leader can recognize that his work develops his head but not his heart."

This arresting passage from *The Gamesman*[3] epitomizes Michael Maccoby's bold new departure from the old "organization man" and "lonely crowd" depictions of the corporate personality. Some thirty years ago, psychoanalyst Maccoby set out to study the personality types running America's advanced-technology firms. He talked to 250 managers at twelve major companies and then made a special in-depth study of two dynamic multinationals that serve as models for other corporations.

Maccoby's background includes a close association with Erich Fromm, and he both draws from and expands on some of Fromm's key concepts. In particular, Maccoby is interested in finding out how work and character influence each other and why—since every organization or society has a "psychostructure" that selects different character types for different roles—certain types of people stay at a given level in a corporation and fail if they rise higher, while other types of people reach the top. When he began his study, Maccoby knew that traditional clinical approaches would produce misleading results, so he adopted two methods used by cultural anthropologists: participant observation and wide-ranging discussion. Personality differences among the managers—their motives, traits, and values —differences that determined their managerial styles and eventually the level to which they could rise in the hierarchy, were discovered during the course of a three- to twenty-hour interview structured around a comprehensive questionnaire, dream analysis, and Rorschach tests.

The managers—and in some cases their wives and secretaries—were perfectly willing to cooperate in the project. They, too, wanted to learn what motivates good managers, because they had an uneasy feeling that their work was developing certain narrow, occupationally useful qualities in them at the expense of broader personal potentials.

Maccoby discovered four basic types of manager, each with a clearly defined set of personality traits. Perhaps surprisingly, he found that neither the perfectionist "craftsman," who competes mainly against himself, nor the "jungle fighter," who competes against everyone else, reaches the top anymore. At least in the corporations he studied, Maccoby found a compelling need for—of all things—trust and interdependence. Moreover, he found that the "company man," who made it big in the 1950s by fitting in and sporting a gray-flannel suit, now accepts a bureaucratic role and expects to go no higher than middle management.

Maccoby's thesis is that a new type of man, the "gamesman" of the book's title, has assumed the leadership of today's most innovative businesses. The higher up the corporate ladder one looks in a large electronics firm, for example, the more likely one is to find a gamesman. Though John F. Kennedy never met a payroll, he seems to be the model and ideal of the breed. Fascinated by technique and a lover of the calculated risk, the gamesman excels at problem solving and coolness under stress. He is fair and open, but lacking in convictions. His independence and inventiveness allow him to adapt easily to changing markets and technologies. He must assemble winning teams, and to do so he must be seductive and supportive, responsive to different human needs. Cooperation is necessary if his gambles are to pay off. But the spirit of cooperation at work does not necessarily foster real caring at home, as Maccoby soon discovered.

After Maccoby had conducted the first round of interviews, he was invited by a friend to visit Bohemian Grove, an executive retreat north of San Francisco where corporate presidents encamp for informal lakeside talks with government officials, military men, university presidents, and a smattering of movie stars. A weekend there, his friend thought, would allow Maccoby to see executives in an atmosphere that would encourage them to express their natural impulses.

"It was a totally male society...and the adolescent *macho* quality was emphasized by the fact that you were encouraged to urinate against the nearest redwood," reports Maccoby. "Every year a play is put on in which men take women's roles. The play I saw was full of anti-feminine digs and humor that expressed the executive's estrangement from home and family. Example: The president of 'Amalgamated Consolidated, Incorporated' calls in his son, who has done poorly as vice-president for public relations. The president tells him he is no good. 'I'm glad', he says, 'that you mother isn't alive to see your failure.' 'But Dad,' the son answers, 'she is alive; I saw her this morning.' 'Is that so?' says the president. 'Well, I can't be expected to know every little thing that happens around here.' Loud laughter."

Of course this story is an exaggeration, at least for the majority of those interviewed by Maccoby. Still, from the start, Maccoby wanted to understand what toll the technological-corporate life took on the managers' emotional lives. Meanwhile, some managers volunteered to participate in the study precisely because they believed their work had caused them to fail as husbands and fathers, and they were eager to find out why. *The Gamesman* is, then, broader in scope than it may at first appear. It tells us not only about managers in relation to their work but also about their personal lives, their feelings about social and political issues, and their larger ideals and concerns.

For the most part, Maccoby found that the gamesman lacks deep self-understanding and shows little concern for the social consequences of his work. The ideals of cooperation and interdependence notwithstanding, in all the companies Maccoby studied he found the spirit of competition rampant. He also discovered that each type of manager is motivated differently: "the craftsmen by interest and pleasure in building and bettering the standard; the jungle fighter by his drive for power over others to escape being crushed by them; the company man by fear of failure and wish for approval; and the gamesman by glory and the need to be in control."

Maccoby concludes that "given our socioeconomic system, with its stimulation of greed, its orientation to control and predictability, its valuation of power and prestige above justice and creative human development, these fair-minded gamesmen may be as good as we can expect from corporate leaders." Throughout the book Maccoby's concern lies in evaluating social systems in terms of how well they help to mobilize the creative energies of different types of people. He thinks that most of the managers he studied were not neurotic but underdeveloped, and he sees the prevalence of gamesmanship as one symptom of a misguided society rather than as an object of moralistic wrath. Fearing that careerism may become our major national pastime, Maccoby appeals for a new corporate type, one in whom the qualities of the heart would be encouraged in addition to those of the head.

*   *   *

It was not so long ago that the title of a book called *Judaism and Psychoanalysis*,[4] ed., Mortimer Ostow, would have raised eyebrows among "orthodox" analysts. Carl Jung had only been one of the earliest and most noteworthy to point out some of the links between Judaism and psychoanalysis. Freud had chosen the Gentile Jung to be his successor precisely because the founder of analysis sought to free his movement from its Jewish origins. The failure of the collaboration between Freud and Jung sealed Freud's determination to present his ideas as a scientifically neutral body of knowledge, to be understood independent of its cultural setting. The quest for universalism in analysis lasted beyond Freud's death in 1939.

Martin Bergmann's essay "Moses and the Evolution of Freud's Jewish Identity," when originally presented in 1974, was sharply criticized for its boldness. Putting Freud in the religious context of the heritage of Judaism seemed to some a heretical line of thinking. Rereading Bergmann's essay now, however, I find it a sound, responsible effort to come to terms with a side of Freud's mind that more rationalistic students of his life have tended to underestimate. Freud sought not only to emancipate himself from the narrow confines of his beginnings but also to criticize the nature of Christian ethics. Doubtless there was in Freud, as Bergmann suggested, an old wish to convert; but in his maturity Freud sought to replace Christianity with a higher, superior form of ethics.

Mortimer Ostow's introductory essay acknowledges the mystical element in the profession of analysis. Ostow also argues that "the structure of the early psychoanalytic community suggests that of a cult, or at least, a dissident sect, secular if not religious." Such a proposition is the only way to begin to make sense of the historical record. It is hardly surprising that Freud and the early analysts were ambivalent about their Jewishness. It is well past the time when to treat Freud and his followers as realistic, struggling human beings invites the charge of desecration. Ostow can also perceive the limitations to Freud's own views on religious matters, without implying disrespect for Freud's pioneering efforts.

Ostow proposes to introduce clinical experience into the well-known theories about psychoanalysis and Judaism. Contemporary studies should see Jewish behavior "as determined not merely by ancient history, but by subsequent history and current experiences." Essays by Ostow and Jacob A. Arlow illustrate clinical psychoanalytic studies and also attempt to "apply" psychoanalysis to social crises and political movements. However, Ostow does not specify clearly enough that every conceptual approach will have its own clinical biases.

A volume of selected essays is difficult to summarize, but the significance of this subject matter helps overcome the usual obstacles. Arlow's "Consecration of the Prophet" gives an account of the invigoration coming from the mystical revelations of a mission, which is compared to a hypomanic state. Richard L. Rubenstein's "The Meaning of Anxiety in Rabbinic Judaism" adds a theological perspective; he raises the question of the significance of an archaic mother figure. Historians and clinicians should be relieved that it no longer needs to be the case (as Ostow tells us it was when he studied at the New York Psychoanalytic Institute) that there be "an unspoken gentleman's agreement that in psychoanalysis one does not discuss Jewishness, except to demonstrate to an occasional religious patient that his piety is a sign of neurosis."

* * *

The state of organized psychoanalysis continues to be worrisome, and to the extent that the practice of psychotherapy is influenced by the ideas of Freud and his followers, the issue has become broadly social as well as psychological. It is therefore to Russell Jacoby's credit hat he has tried, in interviews as well as in his *Social Amnesia* and *The Repression of Psychoanalysis,*[5] to recapture the earlier days of psychoanalysis when its leaders were cultured intellectuals at odds with their surroundings. I do not think Jacoby is willing enough to face up to Freud's own political conservatisms, but Jacoby is certainly correct in detecting a general decline in the vitality of the profession. To be a psychoanalyst was once a calling; too often it is now a career whose advancement is dependent on an organizational hierarchy that distrusts the life of the mind.

And yet the seeds of conformism were implicitly there all along. Freud had a history of quarreling with so-called heretics, and he is not without responsibility for the existence of wooden orthodoxy. Once intellectual historians get over the conceptual roadblocks to understanding what Carl Jung, Alfred Adler, and Otto Rank were protesting about, it should become standard knowledge that fair-minded objections to Freudian theory and technique were being respectfully expressed long ago. Jung's politics in the 1930s were appalling, but the short-term therapy he started to advocate in the 1920s has scarcely been improved upon today. Erich Fromm, too, has a reputation that is now in need of reconsideration. Jacoby's *The Repression of Psychoanalysis* is, in my opinion, more tolerant of diversity and more open to ideological alternatives than his *Social Amnesia*, when he was committed to Herbert Marcuse's particular reading of the history of psychoanalysis.

For those on the political left, it may be worth recalling that in the 1950s some eminent Cold War figures were attracted to features of psychoanalysis. Freud's theories can, I think, serve conservative, liberal, as well as radical purposes, and only if we acknowledge the full range of the theoretical meanings of psychoanalysis can we be capable of making the best possible use of its concepts.

A consensus has grown up about the immense significance of Freud's stature in twentieth-century psychological thinking. It is best to acknowledge our share in that judgment, and then go on to emphasize how different he was from our own preconceptions. Whether he was right or wrong, he laid down some fundamental challenges to Western moral thought. Jacoby justly calls attention to Freud's special stress on "everyday unhappiness." It can do Freud's memory no service to ignore how disturbing, and often profoundly unattractive, some of his attitudes and conclusions were. The more we see Freud as a man of his own time, the better able we should be to use him as a source of our being detached toward today's society.

* * *

John P. Diggins's *The Lost Soul of American Politics*[6] is an important book that aims to reinterpret the whole of American political thought. Its starting point is a negative one, as it seeks to demolish the viewpoints presented by John Pocock and Gary Wills. Diggins is opposed to Pocock's notion that historians have under-estimated the analogies to Machiavelli that can be found in the thoughts of the Founding Fathers, and Diggins thinks that Wills has over-stated the significance in America of the Scottish Enlightenment. Diggins recommends that we turn back to earlier writers such as Perry Miller, Louis Hartz, and Richard Hofstadter in order to understand the American political past. According to Diggins, America has had an ideological consensus stemming from a combination of John Locke and New England Puritanism; instead of America being marked by the presence of a concern with humanist civic virtues, as Pocock has proposed, Diggins notes an absence of enough Christian values. For Diggins liberalism and Calvinism are the main themes in American political culture.

Diggins is a serious worker and his notes refer to the best of recent scholarship on American political theory. Yet one wonders whether the book does not smack of overkill. It is remarkable how the thesis about Machiavelli's significance for America could ever have advanced as far as it has. I think that Diggins might have challenged exactly what the "Machiavellian framework" really amounts to; for the shocking amorality of *The Prince* should weigh as heavily as Machiavelli's republican convictions. As far as Gary Wills goes, he is a wonderfully talented journalist whose books will be influential mainly by virtue of their style. Diggins may be right in thinking that students of American thought have been beguiled by the views of Pocock and Wills, but the alternative approach that Diggins proposes seems so obviously commonsensical that a reader may be forgiven for thinking that in this book Diggins goes on beating a horse long after it has demonstrably died.

However cumbersome the organization of the book sometimes appears, it is a pleasure to follow Diggins's attention to the texts he examines. He is concerned not just with the revolutionary period but writes about the transcendentalists, de Tocqueville, Henry Adams, Melville, and Lincoln.

It is splendid to see American political ideas being treated with such care in the context of the scholarly tradition exemplified by Miller, Hartz, and Hofstadter. Diggins's earlier work, for example, his book on the American response to Mussolini and his study of Thorstein Veblen, to cite only two pieces of his research, made him a name to reckon with; but *The Lost Soul of American Politics* will ensure his being widely recognized as a foremost interpreter of American political thought.

* * *

Cotton Mather's reputation has been tied to his participation in the Salem witchcraft trials of the 1690s. He was, however, immensely learned, an erudite controversialist in defense of Puritan orthodoxy who also maintained monumental correspondences, and he was the author of numerous jeremiads against those he deemed lacking in faith. Although he was unctuous toward authority and extraordinarily anxious to please, he suffered from feelings of isolation and disregard. His public quarreling and prolific scribbling became as famous as his bigotry; even though he deserves credit for pioneering in the early campaign for the use of inoculation against smallpox, he is remembered as a villain in history.

Disputes among psychoanalysts form part of a modern theology, and K. R. Eissler has earned the status of a contemporary Cotton Mather; his past assaults on various "heresies" and "deviations" are as notorious as his actions in sealing much of the Freud Archives from impartial inspection until sometime later this current century. In a 1986 book, *Freud as an Expert Witness: The Discussion of War Neuroses Between Freud and Wagner-Jauregg*,[7] Eissler directed his fire against Julius Wagner-Jauregg, one of Freud's fellow Viennese who became in 1928 the first psychiatrist to win a Nobel Prize. After the conclusion of World War I, official proceedings were instituted to investigate Wagner-Jauregg's wartime conduct as head of the University of Vienna's psychiatric facilities. Freud was asked to testify as to the propriety of Wagner-Jauregg's approach to patients, and in his autobiography Wagner-Jauregg expressed resentment at Freud's contribution.

Although Eissler's book is characteristically huge and oddly organized (it has no less than nine appendixes), its ideological bias is obvious: "Although I never met Freud, he is as much alive within me as though he were still with us. If one owes understanding, profession, and probably psychic survival to one personality, no other outcome is possible." The result is that, as the Viennese psychoanalyst Harald Leupold-Lowenthal pointed out in a review of the original German edition of this text that appeared in the *Sigmund Freud House Bulletin*, Eissler selectively omits critically important parts of the official protocols without even mentioning their existence.

A few key garbled interpretations of Eissler's betray the theological purposes he has in mind. At one point, Freud testified that Wagner-Jauregg had missed out by not making use of psychoanalysis as therapy for the war neuroses, and then Freud ironically added that he could not possibly demand that Wagner-Jauregg do so because even Freud's own students could not do it. The translated sentence, rather different from an earlier version in English, still reads here: "I cannot request it of him, my pupils can request it even still less." Eissler, unable to appreciate Freud's complexities, literally thinks that the sentence makes no sense and raises the possibility of a stenographic error.

It is as easy to laugh at Eissler's sort of ideology as to find it a bore. Freud, for example, testified that "every neurosis has a purpose; it is directed toward certain persons and would disappear at once on a South Sea island or in a similar situation, for there would be longer be a reason for it." Eissler then lamely comments, "It may be doubted whether the South Sea model fits all neuroses." Eissler not only cannot comprehend Freud's understanding of the social bases of suffering, but does not even understand Freud's special sort of morality. When a patient of Freud's, who was carrying on an extramarital affair, found he was impotent with his wife, the man came with concern to his analyst: according to a reliable report Freud congratulated the patient, saying: "Now you are decent." Eissler misses an interesting point, and instead awkwardly quotes Freud: "That is the first sign of honesty that I have seen in you." When Wagner-Jauregg once characterized a patient as "not worth treating," Eissler maintains that it is a "phrase unworthy of a physician," blatantly ignoring how frequently Freud made precisely the same comment, or much worse. The authoritarianism in old-fashioned psychiatry got carried over into the early psychoanalysis that Eissler was later so eager to prettify and perpetuate.

Eissler is thoroughly unreliable as a historian, despite his privileged access to source material at the Freud Archives, and he tries to deny Freud's own prophetic intentions. It is a puritanical brand of religion that Eissler has zealously continued to defend over the years, and in referring to another old-time psychiatrist, Ernst Kretschmer, Eissler tells us that "an adequate polemic against Kretschmer would require a book." Readers of *Freud as an Expert Witness* are unfortunately apt to forget Eissler's worthy campaign in behalf of the practice of lay analysis. Eissler remarks at the outset of this book that a deceased analyst had intended a paper on the topic of Wagner-Jauregg; such a proposal would have made scholarly sense, provided it was carried out with open-mindedness and without Eissler's own peculiarly unfortunate theological baggage.

* * *

The "Baby M" case, which once attracted such an immense amount of publicity, raised a host of genuine moral perplexities, among them, what is the nature of modern reproductive technologies, and what limits should the humane state set to them? The Baby M case pitted Mary Beth Whitehead, the surrogate mother who wanted to renege on the contract she signed, against William and Betsy Stern, the biological father and his wife. In a grotesque situation, in which Mary Beth had conceived by artificial insemination for the promise of payment, it should not be too surprising that crazy behavior took place. As Murray Kempton so aptly put it, "The Sterns had bought themselves a cow, and the cow had kicked over the milk can."

One of the many oddities of the Baby M case is that, according to current terminology, the birth mother gets characterized as the "surrogate," while Betsy Stern, who hoped and planned to adopt the child, escaped the unnatural-sounding label of surrogacy. If it was dubious for Whitehead to have undertaken such a contract, surely the other, far better-educated parties to the deal engaged in behavior at least as questionable.

Phyllis Chesler's *Sacred Bond: The Legacy of Baby M*[8] deserves credit for early on having seen Mary Beth as a victim of class prejudice and media bias. The early reporting did not highlight the fact that Mary Beth had been breast-feeding the child for more than four months before the police, acting on court orders, took the girl away from her. Few may be unaware that William Stern tape-recorded a telephone conversation in which Mary Beth threatened the child's life as well as her own. Mary Beth was caught in a tortured position, her funds had been legally frozen, and she was about to lose her house to the bank; others in custody difficulties have self-dramatically said things they later regretted, and would not have performed.

Throughout the struggle over Baby M, the Sterns come across as an upper-middle-class couple able to provide the baby with the advantages of stability that go with their socioeconomic status. It seems to me repugnant that, under these circumstances, so-called experts have to be called in to assess the relative fitness of the adults. The initial trial judge held that Mary Beth was "mentally unstable" for refusing to give the baby up.

Chesler's book is the outgrowth of her own active campaign in behalf of Mary Beth's cause. Chesler saw it all along as a custody case, and she ties it with her conviction that mothers unduly suffer at he hands of courts who come up with prejudiced decisions in behalf of abusive fathers. Readers can applaud Chesler's willingness to defend Mary Beth, a rather unattractive heroine, at the same time that one can dissent from some of the rest of the ideology Chesler has fashioned.

Chesler seems unaware of any instances, especially among the middle classes, where fathers and children have been victimized by custody rulings unfairly favoring mothers. Chesler may be right that the case of Baby M is similar to the average custody battle, and that it may even bear resemblances to a "witch trial," as she contends; but Chesler's own stand would be far more persuasive if her general account bore the nuances of examples running contrary to the specific programmatic thesis she seeks to promote.

Sacred Bond: The Legacy of Baby M is not a carefully argued book; it scarcely touches on the philosophic dilemmas that the technologies of modern reproduction present us with. Chesler writes as if Britain's Warnock Committee, or the studies of our own Hastings Center in New York, were not relevant. After all, Baby M's fate was decided on the grounds of what would be "for her own good." Medical ethics may seem a moral nightmare, but they are more acutely with us now than anytime in our past.

Chesler's book, whatever its inadequacies, is passionately written in behalf of a good cause; it was completed after the New Jersey Supreme Court had overturned the trial judge's sustaining of the original contract, but before Mary Beth had succeeded in getting reasonably generous rights of visitation. We need to pay more attention to how often and to what extent the state succeeds in protecting a mother from any man's physical, economic or custodial violence. Both child abuse and sex discrimination are realities, and Chesler uses the Baby M case to highlight their existence. Although Mary Beth sometimes looked a bit dippy on television, at least to me, Chesler and her allies were perceptive enough to find something in her to admire.

Chesler correctly argues, in connection with adoption, that surrendering birth mothers "suffer intensely and forever," and yet I do not think one has to be part of the mother-blaming world Chesler hypothesizes to ask that the logic of her own argument be extended to the area of abortion as well. As a psychotherapist, Chesler must have had clinical experience with the consequences of aborted pregnancies, but I suspect that it is because of her own ideological concern to fight what she sees as the "pro-father and anti-mother biases of our society" that she refrains from exploring that sensitive area.

Some feminists involved in the Baby M case were surprised to find themselves for once on the same side as the Vatican, which has long insisted on the relevance of the value of human dignity and explicitly denounced the practice of surrogate motherhood. I think that the more we come to realize what problems we now have on our hands, the more relevant all traditional moral and ethical teachings are bound to become.

* * *

Philip Pomper is a careful intellectual historian, a specialist in nineteenth- and twentieth-century Russian political thought; he has also written *The Structure of Mind in History: Five Major Thinkers in Psychohistory*[9] that provides a fair and balanced account of the "psychohistorical" line of thought that runs from Freud to Erik H. Erikson, Norman O. Brown, Herbert Marcuse, and Robert J. Lifton. It seems to me extraordinary that in an area so laden with partisanship Pomper is consistently able to give solid summary evaluations of all of these writers.

Pomper provides relatively brief overviews of each of the thinkers he examines, and I cannot think of even an instance of his being short-tempered in his effort to survey the way in which Freud's own work has been changed and built upon. Even though each of the post-Freudian thinkers departs in important ways from the "classical" point of view, Pomper treats these contributions without an ounce of polemics. Nor does he unduly proclaim the achievement of innovations. Pomper neither congratulates nor denigrates.

As a matter of fact I wish Pomper had been more outspoken about the defects in each of the thinkers he writes about. Is it, for example, enough to contrast Erikson's epigenetic scheme with the Oedipus complex in Freud's system, without coming to a considered judgment about the respective weaknesses implicit in each point of view? Pomper is decent and dispassionate, so earnest in his understanding of the works of each writer that he talks about that it is impossible not to ask of him: what do your really think? The chapter on Marcuse and Brown, for example, describes two people who were seriously at odds with each other, but the sound of ideological warfare is muffled by the thin air of the academy. And yet I can think of no better encapsulation of Lifton's work than what Pomper provides us with; in one little chapter he manages to distill the essence of Lifton's special point of view.

For those of us in the lucky position to have had the time to read each of these people as they have tried to cope with the special way Freud's heirs dealt with psychology and history, Pomper's book does not do much more than bring together in a good distillation work with which we have long been familiar. In fairness to Erich Fromm's own pioneering, however, I do think he deserved special treatment; clinicians especially are apt to appreciate the grounds for Fromm's differences from "orthodox" theory, even if Fromm's current reputation among the intelligentsia may suffer from his superb ability to reach beyond existing organizational power structures to appeal to the general public. The fact that Fromm only gets the gesture of a passing mention does make me suspect that Pomper is insensitive to the ideological passions that have unfairly excluded Fromm from so many modern bibliographies. Others, such as Erik H. Erikson, certainly feared the fate of Fromm's de facto excommunication, and it colored their own efforts to maintain formal links with "orthodox" powers-that-be. Marcuse's own assault on Fromm has long struck me as unfair, and deserving of reappraisal.

Those who have been immersed in clinical work will find in Pomper a thoroughly reliable guide to research that has grown up about the implications of psychoanalysis for social and historical thought. I cannot think of a better place for a beginner in this area to start, even if I wish Pomper had been willing to ask rather tougher questions of each of those he examines. In my own opinion "psychohistory" as a modern tradition of thought is important enough, and sufficiently well established, to take more criticism than Pomper seems temperamentally interested in delivering. Still, *The Structure of Mind in History* gives a tolerant overview that is a valuable addition to the literature.

* * *

Michael G. Kenny's *The Passion of Ansel Bourne: Multiple Personality in American Culture*[10] is a demanding, difficult book deserving attention, for the author has tackled the perplexing problem of the diagnosis of multiple personality in American society. Kenny is conversant with the best literature about so-called mental dissociation, and he moves effortlessly through evidence from history, psychiatry, and literary criticism. Nevertheless, more than once I found myself losing track of the structure of the argument, and the curious absence of all proper names in the index did not help matters. Yet the impressive breadth of Kenny's reading, and the sophisticated nature of his reasoning, made me wish that someone had insisted that he differentiate the woods from the trees.

Kenny starts off with an exploration of the concept of the "self," and he tries to understand individuality as an aspect of social culture as well as a term in medical psychology. He sees the disorder of multiple personality much as anthropologists view possession; and he argues that "multiple personality is a culturally specific metaphor, not a universally distributed mental disorder." Kenny is dealing with striking conversion-like experiences, that once seemed miraculous and in our own time have been assimilated to the categories of psychiatric science. Since he is presenting well-documented case histories from past American experience, he interprets his material in terms of what he sees as the characteristically American "idiom of distress." The book is rewarding partly because of Kenny's commitment to the idea that multiple personality "is a socially created artifact, not the natural product of some deterministic psychological process."

He documents the story of Mary Reynolds that first appeared in print in 1816. Readers are asked to follow an extremely detailed account of what sounds like hysteria, with no neurological factors that might account for her condition. Silas Weir Mitchell's report of Reynolds helped spread her fame among psychologists later in the century. Unfortunately, Kenny assumes that readers have paid such close attention to his text that there is no need in his conclusion concretely to remind them how he had started out.

Kenny also tells the dramatic story of Ansel Bourne, a carpenter who underwent an upheaval in 1857 that transformed him into an itinerant preacher for the next twenty years. For no easily explicable reason, he was transformed once again; he had lost his identity and took on another name. After he spontaneously awoke to the newest change that had overtaken him, he had amnesia. The tale attracted William James's attention at a time when he was finishing writing his *The Principles of Psychology*. Americans had a special fascination for the notion of a hidden self, and James was one of Sigmund Freud's earliest readers. Kenny's analysis of the return of George Pellow provides even more material about characteristically American approaches to multiple personality by means of late nineteenth-century spiritualist thinking.

In an effort to put into perspective the general problem of the quest for a normal "true" self, Kenny has resurrected the writings of important neurologists (for example, Morton Prince). Oddly enough, Kenny's genuinely impressive bibliography contains not a single reference to the works of Erikson or to others who contributed to the psychoanalytic theory of identity. Kenny's argument might also have been illuminated by Helene Deutsch's concept of the "as if" personality.

Kenny maintains that the cases that he studied have to be understood as the "co-productions of physician and patient." It is undoubtedly sound of him to think that "the form mental disorder takes is influenced by the acquisition of a culturally specific idiom of distress in collusion with local circumstances."

* * *

Witold Rybczynski's *Waiting for the Weekend*[11] is a fascinating essay on the state of contemporary leisure. The author is full of interesting insights into how we choose to spend spare time, and he relates these pursuits not only to practices in different countries, but to past eras as well.

Rybczynski's most useful contribution lies in detailing the origins of the modern weekend. The sovereignty of this social institution is relatively new. The week itself, he points out, is an artificial, humanly constructed interval. The number seven has seemed since the ancient world to possess magical properties. The seven-day week became popular as a convenient unit around which we could structure life to take both work and leisure into account.

Until the nineteenth century, the workweek consumed six days, leaving Sunday as the only day off. But for many, Sunday was a day of religious observance and rest. With the increasing availability of coffee, tea, tobacco, and reading matter, pressure grew for more time off from labor. Since so many public ceremonies were forbidden on the Sabbath, Monday became the time for secular relaxation. Then Saturday became a half-holiday, but only by the 1870s did people start to talk about spending a weekend.

In 1879, ironically almost at the same time that Prime Minister William Gladstone was imposing heavy taxes on liquor in England, we find the earliest recorded instance of the word "week-end" being used. For the middle classes leisure had become accessible.

Our culture defines not only the time for leisure, but also the place where it occurs. For example, as an architect Rybcznski outlines all sorts of information about the home, showing how the average size of our houses has expanded as leisure time grew. He also appreciates the special role of second homes in the country.

But Rybcznski also has moral concerns. He worries that we may have become enslaved to the weekend, making it an institution that dictates and constrains our experience of leisure and the creative impulses associated with it. In so rigorously organizing our weekend activities, he says, leisure time falls prey to the same kind of standardizing conformity that is a feature of workaday life.

Rybczynski believes that leisure is older than civilization, and therefore basically at odds with it. *Waiting for the Weekend* explains why in detail, using as evidence current social mores. He tells the story of the rise in popularity of movie theaters, reports the astonishing twenty-one hours a week people spend before television sets, and laments how few—only 18 percent in Canada—nowadays read a newspaper every day.

Rybczynski also observes that the five-day workweek seems not so much a product of the labor movement's struggle to obtain it as it was the result of the Depression forcing time off on a society with too little work to go around. Nor, he points out, is the weekend universal; Israelis do not observe it, and many Japanese seem never to take a vacation.

Although there is much to admire in *Waiting for the Weekend* —and I share the author's concern about the squeezing out of choice in both work and leisure—I wonder whether he has communicated a balanced account of today's state of affairs. I do not think most middle-class people endure the lives of joyless drudgery that his line of argument implies. I suspect there is more pleasure in work than he is willing to allow for, and that many people manage to get a good deal of fun out of how they earn their livings.

People do not just rush off on weekends shedding their drab work roles; I would expect that it would prove impossible to understand most leisure activities unless we also see how they serve to enhance and enlarge our capacities to be creators at work. It is curious that Rybczynski, in an era of so-called sexual liberation, can exclude entirely from his book any attention to the role of sexuality. Surely it is quaint of the author to be citing Francis Bacon writing in 1625 about "the purest of human pleasures…the greatest refreshment of the spirit of man," when the great philosopher had in mind gardening. Hobbies such as gardening are capable of providing fulfillment. A variety of means exist, aside from drugs or drink, by which we can step back from everyday life and return with an enhanced sense of competency and efficacy. Yet one would have thought that the subject of human sexuality was not to be swept under the conceptual rug.

In line with Rybczynski's anxiety about the over-regulation of modern experience, for example, it could be pointed out that some current sex manuals are so puritanical as to turn sexuality into a form of work; one must be performing, or else run the risk of being considered abnormal. I am not trying to suggest a book that the author legitimately chose not to write. Rather I am pointing out a limit to the argument he develops. That he chose to separate sex from leisure deserves to be explained.

Leisure is a subject that has received less attention than it deserves. Rybczynski is correct in paying homage to the greatest theorist on the topic, Thorstein Veblen, who made popular around the turn of the twentieth century the notion of "conspicuous consumption." While Veblen was apt to make fun of the shenanigans of the middle class, Rybczynski has no such polemical intent. He is genuinely concerned with alerting us to the preciousness of maintaining an area over which we can exercise choice meaningfully

Although Rybczynski is no doubt right in thinking that any sensible person ought to seek self-development in solitary pursuits, I wonder if by his exclusion of sexuality he has not taken the point too far. Everything he writes about the characteristics of true play can also extend to sex. It is well to praise idleness as an end in itself, as the author does here, as long as we do not exclude areas of experience such as sex in which time stands still.

* * *

Matt Cohen's *Freud: The Paris Notebooks*[12] is a thoroughly engaging short novel that I found impossible to put down. Along with other notable modern writers, such as Simone de Beauvoir and D. M. Thomas, Cohen has drawn fictional inspiration from the situation of analyst and patient, and in particular the historical Freud. His novel concerns an Italian nephew of Freud's ("Robert") who has become a practicing analyst in Paris. The scenes in which Robert remembers his Uncle Sigmund are poignant, since they were in Sigmund's last pathetic dying months in London. Cohen's novel is as much concerned with the polarity of death and life, including sexuality, as Freud's theories themselves.

Robert Freud is living a frustrated and empty life as a married practitioner, and has a writer's block even about an unusual patient. Robert breaks free enough to fall in love with his wife's sister. The implication is that Robert is following in a family tradition, behaving like Freud himself in the rumored relation to his own sister-in-law Minna.

Ironically here, however, Robert's wife balks at the arrangement once she soon discovers what has been going on; and it is only after Robert has both shaved off his Freud-like beard, and abandoned his profession as an analyst, that the three people get together in the book's happy ending. Before then, in this well-written, unusually entertaining book, we have also been shown how Robert's life grows increasingly intertwined with that of one of his addictive and adulterous patients.

Cohen does not proceed from the illusory premise that analysts are somehow superhuman. On the contrary, he searches for the common humanity between Robert and those he had sought to help. Unlike the psychiatrist in F. Scott Fitzgerald's *Tender Is the Night*, Robert Freud is not dragged down by those he treats but ultimately liberated by them from what they felt to be unacceptable.

It is a key to Cohen's talent in *Freud* that he can move around from one character's inner world to that of another, without formally announcing what has changed. And he goes back and forth in time, so again it is not immediately clear where the story is. But Cohen's strength as a writer is that none of this is confusing, and he succeeds, instead, in holding the reader in suspense.

Cocaine plays a special role in the story, and the historical Freud did in fact use rather more of it than was good for him. One of Robert's alcoholic patients provides him with some of the drug, and it produces some special surrealistic passages. I found *Freud: The Paris Notebooks* an unquestionable success.

*   *   *

Lisa Appignanesi's *Memory and Desire*[13] seemed to me a masterpiece of a novel, written by a British author who up to now has written only non-fiction;

the book held me in its grip throughout all its 568 pages. I found it impossible to read anything else until completing *Memory and Desire*.

The story starts out in Paris in the 1930s. It concerns a psychoanalyst, Dr. Jacob Jardine, and his obsessive sexual love for the mysterious Sylvie. Their daughter, Katherine, who seeks to cope with the horrors of her childhood, is the heroine of the second half of the book that is set in modern New York.

Once France has been occupied by the Germans during World War II, the characters take part in the underground Resistance movement. Here we see some unexpected changes in people; for those who were weak and incapable of normal love under peacetime conditions behave heroically in opposing the Nazis.

Memory and Desire takes the reader on a number of surprising turns. The European past with its richly textured history is set off against the relative blandness of New World culture, where some of the characters emigrate after the war. The book is an account of how the past continues to live on in the present, and how individual history shapes who we are. But it also a novel of how some people succumb to their own stories, while others manage to rise above troubled beginnings. And it is a sort of detective story about people trying to uncover the truth of their origins.

Several characters are recognizably based on historic figures. The Princess Mathilde, obviously modeled on the Princess Marie Bonaparte, one of the favorites around Freud in his last phase, is a superb example of a cultured European who knows the significance of intimate friendship.

Nothing in this book seemed to me contrived or out of place. Anyone who liked A. S. Byatt's *Possession* should also savor *Memory and Desire*. Lisa Appignanesi's novel also bears some comparison, because of the subject matter, with D. M. Thomas's *The White Hotel*. Although Appignanesi lacks Thomas's capacity for technical fireworks in her writing, the vision of life she holds up seems to me truer and more profound.

We are not only taken through the world of Parisian psychoanalysis, and the wartime Resistance, but also into the milieu of wealthy European aristocrats, art collectors, and industrialists. It is a sprawling and old-fashioned novel, with characters in it that one comes to love, others that one hates. Yet the author is compassionate toward all her struggling people.

Though the novel recounts some obsessive emotional entanglements, Appignanesi has a healthy-minded approach toward the human condition. And, despite all the sad tales that fill the book, she manages to keep the reader in an up-beat mood. There is even a happy ending. I cannot recommend this book too highly.

* * *

Human curiosity about the infinite varieties of sexuality means that the compendium of the latest scientific information, published as *Heterosexuality*[14] by William Masters, Virginia Johnson, and Robert Kolodny, ought to pique the imagination of almost anyone. The senior authors, Masters and Johnson, whose own celebrated marriage broke down, once shocked the world as sex therapists by recommending the use of surrogate partners to help people get over whatever hang-ups they might be suffering from. Such a novel-sounding device, undertaken for the sake of neutral therapeutic purposes, seemed to many like a disguised form of prostitution, and now in the era of AIDS has been abandoned by the authors as a recommended technique.

This text is, as advertised, an up-to-date and comprehensive book about male-female love, covering pleasure, health, and well-being; it is authorized by the world's foremost team of sexual researchers-therapists. It is full of valuable information, not just about sexual dysfunctions but also concerning abortion, contraception, HIV infection, aging, and constitutes a veritable encyclopedia that presumably will benefit a wide range of potential readers.

The problem is that the authors proceed with a kind of detached flatness that seems unnecessarily lacking not just in subtle nuances; but they appear appallingly deficient in the kind of spiritual lightness that someone like Alex Comfort succeeded in achieving. *Heterosexuality* demonstrates a degree of humorlessness that is hard to believe. For example, with capital letters and italics they offer *"ONE CAUTIONARY NOTE: it is DANGEROUS to try to use a vacuum cleaner on your penis. Serious injuries have been reported from this activity."*

Nor do the authors escape obvious tautologies; it is difficult to understand what they think they are telling us when they affirm, "The core problem in premature ejaculation is that the man ejaculates too fast." In their effort to be detached and aloof, they, too, often seem to miss the mystery and spontaneity of sex; they mention, for example, that adding lotion can be a means of enhancing sensory awareness; but how many in the midst of passion are likely to benefit from their advice that "it's best to warm the container of oil or lotion in a basin of hot water."

It should be said to its credit that *Heterosexuality* does not hold out any extravagant claims for the benefits of professional sex therapy. The authors put a modest evaluation on what can be accomplished by visits to an office of an "expert," and they advocate the advantages of a couple relying on "self-help."

Moreover, the authors are aware of the significance of "relationship issues," and they maintain that such questions are "so central that working on a sexual problem in isolation without addressing these other matters is almost certain to be futile." They have turned in behalf of merely proposing "brief time-limited sex therapy."

It can do the cause of sexual enlightenment no good to fail to devote special attention to the realities of oral sex. No neophyte could possibly understand, once again without a separate section devoted to it, the significance of the prostate or the role of the anus. If such matters are in principle deemphasized in a text on heterosexuality, I think it inadvertently supports old stereotypes and fears about "deviancy" being for so-called abnormals.

* * *

A wise older woman once tried to convince me that there were only two possible ways of reasonably reacting to Kurt Eissler's writings; either one got angry or laughed. Unfortunately for those of us who have in the past been attacked by Eissler, it is not easy to choose the alternative of humor. And unfortunately for psychoanalysis, Eissler has for so many years been prominent enough, if only as the founding head of the Freud Archives, that it behooves scholars to follow up on what he publishes.

All Eissler's books are curiosities, and yet nothing could prepare one for his *Three Instances of Injustice.*[15] For years, Eissler espoused the most reactionary orthodox thinking about female psychology, and his downfall as director of the Freud Archives came over the controversy connected with the insistence of Jeffrey Masson, Eissler's protégé, that Freud had been cowardly and wrong in abandoning his early theory that neurosis can be traced to childhood sexual seduction.

Now Eissler has become a convert to political correctness, and almost the first half of this book is devoted to the case of Elizabeth Morgan and her custody dispute with her husband. Eissler sounds like a Don Quixote writing in behalf of a woman he deems heroic, and he waxes at length about the perils of sexual abuse, an accusation made against Morgan's oral surgeon husband. Morgan chose to go to jail, in contempt of court, rather than give away the hiding place of the child. I am in no position, nor is Eissler, to weigh the merits of the struggle between Morgan and the child's father. But Eissler appears to live only in a world of dark versus light.

What is worrisome is that Eissler is able to propagandize on behalf of Anna Freud's viewpoint, unquestionably enshrined in so much North American law, that in child custody matters there is such a person as "the primary psychological parent," who should have the ultimate say over the visitation rights of the other parent. Even more troubling is Eissler's contempt for the law itself, with all its necessary procedural complexities. It is well known that formal rules help critically to distinguish between constitutional democracy and tyranny. Eissler, however, is disdainful of how our courts go about their business, and he is eager to rely on so-called expert psychological witnesses. In the course of Eissler's crusade in behalf of Morgan, he indulges in the kind of armchair psychoanalysis of the participants in the legal dispute that has contributed to giving Freud's name such a questionable standing among neutral outsiders. Eissler is even "sure" how King Solomon would have proceeded. And so he would substitute "suspicion" for conclusive evidence, which would have been enough to settle Woody Allen's hash too. The principle of innocent until proven guilty never comes up in Eissler's tirade.

Eissler tells us about his high moral position, including his denunciation of the death penalty, his opposition to racism, his enthusiasm for the right of abortion, and his contempt for Presidents George H. W. Bush and Ronald Reagan; one presumes Eissler also has a fondness for apple pie. Eissler then suddenly moves on to the second of his injustices. We find that having dwelt in the difficult field of law and psychoanalysis we are back to basics, a fundamentalist defense of Freud. For in this second section of the book, Eissler aims his fire at the idea, supposedly first proposed by C. G. Jung, that Freud had an affair with his wife's sister, Minna. It is curious how Eissler can consider this whole matter a weighty injustice. But he proceeds with his argument without even mentioning the names of the contemporary authors who have done so much to keep alive the idea of Freud's supposed sexual misconduct. I happen to agree with Eissler's general conclusion about Freud's sex life, but it would seem inconceivable to go about making the case in the tendentious way he has undertaken.

The third of Eissler's injustices comes down to himself. He deals with the problem of "the maligned therapist," and how he has had to deal with patients of his own who have read stories about Eissler that have led them to disagree with him on policy matters connected with his notorious secretiveness about access to the still sealed portions of the Freud Archives. (Eissler maintained control, right up to his death in 1999, over Anna Freud's bequests to the Library of Congress, and his successor who replaced him as head of the Freud Archives seemed eager to please Eissler.) In *Three Instances of Injustice* Eissler paints himself into a corner by attacking, almost unbelievably, such defenders of orthodoxy as Peter Gay and Elisabeth Young-Bruehl. Eissler has a defense of Janet Malcolm, although he does not use her name; her *In the Freud Archives*, the occasion for Masson's lawsuit against Malcolm, was sympathetic to Eissler, and the powers-that-be within psychoanalytic orthodoxy.

Three Instances of Injustice has to be read to be believed. It will add ammunition to those who, on scientific grounds, are too willing to dismiss all psychoanalytic reasoning. Here is tortuous thinking all too similar to that of a crackpot: Eissler, for example, anticipates "the day when there will be a crime-free world, because there will be no more people desirous of becoming the victims of crime." No one needs to read this book, except to understand how embarrassing the profession of psychoanalysis can be made to seem and how tempting the lure of grandiosity can become.

* * *

Jacques Szaluta's *Psychohistory: Theory and Practice*[16] is a sober and conscientious survey of the term "psychohistory" that is now so widely used that it no longer needs to be hyphenated. Szaluta is primarily concerned with methodological issues, but he gives ample space to the arguments of critics as well as proponents. Freud plays the central theoretical role; Erikson's work gets a full chapter; and there is a chapter on post-Freudian developments as well, covering ego psychology, the British school, French interpreters, and Kohut's self-psychology. Szaluta seems to be firmly in the camp of psychohistory's proponents, yet reviews the primary literature that has examined the pros and cons of creating a special academic sub-field by combining psychoanalysis and history. Newcomers to this subject will find here a fair-minded outline of the whole contour of the major issues that have arisen in connection with psychohistory.

Some reservations about Szaluta's conceptual approach do seem to me to be in order. To what extent, I wonder, does the old debate over the extent to which psychoanalysis is an art as opposed to a science bear on the question of psychohistory? To see Freud's achievements as in good part humanistic should not, I believe, weaken ties to history, but rather might be reassuring to those traditionalists who see history writing as a craft rather than a hard science. I think that Freud's metaphor of so-called applied analysis (which Szaluta does not try to resuscitate) has long been out of date, and may always have been misleading. Erikson, for example, long held the view that psychoanalysts had as much to learn from historians as the other way around; as long as psychoanalysis and social sciences are seen as moving in thorough interaction with each other, it is possible to appreciate how much psychohistory can do to broaden the outlooks of all of us.

It is no doubt a small point, but I would not have thought that the pioneering work of Erich Fromm deserved to be left out of Szaluta's survey. Even if acknowledgments to psychohistory's contributions are too often unspoken or taken for granted, no good contemporary historian could possibly proceed without taking into account all the central accomplishments of the psychohistorical field. But the recent demise of the journal *Psychohistory Review*, only partially compensated for by the creation of the semiannual *Psychoanalysis and History*, should warn us of the need to keep promoting the advantages of a psychohistorical perspective.

* * *

Although there is little in psychoanalytic theory to prepare one for it, different countries continue to have quite separate national psychotherapeutic traditions. When one thinks of France the name of Lacan comes to mind even more immediately than that of Klein or Winnicott crops up in connection with Britain; in turn, the Americans have had ego-psychology as well as

Kohut's thinking about the self. And the Italians are notably receptive and open to a wide variety of different ideological strains. But the Germans—here one is apt to pause in uncertainty about what most characterizes psychoanalysis there today.

The Future of Psychoanalysis[17] is a collection of essays that should help get us started about the nature of some of the most interesting German psychoanalytic thinking. The editor, Johannes Cremerius, opens with a blistering piece that deals with the authoritarian and hierarchical structure of the International Psychoanalytic Association (IPA). He has assembled a variety of arguments, all unfortunately true, about how training at institutes bears too many analogies to the religious instruction of an organized church. Psychoanalysis, he holds, is threatened by its failure to keep in touch with the broadest philosophical, political, and social questions. Above all, the crisis in psychoanalysis can be traced to its unwillingness to cease to be a "movement" and its hesitancy to fulfill Freud's hopes of having created a science.

An unspoken part of Cremerius's thesis is the extent to which the bulk of German psychoanalysts have seemed by and large identified with the powers-that-be in American psychoanalysis. Perhaps such links were inevitable, given the post-World War II role of the U.S. in helping with the reconstruction of Germany. But the present-day gloom within American psychoanalysis has afflicted the German analysts as well; unlike in France, for example, where Lacan managed to keep analysis vital by being in touch with philosophy, literature, and university academic life in general. The Germans, in contrast, allowed themselves to become more narrowly concerned with the middle class-appearing aspects of therapy itself.

And now that the public health insurance is cutting back on its previous generosity to analysts, German analysis is suffering in an acute way. Various of these essays refer in passing to the problems of public payments, and how the decreasing frequency of mandated paid sessions each week conflicts with traditionally accepted expectations. (Right now the most generously supported long-term psychoanalyses anywhere may be in Ontario, Canada.) One wishes that one of the eight sophisticated writers in *The Future of Psychoanalysis* specifically addressed themselves to the problems unique to Germany.

German analysts of course have to deal with a special and ghastly divide in their history associated with the Nazi era. Exactly who in the past of rival organizations can be considered guilty of collaborating in an unsavory way would make for an immensely complicated story, and perhaps finger-pointing about which ancestors did what would be endless. But political events of this past century make it impossible for Germans to enjoy the luxury of entertaining continuities the way the Americans or British can. This is particularly striking in that although the Berlin Training Institute was the first one to be established after World War I, the name of its founder—Karl Abraham—does not once come up in *The Future of Psychoanalysis*.

Yet the level of thought throughout all the essays here is unusually high. Names like Adorno, Horkheimer, Fromm, Mitscherlich, and Habermas keep turning up; the ideas discussed are cosmopolitan. The authors in *The Future of Psychoanalysis* are aware of the dangers of false scientism as well as the perils associated with North American pragmatism. These writers are justifiably harking back to an era of psychoanalytic intellectuality, and to a clinical approach that takes for granted the values of civilized stoicism. Psychoanalysis arose a hundred years ago inextricably as part of the best in Western culture, and if the writers in *The Future of Psychoanalysis* are in any way representative, they demonstrate that analysis in Germany appears to be alive and well.

* * *

In contrast to what has already been undertaken for other countries, such as Germany, France, America, and Russia, somehow nobody has yet written a history of psychoanalysis in Britain. In the absence of any such comprehensive overview, it is particularly welcome to have had Tom Harrison's book, since he has alerted us to the existence of pioneering attempts at using group psychotherapy for British army soldiers during World War II. The novel efforts of analysts like Wilfred Bion, John Rickman, and S. H. Foulkes in constructing a therapeutic community in South Birmingham have until now been legendary rather than examined. Thanks to Tom Harrison's fifteen years of research and writing he has rescued for history an intriguing series of innovative therapeutic efforts at Northfield.

Despite all the literature about psychoanalysis in America, early figures there like Trigant Burrow and J. L. Moreno have so far attracted little attention; yet their interest in group therapy preceded what happened at Northfield. In Britain Wilfred Trotter and William McDougall had been interested in the psychology of groups. Paul Schilder, first in Vienna and then the States, even though he has yet to attract any substantial literature, was another important influence. Since Rickman was such a key figure at Northfield, and had had a lengthy analysis with Melanie Klein, Harrison spells out some of the implications of her ideas. In addition, the pre-World War II pioneer of British group psychotherapy turns out to have been Joshua Bierer who proceeded on principles derived from Alfred Adler's emphasis on the significance of community. Foulkes was influenced by continentals like Kurt Goldstein and Norbert Elias as well as the American Burrow. (Although Harrison emphasizes in general the role of lineage for all the analysts, he does not seem to know that Foulkes had been analyzed by Helene Deutsch.)

Military psychiatry, whose history has somehow attracted only episodic interest, is in itself a fascinating subject. The problem of morale is obviously a crucial matter in wartime. Despite the fact that Churchill took a dim view of experiments along psychological lines, as during the First World War necessity once more mothered invention. Harrison tells us how "the psychiatrists involved sought methods that encouraged and supported rather than humiliated or frightened." Rickman had tried to build on the abilities of patients while taking pragmatic steps to deal with recent traumas. Combatant disorders were a real challenge for psychotherapists used to treating patients individually.

The reader will find here several names of important early British psychiatrists who have already unfortunately slipped into oblivion—such as Dennis Carroll, Emanuel Miller, E. A. Bennet, Martin James, and Tom Main. Harrison has also conducted numerous interviews with patients and staff who were involved at Northfield. The objective of using psychiatry to defeat the enemy entailed a variety of fresh technical procedures. The rival theories of Foulkes and Bion not only led to different approaches, but were later represented at the Institute of Group Analysis and the Tavistock Clinic. Central clinical issues like idealization and dependency prominently came up at Northfield. When the time comes for some histories of British psychoanalysis, the field work which Harrison has conducted will provide an invaluable addition to a tale which is now rather less exotic.

* * *

I picked up Philip F. D. Rubovits-Seitz's *Kohut's Freudian Vision*[19] in the hope that it could help clarify the long-standing mystery in my mind about just why Kohut's self-psychological ideas have come to be so innovative and controversial. The only time I met him, in the early 1960s, never gave me any hint to anticipate that he could have become the leader of a movement in any way at odds with what then were the powers-that-be within psychoanalysis. Anna Freud in the mid-1960s went out of her way with me to single out Kohut, a native Viennese, for the highest praise. Yet in the end she came to deem his work as "anti-psychoanalytic." At a meeting of the Toronto Psychoanalytic Society in the early 1990s Anna Ornstein seemed to me to be trying hard to be conciliatory about the implications of Kohut's work, but Anne-Marie Sandler steadfastly refused to accept the olive branch of peace she was being offered. So I have continued to wonder what has been going on.

Kohut's Freudian Vision does help get one started understanding the background of Kohut's most original work. However, the reader needs a great deal of patience to plow through the first 160 pages of this book since Rubovits-Seitz has chosen to present the case for Kohut's loyalist continuities with Freud's theories. The book opens with a transcript of Kohut's lectures on psychoanalytic psychology that were presented to candidates at the Chicago Psychoanalytic Institute from 1958 to 1960. Rubovits-Seitz has painstakingly reconstructed these lectures, which take up approximately half of *Kohut's Freudian Vision*. I found myself pitying not so much the candidates of four decades ago who were subjected to such a stale run-through of the conceptual contours to Freud's thinking, since I feel confident that Kohut's lively presence must have infused the words with more interesting meaning. But I could not help wondering why we today are being subjected to such a tortured exercise? Although the idea never crossed my mind as I slogged my way through the pages of these lectures, in hindsight it appears to have been an attempt to legitimize Kohut's Freudian credentials. I would not have thought anyone could have challenged how deeply rooted in psychoanalytic thinking Kohut had been.

Then we are offered in Part II an article that Rubovits-Seitz and Kohut wrote in 1963, "Concepts and Theories of Psychoanalysis." Once again, there is nothing new here, and Part III consists of a short piece on "Kohut's Method of Synthesizing Freudian Theory." The real interesting meat of the book comes only in Part IV, "Kohut's Concepts of Narcissism and Self Psychology: Continuities with Freudian Theory." But Rubovits-Seitz never tells us who he might be arguing with.

The dread name Jung is never used by Rubovits-Seitz, although it does appear in one of the interesting-looking articles in the bibliography. Paul Federn was a Viennese analyst with a following in Chicago during Kohut's time there, but not a word about Federn comes up, although he too was early on, like Jung, trying to work out a conceptualization that sought to embrace the self. Erik H. Erikson also gets passed over in silence, although I remember Kohut's having singled out Erikson as "full of ideas." Surely intellectual historians should be as interested in the parallels and analogies between Erikson and Kohut as Jung (or Federn) and Kohut. When Rubovitz-Seitz cites Herbert Silberer's work as having analytically anticipated Kohut's, he would have to be unaware of how unhappy personally Freud became with Silberer.

It also occurred to me, in reading Part IV, that Otto Rank and Karen Horney were also directly relevant as anticipators of Kohut's thinking. But intellectual history is evidently not the same thing as organizational loyalism, and Rubovits-Seitz has chosen to walk a straight-and-narrow path. It would be good to be in a position to learn more of what went on behind-the-scenes in Kohut's struggle to present his original work. One might have thought that the time should have long since arrived when it was possible to discuss all these issues without unnecessary fear of ideological excommunication. As it is, *Kohut's Freudian Vision* mainly serves to remind us once again how absolutely central the problem of lineage and legitimacy is in the historiography of psychoanalysis.

* * *

Bruno Bettelheim's standing used to be more securely established among the general reading public than with professional analysts. He succeeded in writing a series of interesting and provocative books that attracted worldwide interest. Since his self-inflicted death as an old man in 1990, however, his reputation has gone into an abrupt eclipse. Harsh publicity about his reliance on physical and psychological abuse at his orthogenic school at the University of Chicago has been followed by close biographical scrutiny that has been sometimes so severe as to leave his previous public renown in tatters.

The merit of Paul Marcus's *Autonomy in the Extreme Situation: Bruno Bettelheim, the Nazi Concentration Camps and the Mass Society*[20] is that Marcus concentrates on examining both the pros and cons of Bettelheim's famous argument on the Nazi concentration camps and what they have to tell us about life in mass societies. Bettelheim was also enlarging traditional psychoanalytic theory, which has always been inadequate when it comes to acknowledging the full social role of forces outside strictly individual development. Offhand, I cannot think of psychoanalysts, including Freud, who have even paid attention to the role of nannies and house-keepers in the raising of children; yet I would hazard the guess that more children in human history have been raised by people other than biological parents than one might ever guess from examining the professional literature. More generally, however, it has remained a controversial issue among psychoanalysts how to deal with society as well as psychology. Starting with Alfred Adler's socialism any attention to social realities has been apt to be dismissed as "mere" sociology, and that became a standard way of handling a whole line of so-called apostates such as Erich Fromm and Karen Horney. Bettelheim's tack was to start off with his own experiences as a prisoner, to deal also with what it could tell us about the struggle to maintain individuality under twentieth-century conditions, and to connect that with his recommendations about how to treat severely disturbed youngsters.

Most of us would be sympathetic to what Marcus calls "the dangers of impersonal bureaucracy, the trend-setting mass media and intrusive surveillance in undermining the individual's autonomy and integration...." Technological developments have made privacy and self-determination seem to become harder to defend under conditions of modern life. (I did feel amused to read Marcus quote Bettelheim about the example of "the boss in our society who lets an inferior wait before seeing him," since that is what Bettelheim once did to me when I interviewed him.) Conformity to social norms can become deadening; Marcus quotes a famous sentence from Bettelheim's *The Informed Heart* (1960): "To pattern one's way of life on that of others is not a truly free choice, even if nothing is openly forced on the individual." The impact of "experts" on a variety of subjects can come to overwhelm our genuine internal experience. And in Hemingway's *For Whom the Bell Tolls* the hero, sleeping out-of-doors in romantic Spain, dreams about a beautiful

Hollywood movie star; she had become a standard and uniform symbol, as public and private areas began to dissolve in the modern world. John Stuart Mill and others had warned about what might happen to personal freedom under conformist pressures, and Fromm had talked about "automaton conformity" and how a pseudo-self could make up for the loss of spontaneity. Bettelheim thought that the average citizen becomes unconsciously supportive of the very system that robs us of our autonomy. Consumers thereby become participants in their own social control.

Marcus defends Bettelheim against the charges, leveled for example by Terrence Des Pres, that inmate behavior in concentration camps was not after all lacking in self-respect. But Des Pres was right that dramatic self-assertion and old-fashioned heroic resistance were by no means the only options for remaining human in the camps Bettelheim was talking about. Bettelheim did err in the direction of blaming the victim, and in underplaying the extent of subtle cooperativeness, mutual social bonding, and collective opposition to the Nazi captors. Marcus's interpretation focuses on the aspects of Bettelheim's argument that acknowledged the variety of ways of remaining recognizably human under concentration camp conditions. (Bettelheim never intended to be describing death camp life, since he was imprisoned before the camps turned into factories of extermination.) Marcus is fair in presenting the arguments of those who have criticized Bettelheim for ignoring the degree to which inmates were living in a world of "choiceless choice."

Marcus is consistently evenhanded in presenting some of Bettelheim's most condescending and judgmental sides, such as his pronouncement that "millions of people, like lemmings, marched themselves to their own death," and that this was "the final step of surrender to the death instinct." Long ago Dostoevsky wrote about how when one is humiliated it becomes almost impossible to maintain what we think of as normal human dignity. But Bettelheim had notoriously claimed that inmates in the camps had regressed, become infantile, and thereby taken on the values of the SS guards. Marcus gives plenty of space to Bettelheim's harshest critics, and Marcus tell us "I regard Bettelheim's Jewish passivity argument, his comments on the so-called ghetto mentality and his attack on Anne Frank to be examples of the worst of Bettelheim's mode of analysis...." It should not be surprising that Bettelheim was one of the defenders of Hannah Arendt's controversial thesis in *Eichmann in Jerusalem*. But Marcus is also able to find in Bettelheim's reasoning valuable insights into the effects of the "depersonalizing, conformist, egoistic and dehumanizing pressures" of mass society.

I think that Marcus might have gone on not only to discuss the severe limits to the whole mass society line of thinking, but to explore how Bettelheim's approach to psychotherapy needs to be reexamined. I found it surprising that Marcus devoted so little attention to Bettelheim's writings about treating children and adolescents; after all, Bettelheim thought that at

the orthogenic school he had found a way to use the environment construc-
tively, to build people up, as opposed to how the Nazis had specialized in
tearing them down. To my mind Marcus would have done better to extend his
argument in this direction rather than to try to make Bettelheim more attractive by comparing him to the currently fashionable ideas of Michel Foucault
about how "disciplinary society" can become "normalizing." I find it hard to
believe that Bettelheim, following Freud here, could have endorsed the extreme forms of relativism that come up in Foucault. To me Foucault's idea that
we "have to create ourselves as a work of art" sounds closer to fascistic ideas
about "transgression" than it does to Bettelheim's more classically liberal
defenses of the ultimate value of freedom. But Marcus has performed a real
service in taking so seriously Bettelheim's social theorizing, which may help
rehabilitate a thinker whose ideas have appeared to be swamped by a series of
scandals. I believe that even with all the serious and undeniable limitations
to Bettelheim's writings, he does deserve better than what he has gotten
lately. His work, as well as the secondary literature it has spawned, illustrates
key problems to the broad methodology of using psychological concepts to
understand politics.

Notes

1. Robert J. Lifton, *History and Human Survival* (New York: Random House, 1970).
2. Benjamin B. Wolman, ed., *The Psychoanalytic Interpretation of History* (New York: Basic Books, 1971).
3. Michael Maccoby, *The Gamesman* (New York: Simon & Schuster, 1977).
4. Mortimer Ostow, ed., *Judaism and Psychoanalysis* (New York: KTAV Publishing House, 1982).
5. Russell Jacoby, *Social Amnesia: A Critique of Conformist Psychology from Adler to Laing* (Boston, Beacon Press: 1975); Russell Jacoby, *The Repression of Psy-choanalysis: Otto Fenichel and the Political Freudians* (New York: Basic Books, 1983).
6. John P. Diggins, *The Lost Soul of American Politics: Virtue, Self-Interest, and the Foundations of Liberalism* (New York: Basic Books, 1985).
7. Kurt R. Eissler, *Freud as an Expert Witness: The Discussion of War Neuroses Between Freud and Wagner-Jauregg*, translated by Christine Trollope (Madison, CT: International Universities Press, 1986).
8. Phyllis Chesler, *Sacred Bond: The Legacy of Baby M* (New York: Times Books, 1988).
9. Philip Pomper, *The Structure of Mind in History: Five Major Figures in Psychohistory* (New York: Columbia University Press, 1985).
10. Michael G. Kenny, *The Passion of Ansel Bourne: Multiple Personality in Ameri-can Culture* (Washington, DC: Smithsonian Institution Press, 1986).
11. Witold Rybczynski, *Waiting for the Weekend* (Toronto: Penguin, 1991).
12. Matt Cohen, *Freud: The Paris Notebooks* (Toronto: Quarry Press, 1991).
13. Lisa Appignanesi, *Memory and Desire* (New York: Dutton, 1992).
14. William Masters, Virginia Johnson, and Robert Kolodny, *Heterosexuality* (New York: Harper Collins, 1994).

15. K. R. Eissler, *Three Instances of Injustice* (Madison, CT: International Universities Press, 1993).
16. Jacques Szaluta, *Psychohistory: Theory and Practice* (New York: Peter Lang, 1999).
17. *The Future of Psychoanalysis*, ed. Johannes Cremerius, translated by Jeremy Gaines (London: Open Gate Press, 1999).
18. Tom Harrison, *Bion, Rickman, Foulkes and the Northfield Experiments*: *Advancing on a Different Front* (London: Jessica Kingsley, 2000).
19. Philip F. D. Rubovits-Seitz, *Kohut's Freudian Vision* (Hillsdale, NJ: The Analytic Press, 1999).
20. Paul Marcus, *Autonomy in the Extreme Situation: Bruno Bettelheim, the Nazi Concentration Camps and the Mass Society* (Westport, CY: Praeger, 1999).

11

Hannah Arendt

Hannah Arendt's reputation has continued to climb almost without interruption in the years since her death in 1975. One immense volume of her correspondence with her old teacher Karl Jaspers[1] is only a portion of all the extant Arendt letters. In addition, books made up of Arendt's occasional pieces have come out.[2] And the secondary literature about Arendt has been becoming dauntingly large.[3] In her lifetime she was known mainly for her *The Origins of Totalitarianism* (1951), and she published some striking individual pieces. I will never forget the controversy set off by her Winter 1959 *Dissent* article "Reflections on Little Rock," which seemed to put her against President Eisenhower and instead on the side of Governor Faubus as she expressed her reservations about court-mandated school desegregation. Nothing could match the storm of outrage set off by her *Eichmann in Jerusalem* (1963), which first appeared in the *New Yorker*. Whatever one's political preferences, her account of Eichmann's trial, subtitled *A Report on the Banality of Evil*, has ensured that she will be remembered. I believe few would contest her right to be considered among the most significant political theorists of the past century. (Sir Isaiah Berlin did, following her death, single her out in a *Times Literary Supplement*'s survey of overrated thinkers, and we will be returning to the possible sources of the differences between Arendt and Berlin.)

While Arendt's position among academics has been soaring, Karl Jaspers himself seems to have fallen on hard critical times. Although he was trained as a psychiatrist, and wrote a memorable textbook on psychopathology that went through several editions but still remains undervalued, his standing in that field seems to be confined to specialists in the history of psychiatry who have been so far unsuccessful in explaining to more general readers why Jaspers should matter today. He wrote a pack of other books, about the history of philosophy as well as issues like German war guilt, but as a figure within the tradition of continental thought he has not been in the ascendancy. As the letters between Arendt and Jaspers demonstrate, she appeared to regard him with the utmost reverence and respect. The editors of the Arendt-Jaspers correspondence think that Jaspers was one of the two "main representatives of existentialist philosophy" originating in Germany in the 1920s—the other being Martin Heidegger. But Heidegger continues to attract incomparably more attention than Jaspers. Heidegger's success can be at least partly attributed to how Arendt helped promote him, even as she partly disguised from Jaspers the nature of her enduring commitment to Heidegger.

The letters between Arendt and Jaspers start off in 1926, and only conclude with Jasper's death in 1969. Arendt's cautiously correct approach to Jaspers reflects a bygone era's conception of how teacher and pupil should relate to one another. But inevitably one pays special attention to every occasion on which Heidegger's name comes up here. For it not only was true that as a young woman Arendt was romantically involved with Heidegger (who was married with two children), but the correspondence they exchanged was only belatedly released. Arendt renewed her acquaintanceship with Heidegger after World War II, despite his having been a Nazi party member right up until 1945; on at least one occasion when she saw Heidegger after the war she tells Jaspers nothing about the encounter, which has to be all the more striking since Arendt and Jaspers kept coming back to the problem of Heidegger's unfortunate politics and its relation to his philosophy.

The fate of Germany, both as a culture and a nation, may be the single most striking theme in the Arendt-Jaspers letters. She had fled her native country shortly after the Nazis took power, and then spent years as a stateless person until becoming an American in 1951. Jaspers, married to a Jew, remained in Germany throughout the war, after which he moved to Basle, Switzerland. Arendt had shown early interest in Jewish issues, although her dissertation was on St. Augustine. Before emigrating to the States in 1941 she worked for a Zionist organization in Paris, and like other assimilated Jews it took the shock of Hitler to alert her to the centrality of the Jewish problem in her whole way of thinking.

Unlike in previous centuries, when it was possible to view the state as the enemy of human liberty, Arendt came to conclude that what was unique about twentieth-century conditions was the extent to which politics had become the fundamental source of freedom. Statelessness is a only a phenomenon of fairly recent times, and Arendt's personal experience led her to appreciate not only what she had lost in Germany, but what she later gained through citizenship in America. She and Jaspers were both—despite how bitter they could be at times about particular developments in the United States—convinced that America remained a special source of hope for the future of humanity.

The problem of emigration, however, remains central to all Arendt's thought. It is hard not to think that she perceived the break in her own life history, which entailed exile from Germany, as a reflection of a larger shift in world history. The rise to power of the Nazis was not just a revolutionary change within her country of origin, but a permanently shocking blow to

Western culture as a whole. The most highly educated country in central Europe had voluntarily opted for an unprecedented form of barbarism; the best minds in German political science had drafted a constitutional system that Hitler could use to facilitate his own electoral success. Both Arendt and Jaspers, correctly I think, were lastingly scarred by the implications of Hitlerism for political thinking.

Right after World War II Jaspers could count on Arendt for regular packages of provisions. And he writes her about the whole history of anti-Semitism, lest she think of it all as fascistic. (Her *The Origins of Totalitarianism* is really as much concerned with the place of the Jews in modern culture as with the concept of totalitarianism itself.) Both Arendt and Jaspers were horrified by the way the old German university system collapsed into obsequiousness in the face of the coming to power of the Nazis. She offered Jaspers no intellectual sustenance at all as he revised his work on psychopathology; she remained fiercely anti-Freudian, and one wonders what she truly thought of Jaspers's strictly psychiatric contributions, which were to be sure non-Freudian. Jaspers could always rely on Arendt to manage his business affairs in the English-speaking world, and in effect she functioned as Jaspers's literary agent, advising him on the terms of book contracts, suggesting alternative publishing companies, and generally keeping his spirits up about the fate of his books abroad.

Often Arendt and Jaspers are commenting here about contemporary writers and their books: Czeslaw Milosz, Jean-Paul Sartre, Albert Camus, and Ignazio Silone are only a few of the people they talked about as acquaintances. Sometimes Arendt and Jaspers exchange views about past thinkers like Max Weber (whom Jaspers had once treated) or Spinoza. Arendt saw it as her special function to keep Jaspers informed about American current events, and she was savage about Dwight D. Eisenhower, seeing him too often in the light of Germany's Hindenburg. But then she was prescient about the kind of disaster President Lyndon B. Johnson got involved in through his promoting the war in Southeast Asia. Both Arendt and Jaspers shared a Germanic conviction about the central significance of their native philosophic tradition that to outsiders is bound to smack of dogmatism if not hubris. They can move from the most mundane matters, regardless of how idiosyncratically observed, to the exalted level of the philosophy of Immanuel Kant, as if any civilized person had to reason in their own favorite categories. (Arendt's letters to her second husband, Heinrich Blücher, are sometimes almost comic in their shared Germanic chauvinism, really a form of provincialism.[4])

For me the high point of the book of correspondence between Arendt and Jaspers has to do with the Adolf Eichmann trial. Even before it started Arendt viewed Eichmann as "a walking disaster...in all its bizarre vacuousness." As early as 1946 Jaspers had noted of the Nazis "their total banality...their prosaic triviality." For both Jaspers and Arendt, Eichmann's actions stood "outside the pale of what is comprehensible in human and moral terms," so that "the legal basis of this trial" seemed at best "dubious." Jaspers thought that the Israeli kidnapping of Eichmann from Argentina was "itself illegal." Jaspers held that the trial was "wrongly conceived at its very root," in that the events themselves lay "beyond the scope of any one state's legal jurisdiction." For Jaspers the case was of concern to all humanity, and he regarded the proceedings as a political, as opposed to a legal, matter. Arendt was less "pessimistic" than Jaspers about the legal basis of the trial, but she questioned whether Israel had "the right to speak for the Jews of the world." And she conjectured that one major Israeli motive was to secure renewed reparations payments from Germany.

The publication of *Eichmann in Jerusalem* created an "uproar in Jewish circles" even while it was appearing in the *New Yorker* during 1962. (Arendt was refreshingly honest about her commercial successes, and the various honors she later earned.) From the time she began thinking about Eichmann, Arendt had been impressed with "the huge degree" to which "the Jews helped organize their own destruction." And in witnessing the trial itself she stressed "the fact of Jewish collaboration" in the ultimate holocaust of European Jewry. In the controversy over her book, Arendt felt beleaguered and trapped, for example when Gershom Scholem published their exchange of letters; Jaspers loyally backed Arendt against Scholem's powerful critique. Arendt's argument was taken as an assault on the very "existence" of Jews and Zionists, and Arendt had to defend herself against the allegation that she had implicitly let Hitler and the SS off the hook for the crime of murdering Jews. To many it seemed that Arendt, like Bruno Bettelheim in a psychoanalytic context,[5] was blaming the victims for their own destruction.

Jaspers appreciated Arendt's characteristic use of irony, and he referred once to "the style that some people reproach you for, calling you ironic, cold, heartless, know-it-all, misanthropic...." Neither Arendt nor Jaspers had much perspective on themselves, or on the tradition of thought from which they emerged. Jaspers, for example, found himself fascinated in 1964 by Shakespeare's *The Tempest*, and thought it fitting to add that even if he, Jaspers, could "write it down," he "would never achieve Shakespeare's profundity." One would hardly have thought such a point amounted to a legitimate concession on Jaspers's part, but neither he nor Arendt took themselves lightly.

Still, Arendt and Jaspers were acutely concerned with some of the most central moral dilemmas of the twentieth century. They brought to bear perhaps the best of Western thought onto the key ethical problems of our times, and therefore the private exchanges between them make for fascinating and rewarding reading.

* * *

A generation ago Mary McCarthy was famous as a best-selling novelist and short story writer, a trenchant political critic, and perhaps most memorably as an outstanding autobiographer. Her moving *Memories of a Catholic Girlhood* (1957) and *How I Grew* (1987) may outlast the temporary notoriety of *The Group*, which in 1963 seemed a scandalous portrait of her class at Vassar. Yet by now, so few years after her death in 1989, she seems scarcely known to the youth of today. She once claimed that when she was an orphaned child her caretaking relatives had tried taping her mouth at night, and at her best she remained unforgettably biting, wickedly acerbic. When in 1980 she remarked about Lillian Hellman on the Dick Cavett show that "every word she writes is a lie, including 'and' and 'the,'" Hellman responded with a defamation suit for $2,225,000 which expired only with the plaintiff. One would have thought that McCarthy's sparkling command of colloquial English, a basis for rivalry with Hellman, would have better ensured her being remembered.

Arendt, on the other hand, who died earlier in 1975, has as we have noted already become one of the most famous social theorists of the twentieth century. In 1995 alone there were said to be five international symposia scheduled to examine Arendt's work. Although a handful of distinguished philosophers have raised objections to Arendt's capacity for windy metaphysics, and some historians have bitterly protested how high-handed she could be in shuffling facts to suit her various ideological agendas, none of this minority opinion has deterred young academics from publishing efforts to explain the ins and outs of Arendt's complex theorizing. The intimate friendship between these two women would seem surprising if only because McCarthy had so concrete and light a stylistic touch whereas Arendt could be as heavy-handed as the tradition of German philosophizing from which she came. Although there are plenty of memorably written passages in Arendt's letters to McCarthy, Arendt's friend was someone who (along with the literary critic Alfred Kazin) helped with the "Englishing" of Arendt's published prose. *Between Friends: The Correspondence of Hannah Arendt and Mary McCarthy 1949-1975*[6] records the closeness of their relationship; Arendt chose McCarthy as a literary executor, and McCarthy had Arendt in mind to replace, if necessary, her own literary executor, Elizabeth Hardwick.

Carol Brightman, McCarthy's 1992 biographer, has written a solid introduction to this fascinating account of a literary alliance between two embattled writers who, however much they each may have complained about how time-consuming fame could be, did not mind getting involved in their various respective public fights. When McCarthy took a beating from those jealous of her commercial successes, Arendt was there as a friend to take McCarthy's side. And when the pro-Zionist Jewish intelligentsia turned savagely on Arendt—because of her thesis in *Eichmann in Jerusalem* which condemned the Jewish response to the menace of Nazism as self-destructive—McCarthy published an article denouncing Arendt's detractors. (Literary politics are such that Arendt sent McCarthy a detailed response to a *Partisan Review* attack on her, although regrettably that four-page, single-spaced document is not reproduced here.)

The relationship between these two women was, as Brightman says, "improbable on the face of it." McCarthy, who hailed originally from Seattle, was as American as apple pie and told Arendt that she hated prophets, while the German-born Arendt, who first escaped to France in 1933, thought of herself as the standard-bearer of the best spiritual German culture, a tradition all but destroyed by the rise of the Nazis. In spite of the seeming incompatibilities between them, the relationship between McCarthy and Arendt flourished passionately. (Randall Jarrell's 1954 novel *Pictures From an Institution*,[7] dedicated to both women, perceptively saw more of the similarities between them.) And this large volume of their correspondence, which McCarthy helped get into print, records the tale of their long-standing loyalty and devotion.

Part of the special joy of reading *Between Friends* comes from how McCarthy and Arendt could join in shared gossip about their most illustrious contemporaries. Scarcely anyone seems missing here, from Americans (like Robert Lowell, Saul Bellow, and Truman Capote) to those abroad: Sartre, Silone, Raymond Aron, W. H. Auden, Isaiah Berlin, Simone de Beauvoir, and George Orwell's widow, to mention only a handful of the interesting figures who come up. The names one picks out are apt to reflect the knowledgeability of the reader and how telling (or wide of the mark) were the chatty remarks Arendt and McCarthy chose to make.

In terms of their respective lives, and how open they are to each other, it is McCarthy who feels more able to bare her soul, or who has more need of the other's emotional help. At the time they first met in 1944, McCarthy was still married to the eminent literary critic Edmund Wilson, but for at least part of *Between Friends*, which first begins in 1949, McCarthy is undergoing a series of domestic crises. When she has an adulterous affair, Arendt is supportive but apt to be moralistic and finger-wagging; whatever she might have felt about McCarthy's romantic conduct did not mean Arendt would not be willing to help cover up the traces of McCarthy's infidelity, conniving in helping her friend in need. Arendt rather touchingly refused to abandon one of McCarthy's discarded husbands; in 1960 Arendt wrote that she had

> looked to him as a friend and I did not lie. For to me the fact is that you brought him into my life, that without you he never would have become—not a personal friend which, of course, he is not—but a friend of the house, so to speak. But once you placed him there, you cannot simply take him away from where he is now.

With McCarthy's fourth marriage, to an American diplomat in Paris, her life seemed to settle down. Arendt's own existence with Blücher sounds reasonably untroubled, and we find Arendt mainly worrying about her husband's health problems, which culminated in his 1970 death. Arendt was remarkably uncomplaining about her own illnesses, and whatever her heart troubles nothing appears to have slowed down her smoking addiction.

My own reaction to these letters may be idiosyncratic, but despite my background as a political theorist I came away from them more impressed, if I had to choose, by McCarthy than Arendt. Perhaps it is mainly a question of McCarthy's superb command of her native language, whereas Arendt always had to struggle to express herself in a foreign tongue. But it is not just McCarthy's capacity to write American English that comes through so notably here; I was surprised at how politically sophisticated she was. Of course I knew about her books of essays in connection with the Vietnam War, an effort that both Arendt and McCarthy early on viewed as colossally misguided. And McCarthy also published journalistically about Watergate. But I had not realized how substantial was the moral content to all McCarthy's thinking, and how thoroughly concerned with social and political issues her fiction was. In 1971 she is still reacting to Arendt's Eichmann thesis, although distinguishing her approach from that of Arendt:

> One has to assume that every man is a thinking reed and a noble nature, even if only part time....Perhaps I am dull-witted, but it seems to me that what you are saying is that an Eichmann lacks an inherent human quality: the capacity for thought, consciousness—conscience. But then isn't he a monster simply? If you allow him a wicked heart, then you leave him some freedom, which permits our condemnation.

No record exists of any reply of Arendt to this telling, and Catholic sounding, point, but it should come as no surprise that after Arendt's death McCarthy saw into print the two volumes of Arendt's *The Life of the Mind*, and helped facilitate the publication of Arendt's lectures on Immanuel Kant.

The geography of where they each lived meant that McCarthy was apt to be commenting about European matters while Arendt appeared to become a spokesperson on American developments. They both went back and forth across the Atlantic, and saw each other regularly (they spoke on the telephone every couple of weeks). No matter how intellectually hard to please McCarthy may have been, Arendt's standards were even snootier. In 1962, for instance, McCarthy reports having written a couple of book reviews, one of Nabokov's *Pale Fire* and the other of J. D. Salinger's *Fanny and Zooey*: "The last I did in two days and it is very viperish and mean and gave me no pleasure, except to get it out of the way, but I really fell in love with the Nabokov book and worked very hard on it, with pure joy." Arendt's own reaction to this news was characteristic for her:

> There is something in N. which I greatly dislike, as though he wanted to show you all the time how intelligent he is. And as though he thinks of himself in terms of "more intelligent than." There is something vulgar in his refinement, and I am a bit allergic against this kind of vulgarity because I know it so well, know so many people cursed with it. But perhaps this is no longer true here. Let me see. I know only one book of his which I truly admire and that is the long essay on Gogol.

Arendt might have been right about Nabokov as a show-off (which was true of Arendt too), but that ingrained trait should not be enough to settle his artistic or critical standing, and it is striking to me that Arendt does not even feel the need to stoop to comment about Salinger.

Although Arendt came to be a great admirer of American freedoms, she remained curiously insulated from the country's political events. For example, after the Cuban missile crisis she wrote McCarthy that she was in no mood to discuss it: "I never believed that this thing could get really serious." One might never have guessed from Arendt's observations how close to deadly nuclear confrontation America and the Soviet Union had come.

Between Friends is bound to be fascinating for what it tells us in connection with the publication of *Eichmann in Jerusalem*. (The letters here need to be put alongside Arendt's comments to Jaspers.) Somehow the editor is singularly unhelpful in providing the context of the uproar that greeted Arendt's book, which first appeared in five issues of the *New Yorker*. Brightman blandly asserts that Arendt's "text...was based on the transcript of the trial and was not an inquiry into the massacre of European Jews." She also puts in a footnote trying to summarize Arendt's argument, but does so in a way that extracts all the teeth from Arendt's singular point of view: "Resistance wouldn't have prevented the extermination policy, she contended, but it might have made it harder to put into effect." It seems to me striking how Arendt, with McCarthy, could adopt the "position...that I wrote a report and that I am not in politics, either Jewish or otherwise." Arendt went on to say,

> As I see it, there are no "ideas" in this Report, there are only facts with a few conclusions, and these conclusions usually appear at the end of each chapter. The only exception to this is the Epilog, which is a discussion of the legal aspects of the case. In other words, my point would be that what the whole furor is about are *facts*, and neither theories nor ideas.

Arendt, living in the States, was attempting to adopt the most anti-theoretical American pragmatism, which left her unable to understand the horror her book aroused among the Jewish-American powers-that-be. Although she had a long history of being suspicious of Zionism, she thought that the Eichmann book was mainly an occasion for her enemies to strike back, and she suspected that someone like Isaiah Berlin, for instance, was responsible for manipulating reviews in Britain on behalf of the government of Israel. (Unlike Arendt, Berlin was a defender of classic liberal values, and he viewed the German philosophic tradition, at least as epitomized by Heidegger and Arendt, as a source of political and social poison.)

For all their mutual sophistication, both Arendt and McCarthy could be beside the point about politics. McCarthy actually writes that "the Kennedy assassination is going to be one of those litmus-paper or goat-and-sheep dividers, like the Moscow trials and Pasternak and your *Eichmann*." If McCarthy is flattering Arendt about the stature of her controversial book,

Arendt too can make equally odd judgments. In the spring of 1965, like others concerned about the sharply mounting American involvement in Southeast Asia under President Lyndon Johnson, Arendt writes, "Do you ever see Lippmann's columns about Vietnam? I thought them pretty good, but I must confess that I am less concerned than almost all the people I know. Informed opinion here is quite unanimous against our politics—there is a consensus if that is what Johnson wants." This is the kind of irony in Arendt's way of thinking that it has been so easy for critics of her work to overlook. But then she goes on with a completely irrelevant bit of theorizing: "The chief trouble seems to me still that no American statesman or politician is able to understand what a revolution is all about." (That year Arendt published her *On Revolution*.)

Arendt cannot restrain her penchant for broad-stroke pontificating: "I do not doubt," she writes a couple of weeks later, "that in the very long run, the whole of Asia will fall under Chinese influence but not necessarily under Chinese domination." No effort was made to weigh or assess the role of the Japanese, or even to distinguish between Chinese "influence" as opposed to "domination." And for a woman who hated everything connected to Freud, Arendt did not feel inhibited about making use of diagnoses when it suited her political dislikes: for instance, she wrote in 1968 that she had "the impression that Johnson is not just 'bad' or stupid but kind of insane." (McCarthy's own dislike of psychoanalysis at least was based in several down-to-earth bad experiences with analysts, while Arendt's objections were abstract.)

* * *

The relaxing scintillation of *Between Friends*, which makes a leisurely read, comes as a sharp contrast to the disquieting impact of Elzbieta Ettinger's *Hannah Arendt/Martin Heidegger*[8], a short book that is almost impossible to put down. We have known since 1982 that as a young woman Arendt had that love affair with her philosophy teacher, Heidegger, who at the time was about twice her age; in 1924 he appears to have started the liaison, which was secret and went on for some four years until he broke it off. He later joined the Nazi party, about which he never apologized, nor did his politics interfere with his becoming known as one of the twentieth century's most influential thinkers. (Curiously the French did not hold his Nazi past against him, and Sartre, supposedly a man of the left, helped popularize Heidegger in Paris.) Although Arendt's books so often centered on the moral position of Jews, she continued to treasure her bond to Heidegger.

The reader of *Hannah Arendt/Martin Heidegger* is bound to feel frustrated, since unlike the correspondence with McCarthy and that with Jaspers we do not get the transcripts of the letters themselves, but only Eittinger's description of them. Heidegger's widow, who has been reported to have been even a worse Nazi than her husband, lived on for many years after his death in

1976, and in her behalf the evidence about the affair with Arendt was kept back. Ettinger had undertaken a biography of Arendt, and lucked out when she was given permission to read Arendt's letters as well as those of Heidegger. Ettinger decided, though, to focus exclusively on Arendt's involvement with Heidegger, even though Arendt's executor (who took over after McCarthy's death) was startled at Ettinger's decision. One of Heidegger's sons was also displeased; he had only given permission for his father's letters to be read, not intending that they be quoted, and he was reported to be claiming that there are numerous errors in Ettinger's rendition. Arendt's executor and Heidegger's son then agreed to publish the complete letters themselves, although it will be awhile until they appear in English, and it is unclear whether it will alter the unfavorable impression many have taken away from Ettinger's *Hannah Arendt/Martin Heidegger.*

The notoriety that Ettinger's book has aroused will inevitably lead to Arendt's writings being thoroughly combed for the Heidegger matter to be further explored.[9] His own reputation, as the specifics of his collaboration with the Nazis continues to be further documented, has not been faring well lately. But Arendt first made her scholarly reputation with her *The Origins of Totalitarianism*, and the central if not exaggerated role she assigned there to the power of anti-Semitism is bound to be read now in a fresh biographical light.

Arendt's whole involvement with Heidegger may well cast a shadow over her prominent recent stature. Arendt, so free in expressing ethical judgments about others, nonetheless kept intimately connected with such a dubious creature as Heidegger. One might speculate about whether she was, somewhere in herself, ashamed of the continued tie with Heidegger. (She once wrote to McCarthy, at a time when McCarthy sensed their friendship was in trouble: "I am not sensitive and rather obtuse in all purely psychological matters.") And it is possible to conjecture how much of the bond to Heidegger should be accounted for by their romance, or instead attributed to the opportunism that is part of intellectual life.

After Arendt has resumed her correspondence with Heidegger some years after the end of World War II, she withdrew from her earlier public and private reservations about him; she helped, in Ettinger's judgment, to whitewash Heidegger's politics. As I have mentioned, Arendt was capable of disguising from Jaspers some of her own meetings with Heidegger, and the intensity of her continuing involvement with him. Eittinger suggests that Arendt was protectively acting so as not to hurt Jaspers's feelings, but she was privately outspoken about Heidegger's pathological lying, even as he carried on his own obsession with authenticity. (The subject of bad faith would seem to attract those most capable of committing it.) It appears that Arendt was eager to visit Heidegger as often as he would permit, and she was open with McCarthy about her distress at his declining powers in old age. Eittinger adopts the gentle approach of interpreting Arendt's behavior as an expression of the irrationality of love, but one wonders whether Eittinger has been inadvertently successful in killing Arendt with such kindness. Either Arendt was extraordinarily duplicitous, or else a silly lovesick goose, and neither alternative is likely to add to her reputation as a moralist. The one possibility that Ettinger declines to explore is that Arendt and Heidegger pursued a mutually exploitive relationship.

Arendt gave Heidegger publishing advice, helped promote his writings abroad, and assisted with his translations; when the Heideggers needed money, they sought her advice on maximizing the return on selling the manuscript of Heidegger's *Being and Time*. Eittinger cuttingly underlines that where money was involved, the former Nazis turned to a Jew for help. Such a request did not lead to Arendt's skipping a beat in her relationship with Heidegger; she was fully obliging and cooperative.

Arendt, so apparently heartless about the helplessness of the Jews in the face of the Nazi terror, like others of her generation of German Jews sounds more German than any of her former countrymen could aspire to be. The Eichmann book is as much about the collapse of old German culture as it is concerned with the fate of Jewry. Arendt took the disruption of her own life when she was forced to flee Germany and blew it up into a rupture of Western society as a whole. Arendt is nothing if not a grand theorist, even though I think she is at her best in her essays. One reason why the Eichmann book has been so enduringly successful is that the author had something concrete to deal with, and this work always proves engagingly provocative to students. The coming to power of the Nazis is, in my view, the most significant political event in the history of this past century; it should be permanently disturbing for all friends of democratic theory that the highly educated German nation could willingly choose to vote into office a monster whose views and agenda were well known.

Arendt's letters to her second husband, Blücher, indicate that she primarily blamed Heidegger's wife Elfride for blinding him to the profound evil of the National Socialists; indeed, Arendt seemed determined to rationalize his noxious beliefs and misconduct. One rumor (promoted by Isaiah Berlin) had it that Arendt and Heidegger renewed their physical liaison after the Second World War, although Ettinger does not explore this possibility; as far as I can tell Eittinger is dismissive of any such avenue of thought, but she does report that in the same period Arendt's husband Blücher "erroneously considered her affair with Heidegger as ended." Presumably what Ettinger had in mind was the extent to which Blücher underestimated the depth of Arendt's continuing involvement with Heidegger, even if Ettinger gives little credence to the likelihood that even more might have been involved.

It should be impossible, I think, to dissociate a philosopher's work from the life itself; of course the validity of insights can in principle be independently tested and evaluated, but the meaning ideas possess comes partly from the intentions of historical actors. Students of political theory often like to think that ideas can be treated in a vacuum, apart from normal human experience. But if Heidegger's reputation has suffered as his past political commitments have been put under scrutiny, Arendt too might be tarnished as a result of her unflagging attempts to curry his favor.

In hindsight the whole friendship between McCarthy and Arendt could have appealed to Henry James's characteristic sensibilities. European complexities, like those involving Arendt, the Heideggers, Jaspers and his wife, as well as Blücher, are much more complicated than the more stereotypical divorces in which McCarthy was involved. McCarthy may have intuited the significance that Heidegger achieved in Arendt's life, but it is hard to believe that she could have absorbed the political and social ramifications of what Arendt was bent on justifying. On what possible basis, one wonders, could McCarthy share the leftist moral high ground with Arendt on such issues as Vietnam or Watergate when Arendt had so compromised herself with someone possessing Heidegger's apparent thoughtlessness, especially since Arendt herself knew banal self-deception from first-hand experience? The lesson we ought to take away, however, should not echo moralistic judgment-making; compassion tells us that Arendt was doing the best she could, and when the text for the Arendt-Heidegger correspondence finally appears, perhaps the relationship will seem less distasteful. But for now the surprising delight of Arendt's friendship with McCarthy appears shadowed by the menacing nature of her alliance with Heidegger.

* * *

Eittinger's *Hannah Arendt/Martin Heidegger* made such a compelling narrative that it could be read through in an afternoon, and naturally it provoked wide publicity and intense controversy. To recapitulate the details— Heidegger was Arendt's first philosophy mentor; Heidegger allegedly initiated an affair that was clandestine and lasted years; he appears to have been responsible for breaking it off. Heidegger went on to become, for more than a decade, an enthusiastic member of the Nazi Party, about which he remained afterwards unapologetic; he also is known as one of the twentieth century's most influential thinkers. We have already noted how oddly enough Arendt herself went on to write widely discussed books that often centered on the moral position of Jews, although she continued to treasure her bond with Heidegger. That correspondence between Arendt and Heidegger, which started up again after World War II and lasted until their deaths (she died in 1975, he in 1976) had been embargoed until Ettinger scooped everyone in the field by her account of the letters they exchanged. One might say she was strikingly lucky in being able to read the Arendt-Heidegger letters. Heidegger's widow (a devout Nazi since the 1920s) lived on long after her husband, and for her sake the details of the affair were withheld. Ettinger, who successfully approached Arendt's second literary executor, was allowed to read copies of Arendt's letters as well as the Heidegger side, for the sake of a full-scale biography of Arendt. Ettinger decided, instead, to concentrate on Arendt's relationship with Heidegger, to the shock of Arendt's executor, as well as the displeasure of one of Heidegger's sons. I am unclear whether it is the historical story of the relationship between Arendt and Heidegger that is so unsavory, the interpretation of it that Eittinger has provided, or a combination of the two. It remains to be seen how much the full documentation, which it would appear wiser for the respective executors to have allowed out initially, will change the terrible first impression one takes away from Ettinger's *Hannah Arendt/Martin Heidegger*.

Although philosophers as distinguished as Stuart Hampshire and Isaiah Berlin have been spokesmen for those who object to the credulous popularity of Arendt's capacity for metaphysical wordiness, that has not deterred aspiring academics from repeated efforts to explicate the complexities of Arendt's thinking. I can think of no recent political theorist who has attracted so much of a secondary literature. And historians who have objected to Arendt's theses have been lumped together as biased, not because they are like legendary dry-as-dust British analytic philosophers bound to be hostile to the scope of Continental theorists, but as representatives of the Jewish pro-Zionist intellectual establishment, permanently offended by Arendt's 1963 *Eichmann in Jerusalem*. Arendt's pride was to be a representative emissary of pre-Nazi German culture for the rest of the world. Although she had consistently despised all forms of psychoanalytic thinking, and expressed her abhorrence even of introspection and romanticism, in her examination of Eichmann's trial she allowed herself to blame the victims of Nazism for their own self-destruction, and she could not skip the tastelessness of dismissing Eichmann's prosecutor as a Galician Jew not up to the high standards of her own German background.

At the time Arendt first started publishing books—for example, with her 1951 *The Origins of Totalitarianism*—she was by no means out of step with the prevailing winds of dominant thought. "Totalitarianism" as a concept is no longer now in vogue, but at the time Arendt was writing, it was a modish way of describing both Nazi and Stalinist dictatorships, even if she was mainly concerned with the roots of the German regime. The Cold War was then at its height, and the belief was prevalent that so-called totalitarianism could only be toppled from the outside pressures of war. George F. Kennan, who now stands as the one expert to predict prophetically that the Soviet system might collapse from internal pressures, then was stigmatized by his peers as a quasi-religious seer caught up in mysticism instead of hardheaded political realities.

Although Arendt began fashionably enough, it was not long before all the idiosyncrasies of her thinking became known. As Ralph Ellison later observed, the brouhaha over her Eichmann book had been preceded by her perverse defense of the position of Arkansas Governor Orval Faubus, who fought to preserve segregated schools until President Dwight D. Eisenhower sent troops, enforcing desegregation in Little Rock, as part of a response to the greatest challenge to federal authority since the Civil War. In that *Dissent* piece Arendt manipulated elevated-sounding concepts of "public," "private," and "social" in a breathtakingly high-handed manner. "Since the Supreme Court decision to enforce desegregation in public schools," she somehow claimed, "the general situation in the South has deteriorated." At the time it was hard to imagine where Arendt, who had been in the States since 1941, had been spiritually living, or what her true values were.

Now Hannah Arendt's involvement with Heidegger, as best we can understand it thanks to Ettinger's excellent book, casts new light on Arendt's current standing. It has to be striking that Arendt, so free in expressing ethical judgments about the actions of others, could have remained so enmeshed with Heidegger. As I have already intimated, how much of the tie can be attributed to romance, as opposed to opportunism, may inevitably be impossible to reconstruct. We do know that once Arendt got back in touch with Heidegger after World War II, she reversed some of her earlier criticisms of him as she helped rehabilitate Heidegger's politics in the post-Nazi period. To repeat: she disguised from Jaspers, her other teacher, some of her meetings with Heidegger, perhaps, according to Ettinger, out of protectiveness as she sought not to hurt Jaspers. In notes to herself, as well as in communications with Jaspers, she was open about Heidegger's capacity for mendacity, yet she herself continued to visit him as often as he would permit. The kindest approach, which Ettinger adopts, would be to interpret Arendt's behavior as part of the irrationality of love, the way passion could take control of her.

As she did with Jaspers, Arendt gave Heidegger publishing advice and worked on behalf of his translations. She was tempted to dedicate the German edition of her book *The Human Condition* to Heidegger, but held back. (*On Revolution* was dedicated to Jaspers and his wife.) Arendt's letters to Heidegger sound profuse, although in writing to Jaspers she could be savage about Heidegger. It is true that the full details of Heidegger's activities as a Nazi have grown substantially worse with close historical inspection, but one suspects that Arendt must have known how bad the real story was; Jaspers, for example, remained adamant about not recommending that Heidegger be allowed to teach in Germany right after the end of World War II. Heidegger's address in 1933, on becoming rector at Freiburg University, was notorious, and she, in writing to Jaspers, was unremitting about Heidegger's misbehavior toward his former teacher Edmund Husserl. Eittinger provides disquieting particulars to Arendt's twists and turns connected with Heidegger, even if she does not seem to want to acknowledge the extent to which Arendt and Heidegger might have been mutually cannibalizing each other.

Other of Heidegger's students—Herbert Marcuse, for example—were less forgiving of his Nazi activities. It is striking how Arendt, so unsympathetic to the Jewish plight in Central Europe under the Nazis, found ways to rationalize Heidegger's beliefs and misconduct. One tack was for her to put the weight of the responsibility on Heidegger's wife, although Heidegger himself late in life insisted that the three of them be on the footing of intimate friendship. According to Arendt, Heidegger was like Plato in turning to a tyrant in practical affairs. Somehow she convinced herself that Heidegger had never read *Mein Kampf*, as if that would have been somehow to his credit. One has to question the alleged wonders of old German cultural life if the failure to read such a book should have somehow counted in Heidegger's favor. (In reality he had read *Mein Kampf* as early as 1931.)

Partisans of Arendt, and Heidegger too, are apt to want to dissociate philosophy from practical politics. Arendt's first biographer, Elisabeth Young-Bruehl, has been quoted maintaining that even now the affair between them cannot be shown to have had a strong influence on her thought. One has to wonder how distant from human experience it is possible for intellectual historians to become. The initial news of the involvement between Arendt and Heidegger came as traumatic to some of Arendt's most morally sensitive students. Academic philosophers may continue to be inclined to minimize the significance of Heidegger's politics; and other German intellectuals did collaborate with the Nazis, too. About Arendt, however, no one can lay claim to her equaling Heidegger's technical philosophic originality; and in the light of her Eichmann thesis, it may be hard not to wonder if she was not engaging there in a subtle if unconscious form of self-criticism. If Eichmann were simply following orders, and his conduct certifiably normal within the context of Nazi Germany, her own defense of Heidegger can reflect the way a social thinker such as herself might be conditioned by circumstances and advantage to curry favor in the midst of the most vile forms of evil. Having as a Jew escaped from Germany in 1933, Arendt remained for the rest of her life loyal to the whole philosophic tradition that had helped lead to Hitlerism, and the tale of how she continued to dance around Heidegger's reputation may have permanently damaged her ethical standing.

It is not clear to me that Ettinger is fully conscious of the blow she had administered to Arendt. Ettinger is surely aware of how much she detests Heidegger. Yet when we are told that Heidegger's zealously pro-Nazi spouse was "perhaps the ideal wife for Heidegger," Eittinger has undercut Heidegger in a special way. While Ettinger tells us that "Heidegger's apologists (including Hannah Arendt) endeavored to portray him as a helpless victim of her [his wife's] sinister obsession," Ettinger herself believes that Heidegger was "never a tool in the hands of his wife or anyone else."

Ettinger may be correct that Arendt "exculpated' Heidegger "not as much out of loyalty, compassion, or a sense of justice as out of her own need to save her pride and dignity." Yet I suspect that Arendt would be shocked to see herself as such a stereotypical love-stricken creature, silly even in her old age. Somehow Arendt was taken aback by Heidegger's wife's jealousy of her. Even if Arendt seems not to have been the only instance of Heidegger's adultery, it is hard to believe that she can have expected anything other than jealousy on Elfride Heidegger's part. Yet the Nazi ideology that the couple shared brought them closer together. It should come as no great surprise that Arendt could disguise from her own second husband, Blücher, as she did from Jaspers, what was going on between her and Heidegger after World War II.

The complexities of Central European manners are bound to sound, from the point of view of straight-shooting Americans, like whirlpools of treacherous friendships. To take just one example, when Arendt was in 1961 reading the galleys of Heidegger's Nietzsche treatise for her friend Kurt Wolff, who was not by chance Heidegger's own American publisher, "she did not mention it to Jaspers," lest she upset her ailing teacher.

Intellectuals make at least as many political, moral, and personal mistakes as anybody else. Ordinary folk, however, may not have the same capacity for self-deception as more high-powered minds. For the sake of Arendt's reputation—and it is the quotations from her letters that do so much damage – one wonders if she would not have been shrewder to have destroyed this whole correspondence. For a politically savvy woman, who wrote repeatedly about authenticity and lying, it may have been humanly impossible for her to destroy a past she did not see as damaging. Heidegger, too, had his own ways of self-deceit. There has been a longstanding Heidegger controversy, and now Arendt is a secure part of it. One only hopes that in time professional philosophy will come closer to attaining the ideal of impartiality, so that the story of Arendt and Heidegger will get put in proper perspective without either apologetics or undue moralizing. Although Arendt would not have liked the help that Freud's writings could offer, in a warning to one of his own loyal potential biographers Freud reminded us how Hamlet might have been right when he wondered who would escape whipping were he used after his desert.

* * *

Unlike how some like to talk about Hitler's "seizure" of power in Germany, I would emphasize instead the extent to which the Nazis succeeded in functioning within the context of the democratic rules of the game. Of course they took unfair advantage of political opportunities, and intimidation or violence played a part in their electoral campaigns. But according to the traditional standards of parliamentary democracy, Hitler's party received more popular support than many other democratically elected parliamentary governments. So the failure of the post-World War I Weimar regime to preclude Hitler's success remains an enduring mark against the vitality of democracy.

The German system can be seen as having self-destructed; proportional representation, which was viewed as democratically more fair than winner-take-all single-member districts, helped to promote the recognition of radical fringe parties like the early Nazis. I wonder how many of us would continue to put such a premium on the ideals of free speech and minority rights in North America if we really thought there was a chance of neo-Nazism flourishing here. In France today *Mein Kampf* still cannot be published. Toward the end of the Weimar republic it was, given the combined power of the Nazi right and the communist left, impossible for a government to manage without invoking emergency power decrees that Hitler, once in office, was able to use with notorious advantage.

Hitler was proceeding to implement the objectives he had stated since the end of the First World War. Yet the enormity of the Holocaust that resulted still remains staggering, over half a century after the world learned the worst about what had happened. Recent comparative studies of genocide, which have, for instance, looked at the Armenians destroyed in the Ottoman Empire, or Stalin's assault on the kulaks, still do not match the horror of what the Nazis perpetrated.[10] Even when the continuation of the Holocaust toward the latter part of World War II was consuming vital German military resources, self-interest did not slow down the accelerating force of the Nazi determination to fulfill the Final Solution. That Germany, despite its great contributions to music, philosophy, and literature was capable of being responsible for the Nazis remains a permanent blot on the efficacy of nineteenth-century liberal ideas of enlightenment, progress, and rationality.

Psychoanalysis is supposed to be able to deal with irrational drives. From Hitler's point of view, the Nazis had a well-worked out rationale behind the policies of his government. And the dislocations his regime inflicted on Central Europe had pronounced effects on the movement Freud had created. Although, with the help of supporters abroad, Freud and his immediate circle escaped into exile in London, by the time he got there and adequate thought was given to his four sisters left behind in Vienna, it was already too late to save them from the clutches of the Nazis. (Freud and his younger brother had left them with substantial money, which proved an inadequate safeguard.) Although relatively few analysts died in concentration camps, psychoanalytic thinking has been prominent in accounts of the psychology of camp life. As Nazi terror sent analysts to the United States, Britain, and elsewhere, it doubtless helps to account for the spread of Freud's teachings.

One sign of the impact of psychoanalysis on the intellectual life of our time is the extent to which even those most explicitly hostile to depth psychology share in some of its central premises. Arendt, for example, was as fiercely anti-Freudian as one can image. On having taken a look at J. B.

Watson's *Behaviorism*, she wrote Blücher: "One can't actually read it. Compared to him Freud is a deep thinker, no, a genius, God himself." A few years later Blücher was ineffectively trying to get one of their friends to see Erich Fromm therapeutically, but the anti-psychoanalytic propaganda of Arendt and Blücher was defeating a specific worthy purpose; as Blücher wrote Arendt, "the poor man keeps quoting our own arguments against psychoanalysis. We should never talk to others the way we talk to each other —and in this case we have helped wreak havoc." For Arendt, psychoanalysis had attempted to usurp the role of traditional continental philosophy. While someone later like Jacques Lacan, unlike Freud, sought to bring philosophy and psychoanalysis closer together, Arendt was stupefied at the naïve credulity with which, especially in America, Freud's teachings could become a substitute for what she regarded as genuine philosophizing.

I can still remember how shocked I was by Arendt's Eichmann thesis—for the tale of the Holocaust that it recorded, for the trial she recounted, and for the special viewpoint that she developed. Even though experts had been, I think, correct to pounce on Arendt's lack of compassion for the victims of Nazism, the Eichmann book posed fascinating theoretical issues. And this remains true even though historians were able to tear apart Arendt's contention that had the Jews been leaderless, fewer of them would have had to die; Arendt was adopting an almost crude psychoanalytic blaming-the-victim approach, as she recounted how the Jews had supposedly collaborated in their own destruction. Although she never publicly acknowledged the reviewing support that the analyst Bettelheim offered her, Arendt's reasoning was similar to his own about how the Jews had allegedly behaved like sheep in the face of Nazi aggression.

Arendt not only disdainfully passed over historical evidence contrary to her argument, but she went on to charge that Eichmann himself, centrally in charge of the transportation side of the destruction of European Jewry, was "banal." Arendt had luxuriated in the proposition that before the trial itself half a dozen psychiatrists had certified Eichmann as "normal." Arendt commented, "Behind the comedy of the soul experts lay the hard fact that his was obviously no case of moral let alone legal insanity." She brushed aside evidence that Eichmann had been thought by the psychiatrists to be "a man obsessed with a dangerous and insatiable urge to kill," and was "a perverted, sadistic personality," in which case Arendt thought he "would have belonged in an insane asylum" instead of getting the death penalty. Arendt passed over such psychiatric opinion because she found more challenging the proposition that an average person could be incapable of telling right from wrong. She was bent on denouncing middle class, "bourgeois" society, and Germany was only part of her disappointment. Although in her earlier *The Origins of Totalitarianism* she had advanced the idea of "radical evil," her outlook on the masses ("men who can no longer be psychologically understood") was consistent with her chosen view of Eichmann.

Although the controversy over Eichmann really started over the propriety of his 1961 kidnapping in Argentina, Zionists have continued to be offended by Arendt's critical attitude toward Israeli politics, her contempt for the Galician-sounding speeches of the chief prosecutor, and her ignoring the heroism of the Jewish resistance to the Nazis. One does not have to be a blind advocate of Zionism to take exception to Arendt's judgments, many of which seem off-the-cuff.

The bitter controversy over Arendt's book was different than the more recent intellectual tempest occasioned by Daniel Jonah Goldhagen's *Hitler's Willing Executioners: Ordinary Germans and the Holocaust.*[11] It seems striking that Arendt's own theses were so widely influential that Goldhagen did not feel the need to challenge her frontally. In his account, which focused on the psychology of the perpetrators, and how they willingly carried out Hitler's Final Solution with extraordinary brutality, Goldhagen noted, "Even though the full character of the perpetrators' social and cultural existence is hard to recover, the unreal images of them as isolated, frightened, thoughtless beings performing their tasks reluctantly are erroneous." In a note to this passage, Goldhagen observed: "The person most responsible for promulgating this image is, of course, Hannah Arendt." Goldhagen's version of Arendt's "image" is somewhat tendentious; but his book remains so riveting precisely because he highlighted the extent to which the perpetrators' behavior was anything but "banal." Clearly Goldhagen does not look on someone like Eichmann as a perfect bureaucrat.

The problem of comparing and contrasting Arendt and Goldhagen is complicated by their very different professional backgrounds. While Arendt was reared philosophically in Germany, Goldhagen is a young social scientist whose career is just getting started. The dispute over his book has in a way already far exceeded that connected with Arendt's text. For Goldhagen had indicted Germany itself, and its supposedly special tradition of anti-Semitism, in such a way that his book became the subject of international political interest. I am presuming that the sales of his book not only exceeded those of Arendt's, but surely the German national reaction to his writing was more public and sustained than what Arendt had achieved. It still remains to be seen how his book fares over the long haul.

Far from having stressed the bureaucratic nature of the Holocaust, Goldhagen highlighted the exceptional cruelty involved in the German practice of genocide. Such destructiveness confirms, alas, the most disheartening features of the classical psychoanalytic view of the barbarous potentialities of human nature, which Freud commented on during World War I. It is not often noted that Goldhagen even challenged the old figures, stemming from the Nuremberg trials, which hypothesized what proportion of the six million dead died in concentration camps. The "killing units" were responsible, Goldhagen argues, for over 40 percent of the Jewish victims. Goldhagen insists that had the Nazis "never deployed gas chambers, they would likely have killed almost as many Jews."[12]

While representatives of the international Jewish establishment (including, according to Arendt, Isaiah Berlin) rose up to attack her, in Goldhagen's case he became chiefly embroiled in what looks like a turf-war with historians. He has been accused of radically oversimplifying the motives behind the mass murder of Jews. Why, for example, indict the Germans so strongly when the Austrians, who made up under 10 percent of the population of Hitler's regime, were involved in half the genocidal crimes?[13] Anti-Semitic beliefs seem to many as only one explanation for the destruction of European Jewry. The public's favorable response to Goldhagen's work has been enough to sicken professional rivals, who might be presumed to be jealous of his immense success.

Arendt drove her conception of Eichmann, part of her indictment of modern culture, hard enough that she distorted the nature of the Holocaust and those who were most responsible for the deaths of millions. But if Goldhagen has definitively corrected her conception of what happened, his own account would appear ultimately to diminish Hitler's own responsibility for what took place. The popular conviction, which still continues, that Hitler was insane or somehow unbalanced at least focuses on his own special role. Besides giving us a Hamlet without the Prince of Denmark, Goldhagen has also not succeeded in supplying the diverse motives people had for voting for the Nazis in the first place.

Let us assume that both Arendt and Goldhagen were both guilty of oversimplifications, and that their respective critics were sound in raising heated public objections. Yet *Eichmann in Jerusalem* and *Hitler's Willing Executioners* make, I think, for mesmerizing reading. The study of the Holocaust has surely not been retarded by the biased popularizations of each of the two authors. I do not want to evaluate their work only in terms of the social consequences of what they accomplished, but I believe that it is undeniable that the publication of these two books, and the extended controversies they gave rise to, have signally illuminated successive generations about what happened under the Nazis.

An old teacher of mine, who had with her family fled from Central Europe in the thirties, remarked at the time of the Eichmann trial that she hoped that periodically some ex-Nazi or other could be found and put on trial so that the world would be reminded anew what had once taken place. Revenge can lead to curious politics. How many of us generally endorse kidnapping people from one country and taking them abroad to face trial under a different legal jurisdiction? I am amazed that there was not more opposition to even what happened to Panama's General Noriega, who now languishes in an American jail. And many of us are apt to be skeptical about the ethics of capital punishment, yet in the face of what the Nazis did I find it impossible to take what might seem the most humanitarian position. The whole concept of war crimes, and political trials in general, will continue to haunt modern liberal jurisprudence. In 1970 Telford Taylor, who had been the United States Chief Counsel at Nuremberg, shocked supporters of the War in Southeast Asia by looking at the American venture in the light of Nuremberg principles.[14] What to do with captured Taliban and al-Qaeda fighters has reawakened the problem of meting out political justice.

Psychoanalysis has obviously had something important to say about aggression; the early Freudian concentration on pathology was such that it was some years before someone like Anna Freud started talking about how aggression can be a healthy and essential part of personality development.[15] But no armchair theorizing, even about the supposed existence of a "death instinct," can prepare us for the realities of the barbarism illustrated by the Holocaust. The capacity for wickedness, too often muffled in professional terminology, should remind us that nothing in the jargon of modern psychology should be taken as a replacement for traditional moral philosophizing. It still remains for me a mystery how the Holocaust, or other genocides, could have taken place. Henry Adams once wrote in his *Education* that "the stupendous failure of Christianity tortured history,"[16] and his adage seems to me pertinent in connection with the Holocaust. Inadequate though both Arendt and Goldhagen may be, they were dead right in addressing a problem that may well remain permanently incapable of being resolvable but nonetheless a real dilemma.

Shortly after the Nazis took power, and started their book-burning, Freud is supposed to have ruefully commented: "What progress we are making. In the Middle Ages they would have burnt me; nowadays they are content with burning my books." For all his skepticism about human motives, and his suspicions about the advance of enlightenment in history, Freud like so many others not only did not anticipate the worst of the Holocaust, he missed out on the original danger that Hitler posed. Before the Nazis took office he was said to have remarked that the nation of Goethe could never go to the bad. And after the Nazis were in power Freud credulously joined others in believing all sorts of stories about Hitler's alleged sexual perversities. When Wilhelm Reich made orgastic sexuality the key to normality, he was defending a genuine aspect of Freudian thinking. But Hitler, and Stalin too, have given rise to renewed interest in the figure of Satan. Mikhail Bulgakov's famous novel *The Master and Margarita* is only one example of how realistic the belief in the supernatural powers of the devil can be.

When Freud playfully identified himself, on a number of occasions, with the devil, he was doing so in the spirit of Nietzsche's kind of celebration of the virtues of transgression. No matter how offensive the lack of natural piety in Freud may be, and it would be legitimate to wonder whether Christian ethics deserve to be assaulted by people like Nietzsche and Freud (or Heidegger), at least Freud's thinking, and that of other continental figures, did not leave us unprepared for the clashes between alternative moral values that can be striking in connection with the Holocaust. Jean-Paul Sartre used to rely on the example of the philosophical dilemma of a young man forced to choose between staying home to defend his aged mother as opposed to joining up with the Resistance.

North American conceptions of normality ought to be suspended in the light of the different exaggerations that Arendt and Goldhagen offer. Only if we appreciate the full capacity of human beings to behave in shockingly disappointing ways are we going to be in a position also to appreciate their capacities to transcend experience in a truly heroic way. The good fortune we have enjoyed on this continent, marred to be sure by the destruction of the Indians, slavery, and the Civil War, needs to be balanced by an awareness of what has happened even worse elsewhere. In the face of the reality of the Holocaust I think that those who have tried to revive moral and philosophic teachings have been performing a real service. It took courage for example for someone like Otto Rank to have tried to legitimize altruism psychoanalytically. And an ego psychologist like Erik H. Erikson, whom Lacan disdained as the most dangerous, because the best, of that school of thought, was trying to import Christian ethics within psychoanalytic theory. I think it is no surprise that Lacan's Benedictine monk brother, to whom Lacan had dedicated his dissertation, was able to describe all Lacan's teachings within Catholic theology.[17] Although psychoanalysis has had a special appeal for the left, we ought not to ignore the essential ways in which it also helps enrich some of the most ancient aspects of Western culture. One need not go as far as Arendt in her reaction to the behaviorist Watson to conclude that either Freud, or she herself for that matter, can be considered "a deep thinker, no, a genius, God himself"; but any thinkers like she or others like her do help awaken us to the necessity of confronting the fundamental challenges of moral life.

Notes

1. *Hannah Arendt/Karl Jaspers Correspondence 1926-1969*, ed. Lotte Kohler and Hans Saner, translated by Robert and Rita Kimber (New York: Harcourt Brace, 1992).
2. Hannah Arendt, *Essays in Understanding 1930-1954*, ed. Jerome Kohn (New York: Harcourt Brace & Co., 1994).
3. *Hannah Arendt: Critical Essays*, ed. Lewis P. Hinchman and Sandra K. Hinchman (Albany: State University of New York Press, 1994). See also Margaret Canovan, *The Political Thought of Hannah Arendt* (New York: Harcourt Brace Jovanovich, 1974), Stephen J. Whitfield, *Into the Dark: Hannah Arendt and Totalitarianism* (Philadelphia: Temple University Press, 1980), Maurizio Passerin d'Entrèves, *The Political Philosophy of Hannah Arendt* (New York: Routledge, 1994), Larry May and Jerome Kohn, editors, *Hannah Arendt: Twenty Years Later* (Cambridge, MA:

MIT Press, 1997), Craig Calhoun and John McGowan, editors, *Hannah Arendt and the Meaning of Politics* (Minneapolis: University of Minnesota Press, 1997), Dana R. Villa, *Politics, Philosophy, Terror: Essays on the Thought of Hannah Arendt* (Princeton, NJ: Princeton University Press, 1999).

4. *Within Four Walls: The Correspondence Between Hannah Arendt and Heinrich Blücher, 1936-1968*, ed. with an introduction by Lotte Kohler (New York: Harcourt, 2000).

5. See Paul Roazen, *Political Theory and the Psychology of the Unconscious* (London: Open Gate Press, 2000), "The Rise and Fall of Bruno Bettelheim," pp. 124-51.

6. *Between Friends: The Correspondence of Hannah Arendt and Mary McCarthy 1949-1975*, ed. with an introduction by Carol Brightman (New York: Harcourt Brace, 1995).

7. Randall Jarrell, *Pictures From an Institution* (London: Penguin Books, 1959).

8. Elzbieta Ettinger, *Hannah Arendt/Martin Heidegger* (New Haven, CT: Yale University Press, 1995).

9. See, for instance, Richard Wolin, *Heidegger's Children: Hannah Arendt, Karl Löwith, Hans Jonas, and Herbert Marcuse* (Princeton, NJ: Princeton University Press, 2001).

10. Alan S. Rosenbaum, *Is the Holocaust Unique? Perspectives on Comparative Genocide* (Boulder, CO: Westview, 1996).

11. Daniel Jonah Goldhagen, *Hitler's Willing Executioners: Ordinary Germans and the Holocaust* (New York: Vintage, 1997).

12. Daniel Jonah Goldhagen, "Motives, Causes and Alibis," *New Republic* (Dec. 23, 1996), p. 45.

13. Fritz Stern, "The Goldhagen Controversy: One Nation, One People, One Theory?" *Foreign Affairs*, Nov.-Dec. 1996, p. 129.

14. Telford Taylor, *Nuremberg and Vietnam: American Tragedy* (Chicago: Quadrangle Books, 1970). See also Gary Jonathan Bass, *Stay the Hand of Vengeance: The Politics of War Crime Tribunals* (Princeton, NJ: Princeton University Press, 2002).

15. Anna Freud, *Normality and Pathology in Childhood* (New York: International Universities Press, 1965), p. 180.

16. Henry Adams, *The Education of Henry Adams* (New York: Modern Library, 1931), p. 472.

17. Paul Roazen, *The Trauma of Freud: Controversies in Psychoanalysis* (New Brunswick, NJ, Transaction Publishers, 2002), ch. 8.

12

Geoffrey Gorer

Political history follows the ebb and flow of public events; while in earlier eras the dates of the lives of monarchs become the point of departure for narrative history, by the twentieth century, at least in the democratic West, elections are the benchmarks by which the past is remembered. The study of intellectual history has necessarily been a more amorphous inquiry. People from a variety of academic disciplines have an interest in the subject—sociologists as well as historians, political theorists, and also literary critics. But the history of ideas has inevitably an insecure foundation, since after all there can be little consensus about what deserves to constitute an idea.

It has long seemed to me that one of the central problems with intellectual history is the comparatively capricious way in which it gets constructed. I have chosen now the writer Geoffrey Gorer to illustrate how haphazard is the way in which we remember the past. In his lifetime (1905-85) Gorer was a prominent man of letters, a gentleman-scholar who was widely known in England and America. For example, if one picks up the multi-volume collection of George Orwell's correspondence and essays, numerous illustrations can be found there of the solid friendship between the two men. Further, Gorer was a close associate of Margaret Mead, a surrogate husband who was known to Mead's daughter Catherine Bateson as "Uncle Geoffrey." Gorer was also well known back in England to the family of writing Sitwells. During World War II, Gorer had served at the British embassy in Washington, D.C., during a time when intellectuals were patriotically helping both American and British governments. It is surprising that nothing adequate has yet been written about the part men of ideas played during that great world conflict; Herbert Marcuse's stint at the American State Department, for instance, has attracted no scholarly interest. (It is now known, however, that the Marxist Franz Neumann was, at least for a time, spying for the Soviets while working for the OSS, the predecessor to the CIA.) Gorer claimed himself to have personally cut six months off the Second World War, once he successfully lobbied so that the Japanese Emperor would not be attacked. (It is now generally acknowledged that the failure to indict the Emperor as a war criminal has had momentous implications for the way postwar Japan could evade its history.)

But Gorer has now completely vanished from public memory. At the time I first got in contact with him in London, England during the summer of 1965, I was doing interviewing research, as well as archival work, on the early history of psychoanalysis. Before then when I was initially drawn to the contrast between the reception of Freud's school in America and England, Gorer had in 1961 published "Are We 'By Freud Obsessed'?" in the *New York Times* Sunday magazine section; Gorer was comparing the American love affair with some aspects of psychoanalysis to the overt hostility on the part of so many Europeans, and he alluded, as part of the explanation, to different attitudes toward babies in Britain and America.

Perhaps Gorer's most popular book was his 1948 *The American People*, an impressionistic and highly readable text based on the nine years Gorer had spent in the States. National character studies were in their heyday then, and social anthropologists were centrally concerned with the inter-connections between culture and personality. Although Gorer, who had been an undergraduate at Charterhouse, Cambridge, had also studied at the Sorbonne and the University of Berlin, he remained without any straightforward professional training.

He had nonetheless authored a number of remarkable works. In the 1930s he published a book about the life and writings of the Marquis de Sade, and then an account of a Himalayan village, as well as a sustained discussion of English character. (Although it might seem out of keeping with his greatest strengths, and perhaps in reaction to criticism he had felt, in his later years he grew enamored of using social scientific survey material.) Gorer had also collaborated with a British psychoanalyst, John Rickman, in writing about the psychology of Russians. This last book evoked considerable derision among social scientists because of the causal linkage it proposed between childhood swaddling practices and Russian political authoritarianism, and this hypothesis was regarded as a gross illustration of how psychology could get exaggerated in social science. (Yet a serious Finnish cultural psychologist has been alone in having revived Gorer's name in the course of a recent book: *Swaddling, Shame and Society: On Psychohistory and Russia*.[1]) Gorer had in addition managed to publish travel books, and he remained a considerable essayist; W. W. Norton was his publisher in New York City. *Death, Grief, and Mourning* had come out the same year as I met him, and he later wrote a collection of articles around the theme of the "dangers" of equality. In Britain he regularly reviewed books in the most prominent literary weeklies, and remained a name to be reckoned with.

Gorer had told me, and others I knew as well, about his ill health in the mid-1970s, and he had required a pacemaker to be installed. Although my files indicate that we were in touch by mail through 1979, I recall that my last attempt to be in contact with him resulted in a letter of mine being returned by the British postal system, at which time I concluded that the worst must have happened. I know that I had never seen an obituary notice of Gorer in the *New York Times*, and when I asked some mutual acquaintances of Gorer's in London, they were also in the dark about what had happened. So too was Lord Annan, an expert in twentieth-century British intellectual life.

It was only in 1994, on my way to give a talk at Sussex University, that I happened again to pass by train through Haywards Heath, the town Gorer had once lived in. His exquisite house, dating from 1692, was sufficiently well known that at the railroad station there had been, at least in 1965, a sign directing tourists to the place. When I wrote to the current owner, he reported Gorer's death in 1985: "he was a fine, if somewhat individual gentleman." Subsequently I contacted Somerset House to get a copy of Gorer's will. After rewriting it several times toward the end, the bulk of his money (he remained unmarried and childless) went to Cambridge University. His papers, which I had primarily wanted to find out about since they might be a rich storehouse for intellectual historians, went to Sussex University. Although I went there with the idea of perhaps putting together a volume of Gorer's letters, the ones from Margaret Mead were so lengthy, almost field-trip accounts, that I could not imagine how to edit anything for publication; my knowledge of W. H. Auden and J. R. Ackerley was too slim to make much out of the stacks of their letters to Gorer.

Although I only took notes after first seeing Gorer during the summer of 1965, I did save his letters, and saw him off and on as I happened to be in England. My central impression of him remains that he was one of the smartest people I have ever met, and I am writing now because it seems to me appalling that no one has yet made an effort to memorialize him.

When I initially saw Gorer it was after I had written him out-of-the-blue, and he proposed that we meet for an hour at the Atheneum Club. (Once I started seeing him I found that some of the most prominent British analysts were impressed by my having had contact with Gorer.) I immediately found him very perceptive about the social characteristics of the British Psychoanalytic Society. It had been, as he rightly pointed out, predominately Gentile, which had to stand out in a field so generally dominated by Jews. In the 1920s the British analysts had been a "pretty amateurish" group but it had lots of ties then to the intellectual community. After the emigration of continental analysts to Britain just before World War II, the Society became more professional, yet at the same time also cut off from its old outside contacts.

Like others in Britain with a keen interest in genealogy, Gorer was concerned about the "kinship system" among analysts. At one point that summer he proposed that I construct a chart about who had analyzed whom in the history of analysis. (Recently an Austrian psychologist has finally accomplished a version of that complicated task.[2]) Gorer thought he could differentiate between Freud's pupils and those of, for instance, Sandor Ferenczi or Hanns Sachs, members of Freud's so-called secret Committee, although Gorer confessed that if hard-pressed he would be unable to verbalize the contrasting impact that these various analysts had had on their patients. (His own analytic lineage, he told me, went back to Sachs; a substantial stack of letters from the eclectic analyst John D. Sutherland can be found in Gorer's files, along with many letters from the later defrocked Masud Khan.)

It seemed typical of how well established Gorer was that he quietly spoke about his friendship with Freud's grandson Lucian, who was at the time far less well known as a painter than he has become now. (Gorer also seemed to know Lucian's brother Clement, who went on to be a Liberal Member of Parliament and a television personality as well.) When I first visited Gorer's country house toward the end of the summer of 1965, he showed me examples of the art hanging on his walls that he had picked up cheaply in the 1920s and 1930s. Gorer said that all he had to do to make ends meet was to sell off one such painting annually. He seemed almost as proud of his gardening as of his authorship.

Gorer knew lots about the Bloomsbury group, the circle around Virginia Woolf and Lytton Strachey that has now attracted so much interest, and Gorer understood exactly how they had been involved with psychoanalysis. Unfortunately I did not take up Gorer on the suggestion that I see the painter Duncan Grant, who was still alive then, since he seemed to me peripheral to my special interests; only later did I learn of his romantic involvements with Virginia Woolf's sister Vanessa as well as Lord Keynes. I did go through with interviewing James and Alix Strachey, since I knew them to have been personally analyzed by Freud in Vienna. Gorer could be mistaken about who had or had not been in treatment with the creator of psychoanalysis, and at the outset Gorer was curiously credulous about what he thought were the merits of Ernest Jones's official biography of Freud. That summer I was excited about what I was finding in Jones's unsorted files, which lay then in a big cabinet housed in the basement of the British Psychoanalytic Society; Gorer was, as I recall, the only one I confided in without censoring what I had uncovered. I told Gorer, for example, about how Jones had given a wholly false account of the last years of Jones's own analyst, Ferenczi. One of the impressive qualities of Gorer's capacities as an intellectual was that he could be fully capable, given enough evidence, of changing his mind, and Gorer later acknowledged just how partisan Jones had been. I cannot recall exactly when Gorer said the words to me, but I well remember his exclamation: "You've got their secrets!" (We were able to talk about literary matters as well, and I remember differing with Gorer on the merits of George Painter's biography of Proust, the second volume of which had come out in 1965.)

From the outset of my seeing him Gorer was highly critical of Melanie Klein, a Hungarian analyst who had become by then the most distinctive theorist in British analysis, although her work was at the time scarcely known in America. Gorer said that she "devoured" her disciples, demanding complete devotion from them. Paula Heimann, for example, although initially one of Klein's pupils had been formally read out of the Klein group. According to Gorer a patient had to produce psychotic stages for a Kleinian analyst; sometimes these phases could, he said, be reversible, but sometimes not. He claimed that in the course of very long analyses Kleinians would be unhappy until clients performed the way they were supposed to, and he maintained that Kleinian analysis could be "very destructive." Gorer also said that Klein (or her advocates) could "chew up" papers presented by candidates in training with Freud's daughter Anna, or her allies.

Although Anna Freud was Melanie Klein's chief rival in child analysis, and her long-standing opponent within the British Psychoanalytic Society, Gorer was not very positive about her either. It turned out that Gorer had been taken through her house on Maresfield Gardens (later the Freud Museum), where Freud spent his last months tortured by illness, in the company of Ernst Kris, who Gorer felt was among the nicest and most intelligent of the Viennese analysts he knew. Anna Freud herself was, in Gorer's view, too much a vestal virgin in the church Freud had founded, and Gorer thought she ruled the psychoanalytic movement "by divine right." (He dismissed gossip about Anna supposedly having had a lesbian relationship with Dorothy Burlingham on the ground that she and Anna seemed like nuns he had known.)

Gorer was even harsher about what he thought of the Princess Marie Bonaparte, and her anthropologist son Peter who Gorer thought still meddled in French royalist politics. In Gorer's opinion neither of them counted for much in the world of the mind. (I had found Marie Bonaparte's letters to Jones, while he was writing his Freud biography, remarkably dull and uninteresting.) Gorer felt that Freud must have been attracted to Marie because of the fame of the aristocratic social circles she moved in. She was the direct descendant of Napoleon's brother Lucien, and also married to the brother of the late King of Greece; Marie's husband was in addition a member of the royal family of Denmark.

Gorer was helpful in encouraging me to see key other possible informants. Dr. Edward Glover, for example, had gotten "a raw deal" from everyone in the course of the struggle during World War II between the Kleinians and the Anna Freudians. (Glover not only earned the enmity of Klein's group but his temporary ally Anna Freud accepted Jones's offer to replace Glover as Secretary of the International Psychoanalytic Association.) Gorer proposed that it was a "sociological law" that all such "mavericks" as Glover were one's best possible sources of information, and I found Glover to be a wonderfully insightful person.[3] Gorer also insisted that when I got back to the States I go and see Harold Lasswell in New Haven right away, since Lasswell had been such a pioneer in trying to bring together depth psychology and political science; my own professional background in Government was also Lasswell's original field, so it was generous of Gorer to have been thoughtful enough to push me in that direction, one that later proved helpful to my intellectual development. But Gorer also got me to follow up on seeing Freud's former patient Jeanne Lampl-de Groot in Holland, although she turned out to be so firmly in Anna Freud's camp as to be incapable of much independent contribution to my research.

Gorer was himself politically savvy, and that summer of 1965, when President Lyndon Johnson was escalating the American commitment to the defense of South Vietnam, he felt that Johnson seemed to be "riding a tiger." Gorer also mentioned, in an aside, something that I have never found confirmed in the literature but which I think bears repeating; supposedly Franklin Roosevelt's aid Harry Hopkins had been analyzed, and was out to "convert" others. Gorer might have found out such information thanks to his wartime work in Washington. Subsequently I read that the Washington psychiatrist Harry Stack Sullivan had a special White House pass during World War II, although no biographer or political scientist has yet established the reason for that unusual access.

While I had originally been hoping that Gorer would have some anthropological views on the relation between different national cultures and various psychopathological symptoms, he thought there was not yet enough data to write on the problem. Gorer did think it was safe to ignore the work of Geza Roheim, who was the first analyst to undertake anthropological fieldwork (with the financial support of Marie Bonaparte); Roheim was too committed to the "dogma" that there always had to be a central psychological "trauma" to be unearthed. The French anthropologist Georges Devereux was supposedly "more reliable," and Gorer had recently reviewed one of his works at length in the official *International Journal of Psychoanalysis*; still, Gorer was hardly uncritical of Devereux's work. Although Gorer spoke highly of Erik H. Erikson, an analyst who had anthropological interests, Gorer claimed that his own contribution to Erikson's work on Maxim Gorky was only acknowledged in Erikson's *Childhood and Society* because Margaret Mead had "stomped her foot" with Erikson about the matter. (Later Gorer was, in public and private, harsh about Erikson's book-length study of Gandhi.)

To further underline Gorer's special position at the time I first saw him, he was so well established that when he commented on how Vladimir Nabokov and Isaiah Berlin had tried to out-sparkle each other at the British embassy during World War II, I was struck with how modest Gorer had been in putting himself on a lower category of being than those celebrities. Gorer did not know of a generous reference to him in print by Dr. Karl Menninger, nor did Gorer seem to me to be name-dropping when he reported that Supreme Court Justice William Brennan had been "very receptive" to him. Justice Abe Fortas was another of Gorer's acquaintances.

Perhaps the best way to help revive Gorer would be to quote from some of his letters. He, like Orwell's widow, took great exception to the first volume of the study by Peter Stansky and William Abrahams, *The Unknown Orwell* (1972); Gorer was fiercely loyal to his old friend Eric Blair, whose wishes were being sustained by his widow Sonia. I thought then (and now) that Gorer's judgment was too harsh:

> I think that the major reason Sonia Orwell objected to the Stansky-Abrahams book is the same as mine; they were thoroughly dishonest about it. They came to interview me on the explicit understanding that they were writing a book on the involvement of British intellectuals in the Spanish war; they knew he did not wish a biography to be written and pretended they were not thinking of doing so. They got information under false pretences and made underhand use of it. The book itself I think shamefully bad—ill-written and with no sort of understanding of English culture and absurdly padded—who on earth wants to know the full details of the examination for entrants to the Indian police in 1930 or whenever it was? I do not agree that Orwell was in any way a Jekyll and Hyde character which seems to be their main argument; the pseudonym was above all to protect his very conservative family from embarrassment (*Burmese Days* was the first book he wrote, and this was almost blasphemy to the up-holders of Empire, even though it was not the first book published); and I think the attempt to prove Eric a liar by finding old codgers forty years later to say he could not have witnessed a hanging or shot an elephant mean-spirited and not explicable by any decent or avowable motive.
>
> I reviewed some of Eric's book as they came out—I am proud that I launched *Homage to Catalonia* on its success—but I have not, and do not intent to write on him at any length.

I was already thinking about myself writing an essay on the surprising links between the anti-psychoanalytic Orwell and Freud's central contributions. I naturally wanted to know Gorer's impression of Orwell's reaction to psychoanalysis:

> As far as my recollections and knowledge go, George Orwell had no contact with any psychoanalysts nor any interest in the topic; I should have said that he regarded it with mild hostility, putting it somewhat on a par with Christian Science. His wife, Eileen, had a little training in the academic psychology of the late twenties and early thirties—Bartlett and McDougall and the like—the sort of equipment a school teacher would receive. I knew very little on the subject in the thirties, when I was most intimate with Eric; I was full of enthusiasm for the (for me) newly discovered social anthropology; and I think, without boasting, I can see my influence in some of his essays, such as those on picture postcards and school stories.

It was with Gorer's encouragement that when the American edition of my *Freud and His Followers* came out in 1975, I sent him a copy; he then put in writing an anecdote about Rickman and Freud that Gorer had only alluded to in conversation. Gorer was referring to what he thought was Freud's almost complete lack of visual observation of his patients. John Rickman told me that when he had finished his work with the Friends in Soviet Russia (which gave the material for his contribution to *The People of Great Russia*) he stopped in Vienna— I think in 1920—and had some analysis with Freud. He arrived with a bushy beard but shaved it off after he had been about a month in analysis; it was another month before Freud noticed this and commented on it with considerable surprise. Other people have told me this was typical; he worked with people entirely through his ears, reserving sight for works of art or scenery.

Although three places for which Gorer regularly wrote—the *Observer*, the *Listener*, and the *Times Literary Supplement*—had already found reviewers for the British edition of *Freud and His Followers*, Gorer said in 1976 that to his "great surprise" the *Guardian* invited him to do a review: "I had thought that the friends of Ernest [Ernst Freud] and Anna, forewarned by the American publication, had pre-empted every review to make sure that their picture should be re-instated."

Gorer's review was one of the best that book of mine received in England. He told me he thought he had helped break "the rather monotonous Defense Fund which had been mobilized against the book." At the time I had thought of doing some book-reviewing of my own in Britain, since there were so many more serious weekly outlets there than in the States. Gorer did not pull any punches with me about my poor chances:

> Forget about the idea of doing book-reviewing in any English journal. None of them could afford the air-fare to get the book to you on time. *The New Statesman* is so strapped for money it can no longer afford to send its contributors a copy of the paper in which their article/review appears! Your only chance of English publication (outside learned journals) is to submit unsolicited essays on fairly topical subjects on which you have specialized knowledge....

Perhaps it is clear now how I find it more than a little scary that someone of Gorer's stature can have so quickly vanished with scarcely a trace. He was working in the old English tradition of being a cultivated amateur, but without an affiliation with some larger organization, such as a research university, a school of analysts, or cultural anthropologists, it is hard to know how his reputation could have carried on. Although as a self-proclaimed independent writer he might have taken a certain cynical pleasure in the fact that I am now repaying a debt I feel I owe him by trying to secure some posthumous standing for him, I think he also would have acknowledged that I was proceeding with genuine conviction and without the hope of ulterior gain.

Notes

1. Juhani Ihanus, *Swaddling, Shame and Society: On Psychohistory and Russia* (Helsinki: Kikimora Publications, 2001).
2. Ernst Falzeder, "The Threads of Psychoanalytic Filiations or Psychoanalysis Taking Effect," in Andre Haynal and Ernst Falzeder, eds., *100 Years of Psychoanalysis* (London: Karnac, 1994), pp. 169-94.
3. Paul Roazen, *Oedipus in Britain: Edward Glover and the Struggle Over Klein* (New York: Other Press, 2000).

13

Biography

The civil rights movement had a momentous impact on mid-century American society, and no man played a more heroic part in the struggle for racial justice than Martin Luther King, Jr. William Robert Miller's biography[1] presents the great man's legend in all its glory. Miller explains why it was no accident that a preacher should have led this particular cause. The church was the only institution permitted the Negro under slavery, so it naturally became the forum in which the black man's spirits, stifled and stagnant in public life, could come alive. Moreover, the preacher was able to be the freest man in the black community, since no white man could ever cut off his paycheck. And the cause of racial justice was a fit subject for a man of God, because "behind the pathology of race hatred are human frustrations, misspent lives, unhealthy subcultures."

Martin Luther King, Jr. gives a dramatic panorama of the nature and significance of the civil rights revolution of our time. It also presents a moving account of the development of a public man. Miller has succeeded admirably in recounting King as a leader of the civil rights movement, but the book fails as a human biography.

To succeed fully, biography must be interwoven with history. For example, it seems that when King was twelve his brother slid down a banister, accidentally knocking his grandmother unconscious. Thinking she was dead, Martin reacted by hurling himself from an upstairs window. Months later, this same grandmother fell ill and died, and Martin once again jumped out of a window. (Both times he landed unhurt.)

Miller does not give much more information about these two apparent attempts at self-injury. Yet, knowing King the adult as an advocate of nonviolence and pacifism, does not this one incident from King's early life tell us something about his special childhood sensitivity to his own aggressions? Why else would King need to punish himself for his grandmother falling unconscious or dead, if he had not grown up to fear excessively the power of his own destructiveness? In fact the whole subculture of that racial minority grew up with constraints on the normal expression of assertiveness.

It seems fitting that a man like King, with such special sensitivity to violence, should have fashioned out of its renunciation a philosophy adapted to his people's condition. For nonviolence could be a successful strategy in the South, since it was perhaps the only way for that oppressed minority to express resentment without them all risking getting killed.

What of the legacy King left to history? White America did once have illusions about itself that King and his followers succeeded in puncturing and deflating. Toward the end of his life, King became more and more caught between the "moderates" on his right and the growing ranks of the black militants. Not only did the American conscience need much more prodding than King succeeded in administering, but the power of love had more limitations, and unmerited suffering less redemption, than he believed. And yet his faith in persuasion, his combination of militancy and restraint plus the hand he extended to white participation in the cause of civil rights made him indeed "not simply a great Negro leader but a uniquely great leader of the entire American people."

Much about blacks in America went unfortunately unreported in the press, and George Metcalf's *Black Profiles*[2] fills us in on the biographies of eleven black leaders, most of them contemporaries of King. And Lerone Bennett Jr.'s *Pioneers in Protest*[3] is a collection of biographies of leaders in black protest from the more distant past. All three of these books should help push textbooks of American history more into line with racial realities. Surely it is appropriate that we at least start reinterpreting the past in the face of current perspectives.

* * *

Nuel Pharr Davis's *Lawrence and Oppenheimer*[4] is as exciting as any creative work of art, and yet its author has woven his plot out of historical fact. Thanks to a series of uninhibited interviews with leading physicists, Professor Davis has been able to reconstruct vividly the tale of the inventions of both the atomic and hydrogen bombs.

Anyone who has enjoyed James Watson's *Double Helix* or C. P. Snow's versions of modern science will appreciate this book. For *Lawrence and Oppenheimer* gives an exciting glimpse of the austerity of the scientific life. Beginning with two contrasting personalities in modern physics, Ernest Lawrence the experimentalist and Robert Oppenheimer the theoretician, the book presents a cast of scientists, all of them gluttons for work, committed to communal standards of truth and devoted to the impartial task of scientific discovery. Despite their human frailties, these men labored in friendship to produce the terrible weapons intended to protect us.

Perhaps the most memorable passages in this book commemorate Oppenheimer's magnificent leadership of the scientists who assembled at Los Alamos during World War II to create the first atomic bombs. In this group isolated in a desert, each man shared his work. Some of the world's best scientific heads cooperated in the pleasure and excitement of creative work. As one of them said afterwards, "Here at Los Alamos I found a spirit of Athens, of Plato, of an ideal republic." Over it all presided Robert Oppenheimer, a serenely philosophic man, capable of drawing out of widely contrasting people the capacity to accomplish their objective.

And what an objective! These men had assumed that this dreadful weapon of destruction might be discovered by the Nazis, so they unhesitatingly rushed to get there first. By the time the American bomb was near completion, the Germans already had surrendered. But the technical obstacles still to be surmounted held everyone's interest, and the momentum at Los Alamos continued unabated until at last, by the time the bomb was ready, few scientists had either the moral preparation or the political savvy to feel competent to intervene in the decision to drop the bomb on Japan.

The rest of Professor Davis's tale is a good deal darker and more depressing than the bright disinterested quest for scientific advance. All at once scientists found themselves involved at the highest levels of policymaking. Feeling somehow betrayed by the decision to drop the bomb, some scientists feared to remain excessively deferential to military and political leaders, lest the need for international control of atomic energy go unheeded. Oppenheimer in particular, after having been rather offhanded about the use of the atomic bomb, now dug in his heels—perhaps out of guilt—against the development of the super ("H") bomb.

The red-hunt that brought Oppenheimer down and which, incidentally, cost other innocent people in far humbler walks of life their jobs, was joined by his former friend and collaborator Ernest Lawrence. In behalf of his experimental work, for which he won the Nobel Prize, Lawrence had become a scientific promoter. As the inventor of the cyclotron, Lawrence became aware that modern scientific research needs its patrons, whether private or governmental. He built up an extensive chain of connections with men of wealth and power, which enabled him in the end to help damage Oppenheimer's position. The congressional investigation of Oppenheimer's innocent association with some communists before World War II and the decision of the Atomic Energy Commission taking away his security clearance remain the ugly part of the story.

Despite our country's fickle gratitude, nothing could shake the love and devotion Oppenheimer had earned among his colleagues. He spent the last years of his life as the director of Princeton's Institute for Advanced Study, then a retreat for scientists from everywhere in the world. Everyone interested in science and public policy should read this book, since the human drama is so compelling.

* * *

Although some otherwise well-educated may once scarcely have heard of Max Weber (1864-1920), he ranks securely as one of the leading thinkers of twentieth century social science. His classic book on the inner connection between the Protestant ethic and the spirit of capitalism stands as a monumental defense of the important role ideas may play in history.

Weber had set out to construct a rival system of thought to Karl Marx's communism, and succeeded in constructing an alternative way of looking at historical change. Human thoughts were no mere "superstructure" for underlying economic class conflict; Weber instead emphasized the legitimate role of the subjective (and often religious) element in history, and therefore of voluntarism in social action. Through a massive comparative study of world religions, he tried to account for some of the most distinctive elements in modern Western culture. Weber's most famous concepts remain perhaps "charisma" and "ideal type," and his most notable theory his model of how modern bureaucracy has revolutionized our civilization.

Weber is also responsible for most of the methodological justification of a neutral, value-free social science. He cherished, to be sure, his own political convictions. He was a liberal imperialist because of what he took to be the incompetence of the bourgeois leadership in turn-of-the-century Germany. Yet Weber also wanted to protect the universities from the worst of German ideological demagoguery. So he insisted on professors keeping their politics apart from their scholarship. Arthur Mitzman's *The Iron Cage*,[5] a historical interpretation of Weber, stands as a serious book that all lovers of intellectual history will relish.

Without attempting to summarize all of Weber's works, Mitzman interweaves some of Weber's central personal problems with his most outstanding contributions to social thought. Particularly welcome is the subtle use to which Mitzman puts psychoanalytic ideas. For Weber was a man wracked with an unusual, and sometimes incapacitating, degree of human torments, out of which he forged his most original ideas.

Mitzman's discussion of the sources of Weber's psychological collapse after the death of his father in 1897 is especially interesting, as is his account of Weber's sexual difficulties. Like some other famous unions in intellectual history, it seems that the marriage of Max and Marianne Weber (she became his first biographer) was never consummated. One could wish that this new data about Weber's private life, which comes in only at the end of this book, could have been incorporated in the earlier discussion of Weber's career. But putting aside this somewhat odd organization, since evidently Mitzman only came across the fresh biographical information late in his research, *The Iron Cage* provides an outstanding example of the history of ideas at its best.

* * *

In the midst of the American war in Southeast Asia, thoughtful people were tempted to turn back to the past to discover those national writers who warned us about the possibilities and character of American imperialism. Among the critics of conventional American civilization none can surpass Mark Twain – "the Lincoln of our literature." A modern prophet of American culture, Twain's savage irony not only exposed the beginnings of twentieth-century empire building, but also foretold the role racism would play.

Maxwell Geismar was for a generation one of America's most distinguished literary critics, and in *Mark Twain: An American Prophet*[6] he published a fascinating study of Twain, appreciating his artistic genius as well as the social context of his day. Geismar was out of step with a whole school of less radical academic literary critics who have emphasized Twain's neurosis, hesitations, personal failures and bitterness, while neglecting Twain's brilliant social criticism, the triumphant satire that ensured his fame throughout the world. (The literary establishment that takes a drubbing here includes Lionel Trilling, F. R. Leavis, Justin Kaplan, Leslie Fiedler, Bernard DeVoto, Charles Neider, Irving Howe, Leon Edel, and Van Wyck Brooks.)

Geismar chose to focus on Twain's later thinking, "his mature role as America's conscience before the face of the world…that whole later period of penetrating and prophetic social commentary; of that remarkable repudiation of white Anglo-Saxon culture which was based on colonial conquest and oppression, and of that final identification with the darker-skinned races of the world which has made Mark Twain such a revered figure, not merely in revolutionary Russia, but in India, China, Asia and South America today."

Geismar's contention is that Twain was not primarily a novelist or fiction writer, but rather a "bardic poet-prophet, on the model of Walt Whitman." A bardic figure, Twain used his fiction, along with his speeches and essays, for the sake of expressing his unique sense of social, moral, and metaphysical vision.

Mark Twain: An American Prophet does not, however, portray Twain as a saint, but recounts the many ups and downs in the career of Sam Clemens. Even though it is Twain's writings, rather than his life, which are at the center of this book, we do get some intriguing glimpses of the author as a man; his friendship with General Ulysses Grant, his founding of a publishing house, the squandering of his own money and his wife's fortune in trying to develop a typesetting machine, his bankruptcy, and then his world wide lecturing designed to earn the money to pay off all his debts. Just as at the peak of his worldly success Clemens could enunciate his radical social convictions, so at the end of his life, amidst personal sorrow and loss, he retained his sense of irony, balance, and laughter.

In the course of his career Twain championed many causes—the rights of Chinese on the West Coast as well as of blacks—and he denounced many social movements, from Christian missions to the rise of the economic trusts to Mary Baker Eddy's Christian Science. Partly because he himself (especially in the manipulations accompanying his bankruptcy) had participated in some dubious financial dealings, this American moralist could see through the doings of the robber barons of his time. Thanks to his fame and worldly connections, he was in a fine position to appreciate the get-rich-quick mania of late nineteenth-century America and to understand what greed can do to the human spirit. Twain was, as Geismar so well puts it, "the most notorious spy in the house of the American oligarchy."

Twain grew deeply disillusioned with his own society; he was horrified, for example, by the bloody American conquest of the Philippines. In addition, he came to believe that the white man's "civilization" had always been founded on the slaughter of native peoples. Outraged by social injustice, Twain directed all his powers as a writer and prophet on the side of the oppressed: "There were two 'Reigns of Terror,' if we would but remember it and consider it: the one wrought murder in hot passion, the other in heartless cold blood; the one lasted mere months, the other had lasted a thousand years." An enemy of war and able to make fun of it, his "War Prayer" became a favorite among the militant opponents of the Vietnam War.

Geismar has a field day with Freudian attempts to reduce Twain's most powerful social works to his most private tragedies. (Curiously enough, Sigmund Freud himself attended one of his lectures in Vienna.) In rejecting the negativism of the early psychoanalytic formulations on art, Geismar has performed a real service to post-Freudian thought in resurrecting Otto Rank's theories on the psychology of the artist. Despite all the darker sides of Twain, and the frustrations any great writer must have experienced, Geismar sees Twain affirmatively, as a "daylight writer" whose pagan sense of pleasure was permanently at odds with society's norms. Twain was "more sensitive to, and more affected by the baseness of humanity than humanity was," and Geismar is able to integrate Twain's earlier writings with his later bitterness and cynicism while still respecting his basic human trust, his outgoingness, his colorful "celebrating of life despite all life's tragedies."

* * *

Adlai Stevenson and the World: The Life of Adlai E. Stevenson[7], by John Bartlow Martin, is the second volume of Martin's Stevenson biography and a treat for all those who love to follow the intricacies of American national politics, and will be instructive even for those who were regular readers of the newspapers and periodicals of the day. It is never easy to learn the affairs of the party out of power, and during much of the time covered in this volume,

1952 to 1965, Adlai Stevenson was the unofficial leader of the Opposition. The American system does not make it easy, even for a figure with a seat in Congress, effectively to criticize a presidential administration. Even if we cannot wholly accept Martin's contention that John F. Kennedy was, in his policies, Stevenson's heir and executor, Stevenson did play a notable role in trying to challenge Dwight D. Eisenhower's invincible political appeal.

As a biographer, however, Martin leaves something to be desired. Stevenson was "a string-saver, he almost literally never threw anything away." His papers now constitute the largest collection of manuscripts any individual has donated to Princeton. One would have thought that under such circumstances a biographer had to aim at selectivity. Yet Martin tells us that in using Stevenson's papers he has usually left the material to "speak for itself," as if such an abandonment of critical standards would not have predictably bad results. A reader interested enough to finish a nine-hundred-page book covering a few years of Stevenson's life could be spared such details as the time of departure for an airplane flight or the type of aircraft involved. And does it matter what color suit and shirt Stevenson wore at a press conference? Only if Martin were writing about someone from a distant era, hard to re-create imaginatively, might such information serve a purpose.

Martin criticizes Stevenson for having cared too much about his speeches: "He seemed to think extemporaneous remarks unworthy of him." Therefore Stevenson wanted "to speak only formally and for the record." Martin contrasts Stevenson's speeches, which often read better than they sounded, with Kennedy's, which sounded better than they read. It has long been agreed that Stevenson was not a true intellectual—someone who read books and cared about ideas in themselves. But Stevenson did respect the life of the mind, which sets him apart from most other twentieth-century candidates for the presidency. If Martin, who was one of Stevenson's speechwriters, is right in thinking that Stevenson fussed too much over his addresses, this book suffers from a similar defect. We are treated to long quotations from Stevenson's formal deliveries, as well as to lengthy extracts from remarks at press conferences. Stevenson was an avid letter writer, and here again Martin's inadequately restrained use of documentary material threatens to sink his book as a biography.

Despite all this, Martin has succeeded engrossingly in evoking the memory of the frustrated efforts at political criticism during the Eisenhower years. Although Stevenson has gone down in history as a political Hamlet, he could at times be decisive, and he had the knack of attracting illustrious and knowledgeable advisers. Martin describes how, with aptly chosen expert advice, Stevenson quickly saw that the Secretary of State, John Foster Dulles, had enunciated a policy of "massive retaliation" which did not square with the newly presented Air Force budget.

The account of the 1956 presidential campaign makes depressing reading. (That election vanished entirely in Halberstam's 1993 *The Fifties*.) Martin blames Stevenson for not having made Eisenhower's health an issue—"it may have been one of his worst political mistakes"—without indicating how Stevenson should have gone about it. The public was hardly unaware of the president's health problems, and when, at the end of the campaign, Stevenson did raise the point it was rightly seen as an act of desperation. Stevenson was ambivalent about civil rights matters, and called for a policy of gradual de-segregation. Identified with the Southern whites, who were largely Demo-crats, he opposed federal legislation to enforce the 1954 Supreme Court school decision, and it is no wonder black voters were less enthusiastic about him than they might have been.

In 1956 the country was thoroughly complacent and self-satisfied. Whether because of Stevenson's faults as a speechmaker, or the prematurenes of such policy initiatives as a ban on H-bomb testing and the proposal of a volunteer army, it was a Republican year with an indestructibly popular president. The Hungarian revolt, and the Suez crisis, only made Stevenson's final rout the more devastating. Eisenhower's plurality was second only to that of Franklin Roosevelt's landslide in 1936.

In 1960, Stevenson was unable to face political reality. He still yearned for the Democratic presidential nomination. Never realizing that he was offend-ing Kennedy, Stevenson allowed his own candidacy to go forward, even though Kennedy felt entitled to his allegiance. Afterward Stevenson craved to be appointed secretary of state, although the ambassadorship to the United Nations was all Kennedy would come up with. For Stevenson the final years in New York City were frustrating, and more than one friend thought he had gone to seed at his last post. Stevenson hated to think in terms of power politics, and ineffectively tried to moderate Kennedy policy. He was dis-gusted at having been trapped into making false statements about the CIA's cover story on the Bay of Pigs invasion. The Cuban missile crisis was another disaster for Stevenson; although he was largely absent when decisions were made, a press story from within the administration made him look like an advocate of appeasement. Under Lyndon Johnson, never able to accept that he was neither president not head of the State Department, Stevenson counted for even less than during Kennedy's years.

Perhaps too much time has already passed to appreciate the context in which Stevenson lived, but reading this book reminds one of how fundamen-tally conservative he was. Although he was far less suspicious of the Russians than others, still he regarded communism as "the great conspiracy of our century." Domestically Stevenson refrained from trying to break any of the power of existing Democratic Party machine leaders. As late as 1954, Seymour Harris was still trying to convert Stevenson to Keynesian economics on budget balancing, and others in his entourage worked to help him "overcome his upbringing," by which they meant the Lake Forest influence on his thinking.

An early advocate of the domino theory in Southeast Asia, Stevenson disagreed with Pierre Mendès-France's 1953 suggestion that France give up in Indochina. In 1956 Stevenson declared, "There isn't any colonialism, it's all gone." In 1964 he was privately dubious about the Gulf of Tonkin incident, since he wondered what American ships were doing there in the first place. But by then Stevenson was outside the center of policy-making and too tired to think of any new undertakings. Despite reservations about Dean Rusk's policies at the State Department, Stevenson supported Johnson's decision to send combat troops to South Vietnam and to start an air war over the North.

Martin's earlier volume, *Adlai Stevenson of Illinois,*[8] covered Stevenson's first fifty-two years and was more successful in maintaining a balance between his private and public lives. In this second volume Stevenson's ex-wife, Ellen, keeps popping in and out. Despite (or consistent with) her feelings of persecution, she could not be persuaded to see a psychiatrist (except in Boston in 1942). In 1955 she gave a press interview in which she told why she thought Stevenson would not make a good president. No divorced candidate (until Reagan in 1980) had yet been elected president, and in the 1950s women voters in particular were bothered by the failure of Stevenson's marriage. In the end, Ellen squandered her money and needed to be supported by her family. In 1966 her sons and her mother brought suit before a probate court to have her declared incompetent. A bank was appointed to conserve her estate. Another suit was filed by a social worker to have her submit to an examination at a psychiatric hospital; the court complied, but Ellen fled to another legal jurisdiction. Martin, having told the tale of Stevenson's tragic private life in his earlier book, here recounts how dependent Stevenson remained on support from women friends. Although he was closest to women, and had a number of what Martin calls "girl friends," as best one can make out it sounds like a distant kind of love.

In office, American patricians look graceful and urbane, but away from power Stevenson often seemed like a social butterfly. Despite problems with heart disease and high blood pressure, he ate and drank too much. Martin recounts all the "yachts, villas, idolatry, and food" that filled Stevenson's last self-destructive years. Yet until his death in July 1965, Stevenson showed an inner toughness even when he had the best reasons for self-pity. Characteristically, in his worst defeats he grumbled the least; and he succeeded in his capacity for drawing out the best in people in behalf of public service. Martin's book may be better political reportage than a subtle biographical study. But it does remind us that the words politics and politician are still capable of evoking admiration and respect.

* * *

Lillian Hellman's name, even after her death in 1984, still arouses the fiercest kind of controversy. Her dramas—such as *The Children's Hour, The Little Foxes,* and *Watch on the Rhine*—established her as a major playwright, and her best-selling memoirs were memorable for their extraordinary command of colloquial English. But her sense of embattlement propelled her into numerous personal and political quarrels.

A central source of the fireworks surrounding Hellman had to do with her politics, and how she retrospectively went about defending them. In the thirties she had been attracted by communism, and from then on she always bent over backward on behalf of the worst rulers of the Soviet Union. In the early fifties she, along with other Hollywood screenwriters, was victimized by the hysteria associated with the activities of Senator Joseph McCarthy. In a memorable appearance before the House Un-American Activities Committee in 1952, Hellman eloquently fended off her persecutors. But then in her books *An Unfinished Women, Pentimento,* and *Scoundrel Time,* Hellman constructed her own past record with such artistic imagination that even her own civil rights lawyer could not recognize the facts as he had known them. And her enemies, both within the non-Stalinist left as well as on the right, did not want to forget her previous mistaken commitments.

In this context, William Wright's unauthorized biography, *Lillian Hellman: The Image, The Woman,*[9] is as immensely valuable as it is compelling reading. Although Hellman did what she could to obstruct his path, and then also undertook to commission someone she thought would be a devoted interpreter to do an official biography, Wright succeeded in interviewing more than 150 people who had known her. Out of the welter of contradictory material, Wright fashioned a remarkably fair-minded book.

He traces Hellman's origins in a Southern Jewish family, although she was to spend as much of her childhood in Manhattan as in New Orleans. Her formal education remained spotty, and as a young woman she struck people as homely and unhappy. By 1924, when she was nineteen, she landed a job at an innovative New York publishing house, and for the rest of her life she was on intimate terms with the literati.

Toward the end of an unpromising marriage she met Dashiell Hammett, and in the face of a turbulent personal life they essentially lived together for the thirty years until his death. Hammett and Hellman often stayed in classy hotels; he was to use her as the model for Nora Charles in his *The Thin Man.*

Although Hammett's own writing came to a halt, he was able to help Hellman's own work. His alcoholic decline was to be accompanied by impressive royalties from his books and movie rights; Hellman later made no bones about her own capacities for drinking, as well as hobnobbing with the great and famous. Her feistiness became legendary. Hellman's sexual insecurities (she worried about her odors "down there") and her mastery of the plain style suggest a female Ernest Hemingway. Her individual quarrels with—

besides Mary McCarthy—Tallulah Bankhead, Simone Signoret, Arthur Miller, and Diana Trilling became famous, and her public persona was that of an impossibly bickering woman.

In her plays she had ridiculed material avariciousness, but the role of money was so important in them as to be like a separate character. Few intellectuals had less embarrassment about riches they earned. It is impossible to forget her in wrinkled old age, photographed in full-page advertisements wrapped in a black mink with only the identifying line: "What becomes a legend most?"

When her memoirs first started appearing in 1969, the writing was so remarkable and the story so novel that no one rose to challenge her honesty. But her tale of "Julia" in *Pentimento*, subsequently made into a movie in which Hellman is played by Jane Fonda, was to be the proverbial last straw in establishing Hellman's self-portraits as Walter Mitty fictionalizations. Not only has the tale of Julia been taken to pieces, at least as far as Hellman had anything to do with it, but subsequently other so-called events in Hellman's life were to be subjected to line-by-line refutations.

Hellman made her political resistance to McCarthyism sound a good deal more heroic than it was; and financially she seems to have suffered more from the re-examination by the Internal Revenue Service than any congressional inquisition. An evaluation of her politics has to include her public endorsement of the purge trials that Stalin staged in 1937. In weighing up her political involvements, she did defend the Spanish Republic and was fiercely anti-Nazi. Bitter invective, though, was reserved for the "soft-minded" liberals she despised.

At the end of her life she was established as a theatrical presence in American letters. Her terrible eyesight, which as with Joyce probably had made her all the keener a recorder of spoken English, was to be joined to a medley of other physical problems. Near her death at her home on Martha's Vineyard she sounded indomitable. She was blind and in pain, also partly paralyzed; she had strokes, fits of rage and crying spells, experienced great trouble eating and sleeping, and could bite nurses. When an old friend came to visit and inquired how she was doing, she replied: "Not good, not good." When asked to explain further, she added: "This is the worst writer's block I've ever had."

Wright's *Lillian Hellman* cannot purport to be definitive; it does not seem to have occurred to him that if Hellman misbehaved at a particular dinner party it might have been due to intense boredom at a gathering arranged by a particularly obnoxious hostess. Doubtless there will be a substantial literature on Hellman, but in this first biography Wright did a fine job of recreating a remarkable woman's life.

* * *

America is wasteful of its political talent. An underlying democratic myth about the omnicompetence of the average citizen feeds the illusion that an inexhaustible supply of capable actors can always be counted upon. A parliamentary system of government is less likely to discard its former leaders; our ex-presidents and their vice presidents, not to mention the unsuccessful candidates for those and lesser offices, are rarely able to survive in our political system. That devotion to the public service is a rarity among us is part of the general picture, since our culture resists the idea that political experience is anything special or worth cultivating.

In the case of William C. Bullitt, his failed career does seem like high political tragedy, and one that is peculiarly American. It is not stretching things too much to think of him as a version of Gatsby. As George F. Kennan wrote about Bullitt when he became our first ambassador to the Soviet Union in 1933, he was "handsome, urbane, full of charm and enthusiasm, a product of Philadelphia society and Yale but with considerable European residence and with a flamboyance of personality that is right out of F. Scott Fitzgerald —a man of the world...." And although Bullitt's problems did in part stem from the context in which he functioned, certain character flaws dogged him throughout his life and ultimately caused him to be banished to the political wilderness. Yet he would never have been content with merely private gain; it was in the public world that he struggled, and lost.

Bullitt's credentials for historical significance are considerable. When Franklin D. Roosevelt was extending American diplomatic recognition to the Soviets, Bullitt, as American ambassador, chose as assistants men of the caliber of George F. Kennan and Charles E. Bohlen. Next Bullitt was ambassador to France from 1936 until the German invasion toppled the Third French Republic; Bullitt had been really a roving ambassador all over Europe and possessed a unique set of diplomatic sources. (In the confusion of the retreat of the French army at the outset of the war, Bullitt, who refused to leave his post at the American embassy, became the temporary mayor of Paris.)

Earlier Bullitt had been an adviser to the American delegation at the Treaty of Versailles. He went on a special mission to see Lenin on behalf of the British and the Americans. Bullitt's exclamation "We have seen the future and it works!" usually gets attributed to his associate on that trip, Lincoln Steffens. On Bullitt's return from Russia, with peace terms that he thought momentous, the British disavowed his standing as a negotiator and President Wilson even refused to see him. Bullitt resigned and, along with other idealists, was bitterly disappointed by Wilson. Bullitt was subsequently called to testify before Senator Henry Cabot Lodge's committee, and he so thoroughly spilled the beans about Secretary of State Lansing's reservations in connection with what had been accomplished at Paris that Lansing was forced to resign. Bullitt's testimony helped Lodge defeat the League of Nations. It was not a peace treaty, Bullitt complained: "I can see at least eleven wars in it."

Later on, as George Kennan has underscored, Bullitt was equally prescient in suspecting the wartime intentions of Joseph Stalin; had Roosevelt heeded Bullitt's 1943 written advice to strike deals before Germany surrendered, the post-World War II world might have been different.

In the literary realm, Bullitt had been a fine newspaperman before World War I, and then in 1925 he published a novel that sold some 150,000 copies; it was autobiographical and made fun of his old Philadelphia acquaintances. His second wife, Louise Bryant, was the widow of his acquaintance John Reed, author of *Ten Days That Shook the World*. In the late 1920s Bullitt began a collaborative study with Sigmund Freud on Woodrow Wilson, which did not finally appear as a book until shortly before Bullitt's death in 1967.

It still remains a curiosity how Freud and Bullitt came to write so polemical an assault on Wilson. At the time their *Thomas Woodrow Wilson: A Psychological Study* first appeared, the received opinion was to dissociate Freud from his part in the unfortunate book, even though it was known that he had his own special reasons for hating Wilson. Erik H. Erikson was the most prominent authority to question the authenticity of Freud's hand in a book that orthodox analysts preferred never to have seen the light of day. Not even Anna Freud, who had wanted to improve the manuscript with her own emendations, went as far as Erikson. In reprinting his original essay a decade later, however, Erikson took a different tack, and—without alerting readers to his changing ground—gave greater recognition to Freud's active participation in the text itself.[10]

Part of the scholarly problem has stemmed from Bullitt's fascination with intrigue; Freud privately complained about Bullitt's secretiveness shortly after the manuscript was originally completed. Bullitt turned over his share of the royalties to his daughter Anne, and she in turn was reported for years to have been trying to write a book about her father. The result has been that valuable documents have remained inaccessible. *So Close to Greatness: A Biography of William C. Bullitt*[11] by Will Brownell and Richard N. Billings has half-a-dozen tantalizing references in the notes at the back to an interview granted by Anne Bullitt to the authors, and one cannot help wondering how definitive a book might have been possible had they won her full cooperation. (She was known for being litigious, and her name does not appear in the list of acknowledgements.)

It is not even clear exactly what role Bullitt played in helping to get Freud out of Vienna after the Nazis moved into Austria. Bullitt was then temporarily back in the United States; the formal State Department cables make it sound as if FDR took a personal interest in Freud's safety, and it may have only been Bullitt's later bitterness toward FDR that led him to deny that the president had actually done anything on Freud's behalf. (When Bullitt did his about-faces, he could be untrustworthy; for example, he even tried to deny that he once favored the recognition of Soviet Russia.) An old associate of Bullitt's was the American consul in Vienna, and he was personally able to facilitate the rescue of the Freuds.

All the stories about Bullitt are colorful, but the most famous one is the account of the final wrecking of his career. Although by the beginning of the New Deal Bullitt had overcome the stigma of his disloyalty to Wilson, by the outbreak of World War II Roosevelt was disenchanted with him. Bullitt was impulsive and high-handed, mercurial, and impressionistic – altogether not an easy man to work with. It appears that, after the fall of France, Roosevelt was being devious with Bullitt by stringing him along about finding him another job. Brownell and Billings claim that FDR was annoyed at Bullitt's treatment of "Missy" Le Hand, for years the president's private secretary. Bullitt (again divorced) was the one real romance of her life; they had an affair, and then Bullitt broke the engagement. But the ultimate falling-out between the president and Bullitt came over Sumner Welles.

Although Brownell and Billings do not go into why FDR disliked Secretary of State Cordell Hull (they do make plain FDR's disdain for career diplomats), FDR's admiration for Hull's undersecretary, Welles, was legendary. Hull hated Welles because of his special access to the president, and Bullitt craved Welles's job. Somehow it became known that, on a special train trip to Speaker Bankhead's funeral in 1940, Welles, while drunk, had propositioned a train porter. Bullitt, through friends who ran the railway, got documentation on the incident, including an affidavit from the porter, and spread the story. The FBI entered the case on the supposition that Welles was a possible security risk, subject to blackmail. FDR was not hypersensitive to the issue of homosexuality, and he tried to paper over the whole matter until Bullitt eventually forced his hand.

In 1943 Bullitt, whose favorite private secretary Brownell and Billings tell us was homosexual, circulated the Welles documents to a powerful Republican senator, who would then have demanded Welles's resignation if FDR had not accepted it beforehand. After having destroyed the career of Welles, who was a valuable public servant in wartime, Bullitt then went to FDR to get Welles's job. Alternatively, Bullitt wanted the president's support in a run for the mayoralty of Philadelphia. FDR's response to Bullitt became known, and Mrs. Roosevelt included it in her memoirs; but she left out the names, and the specifics of Welles's indiscretion. Drew Pearson, an old ally of Welles's, ran the story immediately after Bullitt's death: "If I were St. Peter and you and Sumner Welles should come before me seeking admission into the Gates of Heaven, do you know what I'd say? I would say 'Bill Bullitt, you have defamed the name of a man who toiled for his fellowmen, and you can go to Hell.'" To FDR, Welles was a patriot, and his sins were only those of the flesh.

Bullitt's attempt at electoral politics was humiliating; he was badly beaten for mayor of Philadelphia. His early disappointment with the Soviets led him to become one of the first of the cold warriors; he then wrote a scathing appraisal of Roosevelt's last days and his foreign policy; by 1946 he was *persona non grata* in Harry Truman's administration. In 1948 Bullitt became a Republican who hoped for office under Dewey.

For the rest of his life Bullitt remained friendly with the great and the mighty, although his high expectations meant subsequent disappointments, and he continued to have his fallings-out. He quarreled with Chiang Kai-shek (they had adjoining houses in Taiwan), and Bullitt, despite his support for the Free French during World War II, managed to insult de Gaulle. Ill health dogged Bullitt; a recurrent back problem and intermittent bouts with leukemia slowed down his last years. Always known for his tremendous energy, Bullitt traveled between his apartments in Paris and Washington, D.C., and a farm in western Massachusetts. It was, his physician said, mainly out of "sheer boredom" that in 1965 Bullitt decided to release the manuscript on Woodrow Wilson.

Bullitt's obvious brilliance did not prevent his becoming known as intemperate and unstable. He was involved in some of the most momentous foreign policy decisions of the century and earned the admiration of such an expert as Herbert Feis; Bullitt could be charming and debonair, and despite his flaws he so appealed to Freud that the creator of psychoanalysis took him as a patient in personal analysis. Like some others in Freud's circle, such as the Princess Marie Bonaparte, Bullitt's pretense to aristocratic lineage was compromised by the existence of Jewish forebears. (His mother was a Horwitz; the family was Episcopalian, but the eighteenth-century maternal ancestry was Polish-Jewish.)

It is hard not to wonder what, in a different setting, the prodigy who was William C. Bullitt might have become. Churchill could have been killed in the 1920s when he crossed an American street looking the wrong way and therefore not had the chance to oppose Nazism. Bullitt wrote some great speeches, and, to look at him in the best possible light, preferred to be a prophet rather than to play the game. Having been an isolationist and an appeaser before Munich, he immediately thereafter became a belligerent advocate of American intervention. Despite all his capacities, he had serious weaknesses of judgment, especially about military matters, and he ended up an outsider, a political exile. Bullitt's character was such that he was unable to fulfill the part he expected to play. Bullitt's ambitions, although he failed to fulfill them, do not sound at all farfetched, and that is no small tribute to the scale of his achievement.

If a full-scale scholarly biography of Bullitt were ever to be undertaken, I suspect that, in addition to new information required, many of the contentions in *So Close to Greatness* would have to be brought into question. It seems to me bootless—since I learned such an immense amount from the book and have relied on it here—to go about developing the errors on fine points that I happened to come across. *So Close to Greatness* is lively and brief and not intended as a weighty enterprise; I think it is one of those biographies that succeeds in capturing the spirit of its subject. Even if Brownell and Billings have not written great history, I found that the book made for compelling reading. One of the most remarkable aspects of Bullitt's career, which may indicate our historical ingratitude, is how the publication of *So Close to Greatness* seems to have gone almost unnoticed.

* * *

With the help of a series of psychiatric therapists, Anne Sexton transformed herself from a suburban housewife into one of the most influential contemporary American poets. Her suicide, in 1974, like poet Sylvia Plath's earlier, helped add to Sexton's legendary stature for having transmuted her spiritual anguish into artistic achievement.

Anne Sexton: A Biography[12] by Diane Wood Middlebrook is so powerful that it makes a captivating reading experience; I put everything else aside to finish it in one long gulp. Part of what made Anne Sexton so attractive as a poet was the way she used her work as a form of confession; she saw herself as an explorer of the unconscious as she delved into forbidden areas of human experience.

It turns out that, although it did not interfere with her winning a Pulitzer Prize, she had been consistently mad ever since becoming a mother. Sometimes Sexton was wholly unable to function and she made repeated suicide attempts and was often hospitalized. In her work, she used sincerity as a special kind of technique, and saw her poetry as a vehicle for describing her therapeutic experiences.

Anne Sexton, authorized by Sexton's older daughter (her literary executor), makes clear that Sexton violated almost every conceivable restraint. She not only was an alcoholic addicted to a variety of drugs, she even sexually abused the same daughter. The biography is especially compelling because that child authorized one of Sexton's psychiatrists, who treated her for eight years, to release tapes he made during hundreds of her therapeutic sessions. Sexton had been unable to remember anything of significance from one session to the next, and he relied on those audiotapes to help her maintain a continuity in their working relationship.

A storm of medical outrage greeted this psychiatrist's breaking of the customary rule of confidentiality. In addition, he wrote a foreword to *Anne Sexton* and subsequently defended himself against the charge of indiscretion by pointing to how a subsequent psychiatrist of hers had slept with her while she was paying him fees for treatment. Still a third therapist authorized Anne Sexton to go through with divorcing her long-suffering husband, even though this took away a pillar of her stability; in another year she was dead.

Anne Sexton is so engrossing partly because it constitutes such a tale of transgression. She not only lived life to "the hilt," as she put it, but her psychiatrists lost their foothold in trying to treat her. Even if she had ever thought to have authorized the release of her therapeutic audiotapes, I wonder about her mental competency to do so. It remains to me disturbing that someone that sick could speak for the experiences of so many others in our time.

* * *

At the time Sylvia Plath committed suicide in 1963 by placing her head inside a gas oven, she was the mother of two small children and married to Ted Hughes, later to become the poet laureate of England. Plath was herself a first-class writer, who had already published some lyric poetry; her novel *The Bell Jar*, which in her lifetime was published only in England and under a pseudonym, later became a bestseller in North America. Honors came to Plath belatedly; her *Collected Poems* won a Pulitzer Prize in 1982—nineteen years after her death at the age of thirty. Her tragic and premature end helped create a special legend about her.

Part of the interest in her derives from the whole vexing issue of the relationship between art and insanity. Plath, whose first poem was published when she was 8-and-a-half years old, made a suicide attempt when she was ten. While at Smith College she suffered from a serious depression and underwent electroshock therapy. Paul Alexander's *Rough Magic: A Biography of Sylvia Plath*[13] shows that she was not well served by psychiatry, and that the series of shock treatments, which one would hope only come as a last resort for a young person, were at first administered carelessly, without first giving her a muscle relaxant. The last doctor to treat her failed to find her a hospital bed in London in time to prevent her final suicide attempt. Plath has, therefore, attracted attention as one of our era's notable victims.

Alexander's solid biography, part of an increasing flood of work about Plath, has added to the conception of her as a martyr by highlighting the degree to which her marriage to the unfaithful Hughes contributed to her suicide. More generally, Plath has symbolized the retribution society seems to inflict on those women who violate the taboo of wanting to have everything, for she sought to be a mother as well as a wife while pursuing a creative career.

Alexander does a fine job of describing her family background, and her youth growing up in Massachusetts. Such has been Plath's success that her moving letters home to her mother, who remained in the U.S. after Plath moved to England, first to attend Cambridge on a Fulbright Scholarship and then to be Hughes's wife, have attracted attention as a book.

The central problem with *Rough Magic* is the unfortunate absence of detailed documentation. For Alexander was constrained by the objections of Plath's estate, which was controlled by Hughes and his sister, from quoting from Plath's writings. Hughes could no doubt be as monstrous as is alleged (Assia Gutmann, the woman for whom Hughes left Plath, later did away with herself and their two-year-old child, and by using the same awful method as Plath) but Alexander has paid a high price for what he achieved in *Rough Magic*, since what we get is a life without evidence of the work.

Any good writer lives through creation, and the day-to-day doings that also go to make up the narrative of any biography are not in themselves enough to convey the essence of a creative spirit. On the other hand, the Plath industry is far enough along, and her writing well known, so that Alexander could pursue his conscientious research with the conviction that an unauthorized biography would have something unique to add to the understanding of a writer about whom there has been so much intense and increasing interest.

Rough Magic is well written and carefully paced, and makes an engrossing read. And it raises some of the same ethical issues as in Diane Middlebrook's biography of Anne Sexton, since a few of Plath's physicians were willing to be interviewed by Alexander. It sounds like medical confidentiality, at least when it concerns those who become publicly successful, is going to have to be re-argued and explained. A cynic might well think that it is better if future patients are aware of the extent to which psychiatrists can talk; but that reality may tragically conflict with the need patients have, in order to get the help they require, to be able implicitly to trust the discretion of therapists.

* * *

Ever since Voltaire in the eighteenth century, France has enjoyed a tradition of having outspoken thinkers who are also public celebrities. *Michel Foucault*[14] by Didier Eribon is an excellent biography, a bestseller when it came out in France; it is an absorbing account of how a recent philosopher (he died of AIDS in 1984) not only was for a time a successor within university circles to the legendary Jean-Paul Sartre, but a popular icon frequently in the company of motion picture stars like Yves Montand and Simone Signoret.

Foucault was a great critic of conventional uses of psychological terminology, and thought that apparently neutral ideas about the mind could easily become instruments in reinforcing pre-existing social patterns. Like other *engagé* French intellectuals, he sought to take stands on contemporary political issues. In *Michel Foucault*, Didier Eribon recounts the numerous petitions that he signed, and public declarations that he helped to forward.

For a North American reader, the crises besetting France since World War II are bound to seem insular. But Foucault and his allies thought nothing of leaving their libraries and standing on barricades in the streets in behalf of some social cause that those of us on this side of the Atlantic are unlikely to have heard of. The attraction that Maoism held for Foucault and other highly educated French mandarins may also seem puzzling to readers today.

Foucault's books, however, did make an impact abroad, and by the end of his life he had become much sought after as a speaker on the North American continent. And his personal influence has by no means begun to wane. There may be more Ph.D. dissertations being written on him in both the U.S. and Canada than on any other recent thinker. One of the most interesting aspects of *Michel Foucault* is the glimpse it gives into the structure of French higher education, and of just how many formal gradations of achievement Foucault had to attain in order to reach the top of the academic heap. He used his superb education and his innate intelligence to compose, in *Madness and Civilization* and other works, a vast portrait of how insanity has been viewed throughout the ages.

He argued that to follow the history of madness, one also has to understand the different cultures that have described the phenomenon. Everything that he undertook to recount in connection with mental illness had the broadest possible social implications, as did his final effort to write the history of sexuality. Foucault had the advantage not only of being immensely learned but also of being a lyrical writer. His works are complex, providing plenty of material for future researchers to explicate for the general public.

Early on Foucault had thought of the insane as a persecuted lot, and I am afraid that however much he may have contributed in forwarding tolerance for the ill, he also managed to lend support to those who misguidedly romanticize the catastrophe of mental illness. Foucault was a philosopher without any medical training, and he seems to have paid no attention to the accumulating scientific evidence that schizophrenia, for instance, can best be understood as a biochemical disorder. His commitment to defending the cause of the deviant and the oppressed led him also to write about prisons, arguing that criminality can be manufactured by the very institutions that are set up to control, correct, and supposedly reform its inmates.

I do not think one has to share Foucault's own radical politics in order to appreciate how legitimately he challenged conventional notions of normality and deviance. Foucault's life, so superbly recounted in this book, reminds us of the validity of the traditional view that philosophy and psychology should be intimately connected. It may require a special effort for us to be able to appreciate the dazzling character of the philosophical arguments that go on in Paris. But in the long run the life of the mind can only be enriched by our becoming better acquainted with one of the leading figures in those arguments.

* * *

Stephen M. Weissman's *His Brother's Keeper: A Psychobiography of Samuel Taylor Coleridge*[15] is a fascinating book. The tale of Coleridge's life, and how it interwove with William Wordsworth's, makes such a compelling narrative that an untutored reader is bound to be grateful for all that is to be learnt. It does not sound to me as if the author, a psychiatrist and psychoanalyst, has any special ear for poetry; but this book is a work of biographical reconstruction, and whatever Weissman's flaws in understanding poetry, he has spun a remarkable human tale.

At the same time I think that it is necessary to point out some key conceptual flaws. First of all, the book appears in a new monograph series called "Applied Psychoanalysis." Now it is one thing for Freud and his early disciples to think that there was such an enterprise—an application of psychoanalysis beyond the strictly clinical realm. But we should all know by now that psychoanalysis does not constitute a body of knowledge that is inherently capable of being "applied." Rather, psychoanalysis is itself in need of the enrichment that might come from contact with the humanities and social sciences.

Secondly, despite the fact that the narrative flow in the book is a powerful one, Weissman has burdened it with more theorizing than should ever be the case in a biography that purports to recreate a human life. Weissman sees the tie between Coleridge and Wordsworth in terms of Coleridge's need to recapture an early fraternal bond. Entirely aside from what a boring approach to any biographical enterprise such a reductive thesis is, the author makes two central contentions in his introduction that he fails adequately to follow up on.

We are told at the outset of the book that Wordsworth, "at a critical turning point in the fall of 1800, actually helped push Coleridge into his addiction, thereby undermining him as both artist and man." Nothing in the text Weissman gives us supports such a damning charge; in reality, the two men, despite artistic and personal differences, remained extraordinarily good friends throughout Coleridge's life; Coleridge's succumbing to opium, and his extravagances with alcohol, have to be attributed to himself.

Weissman also tells us of Wordsworth's sister-in-law, a woman with whom Coleridge became infatuated: "Sara Hutchinson was merely the go-between, fantasy-vehicle for Coleridge's obsessive attachment to William Wordsworth —an unconsciously homosexual attachment which is also traceable in the poetry Coleridge was writing at this time." Nothing that I read in *His Brother's Keeper* was able to support that early claim of Weissman's. I would have thought it was long past the time that accusations of unconscious homosexuality could be so loosely bandied about, especially when all the poetic evidence that Weissman can offer has to do with an account of a poem describing the strange attachment between two women.

Given all the medical problems in Coleridge's life, it is particularly fitting that a physician should undertake to study it; no layperson could begin to understand either the quantities of drugs Coleridge ingested, or the effects these opiates (and Coleridge's struggle against them) could have on him. *My Brother's Keeper* has disquieting flaws that I fear reflect the prevailing state of psychoanalytic psychology; for despite all the sound criticisms that have been leveled at key parts of Freud's earliest doctrines, they still somehow endure and continue to crop up throughout the literature. Yet I would like to repeat that I found the book so interesting as to make for the most absorbing kind of reading. It would not be the first time that a writer's practices are superior to his theoretical commitments. A subsequent set of volumes about Coleridge by Richard Holmes[16] seemed to me to be masterpieces of biography writing that will endure as models of how a writer should proceed.

* * *

Great subjects call forth interesting books, and there seems no doubt that the relationship between Simone de Beauvoir and Jean-Paul Sartre (sexual, emotional and intellectual) is such a commanding topic. These two giant figures, both authors of books, short stories, plays, and novels, succeeded in being intimate friends for some fifty-one years, until his death in 1980 (de Beauvoir died in 1986). Their remarkable alliance, which survived professional as well as sexual jealousy, was pivotal not just within French intellectual life; the existentialist philosophy they elaborated is a significant addition to twentieth-century thought.

All writers appear a bit dippy, at least by the standards of everyday life, and Sartre would appear to have been both more promiscuous and troubled than Beauvoir, although her own bisexuality, and habit of informing Sartre about the details of her various affairs, goes beyond prosaic notions of behavior.

Simone de Beauvoir and Jean-Paul Sartre[17] by Kate and Edward Fullbrook (an English husband-and-wife team) is not an original source of primary data, like Deirdre Bair's *Simone de Beauvoir* (1990) or Annie Cohen-Solal's *Sartre* (1987). We are taken through de Beauvoir and Sartre's lives and works by means of extensive quotation from their writings, so much so that one is tempted to sit down and start rereading them. The authors apparently accept at face value the complete truth of the autobiographical accounts Beauvoir and Sartre gave us. The Fullbrooks seem unable to rise to the challenge of untangling the rich possible meanings that might lie behind any autobiographical self-revelations.

Contrary to the Fullbrooks's rather naïve view of causality, the past is never a straightforward explanation of later developments. For example, when they attempt to explain Sartre's relationship with de Beauvoir, they cite Sartre's bond with his widowed mother as an example of a couple in which partners tell each other everything, then claim that this was the precursor to the "nearly identical" set of rules that later governed his arrangement with Beauvoir.

Sartre himself repeatedly argued against the Freudian emphasis on the infantile factor in explaining what we are like. Instead of North American babytalk about how the past is responsible for creating us, Sartre insisted that we are what we choose to be. His existentialism demanded that we face up to the void of our existence by making key decisions.

Neither Sartre nor de Beauvoir wanted to allow their social identities to become the basis of their self-identities, and they both successfully insisted on retaining their autonomy within the relationship. They were outcasts by choice, even when they participated in left-wing politics and advanced the principle that intellectuals be socially engaged and committed. They finally broke with the French Communist Party over the 1956 invasion of Hungary, but today they look less prescient in their political commitments to other extreme doctrines like Maoism.

The most troubling aspect of *Simone de Beauvoir and Jean-Paul Sartre* is the claim of the Fullbrooks to have uncovered a secret behind the legendary partnership that boils down to the idea that she was the original one and he a plagiarist. The Fullbrooks believe that Sartre built his 1943 philosophical treatise *Being and Nothingness* out of Beauvoir's contemporaneous novel *She Came to Stay*. They seem obtuse about admitting how notoriously difficult it is to establish influences within intellectual history. When two thinkers spend hours every day talking together, reading each other's work, sharing ideas, might not influence be a two-way street?

For some reason, this slim volume has been published separately from a projected second volume that is supposed to discuss the same subject; but what we have here is too slight to sustain the general thesis that the Fullbrooks intend to establish. Although they remain convinced that "this revisionary biography of one of history's most extraordinary intellectual partnerships will stand as an important step in the remaking of a twentieth century legend," I doubt that many readers will be persuaded by the evidence for their theory that they offer here. I think biographies thrive more on good preceding examples of completed works than on any explicit set of possible conceptual guidelines.

Notes

1. William Robert Miller, *Martin Luther King, Jr.* (New York: Weybright & Talley, 1968).
2. George R. Metcalf, *Black Profiles* (New York: McGraw-Hill, 1968).
3. Lerone Bennet Jr., *Pioneers in Protest* (New York: Johnson, 1968).
4. Nuel Pharr Davis, *Lawrence and Oppenheimer* (New York: Simon & Schuster, 1968).
5. Arthur Mitzman, *The Iron Cage* (New York: Alfred A. Knopf, 1970).

6.   Maxwell Geismar, *Mark Twain: An American Prophet* (Boston: Houghton Mifflin, 1970).
7.   John Bartlow Martin, *Adlai Stevenson and the World: The Life of Adlai E. Stevenson* (New York: Doubleday, 1978).
8.   See Paul Roazen, *Encountering Freud: The Politics and Histories of Psychoanalysis* (New Brunswick, NJ: Transaction Publishers), pp. 255-58.
9.   William Wright, *Lillian Hellman: The Image, The Woman* (New York: Musson, 1987).
10. See Paul Roazen, *Freud: Political and Social Thought*, 3rd edition (New Brunswick, NJ, Transaction Publishers, 1999), Epilogue, pp. 300-322; also, Paul Roazen, *Erik H. Erikson: The Power and Limits of a Vision* (Northvale, NJ: Jason Aronson, 1997), pp.13, 201-203.
11. Will Brownell and Richard N. Billings, *So Close to Greatness; A Biography of William C.Bullitt* (New York: Macmillan, 1988).
12. Diane Wood Middlebrook, *Anne Sexton: A Biography* (Toronto: Thomas Allen & Son, 1991).
13. Paul Alexander, *Rough Magic: A Biography of Sylvia Plath* (New York: Viking/ Penguin, 1991).
14. Didier Eribon, *Michel Foucault*, translated from the French by Betsy Wing (Cambridge, MA: Harvard University Press, 1991).
15. Stephen M. Weissman, *His Brother's Keeper: A Psychobiography of Samuel Taylor Coleridge* (Madison, CT: International Universities Press, 1989).
16. Richard Holmes, *Coleridge: Early Visions, 1772-1804* (New York: Pantheon Books, 1989) and Richard Holmes, *Coleridge: Darker Reflections, 1804-1834* (New York: Pantheon Books, 1998).
17. Kate Fullbrook and Edward Fullbrook, *Simone de Beauvoir and Jean-Paul Sartre: The Remaking of a Twentieth-Century Legend* (New York: Basic Books, 1994).

14

Affairs of State

The Price of Power: Kissinger in the Nixon White House by Seymour Hersh[1] is one of those unusual instances of an important book becoming a bestseller. From the first day of publication it was controversial enough to be subjected to intense scrutiny. Present and former State Department officials were immediately interviewed on television before they had a chance to read it. *The Price of Power* was extensively assessed but largely along ideological lines; those eager to defend or please the American foreign policy establishment have expressed their criticisms, while the left has enjoyed the overwhelming documentation of Kissinger's half-truths, lies, and mistakes. The Watergate prosecutors regarded Kissinger as an untouchable, and despite the 1979 publicity about his involvement with the secret bombing of Cambodia, Kissinger's reputation among the general public has until now remain largely unsullied.

Although reading the book can be difficult, it is absolutely fascinating for anyone interested in contemporary affairs. Hersh provides a massively detailed reconstruction of the years 1968-72. The war in Southeast Asia is obviously the single most significant issue of that period; but Hersh covers other matters as well: the opening to China, the intricacies of the SALT negotiations, the "destabilization" of Allende's Chile, Mideast struggles, and the India-Pakistan war. *The Price of Power* is partly so absorbing because of how much has been forgotten from that period. At the same time, it is astonishing how even the most conscientious outside observer could never at the time have known most of what was going on.

The lack of artistic form in *The Price of Power* may be part of a deliberate attempt to persuade through documentary tedium. Hersh's approach seems to me reminiscent of the technique used by historian Charles Beard who once tried to blame the coming of World War II on Franklin Roosevelt. Hersh relies partly on public records, and he has used the Freedom of Information Act skillfully to get access to new material; he also contrasts different memoirs, like those of Nixon and Kissinger, in order to reveal what each tried to distort or conceal.

Hersh's interviews yield some striking results. For example, a member of Kissinger's staff, willing to be identified by name, recalled how Kissinger reacted to the frustration of dealing with Nguyen van Thieu: "We'll kill the son-of-of-bitch if we have to." A few of the people Hersh quotes are, not surprisingly, unhappy with what he has made of their information; and Hersh's critics can point to the inevitability of malcontents feeding damaging information to someone they could count on as a Kissinger-hater. (In India, Morarji Desai sued over the charge that he was a paid informer for the CIA.) No matter what the rest of Kissinger's public career may amount to, Hersh has found out enough to be able to demonstrate the consistent ruthlessness with which Kissinger was capable of operating. He became the embodiment of Machiavelli's belief that the safety of the state is the ultimate norm of political conduct. Perhaps only in the twentieth century, however, could the political uses of threatening to be insane—the "madman theory" adopted by Kissinger—become a recommendation to rulers.

Hersh's ambitions extend to trying to establish that Kissinger's scheming was for his own personal advancement, while every one of his policies failed. Cold-blooded planners like Kissinger may have all along thought in terms of punishing the opponent, as in the Vietnam War, rather than hoped for old-fashioned military success. Yet the tale Hersh has constructed will take considerable effort to undo. Some of the lengthier footnotes make stories all their own. One wonders, though, despite the role that Hersh accords to the individual in history, whether Kissinger really could have performed so much on his own. Curiously enough, unlike in David Halberstam's *The Best and the Brightest*, we learn almost nothing about the background and character of any of the figures in *The Price of Power*.

Hersh's book is testimony to the vitality of investigatory journalism. Perhaps no one could have stung Kissinger more than Hersh, a Pulitzer Prize winner for his exposure of the My Lai massacre. At the same time, given how Hersh shows that Kissinger succeeded in manipulating as publicity vehicles such columnists as Joseph Alsop and James Reston, friends of democratic self-government can hardly feel reassured. Nor should anyone underestimate the political savvy of the leaders in Moscow, who might once again, not just as in 1972, decide to help reelect an incumbent Republican president.

* * *

Franklin Roosevelt's administration marks the highpoint of political idealism in twentieth-century America. In accepting the 1932 Democratic nomination for the presidency, at a time when the economic depression seemed to many beyond human control, FDR promised to pledge himself to "a New Deal," and his message of hope captured the public's imagination. Ironically Roosevelt won the first of his four presidential elections on a platform of reducing federal spending and balancing the national budget, a program that he strikingly failed to fulfill, but he succeeded in attracting to Washington a host of young idealists bent on joining in Rooseveltian experimentalism.

The late Joseph P. Lash was a long-serving publicist in behalf of the New Deal cause. Earlier he became famous for his Pulitzer Prize-winning *Eleanor and Franklin*, which was a touching account of the relationship between the President and his wife. Lash had been a protégé of Mrs. Roosevelt's, and wrote from her perspective. But in *Dealers and Dreamers: A New Look at the New Deal*[2] Lash tackled the significance of the Roosevelt administrations from a fresh viewpoint. He picked two young lawyers, Benjamin V. Cohen and Thomas G. Corcoran, to concentrate on; they both were lawyers who became legislative draftsmen and speechwriters for the New Deal. The story Lash tells ends just before the outbreak of World War II, when both men were edged out in Roosevelt's favor by Harry Hopkins and other advisers whom the president felt he needed in his new role as "Dr.Win-The-War." By then, FDR was concerned with issues of reconciliation and national unity, so the goals of the earlier Neal Deal took a backseat; consequently he felt he could afford to banish both Cohen and Corcoran from his inner circle.

Throughout Roosevelt's first two terms Cohen and Corcoran were among the New Deal's most loyal cohorts. They were workaholics in behalf of the twin objectives of reform and recovery. For a time Cohen and Corcoran even lived together. Although neither of them ever held formal positions that were in any way commensurate with the various tasks they performed, an aura of mystery came to surround their power; they even appeared together on a cover of *Time* magazine in 1938. Roosevelt had wanted supporters who had strong views, even if in the end he insisted that they do his ultimate bidding.

Cohen was more the careful legal craftsman and Corcoran a political hustler, but they made a worthy team and took part in Roosevelt's legislative effort to ensure that Washington and not Wall Street was the directing authority in the world of money and credit. Although early New Deal legislation like the National Recovery Act and the Agricultural Adjustment Act foundered on the constitutional objections of a conservative Supreme Court, in the end the bulk of Roosevelt's program was judicially sustained. Cohen and Corcoran took a notable part in the Securities and Exchanges Act and the Social Security Act; the Fair Labor Standards Act, which governed wages and hours and outlawed child labor, and the Wagner Act, which guaranteed the rights of labor, also benefited from their help. Roosevelt had the conservative objective of reforming through preserving, and sought not to overthrow but to salvage a free economy. Lash successfully uses the figures of Cohen and Corcoran to tell the wonderfully exciting tale of the struggles of the New Deal.

Although I doubt that Lash was fully aware of it, the figure who I think manages to steal the show in *Dealers and Dreamers* is Felix Frankfurter. At the outset of FDR's presidency Frankfurter was a trusted adviser who chose to remain at Harvard Law School rather than accept an appointment with the new administration. Ultimately, in 1939, Roosevelt appointed Frankfurter to the Supreme Court. But throughout *Dealers and Dreamers* it is Frankfurter who is most notably working behind the scenes; both Cohen and Corcoran defer to him as their leader, and Frankfurter's messages to them are continuously scintillating and authoritative. Frankfurter, who was childless himself, inspired in these young men an extraordinary amount of devotion; he was full of ideas and always recommending new talent to send to Washington. Frankfurter's followers, known as his "hot dogs," came to supersede Roosevelt's first group of advisers, the so-called Brains Trusters.

In the end, both Cohen and Corcoran broke completely with Frankfurter. It is not entirely clear what accounted for the falling out, except that Lash tells us that Frankfurter chose to support other candidates than they for high public office. One suspects that Frankfurter, ever attuned to FDR's own wishes, knew intuitively in which direction the president's own inclinations were moving, and it is unlikely that a Frankfurter endorsement could have prevailed in the teeth of Roosevelt's own growing disenchantment with Cohen and Corcoran. In later years, liberals were to be bitterly disappointed with how Frankfurter performed on the Supreme Court, and in his edition of Frankfurter's *Diaries*,[3] Lash has not pulled his punches in criticizing the justice's judicial positions.

But in *Dealers and Dreamers* Lash has given us an unforgettable inside account of the fights during the New Deal years. Being a New Dealer was more a state of mind than an organization, and we are taken through the early legal agonies of getting Roosevelt's program approved by the "nine old men" who made up the Supreme Court. Roosevelt's "court-packing" plan of 1937, which he formulated after his massive reelection victory in 1936, forms one of the book's dramatic high points. (Lash reproduces a Herblock cartoon about Roosevelt's controversial plan to expand the size of the Court that seems to me worth the price of this book.) Frankfurter quietly assisted FDR, and was soon rewarded with his Supreme Court appointment. Although Roosevelt lost the battle to increase the Court's membership, the frightened Court did shift its ideological position and started approving New Deal legislation; soon justices started to retire, and Roosevelt then decisively shaped the nature of the new Court.

Dealers and Dreamers is full of examples of political courtiers who are jealous of anybody else who succeeded in getting access to the president. There are also some startling examples of how Justice Louis D. Brandeis, although already on the Supreme Court, performed extra-judicial activities; he gave teas and spoke with a stream of people who sought his advice and counsel, and therefore ranks as a major New Deal figure. Cohen and Corcoran themselves had later careers that did not fulfill their early promise; Corcoran in particular seems to have descended into being an influence peddlar. But in the 1930s they both had been in the right place and with the best motives, for, as Lash puts it, they had stifled their rebelliousness knowing that "it was in service to Roosevelt and the causes he championed that they were achieving the highest moments of personal fulfillment."

* * *

The words "liberal" and "liberalism" appeared in the U.S. political vocabulary in the early years of Franklin Roosevelt's presidency, and afterward they stood for the viewpoint of his New Deal. In the era of President Ronald Reagan's immense popularity, none of the leading contenders in politics seemed eager to call upon the tradition of liberalism. Yet the Nobel Prize-winning Swedish writer Gunnar Myrdal put his finger on the paradox that liberalism in the United States is traditional; he wrote that "America is conservative...but the principles conserved are liberal, and some, indeed, are radical."

It seems to me that Michael Dukakis has exemplified the way a reformer can also be profoundly conservative. His genuine idealism and devotion to public service have been built on the conviction that those who are truest to fundamental U.S. values are the leaders who return to the ideal purposes for which the country was founded. It is no accident that in his acceptance speech for the presidential nomination that he delivered at the Democratic convention in July 1988, he cited words of Puritan John Winthrop, a spiritual forefather who had reminded his newly arrived flock in Massachusetts of the significance of community.

Dukakis's credentials as a liberal seem to be impeccable, even though over the years he has disappointed some on the left. He once described himself as "a liberal who can count." Especially after he first became governor of Massachusetts in 1974, his commitment to budget balancing forced him to cut social services in order to avoid financial insolvency. "The good thing about Michael," one of his colorful leftist critics put it at the time, "is that he takes the subway to work everyday; the bad thing is that he gets off at the State House."

It seemed, when he was starting out as a state legislator in the early 1960s, that his integrity and personal asceticism made becoming governor impossible. Massachusetts had throughout the twentieth century a pattern of graft and corruption that exceeded that of almost any other state (or Canadian province). The Kennedys in Massachusetts always chose to opt for federal politics, and stayed as far away as possible from the maelstrom of state political races.

Dukakis, however, worked his way from the bottom, with his rectitude intact, by means of immense organizational skill. In the 1988 Democratic primaries he struggled as one of the so-called "seven dwarfs," until he emerged as the victor. But the full story of his rise is even more of a tribute to the American dream that industry and competence are capable of overcoming almost any odds.

He began his career by first becoming an unpaid member of a local town meeting, then by entering the state legislature; in the midst of the Vietnam War he pioneered in enacting the nation's first no-fault automobile insurance law. Finally he started to campaign for statewide office, becoming governor at the age of forty-one. In 1988, when both Gary Hart and Joseph Biden were found to have different kinds of skeletons in their respective closets, Dukakis's character as a do-gooder was bound to be attractive. As his mother once said of him, "What you see is what you get."

Two 1988 books about Dukakis, one by Charles Kenney and Robert Turner,[4] reporters for the *Boston Globe*, and the other by Richard Gaines and Michael Segal,[5] journalists on the *Boston Phoenix*, are both good introductions. Dukakis was born in 1933 in Brookline, a Boston suburb, and the chapters about his early life are fascinating. We are told, for example, that an ancient history teacher in the high school once was so impressed by the young Dukakis that she predicted to the class, "Sometime Michael Dukakis is going to be president of the United States." The educational system in which he grew up was so sheltered it was conceivable to believe that if one did one's Latin conscientiously, it was possible to become president.

Dukakis was not being phony in proudly reminding the public of his Greek heritage. The United States is a nation of immigrants, and the fact that both his parents were born abroad is a tribute to the fluidity and openness of that society. Dukakis does give the appearance of having been born to rule. He was first elected president of his class in the third grade. But his climb has been an individual one; when his opponents underestimated him, it cost them dearly in the end.

Dukakis is himself the product of the best in U.S. higher education, since he attended both Swarthmore College and Harvard Law School; he did not neglect to serve two years in the army as a private, though others at the time either got military deferments or chose to go to officer training school. His career looks like a continuous line of advancing public officeholding. The one great divide came in 1978, when he was defeated for renomination as governor by one of the figures from the unsavory part of the state Democratic Party.

During Dukakis's first tern he became known as "the Duke," and he reformed a chaotic court system. In hindsight, Dukakis's uncompromising righteousness helped undermine him. Somehow he overlooked the warning signals of political trouble. His successor as Governor made a joke out of the office; his appointees were responsible for tax-collecting scandals that fatally tarnished the administration. Once Dukakis returned as governor in 1983, after a stint of teaching at Harvard's Kennedy School, supposedly "Duke II" took the place of the earlier "Duke I," and he proved that he understood that politics is the art of the possible.

Dukakis was reelected in 1986, and was an immensely successful governor. His own book, *Creating the Future,*[6] co-authored with a professor at Harvard Business School, recorded an account of how Massachusetts made its notable comeback. Dukakis used the power of the state, setting up agencies that financed pilot programs to encourage investments in innovators. The man who started out as a political saint was able to work harmoniously with business leaders and bankers to ensure that prosperity and revitalization did not leave pockets of economic backwardness.

Against a background of sordid state politics, he conceived the idea of enforcing the tax laws; in its first two years the program produced $300-million in new revenues, including $85-million that came in during an amnesty period. Unemployment dropped from 12 per cent to less than 3 per cent. No one can alone account for the Massachusetts "miracle," but the state went from being a financial basket-case to the economic envy of the nation and a model of efficiency and creativity. His fellow governors voted Dukakis the most effective governor, and *Creating the Future* called upon his state experience as a laboratory example for the nation.

Both campaign biographies are solid books. Although Gaines and Segal provide the more comprehensive background on Massachusetts politics, Kenney and Turney (who had the interviewing cooperation of Dukakis and his wife) offer more details. Dukakis has been that rare political creature who naturally combines progressive principles with conservative inclinations, and to the extent that character can be electorally decisive, these books go far in defining what qualities Dukakis brought to the offices he held.

* * *

When Lionel Trilling's *The Liberal Imagination*[7] appeared in 1950, and then Louis Hartz's *The Liberal Tradition in America*[8] in 1955, they both were innovatively relating the doctrines of classical European political and social thought to the special characteristics of American life. In searching for the roots of American liberalism it does not take too much historical reflection to turn back to Thomas Jefferson and the early paragraphs of his Declaration of Independence. It is at least as patriotic to think about our dedication to the historical principles of "life, liberty and the pursuit of happiness" as to recite the far more recently appearing Pledge of Allegiance. But I believe that presidential political campaigns ought to be devoted to concentrating on the public issues that are outstanding, rather than working up nationalistic emotional fervor.

No dispute should be necessary about the greatness of America, but its heritage is broader than that implied by those who have been eager, starting especially in the presidential campaign of 1988, to stigmatize the word *liberal* as a politically dirty one. American liberalism has its roots in a European past, embracing such heroes of intellectual history as John Milton, John Locke, and John Stuart Mill.

It is not necessary to exclude any of the great ideological schools of thought from the broad American moral consensus. Long ago, Ralph Waldo Emerson wrote of the liberal and the conservative: "Each is a great half but an impossible whole. Each exposes the abuses of the other but in a true society, in a true man, both must combine."

Any political campaign would rise to a higher level if the use of symbolic behavior (like flag-saluting) were minimized, and the candidates themselves examined. Everyone on the ballot deserves scrutiny to the extent to which they embody liberal as well as conservative commitments. But we will never get far in the direction of sophisticated political discussion as long as the one word, *liberal*, remains tarred and tainted, in spite of its being so intrinsic a part of our nation's heritage.

*   *   *

According to Thomas C. Reeves's *A Question of Character: A Life of John F. Kennedy*[9] the unending saga of dirt associated with what can look like America's most dissolute dynasty all started with the model set by its founding father, Joseph P. Kennedy, who amassed a fortune by hook or by crook. When in the thirties President Franklin Roosevelt appointed him, in recognition of important campaign support, to the Securities and Exchange Commission, FDR had in private told critics: "Set a thief to catch a thief."

Thomas Reeves, a respected historian who has produced a well-documented study, thinks that the amoral character of President Kennedy's father is the key to the story of Jack's own life, but the only improprieties Reeves fails to accuse JFK of committing are those concerned with finances. The "Ambassador," as Joseph Kennedy preferred to be called after having served as Roosevelt's ambassador to Great Britain, handled all his children's money, and pulled the major political strings in their careers. The picture Reeves paints is a terrible one, and Kennedy haters will relish this book. Even JFK's record during the Second World War gets besmirched, for he is portrayed as an incompetent PT boat commander. His father was, in addition to being a ruthless opportunist, a sexual philanderer; and Reeves is unremitting about JFK's own compulsive infidelities.

Politics takes a back seat in *A Question of Character*. For example, we are told virtually nothing about the presidency of Dwight D. Eisenhower, or how JFK's own brilliant style contrasted with the dull last days of his predecessor in the White House. Reeves claims in the first sentence of his book that he has "always liked John F. Kennedy," and that the thought of Richard Nixon becoming president in 1960 made Reeves think about living in Canada. Since the author describes no process of disillusionment, I believe any of his other heroes had better run for cover. But Reeves does think that, starting in 1960, there was a sudden falling-off in the character of American presidents; he lumps JFK, Nixon, and Lyndon Johnson together as reprobates.

Reeves lets up on JFK only during his account of the Cuban missile crisis, perhaps the most dangerous moment in world history. Here, the running narrative on JFK's extramarital affairs suddenly halts. *A Question of Character* indicates that toward the end of JFK's life, there was more to him than the pursuit of pleasure and power that had marked his earlier career. Reeves praises him for growing more sensitive to his family, as his marriage was finally beginning to work. Then Reeves pulls the rug out from under such belated maturity and, although he no longer provides concrete examples of sexual exploits, argues hat JFK was "incapable of monogamy at the time of his assassination."

Reeves believes that not only did the president have a liaison with Marilyn Monroe, but that so did his brother, Robert. Reeves contends that the two brothers shared her, and he lends credence to an old story that linked Bobby to her mysterious-seeming death. JFK, while president, also supposedly shared a call girl with a leading mobster who was involved in plots to assassinate Fidel Castro. And, among other drugs, JFK was injected with amphetamines. *A Question of Character* presents a sordid story; but it has to be surprising to find a professional historian relying in his notes on an early book by a tabloid journalist like Kitty Kelley about Jacqueline Kennedy Onassis.

Reeves is correct in suggesting that before Kennedy, the public had never been given such apparently intimate glimpses of a president's private life. He dwells on the enormous gap that grew up between JFK's image and the real man, who was reckless and often irresponsible. He had exposed himself on numerous occasions to blackmail, and the Kennedys had to kowtow to the FBI's J. Edgar Hoover because of the files he had on them.

Apologists for Kennedy and his brothers have been consistently eager to come forward. The most telling portions of Reeve's book come in devastating asides he cites, rhapsodies that fellow historians have offered in contrast to his own reconstructions of political expediency. When I was growing up in Brookline, Massachusetts. in the 1950s, one side of my family was Republican and the other Democratic. Yet there was unanimity on one subject; no son of old Joe Kennedy could possibly be any good. It has to be with a mixture of misgivings and nostalgia that I realize to what extent they were right.

* * *

A week after President Kennedy was assassinated in 1963 a Gallup poll showed that only 29 percent of Americans believed that Lee Harvey Oswald alone was responsible for the killing. Lyndon Johnson seemed to be politically sensitive enough, and also personally suspicious about the possible ramifications of the Central Intelligence Agency's conspiracies to kill Castro, that Johnson persuaded Chief Justice Earl Warren to head a distinguished commission to look into the whole matter. In time for the 1964 presidential election the Warren Commission had concluded that Oswald alone was guilty. But within a couple of years we learned that the Warren Commission had rather hurriedly reached its findings, and any piece of sloppiness was all the grounds necessary for the most paranoid kinds of advocates of conspiracy theorizing to flourish.

Ever since then there has been an industry of people who have been making a financial boondoggle out of tales of supposed missed clues and suppressed evidence. Oliver Stone's film *JFK* gave a degree of respectability to conspiracy buffs that was bound to be shocking to those most intimately familiar with the case, and responsibly concerned that our youngsters not be misled about the most striking facts. Although I set out to read Gerald Posner's *Case Closed: Lee Harvey Oswald and the Assassination of JFK*[10] for the sake of bringing myself up to date on all the latest ballistics evidence, it quickly became apparent that the Warren Commission, even in an era without today's technical capacities, had done a fair-minded job of evaluating the points at issue.

For me the most impressive aspect of *Case Closed* is the way Posner was able to reconstruct the unbelievable atmosphere associated with the crime in Dallas that not only destroyed a young president's life, but helped poison the political atmosphere of the remainder of the twentieth century. Posner convincingly recreates the personalities of not just the victims of the shooting, but he also traces with compelling attention to detail and psychological plausibility the kind of twisted thinking that could lead Oswald to commit such an unthinkable deed. Oswald's own assassin, Jack Ruby, was another example of the same sort of borderline personality that Oswald himself represented.

It may be hard to imagine that great world events can be precipitated by a couple of kooks who had the opportunity to strike through a surprisingly porous system of security. All presidents since JFK's death have had to bear the burden of the distance that it has proven necessary to maintain between elected officials and the general public. Posner should be congratulated for doing his unbiased best, in a convincing narrative, to allow the next generation to understand the contours of the tragedy that actually happened.

* * *

Paul Kennedy's *Preparing for the Twenty-First Century*[11] is unusually timely. For the author, an historian, earlier argued in his *The Rise and Fall of the Great Powers* that powerful countries have in the past over-reached themselves. Now Kennedy has sought to extend his analysis of the future beyond the confines of the nation state as a central player in world affairs. He therefore examines worldwide forces for change like the growth of population, the nature of new technology, global environmental problems, and movements of people across political boundaries.

The world economy appeared to be in an unusual mess, and Kennedy is as helpful a guide as any in understanding what was going on. Former President George Bush thought that by his buying some silk socks he was contributing to turning around the American recession. Kennedy's approach was in keeping with others who helped provide the underpinnings to the special budget proposals of the incoming Bill Clinton administration, and anyone concerned with public affairs will find here interpretations that seem of great interest.

Part One runs through a series of major trends still affecting us today. Kennedy has revived the old concern of the late eighteenth-century thinker Thomas Robert Malthus, who was pessimistically obsessed with the danger that the explosion in the number of people would exhaust the available food resources. Overpopulation is a particularly acute issue in sub-Saharan Africa, which has fared poorly since the end of Western colonialism. Even if birth rates can be kept down, the decline of infant mortality becomes a paradoxical threat to the possibility of prosperity. Some 95 percent of future population growth will take place within the developing countries. The AIDS epidemic, which seems to be ravaging the poorest areas the worst, would be a grim way for events to resolve the dilemmas posed by the demands thrown up by the power of population.

Agricultural production is threatened by dangers to our natural environment. Global-warming is only part of the crisis. For emerging factory enterprises, in China for example, are contributing to the damage to the world's ecosystem that the more developed areas have been beginning to try to do something about. Pollution of the atmosphere turns out to have been worst in the under-developed places that can ill afford such a handicap. The best part of *Preparing for the Twenty-First Century* is when Kennedy moves away from some well-known generalities to examine the impact of these worldwide forces on specific regions. East Asia has obviously had a developmental jump, and the examples of Japan and Korea, as well as Taiwan and Singapore, have to be instructive about what the future holds.

Kennedy's use of economics fulfils the old idea about its being a dismal subject, and it is typical of Kennedy that he chooses to highlight the special problems of an aging population that threatens even the Japanese. But the fact that Japan now possesses about three-quarters of the world's robots means that through automation it may be able to escape from somber demographic statistical projections. The title of Kennedy's book may sound more pretentiously prophetic than he intends to be; by and large his analysis is aimed only at preparing us for what our situation is going to be around 2025.

The examples of India and China pose special conundrums because their combined populations amount to some 37 percent of the world's total. If there is one cliché that Kennedy succeeds in doing way with it is the notion that any such entity as the "Third World" exists. The problems of the Indians and Chinese are so different, and the gap in performance between East Asia and sub-Saharan Africa yawning, that the term "Third World" becomes redundant. Incidentally, according to Kennedy's survey, Latin America also lost ground in the 1980s.

Kennedy has interesting chapters on the old Soviet Union, whose problems look appalling, and on Europe, which is a relative bright spot. But his whole book is obviously geared to the special dilemmas America found itself in. In the end, Kennedy thinks that the U.S. will continue to "muddle through," but that approach will entail a slow, steady decline like that which Britain went through earlier. Kennedy does conclude on a relatively upbeat mood, that fresh political leadership could in fact make a difference in the prospects we face. One can only hope that public leaders throughout North America will pay attention to the kinds of literature Kennedy's book represents, and that they will be better equipped to come to terms with the challenges he anticipates.

* * *

The 1962 Cuban missile crisis remains indelibly etched in the minds of those of us old enough to have been politically conscious during the most frightening moments of the Cold War. But for decades afterwards, the inner workings of the Soviet side of the story remained almost wholly shrouded in mystery. At the time, Kremlinologists were still looking at group photographs of the Communist Party Politburo and trying to determine members' relative political power by noting who stood where in relation to Khrushchev. Kremlinology had developed after the Second World War as the study of a kind of gigantic Cold War black box. Although by the early 1960s Khrushchev had repudiated the worst aspects of Stalin's dictatorial and paranoid rule, in many ways it was as difficult as ever for Western analysts to determine what was going on within the USSR's holy of holies.

But as the twentieth century drew to a close, nearly everything connected to Soviet historiography changed. Numerous projects were afoot to determine what could be learned from top-level Soviet files. Although some material is almost certainly being still held back, and Western scholars have only recently started independent investigations, it may be that we can now speak more confidently about what the Soviets were up to in 1962 than about what motivated the Americans. Politburo members were used to a situation in which they could expect everything written down to be safe from outside inspection, while American policymakers had to count on their deliberations being subjected to the closest kind of partisan evaluation. (President Kennedy taped some high-level meetings and shared this secret only with his brother Robert.) And then, thanks to Aleksandr Fursenko and Timothy Naftali's extraordinary access to Soviet archives, we also gained insight into the thinking of Castro's regime during the crisis. Their book title *"One Hell of a Gamble":* *Khrushchev, Castro, and Kennedy 1958-1964*[12] comes from President Kennedy's assessment of a proposed invasion of Cuba in the midst of an international confrontation that threatened to touch off a global conflagration.

Back in 1959 there was heated debate over whether, or how much, American policy was helping drive Castro into an alliance with international communism. During the 1960s, so-called revisionist historians were trying to assess the extent to which America deserved to be blamed for the rise of the Cold War as a whole. I remember how outspoken Theodor Draper was at the time in highlighting Castro's special ideological attraction to communism. Often while reading *"One Hell of a Gamble,"* I was struck by how prescient Draper had been—especially when I perused hitherto secret communications between the Soviets and the Cuban government. (Draper's 1962 book *Castro's Revolution: Myths and Realities* is unfortunately long out of print.)

It seems to me like yesterday that one's hopes for a liberated Cuba collapsed as Castro executed over 500 former Batista officials after quick war-crime trials, and then refused to set a date for elections. At the time, U.S. policy in Latin America was still under the cloud of America's role in the 1954 overthrow of the Arbenz regime in Guatemala. According to Khrushchev's 1970 reminiscences, the Soviets were aware that Castro's brother Raul was "a good Communist," although for a long time he kept his deepest political beliefs hidden from Fidel.

At the same time, Khrushchev's doctrine of "peaceful co-existence" with the West had aggravated the rivalry between the USSR and China, still ostensibly allies. For Latin American revolutionaries, the extraordinary success of China's peasant-based revolution was an inspiration, and the Soviets had to worry that Castro might find Mao's revolutionary credentials less musty than the Kremlin's. Starting in late September of 1959, Khrushchev's Praesidium had decided to send Warsaw Pact weapons to Cuba. Secret documents indicate that the Soviets were prepared to provide more assistance than the Cuban leader felt was domestically safe for him to accept, given communism's unpopularity in Cuba. Soviet tanks and rifles, bearing the insignia of various Warsaw Pact nations, gave the Soviets a beachhead in the Western hemisphere.

It appears that Che Guevara, in the fall of 1960, was the first to propose to Khrushchev that the Soviets station missiles in Cuba. After the fiasco of the 1961 Bay of Pigs invasion, Robert Kennedy seems to have been the first within the administration to suspect that the Soviets might be planning on setting up such bases in Cuba. Khrushchev's craftiness had carried him from a modest peasant background to the top of the Soviet hierarchy, but in terms of international statesmanship he was a gambler. In the absence of an agreement between America and the Soviet Union banning the resumption of nuclear testing, President Kennedy was determined to continue such tests. For their part, the Soviets were reluctant to agree to any deal since international inspection would expose their relative weakness, and they feared the possibility of an American pre-emptive strike.

Khrushchev was imaginative and impulsive; Pierre Salinger, Kennedy's press secretary, described him as the "most mercurial man" he had ever met. Castro had indeed requested missiles from the Soviets, but Khrushchev decided that these would be medium-range weapons armed with nuclear warheads. The Soviet leader was taking a great risk in sending his country's most costly and lethal weapons 7,000 miles across the ocean to an island just off the U.S. coast.

The missile project was carried out in the greatest secrecy, even cutting the Soviet ambassador to Washington out of the loop. After American surveillance planes discovered the missiles' presence in October 1962, Kennedy was understandably furious at the deception. Once operational, the missiles would have doubled the number of Soviet nuclear weapons able to reach the United States. In all, eighty-five Soviet ships were involved, along with 40,000 Soviet military personnel. The Soviets knew ahead of time that America's high-flying U-2 reconnaissance planes would spot the missiles, but they hoped the Americans would grudgingly accept the presence of such weapons ninety miles from Key West in Florida, just as the Soviets had been forced to swallow their opposition to American missiles in Turkey.

The crisis started on 16 October, when the president was informed about the missiles on Cuban soil. Very soon the USSR and the U.S. seemed on the brink of war. After five days of the most intense discussion between Kennedy and his advisers, the U.S. administration decided to blockade Cuba and establish a weapons quarantine. The alternative was an air strike, which could not be expected to be totally successful. In retrospect, Kennedy appears to have been correct in expecting the worst from an invasion of Cuba.

On the Soviet side, the worst-case scenario (aside from a nuclear exchange) was that their missiles would fall into American hands. Khrushchev felt himself in a weak position because he could not hope that there was any chance of him prevailing in a Caribbean war. Fursenko and Naftali's investigation of top-secret documents reveals, for instance, which intelligence files Khrushchev read first on each day of the crisis. Khrushchev concluded that

Castro was advocating nuclear suicide. On 28 October, Khrushchev backed down and accepted America's terms; the world heaved a sigh of relief. Meanwhile, Castro was angry that the Soviets had made the final decision without consulting his regime.

From Khrushchev's point of view the incident was a debacle, one that led to his removal from power in 1964. For Castro, the crisis turned out to be only a blip in his construction of a communist regime, while the Chinese crowed about the miserable performance of the Kremlin. The big winner, of course, was Kennedy, who had redeemed himself after the Bay of Pigs disaster, and a whole generation of Cold War thinkers felt vindicated about the necessity of firmness to contain Soviet expansionist moves.

The single most frightening confrontation of the Cold War was over. Almost twenty years of political thinking preceded the American response to Khrushchev's provocation. For those who did not live through those frightening events, Fursenko and Naftali have successfully recreated the high drama of the key days of October 1962. For my own generation, the authors have compiled a deeper background to the fast-paced narrative. More than that, their examination of Soviet sources means that *"One Hell of a Gamble"* has something to teach even the most conscientious students of foreign policy. This work is diplomatic history at its best.

* * *

Howard Kurtz, a media reporter for the *Washington Post*, wrote *Spin Cycle: Inside the Clinton Propaganda Machine,*[13] a lively book that immediately leapt onto the American bestseller lists. It was so up-to-date as to be almost frightening about how modern technology has made books quick to produce. In both his introduction and epilogue he was able to touch on the crisis associated with Clinton's liaison with Monica Lewinsky; and the backgrounds to the Kathleen Willey and Paula Jones cases are also set forth.

One anecdote from *Spin Cycle* has probably outshone all other Clinton jokes. At a Connecticut fundraiser in the spring of 1996 the president made a comment about a five-hundred-year-old Inca mummy that had just then been discovered in Peru. "You know," Clinton said, "if I were a single man, I might ask that mummy out. That's a good-looking mummy." Afterwards the president's press secretary, Mike McCurry, indicated to Clinton that that seemed an unwise comment for someone with his reputation as a philanderer. Clinton snapped at McCurry, and the press secretary decided he needed a break from his boss and rode with the press charter instead of Air Force One. McCurry had at least one drink, and was queried about Clinton's mummy observation, responding: "Probably she does look good compared to the mummy he's been" making love to.

For anyone absorbed with the rise of the tabloid presidency, *Spin Cycle* will be hard to put down. There are abundant and vivid anecdotes about journalists as well as the president's White House staff. I confess I admired the dean of the Washington press corps, Helen Thomas, for asking McCurry, "Don't you think there is a lot of hypocrisy in always advocating reform and doing exactly the opposite?" Clinton was in fact a fairly conservative president underneath all the tawdry sensationalism that accompanied his presidential career.

Spin Cycle concentrates on Mike McCurry, who was the successor to Clinton's Dee Dee Myers and George Stephanopoulos. Anybody who focuses as purely on public relations as Kurtz does is bound to come up with a book that will appear unappetizing to moralists. The Arkansas editor who coined the nickname "Slick Willie" for Clinton would seem to have been as successful as the person who long ago came up with the phrase "Dirty Dick" for Richard Nixon.

Kurtz has written a thoroughly snappy book; "despite his staff's best efforts," we are told, "Clinton seemed trapped in a yo-yo presidency." One doubts that the upswings in Clinton's career will enable him to succeed in his aspiration to match Teddy Roosevelt in history. Over seventy years ago the pundit Walter Lippmann wrote books that worried about the problem of managed news in a democracy, and Kurtz provides such concrete illustrations from recent times that it is hard to believe that the general reading public will not come away from *Spin Control* with heightened cynicism. Clinton could afford to disdain the *New York Times* and the *Washington Post* as long as he knew how to handle *USA Today*.

At the same time Kurtz is surprisingly sloppy in how *Spin Control* got put together. Computers can make writing easier, but not necessarily better; an anecdote that appears about the *Wall Street Journal* on page 6 reappears with some changes on pages 106-7. In my day, no high school English teacher would allow split infinitives, but Kurtz's editor does not seem to object. Still the thesis that White House news spinners are "ultimately joined at the hip in a strangely symbiotic relationship" with journalists would be hard to refute.

Molly Ivins's *You Got to Dance with Them What Brung You*[14] was written with a kind of style and humor that is absent from *Spin Control*. Ivins is a Texan columnist, and put together a book of her pieces from the *Fort Worth Star-Telegram*. She not only has a taste for the bizarre in politics, but shows an underlying kind of human wisdom. Although sympathetic to the cause of liberalism, she worries here about the possibility that Clinton's presidency may turn out to have been crippled. And she concludes the book with a moving tribute to her late mother. The reader can dip in and out of *You Got to Dance with Them What Brung You* and get nuggets of genuine insight in each of these short pieces.

Thinking about the people that appear in both these two books, I wonder whether we have not been misled about politics by some of our greatest writers. Lady Macbeth sleepwalking in an agony of guilt, or King Lear maddened by what he sees as the betrayal of his daughters, are unreliable examples of the psychology of political drama. Such models tell us more about our common humanity than succeed in being instructive about actual political leaders. What is striking about so much of high public life is the extent to which internalized conflict is irrelevant to what goes on politically. That which would be mortifying in everyday life to people of genuine character, financial skullduggery or proven adultery, can be run-of-the-mill to those engaged in great partisan stakes. Abraham Lincoln alas may be the exception that proves the rule: moral sensitivity accompanied by the greatest tactical skill.

Notes

1. Seymour M. Hersh, *The Price of Power: Kissinger in the Nixon White House* (New York: Summit Books, 1983).
2. Joseph P. Lash, *Dealers and Dreamers: A New Look at the New Deal* (New York: Doubleday, 1988).
3. See Roazen, *Encountering Freud*, pp. 251-55.
4. Charles Kenney and Robert L. Turner, *Dukakis: An American Odyssey* (Toronto: Thomas Allen, 1988).
5. Richard Gaines and Michael Segal, *Dukakis: The Man Who Would Be President* (New York: Avon, 1988).
6. Michael S. Dukakis and Rosabeth Moss Kanter, *Creating the Future: The Massachusetts Comeback and Its Promise for America* (Toronto: Musson, 1988).
7. Lionel Trilling, *The Liberal Imagination: Essays on Literature and Society* (New York: Anchor, 1957).
8. Louis Hartz, *The Liberal Tradition in America: An Interpretation of American Political Thought Since the Revolution* (New York: Harcourt, Brace & Co., 1955).
9. Thomas C. Reeves, *A Question of Character: A Life of John F. Kennedy* (Toronto: Macmillan, 1991).
10. Gerald Posner, *Case Closed: Lee Harvey Oswald and the Assassination of JFK* (New York: Random House, 1993).
11. Paul Kennedy, *Preparing for the Twenty-First Century* (New York: Harper Collins, 1993).
12. Aleksandr Fursenko and Timothy Naftali, *"One Hell of a Gamble": Khrushchev, Castro, and Kennedy 1958-1964* (New York: W. W. Norton, 1997).
13. Howard Kurtz, *Spin Cycle: Inside the Clinton Propaganda Machine* (New York: The Free Press, 1998).
14. Molly Ivins, *You Got to Dance With Them What Brung You: Politics in the Clinton Years* (New York: Random House, 1998).

Conclusions: The Psychology of Women

Feminism often seems as much a political movement as an intellectual approach, and therefore we have grown accustomed to feminist writings that transform reality to serve ideological purposes. When it comes to psychoanalysis feminists have already succeeded in achieving a major social impact. Starting in the 1960s and extending throughout the 1970s feminists established once and for all the sexist biases implicit in Freud's framework. Although women themselves held high positions as analysts throughout the twentieth century, and Freud's ideas were long ago challenged by a few "dissident" analysts discontented with his approach to feminine psychology, feminism fundamentally altered the way Freud's work is now perceieved. As a matter of fact feminism has been so influential in making its point that Freud's stature has, I think, unnecessarily suffered a relative decline.

In more recent years, however, feminist writers on psychoanalysis have tended to shift. Now that their battle against Freud has been won, feminism is allowing itself to see other aspects to analysis than those it had been assaulting. Psychoanalysis has come to be seen not just as a defense of patriarchal culture, but as a critical source of insight into traditionalist injustices.

In *Understanding Women: A Feminist Psychoanalytic Approach*[1] we have two therapists who find in analysis a means of challenging contemporary society. It is a balanced, interesting and serious book. Luise Eichenbaum and Susie Orbach use analysis to isolate some typical issues in feminine psychology. The women's movement now seems able to accept a contrast between external and internal experience, without implying male chauvinist prejudices. Eichenbaum and Orbach believe that out of women's social existence can come an understanding of their psychology. They think, for instance, that social role-playing helps account for feminine deference. In the belief that women should be independent, without being possessive or insecure, the authors look to unconscious processes in early family experience. Within psychoanalysis they draw especially on the so-called object relations school of thought, typified by the work in England by thinkers like Fairbairn, Balint, Klein, Winnicott, and Guntrip.

As meritorious as the authors' objectives are, it still should be pointed out that they are curiously credulous in accepting what is a highly speculative (if now fashionable) psychoanalytic perspective. The object relations theorists postulate phases in early infancy that are in principle impossible to verify. It is simply not true, moreover, to write that "Ronald Fairbairn was the first analyst to depart radically from Freud's instinct theory and to revise libido theory." It is worth pointing out, for the sake of keeping the intellectual history of psychoanalysis straight, that Carl Jung, Alfred Adler and Otto Rank —among others—pursued just such a course over eighty years ago.

Understanding Women may be theoretically weak but still it contains many sound points. Motherhood does involve a special kind of caretaking of others; and women, in the construction of ideals of femininity, may have paid too high a price for the ability to nurture. In developing what the authors call "emotional antennae for the desires of others" women may have put their own needs second, resulting in a situation where the experience of receiving nurturance is "not symmetrical for women and men." Psychoanalysis helps explain how mothers identify with daughters, as feminine psychology gets reproduced from generation to generation. Conflicting messages are transmitted, and women may look to men for their exaggerated needs for nurturance, as they are bound to feel false, frustrated and disappointed. A woman's desire for autonomy meets with a special set of obstacles. A daughter's "development toward independence brings feelings of loss as well as pride." The result is that a woman "gives to others out of the well of her own unmet needs."

Eichenbaum and Orbach believe that one of the tragedies of patriarchy is the father-daughter relationship. Both mother and daughter share the experience of weakness in males who do not stand up to women, especially in their behalf; and both mother and daughter feel disillusion with father, as their disdain for men tightens the unspoken bond between adult and child.

The authors, as therapists, illustrate how the buried part of a woman's self can emerge in the context of a clinical situation. The psychoanalytic thinkers they have chosen to emphasize did, in fact, see themselves as maternal objects of affection. Freud knew he had missed a lot about the role of mothering, even though the authors ignore earlier writers in analysis who had tried to correct the imbalances in Freud's theory of the Oedipus complex. When Eichenbaum and Orbach stress that in therapy a woman needs "to have a different experience in the new relationship," it is as if someone like Franz Alexander has been totally forgotten. Feminism ought to be far enough along to become aware of the full range of psychoanalytic thinking, especially when it legitimizes the expression of dependency needs and desires, and how they can be conflictual.

Feminist therapy turns out to be what good analysts have always tried to achieve—allowing the client to grow up and become autonomous, which is especially hard in relation to therapists of the same sex. For a woman to be successfully "validated" by another woman is part of a larger human picture, and if feminism could acknowledge that it is so their cause could contribute to a broader understanding of what it means to be a fully developed person.

* * *

George Orwell once began an essay on Mahatma Gandhi by asserting, "Saints should always be judged guilty until they are proved innocent." Well-meaning idealism does evoke a kind of cynicism, and since Eli Sagan comes across in his *Freud, Women, and Morality*[2] as a self-proclaimed lover of mankind, Orwell's skepticism about sainthood does seem appropriate to keep in mind as one attempts to evaluate what Sagan's book amounts to.

Sagan is against cannibalism, racism, slavery, infanticide, and sexism, ethical conclusions with which few of us will have difficulty. But he follows a series of such dubious steps that I think that his argument threatens the values he upholds. For one thing, Sagan adopts a teleological view of the universe; he not only believes in moral progress but defines a historical perspective by means of an evolutionary process, from lower to higher. To put his outlook baldly, he thinks that past ages were cruel and bad, while we are valiantly struggling toward the light. It seems to me, and most historians, that the essence of a true historical outlook means appreciating diversity, as we learn from the perspective of earlier outlooks. Sagan insists, however, on looking at the past solely through the spectacles of the presumed superiority of the present.

Although Sagan strikes me as philosophically naïve, the center of his book, which criticizes Freud's concept of the superego from the point of view of current feminist thought, does succeed in being both serious and stimulating. Sagan regards Freud as the greatest mind of the twentieth century, even though Sagan believes that Freud's thinking about morality, civilization, science and reason was twisted out of an essential ambivalence about women.

Sagan is no sensationalist eager to court publicity by means of Freud-bashing. On the contrary, if anything Sagan is too naive in his premise that Freud made "discoveries," instead of thinking that Freud's position was one among many possible interpretations of psychological evidence. Sagan is sound, as he explores the ethical implications of psychoanalysis, in arguing that Freud upheld an unduly negativistic position by means of his theories about the superego.

As an alternative to the superego, Sagan proposes the notion of conscience, and while the distinction between the two may seem like a terminological sleight of hand, Sagan is right in searching for some means of softening the harshness of Freud's conviction that values are inevitably in conflict, and that morality can never be defined by any set of health values.

Even if one cannot share Sagan's belief in the existence of a universal human morality, he has performed a service in trying to relate what he calls conscience to the original nurturing situation between the child and its primary caretakers. For Sagan, morality is defined by love, and the existence of aggression, tyranny, and dominance are seen as secondary defenses against anxiety. He thinks that sexism arises out of a repression of the memory of the so-called pre-Oedipal mother, and that the values of compassion and pity are endangered because of the fear of engulfment by the symbiotic mother. Feminism has to be central to Sagan's thesis since he propagandizes in behalf of those qualities that frightened men stigmatize as "feminine." Sagan also thinks that he can spell out the various stages of moral development as conscience awakens in us.

Sagan's effort to understand the relationship between psychoanalysis and ethics is a worthy one, as is his attempt to work out a psychoanalytic sociology by means of adopting the view that shared values are at the core of any social system. But his approach is, for me, fatally flawed by his assumptions about the alleged existence of moral progress. I think that it is hubris to believe that "you and I are capable of a moral vision more far-reaching that that of Plato, Aristotle, Rousseau, and Freud." However emancipated we might like to think ourselves, the history of ideas should teach us that in some basic sense there is nothing new under the sun.

The links between psychology and society are more subtle than Sagan likes to hope. One would have thought that the discredited hypothesis from the 1940s tying the swaddling of babies in Germany and Russia to political authoritarianism could not once again be seriously advanced. But Sagan is so eager for reform that he commits himself to positions that strike me as hair-raising. For example, in citing our time as one of spiritual exhaustion he illustrates the sense of transitional malaise by "the current moral disarray of the Democratic Party in the United States." Sagan is writing from the point of view of the left, but in the context of intellectual history that particular example does sound like a movement from the sublime to the ridiculous. The current state of American politics, no matter how important, cannot settle anything once one proposes to enter the world of values—the universe of Plato, Aristotle, Rousseau, Freud, and others.

The North American continent has not seen enough moral inquiry into how we ought to live, and Sagan's book is a worthwhile attempt to look at where our values come from. But he damages his whole enterprise by the old illusion of moral progress. We are not, despite what he thinks, "tantalizingly close to a real understanding of society," precisely because reality is bound to be defined in different ways by various value perspectives. It is not cynicism, but proper historical humility, that tells us that the future is bound to surprise as well as disappoint, as much as the past should continue to enlighten us. But it is the pastness of the past, the way history can give us critical distance toward ourselves, that eludes the naïve progressivisism implicit in Sagan's thinking. The reader will recall the discussion of tragedy in chapter 4.

*   *   *

Freud's Women,[3] by Lisa Appignanesi and John Forrester, is a remarkable book. The authors begin with the premise that Freud has to be considered this past "century's most influential writer," and on that basis they explore the significance of his various relationships with women. *Freud's Women* is huge and sprawling, like an old-fashioned novel; it is not the result of new primary research, although even well-informed readers will be bound to learn many new points. What we have here is a work of synthesis, as previous studies are rethought and reconsidered. Many of the authors' judgments could be questioned, or occasional historical errors pointed out. But the important point, it seems to me, is that the interpretations of Appignanesi and Forrester are always subtle, and I felt gripped by the power of an original understanding of the subject.

They begin first with Freud's biography. Although in the absence of the full correspondence between Freud and his future bride, now being edited for ultimate publication, our understanding of Freud's marriage has to remain sketchy, I found that *Freud's Women* represents a sensitive handling of the available marital material. The book gets on more solid ground when it describes the invention of psychoanalysis, and Freud's construction of his first published case histories. In keeping with their conceptual intent to describe Freud's attempts to understand women, the authors put on the back burner what Freud had to say about men. It is often mistakenly overlooked how many of Freud's earliest clinical problems dealt with those of males, whatever his publications may have made things sound like. And if, from today's perspective, many of his attitudes toward women sound at best quaint, his outlook on men too was necessarily one that requires genuine historical imagination to understand. The authors do not share the common anachronistic bias that insists on seeing Freud solely in today's terms; at best we should try to overcome the blind spots and limitations of our own presuppositions, with the confidence that the study of the past will lead us to be less parochial in our own outlook.

On several occasions the authors remind us how Freud thought of the task of psychotherapy as if it were trying to match the traditional functions of an old-fashioned Jewish marriage broker. Freud did sometimes think of marriage as a possible therapy for the neuroses, although I think he was rather more cosmopolitan about sexuality than one might suppose from a reading of *Freud's Women.* Some of the most famous examples of couples Freud sought to keep together were not sexually active relationships, and he was known to sanction extramarital arrangements.

Freud's Women does on occasion fall into the familiar trap, that most of us have at some time succumbed to, of uncritically believing in Freud's own version of events. For example, Appignanesi and Forrester seem to accept the proposition that it was Freud's patients, and not also he himself, who produced the transference phenomena. Modern psychodynamic thinking would,

I believe, look more closely at the peculiarities of the therapeutic setting Freud evolved as the crucible that helped create the clinical difficulties he encountered.

The strongest parts of *Freud's Women* consist of the chapters about Freud's prominent female followers. The vocation of being a psychoanalyst was remarkably suitable for women, and within his own circle Freud had to oppose those who tried to block women from becoming analysts. Freud was helping these women defy conventional expectations about the kinds of lives they should lead. I particularly liked the way Appignanesi and Forrester understand Lou Andreas-Salomé and her involvements with Nietzsche and Rilke before her entering Freud's world. But they also interestingly describe the careers of Sabina Spielrein, Loe Kann, Anna Freud, Helene Deutsch, Marie Bonaparte, Joan Riviere, and Alix Strachey, as well as others.

The final section of the book addresses theoretical concerns. The history of psychoanalytic disputes over theories of femininity is an elaborate one, and Appignanesi and Forrester deftly summarive the key positions. I am not entirely confident that the authors are fully aware of what a theological-sounding thicket they have entered.

Freud's Women does successfully conclude with a balanced chapter on feminism and psychoanalysis, illustrating how saturated with psychoanalytic thinking even the most recent theorists of femininity remain. It is not just that one needs Freud's concepts to understand patterns of victimization; even if we concede that the social conditions of patriarchal society are responsible for perceived patterns of inferiority, that simply renders more relevant some of Freud's initial questions:

> Deterministic arguments only make it both more difficult and more imperative to discover a feminine subject who is untouched by the social beyond the roles and rules of patriarchal society. Thus the social determinism of feminist critiques of Freud—deterministic because they posit a direct, unmediated and uncontested translation and transference of patriarchal values and roles from family and social ambience to potential feminine subjects—requires, in a second stage of analysis, recourse to a feminine subjectivity which lies untouched and recoverable, beyond the social.

Appignanesi and Forrester have written a challenging book that should remain a key source for many years to come.

*   *   *

It seems that we are living in a period that is unusually ahistorical. I have been in smallish bookstores where the section on European History is overshadowed by that on Gay and Lesbian Studies. Such an incongruity, appalling to those concerned with the future fate of an educated citizenry, may be facilitated by the seemingly unprecedented pace of change today; as technological developments seem to overleap each other, the past can seem irrelevant. But this would not be the first occasion when it has been tempting for people to be misled by the fallacy of thinking that the present is peculiarly blessed with knowledge and virtue, while the enduring relevance of history gets discounted.

The current precarious state of history is supported by problems that are peculiar to America. As we have discussed, our country was founded on a linear faith in progress. And it has been said that happy countries have little need for history. (One need only talk to Germans, Russians, or Italians to get a wholly different picture of how it is possible to approach the past.) Looking back on our history, it seems to me striking how far we have come, for example in connection with race relations; it took a terrible civil war to destroy slavery, and then the position of blacks was not easy to improve. I hope it does not seem too culturally self-congratulatory for me to wonder how many other societies in world history have come this far, and in a relatively short period of time, on such a rooted matter of prejudice.

Smugness can take a varierty of different and insidious forms. Americans are known for their self-confidence, and interest in short-range change. Stereotyping any nation or group obviously has its dangers, but I think that it is possible to attempt some tentative generalizations; we have been given to a moralistic outlook, which takes an inadequate understanding of the way other cultures function. America has not only, I think, been apt to ride roughshod over the different ways contemporaries have of ordering their affairs, but we have in general been singularly obtuse about understanding the past. (How our country characteristically preserves its historical relics would be a subject all its own.)

Studying history can be likened to an imaginative form of foreign travel. While there are those who seem incapable of learning from the way others do things, history ought to be beneficial precisely because it forces us to enter the minds and souls of people who ordered things quite differently than we do now. The danger is always that it is so easy to fall into anachronisms, failing to understand a culture in its own terms. It is inevitable that we look at history through contemporary eyes, but the objective ought to be to attempt as much as possible to put aside today's preconceptions in favor of understanding the past for its own sake. Too often it seems that we look at history through the wrong end of the moral telescope; we should study the past for the sake of trying to emancipate ourselves from today's presuppositions, instead of using history in order to reaffirm our sense of superiority.

I have a warning in mind: present-mindedness dooms even the best of us to oblivion in no time. For if we set out to judge past thinkers or folkways in contemporary terms, then that same way of proceeding will insure that shortly we too will be assessed as woefully inadequate by the next generation. So that in the year 2013 or 2023, for example, it will be possible for even an average nitwit to see us all in 2003 as nicompoops, or worse. The practice of evaluating the past by harsh ethical standards builds a precedent that means that we too will be necessarily overcome by events. So that in little time our own accomplishments will be able to be dismissed as not only inadequate but ill meant. Everyone who seeks to promote change should be aware of how revolutions have a way of consuming their own pioneering innovators. But even more modest endeavors can be trapped by an ongoing repetition of the cycle by which one generation is able nonchalantly to dismiss an earlier one; it should go almost without saying that the grounds for these sweeping judgments are often unsound, and that too often losses get ignored in the enthusiasm for the latest so-called advances.

* * *

How does this line of reasoning apply to the study of the psychology of women? It seems to me that we have been peculiarly unable to acknowledge the achievements of predecessors on this subject. For example, Karen Horney, after being consigned for years by the so-called psychoanalytic mainstream to the wilderness of the troublemakers responsible for "dissidence," has for some time now been accepted as having been ahead of her time in her thinking. But simultaneously one of her contemporaries, Helene Deutsch, has been having tough sledding in being acknowledged for her early contributions. Horney did found her own training school, with its separate journal, but her success has gone well beyond what that professional group was able to accomplish. Horney wrote for the most general audience, and her books were rewarded by a wide readership that has entailed multiple biographical efforts at understanding her life and work.

Helene Deutsch, a great personal favorite of Freud's and the author, among other works, of an almost encyclopaedic, two-volume *The Psychology of Women*, has been so widely reviled that that landmark in the history of concepts about femininity has been out of print in English for years now. Horney did criticize Deutsch, which was only answered by Deutsch in the most indirect way. But, in order to unsettle today's standards of political correctness about these two women, let me take one difference between them stemming from the 1920s. Horney had argued then that a young woman's identifying with her father was a source of neurosis, whereas Deutsch's position was on the contrary that a woman could legitimately build her career out of such a father identification. We now know that both women were speaking autobiographically, since Horney had a poor relation with her father (which extended also to Freud), whereas Deutsch had found a great ally in her father for her emancipation as a woman, which continued in her ability to use Freud's ideas in order to express her own most intimate experiences. (Although Horney stopped writing about women, Deutsch kept to the subject throughout her extremely long life.)

The specific 1920s point of disagreement between Horney and Deutsch on the issue of a woman's father identification almost never gets discussed today, but if brought to light would probably make Deutsch's position, by today's standards, look the more enlightened. I am not bringing up this disagreement stemming from eighty years ago for the sake of partisanship, but in order to underline how history can confront us with possibilities and complexities that we might not be otherwise aware of. Horney certainly had some splendid slogans, and was prescient in brushing aside aspects of Freud's work that not many would be inclined to defend today.

But while Horney had openly challenged Freud's approach, mainly starting in the 1930s, Deutsch had taken a different tack that requires close attention fully to appreciate. Deutsch was able to use Freud's ideas to express her own most private experiences; of course she was writing as a psychoanalyst, and when she proposed the significance of masochism in the life of women, she—like Freud—was taking for granted the idea that all civilized people are masochistic. And narcissism was, Deutsch retorted to Horney's indictment against her, a woman's self-protection against masochism. Deutsch was proposing to explore the ways in which female masochism was different than that of men, and she did so in the course of a huge text (as well as numerous technical papers) in which her differences with Freud got expressed in indirect ways. The title of her largest work—*The Psychology of Women*—should in itself have alerted sensitive readers to the fact that she had gone beyond proposing the psychoanalysis of women. (Too many readers have picked and chosen slices of Deutsch's sentences for purposes of attack; her writing so many pages thereby became an invitation to be made to look silly.)

But let me focus in even more closely on the substance of Deutsch's argument. In her first book, *The Psychoanalysis of the Sexual Functions of Women* (1925), Deutsch had included a chapter on "The Menopause." In Horney's review of Deutsch's book, Horney singled out this chapter for its rich clinical material. Now eight decades later we might well be inclined to think that modern science has taught us lots of things that Deutsch (and Horney) had not known at the time. But the historical point that I am trying to make is that whatever we might now think of the limitations or merits of what Deutsch proposed then, or later for that matter, it needs to be made explicit that she had done more than anyone else to establish the menopause as a legitimate subject to be thinking about psychoanalytically.

As Deutsch wrote to her husband Felix at the time she first completed the manuscript of that 1925 book, "It brings something new to this *terra incognita* in analysis —I believe, the first ray of light on the unappreciated female libido. But what is more: I'm not making it the central part of existence...."[4] Historically one has to remember how even as late as 1933 Freud had thought that the "juxtaposition 'feminine libido' is without any justification."[5] Deutsch had not publicly crossed Freud, but had been able to pursue her own course within Freud's general framework. And, like Freud, Deutsch was cultured enough to try to put limits to how far one could push the significance of what was known in those days as the "sexual function." Throughout the history of psychoanalysis, it has been the gentle ones who have been apt to get forgotten, whereas some of the system-builders have had an easier time winning their place.

I would like to persue the study of history even more, and point out the relevance of a theorist who is underrated today: Erich Fromm was ideologically allied with Horney, and we now know about their romantic liaison. But Fromm has somehow, despite how involved he and Horney were in their lives and work, remained outside the tent of figures who are commonly cited on the issue of female psychology. A powerful 1949 essay of his on "Sex and Character," that was reprinted in Fromm's *The Dogma of Christ*[6] (1963), remains almost unknown within the feminist literature even though it was a characteristically pungent statement by one of psychoanalysis's great theoreticians. Fromm was so successful as a social thinker that too many have chosen to ignore his early concept of "social character" and its significance for his pioneering as a clinician.

In addition to the examples of the unnecessary neglect of Deutsch and Fromm, I would add still a third example of the kind of error that crops up in the course of the history of women: it has been tempting for Joan Erikson to get talked about now as if she were equally responsible with her husband Erik for all his writings. She was a talented woman, whose editing of Erik Erikson's work was essential to his onetime success. But she wrote enough on her own that got into print for us to be clear that her writings never had the magical attractiveness of his own work. George Eliot long ago made fun of those apt to attribute writing success to others than the proclaimed author.

These different examples connected to the history of women feed into the more general problem of whether today's writers are able to be accurately aware of their predecessors in the field. For example, someone like Carol Gilligan and others write about specific feminine sources of strength without always acknowledging how people like Helene Deutsch and Erik Erikson had long ago preceded her precisely in this endeavor. And those who talk about motherhood do not seem to realize that whatever by today's standards might be lacking in Deutsch's conception of mothering, nobody in the history of psychoanalysis did more than Deutsch to put motherhood on the map of what it is that psychoanalysts are supposed to be concerned with.

* * *

Contemporary feminist journalism lacks an adequate hold on what the history of the whole field has been like. It is easy to take cheap shots at Freud, who was born in 1856. He not only had a spittoon in his office but he also made use of it. (Today's justices of the American Supreme Court have retained the old spittoons for modern purposes.) Nobody seems adequately impressed that when the Vienna Psychoanalytic Society before World War I first discussed the possibility of allowing women members, Freud spoke out in behalf of the proposal. The measure only passed over the objections of such a sizable minority of members (all over a generation younger than Freud himself), so that Freud had to claim that these opponents of the new idea of equality should be respected for their views.[7] Freud then, in fact, proceeded just as he was inclined to anyway, and put in power more women than I think are prominent in today's organized psychoanalysis. But where are the studies of Lou Andreas-Salomé's writings? Anybody as complicated as "Frau Lou" has had to be neglected, along with the subtleties of someone like Helene Deutsch. (I think that Deutsch would have been delighted to read Alix Strachey's 1924 letter to her husband in which she observed that Deutsch's "paper was a great success, only capped by her evening gown [from Paris, they all said].... She's a remarkable woman."[8] Just as Freud had a barber every day to trim his beard, Helene Deutsch needed a daily hairdresser in the Berlin of the 1920s.)

The truth of the matter is that Old World culture was different from ours, and we ought to approach it with an eye to what we might be able to learn. Instead of scorning the past for what it did not know about, contemporaries might well learn something about how complicated European manners were. Our time seems to glorify what I regard as a kind of pseudo-intimacy, whereas the Old World knew something about the complexities and duplicities of human communication. (I see President Clinton's presentation of himself in the Lewinsky scandal as the work of a sincere liar.) Freud, and his early disciples, can be misread through what they might have judged the coarse beliefs and values of today's time. Saying the same thing to a stranger as an intimate would have seemed to them all as a characteristically American species of barbarism. I remember a Parisian analyst being asked by a Canadian candidate in training: "What is 'tact'?" The subject had obviously never come up before in his education for becoming an analyst.

The Japanese today approach human affairs with something approaching Old World delicacy. I am reminded of an epigram that Freud cited a couple of times in his *Jokes and Their Relation to the Unconscious*: "A wife is like an umbrella. Sooner or later one takes a cab."[9] Freud's obvious pleasure in this saying does not mean that he was himself an unfaithful husband, although that is exactly how his citation of this witticism has been misunderstood. I once mentioned it to a male friend at a dinner table in a Hong Kong restaurant, without realizing that a sophisticated woman seated across from me, who had been reared in Japan, would be able despite the linguistic barriers to follow what I had said. Without being seemingly offended, she was though quick in picking up the meaning behind Freud's Viennese cynicism: "a la carte," she restated the epigram, "is better than menu." (I can think of a saintly Episcopalian parish priest who was shocked by Freud's apparent witticism, as this contemporary of ours repudiated the truth of what Freud implied; then again an unmarried American colleague of mine literally did not understand what Freud had proposed.)

Old European culture had something valuable to it that we are apt to miss out on. When Helene Deutsch first wrote about the conflict between motherhood and sexuality, she was proceeding on the unspoken assumption that all good things are not automatically compatible with one another. American have been reared instead on the proposition that our country can be dedicated to life, liberty, and the pursuit of happiness, and that these values need not be in conflict with one another. When we discover that Thomas Jefferson had an affair with a household slave—something that was established satisfactorily as long ago as Winthrop Jordan's *White Over Black*[10]—at least part of the public reacts with indignation at the hypocrisy involved. Freud taught that most people are in conflict with themselves, whereas despite all the lip-service we may pay to his teachings we are inclined to think that we ourselves are less subject to unconscious self-deceptions.

I would like to take one issue that I have never seen discussed in any psychoanalytic journal—the role of servants, and domestic help in general. (I am not confining myself to the problem of nannys, which at least comes up in Freud's autobiographical memory of the significance for him of the woman who was discharged for stealing in Freiburg, or the Wolf-Man's perverse sexual attraction to a household servant.) Why do we assume in our own time that middle-class parents are supposed to do all the childrearing? As far as I know, intellectuals can be the last people to have common sense on such matters, but there is nothing in the literature that tells them that it could be legitimate to delegate responsibility to others. Of course it takes psychological security to do so, but then some articles on the subject might make it more possible for people without guilt to make the kind of decisions that allow domestic help to ensure the carrying on of careers on the part of the biological parents themselves. Why do we continue ambitiously to believe that everyone is supposed to be able to do everything? In fact, I feel certain that the patterns of the Oedipus complex, and family relations in general, are different in the presence of special help. As traditional extended family structure is changed, we seem only aware of the possible role of psychotherapists as sources of assistance. I am not at all sure that the so-called nuclear family provides as emotionally rich a background as the more old-fashioned family life that no longer seems viable.

There are altogether more inescapable conflicts in life than today's ideology seems willing to recognize. And more historical conciousness might alert us to some of the alternatives that exist. Over the last fifty years, which we naively tend to think of as a record of progress in which, say, women (and blacks) have been able to advance, who has lost out? (Chechens are currently suffering from the force of Russian democracy.) I wonder to what extent psychoanalysis has been used to help feed a Western culture that is potentially anomic. At least some middle-class family life has become a potential jungle; Anna Freud's ideas about the significance of continuity in child custody cases have been used legally to give one custodial parent unchallenged authority over the other parent's visitation rights. Ernest Hemingway once wrote a great collection of short stories called *Men Without Women*; are we now prepared to advocate as a sign of moral progress a world in which women are without men? I am old fashioned enough to find the suggestion that gay liberation is automatically good for the women's movement a real puzzlement.

If pressure groups are interested only in short-term gains, that would be one thing. No very principled sorts of reasoning would be required if what is at stake is merely getting ahold of a piece of the action. But such partisanship should not be confused with humanitarianism or justice, not to mention progress. There are losses as well as gains in all realistic social change, and it does nobody any service to disguise what is really going on.

Far too much hot air surrounds the subject of women today. As I think back on the problems associated with history, it seems remarkable to me that so much propaganda about "glass ceilings," "sticky floors," and other banalities like "cutting edge" or the "new millennium" are allowed to pervade the literature. Real role models from the past—such as women like Helene Deutsch or Lou Andreas-Salomé—exist without the need to resort to wholly imaginary ones. One would have thought that Deutsch, the first director of the Vienna Psychoanalytic Institute, one of the great teachers in early analysis, and someone who helped people, for example, of the stature of Norbert Weiner and J. Robert Oppenheimer, would attract the admiration of ambitious young students.

But the invitation to self-indulgence is one of the worst sins of our sort of contemporary culture. And pious moralizing is altogether in keeping with our tendency to think every social problem can be approached from the perspective of victimization. If women only are interested in short-term success, then these more popular avenues of approach are capable of being suitable. But surely such empty-seeming reasoning is not going to be enough to secure the real future of women professionals, or improved family life in general. (I remember in the mid-1960s how Helene Deutsch disdained the idea of men pushing baby carriages, even though to took years for me to realize that in her day servants performed that task.)

Self-criticism can be a sign of maturity, and it is high time that analysts addressed themselves to the real problem of power: for example, what happens within the practice of psychotherapy itself? As Freud wrote in 1937, "when a man is endowed with power it is hard for him not to misuse it."[11] I remain distressed that there are not more studies of how authority is exercised, by women as well as men, within the clinical context itself. The success of biological psychiatry, with its technology of pills, makes these questions as relevant as ever. Research that would involve thinking along these lines would be, I think, more productive than the phrasemaking that seems to be a substitute for the evaluation of where we have gained and what we might have lost.

All we can ask of the future is that people pay a decent respect for the past, which involves reading works despite how politically incorrect they may seem. I have spent now forty years working on the history of psychoanalysis, and in all that period I cannot think of very many scholarly success stories. The one figure who has managed to be wholly rehabilitated in the period is Sandor Ferenczi, who is now widely acknowledged as worthy of increased attention and scrutiny. (I suspect that today's ritualistic incantations of the name of D. W. Winnicott will someday go the way of how Heinz Hartmann's name was once used.) Freud had a canny idea about the power of historical legend, which is why he composed his "On the History of the Psychoanalytic Movement" in 1914. Alfred Adler and Carl G. Jung did not show equal savvy, and they shortsightedly let Freud's side of things get in the history books before it was questioned.

It is still hard to get people to reconsider what happened in those famous pre-World War I historical quarrels, but I am addressing myself now to the narrower problem of how Americans need to proceed. We still don't know some of the worst of what Freud had had to say about America; according to an interview with Franz Alexander I have recently read, Freud disdained America as Indian territory which in fifty years would become a "Negro republic." (The fact that Plato and Aristotle took the existence of slavery for granted does not settle their hash as great philosophers.) Despite Freud's sort of anti-American prejudice, I think we as a culture have lacked an adequately European perspective, so that the power of history, and the reality of tragedy, are too often deemed alien to us. Some people will continue to treat Freud's Dora case as an account of some kind of heroine, while others of us will marvel at Freud's boldness in publishing a therapeutic stalemate for the sake of what he thought he had scientifically understood. (To give some historical perspective on today's reaction to Dora, in the 1950s Alexander thought that case history was a high point in demonstrating how much Freud was willing to rely on contemporaneous emotional reality—as opposed to reconstructing early childhood—in understanding a patient.)

The example that we started off with in chapter 1, concerning Fromm's exclusion from the IPA, should remind us that we ought never to allow bureaucratic politics to define for us who is or who is not worthy of being a memorable psychologist. In chapter 2 on the Hiss-Chambers case, we saw how inevitable an examination of motives, and explicit psychologizing, can be in even the most partisan-seeming political controversy. Chapter 3 brought to our attention the memorable instance of the novelist Virginia Woolf; the Bloomsbury intellectuals did in fact help in a major way to popularize psychoanalytic thinking. But Woolf's life, in the course of how feminism developed, could ironically become a prototype for the crude Freudianism she herself did so much to ridicule.

Different national receptions of psychology, in Britain as opposed to America for example, underline how it can be possible for some cultures to ignore the inevitability of moral choice. In chapter 4, I was suggesting that the American approach to tragedy can be associated with the tendency to use psychology as a more or less straight-forward substitute for ethics. And in chapter 5, I discussed how the secret and publicly funded subvention of *Encounter* was part of the intellectual history of how countries can use their resources; the ethics of what happened then becomes, I think, part of the kind of theoretical debate which political psychology should be part of. Chapter 6 dealt with the reaction of three great philosophers to Freud's innovations, and should help make clear that values and beliefs ought never to remain only implicit.

Chapter 7 reminds us of how central to psychology and politics should be the study of all the great theorists in the grand tradition of social thought; Fromm and Berlin are only two recent representatives of this long school of thinkers. Chapter 8 on Vietnam and the Cold War is one example of a memorable political issue requiring moral thinking to be linked with political psychology. Chapter 9 tried to raise the problem of the possible social supports for the ability to make abstractions, and chapter 10 explored various methodological issues associated with bringing together two different fields like psychology and politics without anticipating that either could emerge unchanged from the encounter.

Few would contest that in chapter 11, dealing with the work of Hannah Arendt, we have a figure that who is acknowledged as someone who ought to be central to a contemporary look at political psychology, while chapter 12 on Geoffrey Gorer attempted to reawaken interest in someone apt to be unduly neglected today. Chapter 13 approached from a variety of angles the tangled issue of biography writing, and chapter 14 provided a series of instances of how practical political studies are inevitably infused with issues having a psychological character.

I make no apology for thinking Freud himself was an absolutely fascinating figure in intellectual history, and for my purposes he deserves I think to rank with the greats like Jean-Jacques Rousseau and others in the tradition of social philosophy. Just because of the importance of feminism I feel distressed when the subject of women gets treated too lightly and apart from the context of the history of ideas. One of the sayings of George Santayana that I have always admired, especially in the course of his critique of American pragmatism, was his conviction that

> To be boosted by an illusion is not to live better than to live in harmony with the truth; it is not nearly so safe, not nearly so sweet, and not nearly so fruitful.... Believe, certainly...but believe rationally, holding what seems certain for certain, what seems probable for probable, what seems desirable for desirable, and what seems false for false.[12]

Part of living the examined life means being willing, I think, to stick my neck out, as I am probably doing with ending this book on political psychology with these reflections of mine about the controversial issue of contrasting ideas about women. Political theory has traditionally been concerned with the hottest topics, and it is within the great tradition of social philosophy that I have tried to present my ideas on psychology and politics.

Notes

1. Luise Eichenbaum and Susie Orbach, *Understanding Women: A Feminist Psychoanalytic Approach* (New York: Basic Books, 1983).
2. Eli Sagan, *Freud, Women, and Morality: The Psychology of Good and Evil* (New York: Basic Books, 1988).
3. Lisa Appignanesi and John Forrester, *Freud's Women* (New York: Basic Books, 1992).
4. Quoted in Paul Roazen, *Helene Deutsch: A Psychoanalyst's Life* (New York: Doubleday, 1985; second edition, with new introduction, New Brunswick, NJ, Transaction Publishers, 1992), p. 231.
5. Freud, *New Introductory Lectures on Psychoanalysis, Standard Edition*, Vol. 22, p. 131.
6. Erich Fromm, *The Dogma of Christ* (New York: Holt, Rinehart & Winston, 1963).
7. *Minutes of the Vienna Psychoanalytic Society*, Vol. II: 1908-1910, ed. Herman Nunberg and Ernst Federn, translated by M. Nunberg (New York: International Universities Press, 1967), p. 477.
8. *Bloomsbury/Freud: The Letters of James and Alix Strachey 1924-25*, ed. Perry Meisel and Walter Kendrick (New York: Basic Books, 1985), p. 87.
9. "Jokes and Their Relation to the Unconscious," *Standard Edition*, Vol. 8, p. 78.
10. Winthrop Jordan, *White Over Black: American Attitudes Toward the Negro 1550-1812* (Chapel Hill: University of North Carolina Press, 1968).
11. "Analysis Terminable and Interminable," *Standard Edition*, Vol. 23, p. 249.
12. George Santayana, *Character and Opinion in the United States* (New York: Doubleday Anchor, 1956), p. 53-54.

Index

Rank and, 9, 158, 260
Reich and, 8–9, 10
reputation, 93, 158
Rickman on, 213–214
Rousseau and, 90, 104
royalties, 49
'saving' psychoanalysis in Germany
and Italy, 8, 16, 19
Schultz-Hencke and, 7, 8, 10–11
self-development and, 95
sexuality and, xv, 65
Silberer and, 177
sister-in-law (Minna Bernays) and,
168, 172
sisters, fate of, 199
social context to, 96
to Strauss, xi
Studies in Hysteria, 64
*Thomas Woodrow Wilson: A Psycho-
logical Study* (with Bullitt), 229
tragedy to, 68
the unconscious, 68, 96, 236
U.S., views on, 272
value conflicts, 261
Vienna and, 149
Wagner-Jauregg and, 160–161
Wittgenstein and, xii, 87, 89–90
on wives, 269–270
Woolf, Leonard, and, 49
Woolf, Virginia, and, 49–50, 273
Freud: The Paris Notebooks (Cohen),
168
Freud, Women, and Morality (Sagan),
261–262
Freud and the Politics of Psychoanalysis
(Bruner), 117
Freud Archives, 170, 171
*Freud as an Expert Witness: The Dis-
cussion of War Neuroses Between
Freud and Wagner-Jauregg* (Eissler),
160–161
Freud's Women (Appignanesi,
Forrester), 263–264
*Friendship and Fratricide: An Analysis
of Whittaker Chambers and Alger
Hiss* (Zeligs), 39–40
Fromm, Erich
Adler and, 27
analysts of, 4
*The Anatomy of Human Destructive-
ness,* 2
The Art of Loving, 1, 121

Berlin, Isaiah, and, 121
Blücher and, 200
conformity and, 179
direct membership in IPA, 17–18, 22–
25, 28
doctorate, 4
DPG, resignation from, 14–18
Eissler and, 10, 18, 23–26
emigration from Germany, 12
Erikson, Erik, and, 3–4
Escape From Freedom, 1, 3, 121
exclusion from the IPA, 1–30
Fenichel and, 121
Ferenczi and, 2, 28
The Forgotten Language, 1, 122
Freudian orthodoxy and, 27
on Freud's disciples, 2
German Psychoanalytic Society
(DPG) and, 5
To Have or to Be?, 1–2
Horney and, 4, 28, 120, 121, 268
intellectual antecedents, xiv
International Federation of Psycho-
analytic Societies founder, 27
IPA, exclusion from, 4, 272–273
IPA dues, 14–15
Jones and, 10, 18
Jung and, 3, 27
as lay analyst, 28
Macdonald and, 122
Man For Himself, 1, 121
Marcuse and, 4, 26–27, 28, 122
Mead and, 122
Menninger and, 3, 26, 121
Montagu and, 122
Müller-Braunschweig and, 10, 14–15,
18
neo-Freudianism and, 2, 27, 120
Peale and, 121
Psychoanalysis and Religion, 1
Rank and, 2, 28
Reich and, 8
reputation, 120–122, 164, 173
Rousseau and, 121
Sachs and, 2, 4
The Sane Society, 1, 121
*Sigmund Freud's Mission: An Analy-
sis of His Personality and Influ-
ence,* 2, 9, 28, 122
social character and, 4, 268
*Social Character in a Mexican Vil-
lage* (with Maccoby), 1